ITALY IN THE AGE OF THE RISORGIMENTO
1790–1870

LONGMAN HISTORY OF ITALY
General editor: Denys Hay

Italy in the Early Middle Ages 600—1216
T. S. Brown

* Italy in the Age of Dante and Petrarch 1216—1380
John Larner

* Italy in the Age of the Renaissance 1380—1530
Denys Hay and John Law

* Italy 1530—1630
Eric Cochrane (edited by Julius Kirshner)

Italy in the Seventeenth Century 1598—1713
Domenico Sella

* Italy in the Age of Reason 1685—1789
Dino Carpanetto and Ginseppe Ricnperati

* Italy in the Age of the Risorgimento 1790—1870
Harry Hearder

* Modern Italy: 1871—1982
Martin Clark

* already published

LONGMAN HISTORY OF ITALY

Italy in the Age of the Risorgimento
1790–1870

HARRY HEARDER

LONGMAN
London and New York

Longman Group UK Limited
Longman House, Burnt Mill, Harlow
Essex CM20 2JE, England
and Associated Companies throughout the world

*Published in the United States of America
by Longman Inc., New York*

© Longman Group Limited 1983

First published 1983
Sixth impression 1992

British Library Cataloguing in Publication Data

Hearder, Harry
Italy in the age of the Risorgimento: 1790—1870.
– (Longman history of Italy)
1. Italy – History – 18th century
2. Italy – History –19th century
I. Title
945′.08   DG678.5

ISBN 0-582-49146-0

Library of Congress Cataloging in Publication Data

Hearder, Harry.
Italy in the age of the Risorgimento: 1790–1870.

(Longman history of Italy; v. 6)
Bibliography: p.
Includes index.
1. Italy – History – 1789–1870.   I. Title.
II. Series
DG467.L67   1980   vol. 6 [DG551]   945′.08   82-23974
ISBN 0-582-49146-0 (pbk.).

Set in 11/12 Linotron 202 Garamond No. 3
Printed in Malaysia by TCP

Contents

List of maps vi
Acknowledgements viii
Preface ix

PART ONE   *The conflict of interpretations and the sources*

PART TWO   *The states and regions before unification: political developments, the economy and the conditions of life*

Chapter One   Lombardy and Venetia 16
Chapter Two   Sardinia-Piedmont 43
Chapter Three The Central Duchies – Tuscany, Parma and Modena   69
Chapter Four   The Papal States 96
Chapter Five   The Two Sicilies 125

PART THREE   *The creation of the nation-state*

Chapter Six   The origins of the Risorgimento; Italy in the era of the French Revolution and Napoleon (1790–1815) 156
Chapter Seven Revolutionary creeds in an age of political stagnation (1815–40) 172
Chapter Eight Rival movements of nationalism and the delusions of 1848 (1840–52) 193
Chapter Nine   Cavour and the achievement of unity (1852–61) 218
Chapter Ten   The integration and centralization of institutions (1861–70) 240

PART FOUR   *The culture of nineteenth-century Italy*

Chapter Eleven Literature and the opera 254
Chapter Twelve The arts and urban development 272

Chapter Thirteen Religion and the Church 283
Chapter Fourteen Beyond nationalism: the end of the Risorgimento 295

Maps 307
Index 313

List of maps

Map 1 Physical features and historic regions of Italy 308
Map 2 Italy in 1815 309
Map 3 North and Central Italy, 1848–59 310
Map 4 Southern and Central Italy in the 1860s 311

For my son, Paul

Acknowledgements

I would like to thank the British Academy for a generous award which enabled me to read in the Museo del Risorgimento e Storia Contemporanea in Milan and the Biblioteca Nazionale Centrale in Florence. I am also grateful for the services of the officers of those libraries and of the British Library (to use the colourless pseudonym of the British Museum Reading Room), and of the library of University College, Cardiff, where the Mazzini collection, bequeathed to the College by G. O. Griffith, was especially useful.

Mr Lewis Allan, who is a considerable authority on nineteenth-century Tuscany, was kind enough to read the typescript of Chapter 3, and to make some invaluable suggestions. Professor Denys Hay, the editor of the series, read the entire typescript, and commented on it with his usual understanding and insight. The staff of Longman have also been a tower of strength in the preparation of this book.

I would also like to thank Mrs Patricia Moffatt and Miss Carmen Larreta who produced the typescript with efficiency and style. Finally I must apologize to my wife and family for spending long hours shut away in my study instead of keeping them company. It is sad that writing a book demands isolation.

Preface

One of the reasons for the popularity of nineteenth-century Italy with historians has been the ease with which it can be interpreted in the form of a single theme, the theme of the Risorgimento. Undeniably the central theme of the period of Italian history covered by this volume was the acquisition by the Italians of a clearly defined national consciousness, political independence and unification. The apparent simplicity of such a theme has attracted many historians, who evidently felt no inclination to write the history of Italy in the seventeenth or eighteenth century when no such direct, epic quality can be traced. But to write the history of a people over a century or even half a century within the limits of a single theme must result in a distortion, if not the total neglect, of many aspects of that history. For the greater part of the period covered by this book the majority of Italians thought very rarely, if ever, of the national question. Even their strictly political preoccupations were centred on the affairs of their own state, and were often unrelated to any movement for the creation of an Italian nation-state.

The problem in writing this book, then, seemed to me to be that of combining an interpretation of the Risorgimento as a central, but not an only or an exclusive, theme, with an impression of developments and life in the various regions — developments and life often unaffected by the unfolding national history. I have attempted to resolve the problem by dividing the book into four parts. Part One considers the sources and historiography for the period. In Part Two the regimes, society and economy of the five principal regions before unification have been considered for their own sake, apart from their rôle in the traditional story of the Risorgimento. The theoretical debate on the national question is omitted from Part Two; there is less on the dreams of nationalist writers and conspirators than there is on social and economic conditions on the land or in the textile industries of the North. The advent of Napoleon I in Italy, or the policy of Cavour, are thus treated in Part Two rather from the viewpoint of Turin or Milan than from an overall Italian angle.

In Part Three an attempt to give the overall picture is made. It is here that a discussion of the origins of Italian nationalism can be found, and an account of the long and complex debate which accompanied the Risorgimento is given. The international perspective, both of Mazzinian revolutionary philosophy, and of Cavour's policy and diplomacy, is provided by Part Three.

Part Four, like Part Two, is a study of Italy and the Italians in the nineteenth century, rather than of the Risorgimento. It is a study of the culture of Italy, a culture to some extent inherited from the days before unification, the days of the European Romantic movement, but to some extent also reflecting the era established by the Industrial Revolution, an era of tension between a triumphant capitalist world and the early socialist response. Part Four is intended to give an impression of the society and culture of Italy after she had emerged as a nation-state.

Part Three aspires to answer the questions: what happened, and why? Parts Two and Four attempt to answer the more diffuse questions: what was it like, and why was it like that?

A word must be added on the policy regarding anglicization of proper names. Italian kings, grand-dukes, etc., have not had their names anglicized. The names 'Carlo Alberto', 'Vittorio Emanuele', and so on, have been used, as I feel that to anglicize them is to suggest false associations – associations, for example, of 'Charles Albert' with English monarchs and the Prince Consort, are obviously very misleading. I am, however, aware that I have not been completely consistent. Thus I have referred to the Grand Duke 'Pietro Leopoldo' when that ruler was an Italian prince, but when he becomes emperor I have switched to 'Leopold', since it would seem strange to refer to a German emperor ruling in Vienna by the name by which the Italians, of course, still knew him. The names of popes, too, have been anglicized, on the grounds that they were not only Italian princes, but also the spiritual heads of Catholics all over the world. Pius IX is the one exception. He is occasionally referred to as 'Pio Nono', since his Italian title is familiar to English-speaking readers in a way that 'Gregorio Sedicesimo', or even 'Pio Settimo', would not be. I have not anglicized Christian names. The Victorians wrote of 'Joseph' Mazzini and 'Felix' Orsini, but that practice has on the whole been abandoned today. Indeed 'Felix' Orsini seems only a little less comic than 'Happy' Orsini would be.

PART ONE

The conflict of interpretations and the sources

The first accounts of historical movements or periods of history are usually written immediately after the events, by the protagonists themselves, as assessments of success or failure, and often as recriminations against opponents or rivals. Thus both democrats and moderates who had taken part in the revolutionary movements of 1848−9 in Italy wrote their post mortems. The work of a socialist democrat, Carlo Pisacane, is considered, in another context, in Chapter 14. Among the apologists for the moderates was Filippo Antonio Gualterio who published his *Gli ultimi rivolgimenti italiani* ('The recent Italian upheavals') in 1850− 1.[1] Born into a family of the papal nobility at Orvieto in 1819, Gualterio had been educated by the Jesuits, but influenced by more liberal Catholic writers. He fought in the war of 1848 against Austria, and eventually settled in Turin with so many other exiles from all over Italy. It was in Turin that he wrote 'The recent Italian upheavals', which made him a champion of the moderate party of Cavour, but hated alike by clerical reactionaries and democrats. His heroes were the political figures who were both devout Catholics and Italian nationalists, like Cesare Balbo, or anti-clerical and liberal nationalists, like Massimo d'Azeglio − two men whose impact on Italian history is considered in Chapter 8. Historians, like Gualterio, who believed themselves to be 'moderates', also believed themselves to be 'realists', and for that reason gave Cavour a central position in the history of Italian unification. Gualterio insisted that economic factors were vitally important, and in this he was in complete agreement with Cavour, whose interest in economics, and specifically the railways, led him into an interest in the Italian national question. In their conviction that economic issues were fundamental Gualterio and Cavour were in agreement, paradoxically, with Marx, but their spiritual companions were, of course, rather the Manchester School in England. Gualterio, however, mixed with his respect for material forces a Catholic piety. Thus Carlo Alberto, a devout Catholic who took up arms against Austria in 1848, was one of Gualterio's heroes, if a tragic hero. On the whole these early 'moderate' interpreters of the Risorgimento would have accepted Mussolini's later exclamation: 'C'è di tutto!' ('There is everything in it!'). Revolution, diplomacy, war, regicide, every species of political activity, went to make up the Risorgimento. And so the interpretation emerged that all the participants in the movement had contributed to some glorious national synthesis. Such an interpretation, which became something of an orthodoxy, undermined early attempts to make a serious analysis of the forces at work in nineteenth-century Italy, and gave later scholars the difficult task of disentangling truth from mythology.

Of the four volumes of Gualterio's publication of 1850−1 two had been printed documents. He thus started a tradition in the historiography of the Risorgimento − that of supporting interpretations with published documents, documents selected inevitably with a bias, although not always a conscious bias. In the nineteenth century the editors of documents usually supported the moderate or pro-Cavour interpretation. Only in the mid twentieth century was a more deliberately impartial approach adopted. The first editors of relevant documents after 1861 were usually either Piedmontese, or exiles from other Italian states who had settled in Piedmont. The editor of a very early, yet impressive, collection of documents was Nicomede Bianchi, who was born in Reggio Emilia in 1810, and actually went to Vienna to study in 1844, but to study medicine, not history. Sympathizing with the Piedmontese cause in 1848, he escaped to Turin as an exile in 1849, and took Piedmontese citizenship in 1850. After 1870 he was principally responsible for founding and organizing the State Archives in Turin, archives which are still important for any student of the international history of the Risorgimento. This formidable scholar did much to give Piedmont and Cavour dominant roles in the historiography of Italian unification. His eight volumes of diplomatic documents, embedded in a commentary, the *Storia documentata della diplomazia europea in Italia dall'anno 1814 all'anno 1861*, were published in Turin over the years 1865 to 1872. In other words he had started to publish them even before Venice and Rome had become part of the kingdom. At the time he was accused of publishing documents written by, or intimately concerning, people who were still alive, or, like Cavour, had very recently died. To this he replied that it was better for friends of the people concerned to edit their writings rather than to leave the task to insensitive editors of the future. His argument unintentionally indicated that his approach was far from impartial. The collection of documents put Cavour in the best possible light, and the Bourbons of Naples in the worst possible light. By printing some passages of documents and suppressing others, Bianchi depicted Ferdinando II as a monster. Nor was he any kinder to Mazzini. He had available the correspondence between Mazzini and his mother, intercepted by the police and kept in the Turin archives, but refrained from publishing letters which would have illustrated the honesty and integrity of Mazzini. In his translation of documents from the French, Bianchi also made elementary mistakes. Yet his eight volumes were accepted as an indispensable source by several generations of historians, and even in the 1950s were still regarded as a starting-point for students of the diplomatic history of the unification of Italy.

The early interpretations, which depicted Cavour and the Piedmontese monarchy after 1852 as being almost infallible, but Mazzini and the republicans as being always misguided and subversive, were the work not only of Piedmontese historians, but also of men from other parts of Italy who had settled in Piedmont and felt a debt of gratitude for their new homeland, which had treated them sometimes with suspicion but more often with generosity. Gualterio and Bianchi fell into this category, as did Massari, who will be considered in a moment. Luigi Chiala was a native of Piedmont. Born in Ivrea, in the far north-west of Italy, in 1834, he was to live into the twentieth century, but he had known Cavour and was to do great services for the Piedmontese statesman by his writings and editorship. He fought in the war of 1859, and was a deputy in the Italian parliament from 1882 until 1902, when he was made a senator, and sat in the senate for the last two years of his life, from 1902 to 1904.

Like Bianchi's, Chiala's editorship of documents is slanted by the judicious omissions which he makes. Between 1884 and 1887 Chiala published six volumes of Cavour's letters, *Le lettere edite e inedite di Cavour*,[2] preceded by an introduction which was in effect a sizeable biography of Cavour. Since Cavour died so suddenly, aged only fifty-one, and at the peak of his political struggle, he had no time to write his own memoirs nor, probably, any inclination to do so. There is therefore no parallel with Bismarck's long and elegant, if acrimonious, reminiscences. Cavour's early death meant that his reputation had to depend on writers who had known him, worked with him, and admired him. They certainly did not fail him.

One last friend of Cavour, Giuseppe Massari, who left copious records and writings, must be mentioned. Massari, a Neapolitan, was born in 1821. His first hero was Gioberti, of whom he published some correspondence and biographical memoirs in 1860. Exiled in France and then in Turin, Massari became a close associate and apologist of Cavour. Perhaps his most important work was *La vita e il regno di Vittorio Emanuele II, primo re d'Italia*, published in Milan in 1878.[3] Already in 1875 he had published his life of Cavour, *Il conte di Cavour. Ricordi biografici*.[4] Both works fall well short of the standards of scholarship adopted even by Bianchi or Chiala. Massari is quite happy to give verbatim reports of conversations which he did not hear, nor does he bother to give any indication of his sources for such accounts. For the historian, Massari's most interesting publication is his own diary, a diary which provides great detail on the activities of Cavour, Vittorio Emanuele II, the British minister in Turin, Sir James Hudson, and countless others, during the culminating years of Italian unification, 1858–60. For many years historians had to content themselves with a very inadequate and inaccurate edition of this massive work, but in 1959 a fine Italian scholar, Emilia Morelli, produced an excellent edition which she entitled *Diario dalle cento voci* ('Diary from a hundred voices') *1858–1860*.[5] Chiala had on the whole limited himself to praising his own party – the Piedmontese moderates – without attacking their Italian republican enemies. Massari, on the other hand, makes Mazzini, in Dr Morelli's words, 'enemy number one'. Two eminent Italian historians, Adolfo Omodeo and Luigi Salvatorelli, both judged Massari to have a mediocre intelligence, and it is certainly as a diarist rather than as a historian that Massari has value, but his detailed day-to-day account of activities in Turin did much to support the picture of Cavour as the controlling mind during these two vital years.

Those English-speaking historians of the Risorgimento who wrote in the nineteenth century were inevitably influenced by the powerful pro-Piedmontese school which had preceded them, but they were also by temperament prepared to accept an interpretation favouring a moderate, quietly constitutional, tradition. However, they liked to see the history of the Risorgimento as a romantic epic, which contrasted with the somewhat prosaic nature of the history of Victorian England. Epics have heroes and villians, and are not improved if the heroes are sometimes noble but sometimes misguided or self-centred, nor if the heroes have complex disputes among themselves. The Victorian historians were on the whole prepared to see the Risorgimento as a struggle between good and evil forces, a struggle in which the good forces eventually triumphed. One of the more influential English historians was

H. Bolton King, who wrote at the end of the nineteenth century. He published his *History of Italian Unity* in 1899, a work translated first into French and then into Italian. After graduating at Balliol College, Bolton King had worked for eight years at Toynbee Hall. For ten years, from 1888 to 1898, he worked on the extensive Risorgimento material in the British Museum, the material collected mainly by Sir Antony Panizzi, the Italian émigré who had been appointed director of the museum by Gladstone, and who had been largely responsible for the creation of the splendid Reading Room. The positive and original feature in Bolton King's history is his awareness of the social question. He quotes, with approval, Cavour's perceptive comment: 'To harmonize the North with the South is more difficult than to fight Austria or to struggle with Rome.' But so far as his interpretation of the political history of unification is concerned, his work established in Britain the pro-Piedmontese tradition which was not to be seriously revised until after the Second World War. His avowed intention in writing his two-volume history was to encourage Italians to return to what he believed to have been the liberal democratic tradition of the Risorgimento, instead of pursuing the reactionary tendencies of the end of the century or the chauvinism which, in 1896, had led them into disaster in Africa. Italy needed, according to Bolton King, 'another Cavour, wise, honest, and a lover of freedom'.

In addition to his *History of Italian Unity* Bolton King wrote a study of Mazzini of considerable depth and understanding.[6] He recognized the sincerity and selflessness of Mazzini, and pointed out that the not uncommon impression that Mazzini was simply a fanatical conspirator was absurdly superficial. Bolton King stresses that Mazzini was a 'puritan', and this is intended as high praise. Another of Bolton King's principal heroes – Ricasoli – is also considered to be a puritan, as, in some respects, he was. Bolton King is perfectly aware of Mazzini's failings and yet, by concentrating on his virtues, and at the same time considering Cavour an honest lover of liberty, he gives a misleading picture, a picture which understates the conflicts between Italians at the culminating moment of the creation of Italy.

If Bolton King was the first serious English historian of the Risorgimento, the first to have a great impact on the reading public was without doubt George Macaulay Trevelyan. The grandson of Macaulay, Trevelyan was born in 1876, and was to live until 1962. No longer a young man at the time of the First World War, Trevelyan formed a remarkable link between the Victorians and the immense historiographical activity which followed the Second World War. His career thus bridged several generations of historical writing. He inherited from his brilliantly successful grandfather a felicity of literary style which carried his books far beyond a purely academic readership. In the Second World War in the tiny libraries of British army units all over the world Trevelyan's books were always prominent, and always read. So fluent is Trevelyan's prose that the reader can easily forget the precise and painstaking research on the primary sources which Trevelyan had carried through before writing his elegant narrative. He chose Garibaldi for his earliest works because, he says in his autobiography, 'his life seemed to me the most poetic of all true stories'.[7] But having selected his topic for a romantic reason, he carried through an exhaustive programme of research on it. His famous trilogy on Garibaldi, *Garibaldi's Defence of the Roman Republic, Garibaldi and the Thousand*, and *Garibaldi and the Making of Italy* were published by Longmans, Green and Company in 1907, 1909, and 1911 respectively. He believed them to be his best works, because their inspiration was a poetic one. He visited Garibaldi's battlefields outside Rome and in Sicily, and interviewed many survivors of the Risorgimento. He was perfectly aware of the bitterness of the conflict between the moderates and the democrats, between Cavour and Garibaldi, yet in his total interpretation he seems to understress it. He argued that if Cavour had been able to annex Sicily to Piedmont in the summer of 1860 the Great Powers would have prevented him from taking Naples, while if Garibaldi had marched on Rome in the autumn Napoleon III would have intervened against Italy. Although the two points are probably valid ones, by linking them in a single argument Trevelyan was reinforcing the familiar interpretation of the movement of unification according to which apparently conflicting forces were in effect complementary as though Cavour and Garibaldi needed each other without realizing it. The argument has a certain seductive elegance about it, but it underestimates the fundamental contrast between the aims of the moderates and those of the democrats.

After the First World War Trevelyan wrote one more work on the Risorgimento – *Manin and the Venetian Revolution of 1848*.[8] Although less impressive than the great Garibaldi trilogy, Trevelyan's book on Manin had less success than it deserved. But by today's standards and today's interests it is inevitably dated. It is interesting to contrast it with a book written by a young English historian, and published in 1979 – Paul Ginsborg's *Daniele Manin and the Venetian Revolution of 1848–49*.[9] While Ginsborg gives a sympathetic picture of Manin, he is far more aware of Manin's limitations than was Trevelyan. Ginsborg is also interested in the peasant movements on the Venetian mainland, movements with which Trevelyan did not deal. But if Trevelyan's view of the Risorgimento seems today dated, if not a little quaint, his three books on Garibaldi will surely remain respected classics, very much as the works of Macaulay have done.

The thought of several writers in the democratic or socialist tradition, writers who played a role in the political movements of the mid nineteenth century – Giuseppe Ferrari, Carlo Cattaneo, Carlo Pisacane – are considered later in the book. They were already starting to criticize the essentially political arguments of the pro-Piedmontese moderates, and to suggest that social and regional questions, as well as the purely national one, should be considered. They already had a concept of 'class struggle', although their definitions of classes were somewhat broad and ill-defined. Perhaps the first very moderately socialist historian with the academic qualifications and the intellectual precision needed to define the Risorgimento in terms of social classes was Gaetano Salvemini. In his penetrating study of the political thought of Mazzini, Salvemini praises him for his successful preaching of the need to create a unitary state, and then, in the more original part of the book, discusses Mazzini's relations with socialism.[10] In spite of Mazzini's declared aversion to socialism, and Salvemini's own socialist convictions, Salvemini believed that a united democratic state, a state which would be created by the bourgeoisie, like the one recommended by Mazzini, was a necessary forerunner of a socialist state, which would eventually be created by the working class. He was thus reconciling a positive interpretation of Mazzinianism with a mildly socialist approach.[11] After the Fascists came to power Salvemini went into exile, but he survived Fascism to become a much respected historian after the birth of the Italian Republic. He was perhaps the first Italian historian to make clear that the nationalism of Mazzini had nothing to do with the nationalism of Mussolini. Much of Salvemini's life was dedicated to a condemnation of Italian imperialism, but that struggle is clearly outside the terms of reference of this book.

Salvemini had been born in 1873 and so, like Trevelyan, knew many of the survivors of the Risorgimento. A younger left-wing historian, born near Perugia in 1886, was Luigi Salvatorelli. Combining academic and journalist activities Salvatorelli rapidly moved from an interest in the political and social aspects of the history of early Christianity to an interest in the history of modern Italy. In 1925, when Mussolini established complete control in Italy, Salvatorelli was obliged to give up his journalistic activities, and then produced at great speed works on the Middle Ages, but also, in 1939, a study of the Triple Alliance. He claimed that his roots were in the eighteenth-century Enlightenment. In a world which was turning against rationalism he proclaimed himself an unrepentant rationalist. So far as the history of the Risorgimento was concerned he started an important variation in interpretation. 'It would not be exact', he argued, to say that Cavour and Mazzini complemented each other in the work of unification. Such an interpretation would be 'a beautiful construction in historical reconciliation, but an arbitrary one: a little poem, a pastoral eclogue, not history. In reality there was in the struggle a winner and a loser; the winner was Cavour, the loser Mazzini.'[12]

But the central figure among Italian socialist historians in the twentieth century has without doubt been Antonio Gramsci, who used an orthodox Marxism as a substructure of his interpretation of the Risorgimento, but built upon it a highly original and sophisticated superstructure. He was born in the island of Sardinia in 1891. He joined the Socialist Party in 1910, founded the newspaper the *Ordine Nuovo* in 1919, and was one of the principal founders of the Communist Party in 1921, and a guiding spirit in the workers' occupation of the factories in Turin, an occupation which could well have led to a communist revolution. He was condemned by the Fascists in 1928 to twenty years' imprisonment, which was later reduced to ten. He died in a prison hospital in 1937. His writing on the Risorgimento while he was in prison, where he managed to obtain many recently published works of history, have since been published in a single volume.[13] His prison notebooks became a classic of Italian historiography, just as his letters from prison became a classic of Italian literature. The historical commentaries are often little more than jottings, but so full are they of stimulating ideas that they have been the basis

7

of a school of socialist history, and the starting-point of sharp polemics.

Gramsci's introduction to the study of philosophy and of history had been in the school of Benedetto Croce, much as Marx's had been in the school of Hegel. But Gramsci had quickly rejected Croce's Hegelian idealism, and turned to the materialism of Marx. He accepted the Marxist interpretation of the great French Revolution of 1789 as a 'bourgeois' revolution, but he added a modification of his own to that interpretation: he pointed out that the middle-class leaders of the Jacobin revolution had recognized the needs of the peasants, and so had created an active, national revolution. The bourgeois leaders of the Risorgimento – including Mazzini and his followers – had failed to do the same in Italy. He realized, however, that the lack of national unity in Italy made it impossible for Mazzini's Party of Action to act as the French Jacobins had acted. However, he believed that the peasants could, and should, have been involved in the movement for independence and unification. The Risorgimento in Gramsci's eyes was 'an agrarian revolution *manqué*'. The role of the peasants in the Risorgimento will be considered in several different contexts in the course of this volume. Sometimes they supported the middle-class nationalists, and sometimes their support was rejected; sometimes they opposed the middle-class nationalists, and were concerned only with their own needs: and on those occasions the middle-class nationalists – whether 'moderate' or Mazzinians – showed no understanding of the peasants. There was then much to be said in support of Gramsci's thesis of an 'agrarian revolution *manqué*'. However, he overstated and oversimplified it. The arguments against it from the right will be considered in a moment, but it must be said that some Marxist historians have since rejected the 'agrarian revolution *manqué*' interpretation. Aldo Romano, in his *Storia del movimento socialista in Italia* (3 vols., Milan, 1954–55), discarded the interpretation, although without mentioning Gramsci. It was unrealistic, Romano believed, to expect the peasants in the nineteenth century to contribute to a revolution. It was with the urban workers, in Romano's eyes, that hope lay, and the prominent rôle played by urban workers in Rome in 1848–49 and in Florence in 1859 lends some strength to his argument. Gramsci had inspired and led the urban working class in the attempt to start a communist revolution in Italy after the First World War, but the employees he had known were working in the motorcar industry – in other words they were genuine members of a modern proletariat. The urban workers of the Risorgimento were pre-industrial – artisans, shopkeepers – no more members of a proletariat in the Marxist sense than were the peasants.

Gramsci's interpretation of the rôle of the peasant in the Risorgimento was less specific and less original than his explanation of the success of the moderates and the failure of Mazzini's Party of Action. The moderates, he explained, were a tightly cohesive social group. They were, in fact, mostly Piedmontese aristocrats. The Mazzinians came from a wider geographical and social background. After 1848 the Piedmontese moderates had a hold on political power, including control of an existing army. It was therefore not difficult for them to start seducing Mazzinian leaders into their ranks. The term *trasformismo*, or 'transformism', was first coined to define the corrupt methods by which De-pretis, prime minister of Italy after 1876, bribed political leading figures and deputies to join his ministries, or to vote for him in parliament. Gramsci extended the use of the term in an effective and illuminating manner: 'It could be said that Italian political life since 1848 has been characterized by trans-formism, that is by the elaboration of an ever larger ruling class within the framework fixed by the moderates after 1848 and the failure of the neo-guelph and federalist utopias with the gradual but continuous absorption of rival and often hostile elements.'[14]

In other words Cavour, the National Society, and the moderates splintered away the intellectual leaders of the Party of Action except, of course, the rock-like Mazzini himself, who became ever more isolated. The concept of a central political force which attracts to itself potentially rival forces seemed not to apply to the period in which Gramsci himself was writing – the fascist period. Yet, astonishingly, it seems to apply very eloquently to the period of Italian history since the Second World War, a period long after Gramsci's death.

The best known philosopher of modern Italy, Benedetto Croce, wrote little on the period of history covered by this book. His major work on nineteenth-century Italy, the *History of Italy from 1871 to 1915*, clearly has only an ob-lique relevance to the period 1790–1870, and his history of Naples has only a few perceptive pages at the very end which are relevant. Among his more immediate followers Federico Chabod wrote primarily on the twentieth cen-tury. Only Adolfo Omodeo deserves mention here. A Sicilian, born in 1889, he fought with distinction in the First World War. He did not for long survive the Second World War, dying in 1946. Like Croce he had no intellec-tual sympathy for fascism but, like Croce, he remained in Italy during the fascist period. Croce's school could not be termed Hegelians of the Right, since they disapproved of the aggressive imperialism of Mussolini, nor could they be termed Hegelians of the Left, since they disapproved of socialism. But since they disapproved of the aggressive imperialism of Mussolini, nor could be considered Hegelians of the Centre. Omodeo lacked the literary elegance of Croce or Chabod. His books tear and bluster their way through his argu-ments. Yet he had a strong and robust understanding of the Risorgimento. One of his most important themes – expressed early in his career – was that there was a striking contrast between the nationalism of Mazzini, planned as a vehicle for securing freedom and civilization, with the nations of the world living together within their frontiers at peace, and the nationalism of Bis-marck's Germany, which assumed permanent rivalry and hostility among na-tions and twisted Darwinian ideas into a justification for this assumption. The myth surrounding Carlo Alberto – that he was a great, if tragic, hero of the Risorgimento – was also destroyed by Omodeo, who considered him 'a figure in historical and human terms interesting . . . in his mystical-romantic dream, in the inadequacy of his gifts, in his struggle with a hard world, in his tragic fate'.[15] A note of realism was beginning to creep into the historical account of the Risorgimento.

But Omodeo's major work was his *Opera politica del conte di Cavour*.[16] The book was never finished, but the commentary to 1857 was published in a volume entitled *Difesa del risorgimento* (see note 15). Omodeo depicted Cavour as a liberal – first a Piedmontese liberal, and then a liberal as regards the Italian question. He stressed that Cavour refused to serve as a minister under the absolutist régime of Carlo Alberto but, although in this sense he was an idealistic liberal, once he came to power Cavour was a realist and was prepared to secure his aims by methods of which Machiavelli would have approved. Omodeo's account of Cavour and his policy was a balanced one: he recognized that Cavour made mistakes, but he underlined Cavour's achievements. He modified the extravagant eulogies of Chiala, Bianchi and Massari, but he repeated the misleading general theme that Cavour and Mazzini complemented each other.

After the Second World War a number of Marxist historians developed Gramsci's thesis of the agrarian revolution *manqué*, although, as has been seen, not even all Marxist historians accepted it. From the right the thesis was virulently attacked in the 1950s by a young Sicilian historian, Rosario Romeo. An extension of Gramsci's thesis, an extension which he himself had expressed, had argued that because the bourgeois leaders of the Risorgimento had ignored the interests of the peasants, the Kingdom of Italy created in 1861 had also ignored those interests. Romeo, on the other hand, argued that there was no possibility of Italy becoming industrialized and prosperous except on the basis of capital accumulated by agriculture. The new state had to extract its revenue from agriculture, and this meant that heavy taxes on the peasants were unavoidable. On the other hand, even some non-socialist economic historians have argued that the grinding taxes on the peasants after 1861 deprived them of money for all but the bare essentials of life, and so prevented the growth of a domestic market for manufactured products – an argument which has a Keynesian rather than a Marxist flavour about it.

Romeo's approach was perhaps slightly suspect. His critique of Gramsci is contained in a volume entitled *Risorgimento e capitalismo*,[17] which consisted of two articles which had already been published: 'La storiografia politica marxista' and 'Problemi dello sviluppo capitalistico in Italia dal 1861 al 1887'.[18] The second article had appeared two years after the first, two years during which much was published and Romeo himself had carried out further investigations, yet his interpretation had not been modified in any way. But this is perhaps to judge Romeo by harsh standards. He himself wrote in 1959 that the question is still an open one, and it would be well to regard it as an open one in 1982. The vitality of the writing of history can be only harmed by closed minds.

In the period between the two world wars English-speaking historians continued to write within Trevelyan's interpretation, according to which the Risorgimento was a great epic story with the activities of the leaders complementing each other. A. J. Whyte wrote two scholarly and detailed volumes on Cavour,[19] and a more general history of the Risorgimento entitled *The Evolution of Modern Italy*, which is still sometimes cited in bibliographies of

British textbooks as though it were still relevant and authoritative.[20] But all Whyte's writings are, by modern standards of historical interpretation, very dated in their approach.

The breakthrough in British historiography of the Risorgimento came with the publication in 1954 of Denis Mack Smith's *Cavour and Garibaldi, 1860*.[21] Mack Smith did not follow a Marxist interpretation, nor did he glorify Mazzini or Garibaldi, but he did not hesitate to suggest that Cavour had retarded the development of Italian democracy. The significant aspect of Mack Smith's interpretation, both in this first work of detailed research and in the many books and articles which he has written since, is that the unification of Italy resulted from bitter struggles between Italians rather than from a glorious synthesis of forces which were basically in agreement though, for the moment, rivals.

The documentary sources of Italian nineteenth-century history, sources from which all these historians have drawn in such full measure, are scattered among many archives. A country, like Britain or France, which has been united for centuries, will have a central national archive. Clearly this cannot be the case with Italy, where the state archives, the *Archivi di Stato*, of the formerly independent states, still retain a great deal of important material. Perhaps the most important *Archivio di Stato* outside Rome is the one in Turin, where many drafts or autographed dispatches of Cavour are kept. In the same way museums and archives of the Risorgimento exist in every large Italian city, and contain priceless collections of private papers. The Central Archive and Museum of the Risorgimento in Rome was founded in 1906. Acting also as the headquarters of the *Istituto per la storia del risorgimento italiano*, the archive, which has some 500,000 documents, must be one of the most remarkably situated in the world. It is at the top of the Victor Emmanuel II Monument, familiarly called the 'Wedding Cake'. A lift carries the researcher far above Rome or, if the lift is not working, he or she must climb several hundred steps. The Institute is presided over by two eminent historians – Professor Alberto M. Ghisalberti and Dr Emilia Morelli, who are also responsible for the publication of the most important journal dealing with the Risorgimento – the *Rassegna storica del risorgimento*, a journal whose articles are often quoted in these pages. In the *Rassegna* Dr Morelli has contributed many articles surveying the various collections of private papers in this central archive. Also deserving of special mention among the many museums of the Risorgimento in Italy is the Library, Archive and Museum of the Risorgimento and Contemporary History in Milan. It has a valuable collection of nineteenth-century pamphlets and journals. So far as diplomatic documents go the archives of the Foreign Ministry in Rome are central, but many important despatches and papers are scattered around Italy in the various state archives.

A great number of diplomatic documents have been published. Those published in the nineteenth century – like those edited sometimes not too reliably, by Chiala and Bianchi – have already been mentioned. In 1913 a royal commission was instituted to publish those of Cavour's papers which were concerned with his political, rather than his personal, existence. The work of the commission was halted by the First World War, but started again in 1920. The volumes were published by Zanichelli of Bologna. The first four volumes contained Cavour's correspondence with his confidential agent, Costantino Nigra, in Paris, over the vital years 1858–61: *Il carteggio Cavour-Nigra dal 1858 al 1861*. Two volumes dealt with the Roman Question: *La questione romana negli anni 1860–1861*. Two further volumes dealt with relations with Britain, through Cavour's correspondence with his minister in London: *Cavour e l'Inghilterra. Carteggio con V. E. d'Azeglio*. One volume contained Cavour's correspondence with his friend Salmour, who was also in Paris at this culminating moment of the movement for Italian independence: *Carteggio Cavour-Salmour*. Finally five volumes dealt with the crisis of 1860 and the creation of the Kingdom of Italy: *La liberazione del Mezzogiorno e la formazione del Regno d'Italia*. The whole series was immensely important since it made apparent the omissions in the nineteenth-century editions, and provided much material for a proper understanding of the process by which Italy was united. At least one good thing had come out of Fascist Italy.

One important source for the history of the Italian Question was the British Blue Book. In the nineteenth century a great number of diplomatic papers were printed in London, 'laid on the table of the House' – in other words, made available to MPs – and sold to the public. Publication reached a peak in the Palmerston period, and many volumes and single printed despatches dealt with Italy. They were, of course, edited by the Foreign Office, but comparison with the original manuscripts shows that they were often edited with a surprisingly light touch. Often only references to individuals, references of a disparaging kind, were omitted.

Since the Second World War an even more scholarly generation of Italian historians than that of the 1930s have edited many volumes of diplomatic documents. Two or three samples can be mentioned here, as an indication of the kind of material which has been made so readily available to historians, but several other equally excellent series have been published. Relations between Piedmont and Britain were covered in eight volumes. Federico Curato edited *Le relazioni diplomatiche fra la Gran Bretagna e il regno di Sardegna* in five volumes, taking the story from 1848 to the end of 1856. Giuseppe Giarizzo edited three further volumes in the series, covering the period 1857 to March 1861, in other words to the amount of unification.[22] The diplomatic relations between other Italian states, and with other Great Powers, have been illustrated by other series of volumes. As a final example, one of the more recent publications can be mentioned: *Le relazioni diplomatiche fra il regno Due Sicilie e il regno di Prussia, 1814–1848*, edited by Giuseppe Coniglio.[23]

Of the national editions of the writings of Mazzini and Garibaldi the former appeared on the more massive scale, running into a hundred volumes.[24] Garibaldi's writings, which have appeared in diverse, fragmentary forms in the past, are now appearing in a national edition published by the *Istituto per la storia del risorgimento italiano*. The most recent volume, *Epistolario di Giuseppe Garibaldi*, vol IV: *1859*, appeared in 1982 (Istituto per la storia del risorgimento italiano: Rome). There is a centre for the private papers of Cavour at

Santena in Piedmont, which has produced several monographs and printed documents. Perhaps it is sufficient to say here that an inventory of the papers at Santena has been edited by Giovanni Silengo. It runs into three volumes and over 900 pages.[25] While Cavour never wrote his own memoirs, there is a considerable wealth of autobiographies, memoirs and diaries of other figures of the Risorgimento. Reference will be made to many of them in the course of this book.

The Risorgimento has attracted more attention from historians than any previous period of modern Italian history after the Renaissance. It has been a happy coincidence that a period which has so fired the imagination of historians has also provided such rich sources.

NOTES

An excellent survey of writings on the Risorgimento until 1960 is Walter Maturi, *Interpretazioni del risorgimento*, Turin, 1962. The book was made up from lectures given by Maturi over the years 1945 to 1960, the first two at the University of Pisa, the others at the University of Turin. It is a masterpiece of balanced and lucid interpretation.

Still an admirable introduction to the Risorgimento is Alberto Maria Ghisalberti, *Introduzione alla storia del risorgimento*, Rome, 1942.

Three general histories with very differing approaches must be mentioned here. Giorgio Candeloro's *Storia dell'Italia moderna*, Milan, 1956– , is an invaluable detailed narrative history. The most recent volume to be published, volume IX, appeared in 1981. After a tenth volume there is to be a final volume containing a chronology and index, which will convert the series into an extremely useful work of reference. The volumes relevant to this book are: I. *Le origini del risorgimento 1700–1815*; II. *Dalla Restaurazione alla Rivoluzione nazionale 1815–1846*; III. *La Rivoluzione nazionale 1846–1849*; IV. *Dalla Rivoluzione nazionale all'Unità 1849–1860*; and V. *La costruzione dello stato unitario 1860–1871*.

The second general history deserving of mention is Cesare Spellanzon's *Storia del risorgimento e dell'unità d'Italia*, 7 volumes, Milan, 1933–60. Like Candeloro, a historian of the left, Spellanzon, who died in 1957 leaving his great work unfinished, gave an immensely detailed account of the Risorgimento, but an account less balanced and less controlled than Candeloro's.

The third general history which must be mentioned is the impressive if idiosyncratic Einaudi *Storia d'Italia*. Volume III, *Dal primo Settecento all'Unità*, published in 1973, is the relevant one for this book. It contains four sections – Stuart J. Woolf, *La storia politica e sociale*, which is mentioned again, in its revised version in English, in the notes to Chapter 6; Alberto Caracciolo, *La storia economica*; Nicola Badaloni, *La cultura*, which deals rather more with the eighteenth than the nineteenth century; and Franco Venturi, as lively and brilliant as always, *L'Italia fuori d'Italia*, placing Italy in the European context.

The economic history of Italy as a whole throughout the period has not been well handled, but two works deserve mention: Shepard B. Clough, *The Economic History of Modern Italy*, New York, 1964, is important for its first two or three chapters, and the first two chapters of Rodolfo Morandi, *Storia della grande industria in Italia*, Turin, 1966, give a good sketch of industrial development from Napoleonic times to 1870. A young generation of historians is now doing valuable work on Italian economic history.

1. Le Monnier: Florence, 1850–1, 4 volumes.
2. Roux e C.: Turin, 1884–7, six volumes, with a seventh containing the index.
3. Milan, 1878.
4. Turin, 1875.
5. Rocca San Casciano, 1959.
6. *Mazzini*, London, 1903.
7. *An Autobiography and Other Essays*, London, 1949, p. 13.
8. London, 1923.
9. Cambridge, 1979.
10. *Mazzini* (original Italian edition 1905, English translation by I. W. Rawson: London, 1956).
11. The question is considered for its own sake, outside the context of Salvemini's interpretation, in Ch. 14.
12. Luigi Salvatorelli, *Prima e dopo il quarantotto*, Turin, 1948, p. 189.
13. Antonio Gramsci, *Il risorgimento* (*quaderni dal carcere*), 3, Turin, 1949, rpr. 1966.
14. Ibid., 1966, p. 70. Gramsci's general conclusions on the nature of a ruling class, conclusions which go far beyond a consideration of the history of Italy or, for that matter, of Marxist orthodoxy, follow on from page 70, and reward consideration.
15. Adolfo Omodeo, *Difesa del risorgimento*, Turin, 1951, p. 222.
16. Florence, 1940.
17. Bari, 1959.
18. In *Nord e Sud*, August–September 1956 and July–August 1958.
19. *The Early Life and Letters of Cavour*, London, 1925, 2 vols, and *The Political Life and Letters of Cavour*, London, 1930.
20. A. J. Whyte, *The Evolution of Modern Italy*, was published in a heavily revised and modernized version by the Cambridge University Press in 1963. It constituted the second half of the volume *A Short History of Italy*, edited by H. Hearder and D. P. Waley. In this book the antiquated aspects of Whyte's account have been eliminated.
21. Cambridge, 1954.
22. The eight volumes were published by the *Istituto storico Italiano per l'età moderna e contemporanea*, Rome?
23. Also published in Rome for the *Istituto storico italiano per l'età moderna e contemporanea* in 1977.
24. *Scritti editi ed inediti di Guiseppe Mazzini*, ed. M. Menghini (edizione nazionale), Imola, 1906–1940.
25. Fondazione Camillo Cavour: Santena, 1974.

PART TWO

The states and regions before unification: political developments, the economy and conditions of life

CHAPTER ONE

Lombardy and Venetia

The capital of Lombardy, Milan, with a population of 131,000, was the second city in the Habsburg Monarchy in 1790. Like the rest of the Monarchy, Lombardy had experienced the reforms of the enlightened despot, Joseph II, who died in 1790 after a reign of ten years. His brother, who succeeded him as Leopold II, preserved the more constructive of his reforms, but abandoned the less popular. The effect of the reforms had been to rationalize the legal codes – in particular humanizing the penal code to some extent – and to limit the power of the Church by placing it under the control of the state. Before the French Revolution the social structure of Lombardy, which had never been 'feudal' in the full sense of the term, was a more advanced one than that of France.

A small group of Italian intellectuals in Milan had, in the second half of the eighteenth century, discussed the need for economic and administrative reform in Lombardy, and their discussions, especially in their journal, *Il Caffè*, which was published briefly in the 1760s, had eventually exerted some influence on the reforms. The editor of *Il Caffè* and the leading spirit in the group was Pietro Verri, who lived through the era of the enlightened despots into the age of the French Revolution. Verri recorded the reactions of the Milanese to the events of 1789 in France. He noted that they first applauded and then, like most people outside France, condemned what they regarded as extremism. But Verri himself believed that the creation of a constitution for France must bring progress and prosperity. In his *Thoughts on the political state of Milan in 1790* (in *Scritti vari*, Carcano: Florence, 1854, vol. II) he recommended a constitution for Lombardy, but a constitution based on a franchise limited to property owners. The new emperor, Leopold II, had asked the local governments of the Lombard towns to submit lists of their needs, and Verri seized the opportunity to suggest a constitution, but the Milanese dignitaries did not forward his suggestion to Vienna. Leopold II was frightened of the possibility of revolution in Lombardy. Involved in a war with the Ottoman Empire, and preoccupied by events in France where his foolish niece, Queen Marie Antoinette, was in a dangerous situation, he was only too ready to placate his Italian subjects. The Austrian officials who had governed Lombardy in the days of the Empress Maria Theresa (1748–80) had enjoyed a certain amount of autonomy from Vienna, and there had even been an element of representation for the richer Italian inhabitants in bodies known as 'general congregations' and 'patrimonial congregations'. Maria Theresa's benevolent system had been abolished in 1786 by Joseph II, as an aspect of his frantic effort to centralize the empire, but Leopold II brought it back in 1791, partly because of petitions from the Lombards.

Leopold died on 1 March 1792, and was succeeded by his son Francis II. The change in emperors meant that the age of the Enlightenment in the Habsburg Monarchy was over. Francis II was quickly identified throughout Europe as a principal leader of the *ancien régime* against the 'ideas of 1789'. But the Jacobin movement of 1792–4 in France, which so quickly spread to Naples, took longer to stimulate conspiracies in Austrian Lombardy. However, in 1794 a republican group in Milan was forming around a lawyer, Fedele Sopransi, while another was centred on students of the University of Pavia, some of whom were arrested and tried in February 1795. Much more numerous and typical than the Lombard Jacobins were the groups of Milanese who disapproved equally of the Jacobin phase of the revolution in Paris, and of the severe rule of the Austrian archduke, Ferdinand, who had been made governor of Lombardy. Among these so-called 'moderates' were Pietro Verri, who was sixty-six in 1794 and died three years later, and Count Francesco Melzi d'Eril, who was only forty-one and had a distinguished future ahead of him.

The Venetian Republic in its last days of independence was not so decadent that there was no response at all to the startling developments in France. Already in 1794 trials of Jacobin sympathizers were held in Brescia, most of the accused being noblemen, though some were priests and some were from the middle class. In Padua as early as 1791 there was a 'democratic club'.

The state and society of eighteenth-century Venice had undeniably reached a condition of extreme decadence. Two familiar symptoms of social decadence were present – an extreme ostentation in clothes and manners, and a distaste for that pursuit of trade which had made the Republic great in past centuries. The régime and constitution of the Republic had become increasingly exclusive and ossified over the centuries. The middle class was permitted no political nor administrative responsibility. The aristocratic ruling class in the city of Venice itself dominated all other classes, and even the nobility of the mainland. The sovereign body in law was the Grand Council, meetings of which all the thousand or so patricians over twenty-five could attend. The Senate – the real ruling body – was elected by the members of the Grand Council. The executive government was still known as the *signoria*, and the Council of Ten still held intelligence and security powers as it had done in the sixteenth century. The head of state, performing the functions of ceremonial figurehead, was still the Doge. In short the constitution of the Republic of St Mark had changed little since the Renaissance, except that the ruling class had become even more restricted and inward-looking. Rarely has a constitution proclaimed so blatantly the belief that one class is born to legislate and to govern.

Italy became involved in the wars of the French Revolution when, on 21 September 1792, the French attacked the Kingdom of Sardinia, without declaring war, and occupied Savoy and Nice. Yet even this was a false start to the wars so far as Italy was concerned. The revolutionary government in Paris in 1792 thought in terms of securing France's natural frontiers rather than of liberating the Italians. Only with the arrival of the government of the Directory in 1795 did French policy become more ambitious. The plan for 1796 was to force the Austrians to come to terms, after the French had signed an alliance with Piedmont and had secured a promise from the Piedmontese king, Vittorio Amedeo III, that he would recognize the French acquisition of Milan from Austria in some unspecified future.

On 2 March 1796 General Bonaparte, at the age of twenty-seven, was given command of the army of Italy. Within two months he had defeated the Piedmontese, and forced Vittorio Amedeo to sign an armistice allowing for the French occupation of all Piedmontese fortresses. On 8 May the Austrian governor in Milan, the Archduke Ferdinand, fled, and a few days later Napoleon won his first great victory against the Austrians at Lodi. The government of the Directory in Paris were not interested, at this moment, in occupying Lombardy, but intended Napoleon to move into Tuscany, to occupy Leghorn, and to threaten Rome and Naples. Napoleon believed such limited aims to be beneath his genius, which should be devoted to a march on Vienna. Meanwhile in Milan a revolutionary atmosphere was forming, and Jacobin ideas, which had been proscribed in France, were still being expressed. But on the whole the upper classes, led by Francesco Melzi and Paolo Greppi, were opposed to any violent movement, and were determined to keep the national question separate from the social question. Greppi, who had been studying in Paris at the time of the revolution, had a horror of Jacobinism.[1] He had no thoughts of uniting Italy, and would one day collaborate with Bonaparte. More far-seeing than Greppi, but not less cautious, was Melzi. Distrustful both of the republicans and of the French, Melzi still hoped for a constitutional state based on a restricted franchise. While in Melzi there was a stronger element of Italian nationalism than in Greppi, neither man had any links with the democrats.

Bonaparte had found Italian Jacobinism useful against the Piedmontese, but in the long run he was to turn for support to men with the more conservative convictions of Melzi and Greppi. Once the Piedmontese were defeated he decided to break with Italian radicalism. The Italian Jacobins adjusted to the change by moving their centre of activities from Turin to Milan. In May 1796 the Directory in Paris suppressed Babeuf's communist conspiracy, and when Babeuf was executed, Filippo Buonarroti, the Italian exile who was Babeuf's friend and supporter, was imprisoned. Thereafter the Directory were inclined to identify Italian Jacobinism with Babeuf's communism.

On 9 May the French crossed the Lombard frontier and were warmly and politely received by the Lombards. Napoleon announced that the 'religion, property and customs' of the Italians would be respected. 'We are enemies only of the tyrants who keep you slaves.' The aristocracy and bourgeoisie of

Milan probably did not really feel that they were anyone's 'slaves', but they accepted the conventions of rhetoric with their usual good manners. Francesco Melzi was chosen to lead a mission to Bonaparte to congratulate and welcome him. A highly cultured man, a cosmopolitan whose French was impeccable, Melzi seemed a good choice; he respected the peace and order of the old régime, but was to some extent in tune with the new ideas. If his meeting with Bonaparte was a somewhat strained and uncomfortable one, it yet contributed to Melzi's growing conviction that Lombardy had to break with Austria and seek an alliance with France, no matter what her own constitutional future in Italy was to be.

The democrats in Milan were in 1796 led by an aggressive and courageous journalist, Carlo Salvador, who had founded the first Jacobin club, the 'Society of the Friends of Liberty and Equality', or more familiarly, the *Società popolare*. Salvador independently secured a meeting with Napoleon, and asked him for freedom to act against the Milanese nobility, a freedom Napoleon firmly refused to grant. But he was not yet prepared to antagonize either Salvador and the Jacobins, or Melzi and the moderates. The Milanese democrats, for their part, also preferred for the time being to identify themselves with the French. Napoleon's army, after all, was still the army of the Revolution, civilian if not *sansculottes* in appearance — cheerful, friendly and spontaneous, in sharp contrast to the Austrian army, which had been uniformed and severely disciplined. After his arrival in Milan in 1796 Napoleon wrote back to the Directors in Paris saying that he was favourably impressed by the advanced political ideas of the Milanese, and he believed that they were ready for the creation of a republic. The Directory did not react to his suggestion. They were thinking of Lombardy in a totally negative sense — first as a source of loot, and second as a pawn to exchange with Austria for a more valuable piece or for an advantageous position. Napoleon himself was certainly not averse to sending Italian loot back to Paris: works of art, cash and precious metals were soon on their way. Anything of use to the French army in Milan — for example, horses — was at once requisitioned. The chests containing the public wealth of Milan were broken into, as were all offices of the government, of the Cathedral, of banks, of the *Monte di Pietà*, which provided a pawnbroker's service for the poor on reasonable terms, and other charitable institutions. Napoleon and the Directory were fighting a total war against Austria in the modern manner, and did not scruple to secure resources wherever they found them. The initial irregular mass looting by Napoleon was soon to be replaced by regular, but no less onerous, taxation. The vast scale of organized looting over the next three years — in Lombardy as elsewhere in Italy — gravely damaged the arguments of those Italians sympathetic to the French.

Support for the French in Lombardy initially came almost exclusively from the towns. The rural regions were often bitterly hostile. Only a week or so after Milan had warmly greeted Napoleon, great numbers of peasants, led by the rural aristocracy and priests, marched on Pavia, and forced the French military government there to surrender. Napoleon suppressed the rising with some brutality. Since initially he had no idea what the Directory would let him do with Lombardy, he was obliged to establish a military government in Milan. On 19 May 1796 he appointed three Frenchmen to form a 'Military Agency' to administer Lombardy under his own ultimate authority. So far as local government in Milan was concerned, he renovated the municipality, pensioning off the older councillors who had served under the Austrians, and appointing sixteen members of the Società popolare as the new officials. The Society's founder, Salvador, had French connections, though they were not connections likely to make him very popular in Paris at that moment: during the years he had lived in France he had been a friend of Marat, and had in fact been sent back to Italy by the French foreign minister. He made the principal aim of the Società popolare the creation of a French-type republic in Lombardy, but most of the other members were less radical than Salvador. A few noblemen joined, among them Duke Giovanni Galeazzo Serbelloni and Count Gaetano Porro, though they were initially not made very welcome. Porro felt obliged to renounce his titles and take a public oath that he would exchange his aristocratic clothes and way of life for those of an average citizen. A priest, Father Lattuada, joined the Society, in spite of its strongly anti-clerical attitude. One or two of the branches of the Society used churches for their meetings, which were open to the public and well attended. Trees of liberty were planted. Bonaparte reported to the Directorate: 'Ce pays c'est beaucoup plus patriote que le Piémont; il est plus près de la liberté'.[2] He tried to create the impression that he was forming a democratic government, but real power of course remained in his hands or in those of his military subordinates. In the other towns of Lombardy the old municipalities were left in existence, though all their public announcements were made in the name of the French Republic.

At the end of August 1796 Napoleon suppressed the 'Military Agency', and founded a 'General Administration of Lombardy', which quickly acquired the character of an authentic local government. On 9 October a Lombard legion was formed. Fighting beside the French, it flew the new Italian tricolour with its green, white and red stripes. The municipality of Milan and the General Administration of Lombardy were both eager for the creation of a republic. Milan was now the centre of lively political discussion, and had become the most politically conscious city in Italy. Exiles settled there from Piedmont, Naples and the Papal States, and many newspapers appeared. On 14 November, while Napoleon was occupied with his military campaign against the Austrians, a meeting of Italians in Milan solemnly declared the independence of Lombardy, its alliance with the French against the Austrians, and the intention of the meeting to organize a general election. The French military authorities closed the meeting, and its leaders – among them Carlo Salvador and the socialist, Enrico l'Aurora – were arrested, though released shortly afterwards. On 28 December Napoleon, with his usual lucidity, wrote to the Directory that there were in Lombardy 'three parties: 1st that which allows itself to be led by the French; 2nd that which would like freedom and even demonstrates this desire with some impatience; 3rd the party which is a friend to the Austrians and an enemy to the French. I support and encourage the first; I contain the second; and I repress the third . . . .' In other words he had not yet formed a clear idea of the political organization he wished to see in Lombardy, but had merely decided how he would treat the various political groups which had formed. It did not, however, take him long to come to more forceful conclusions. By April 1797 he felt sufficiently independent of the Directory to decide on the creation of the Cisalpine Republic in Lombardy. Meanwhile his relations with the Venetian Republic were reaching crisis point.

There was a certain proud lack of a sense of reality in Venetian policy in the last years of the Republic. The ambassadors in Paris, Antonio Cappello and, after him, Alvise Pisari, both implored the Venetian government to recognize the danger of her isolation and come to some arrangement with one of the Great Powers. The Republican government in Venice preferred to persist in its claim to be wholly neutral. But if Venice was neutral as between one Great Power and another, she could not be neutral as between the opposing ideologies. She was inevitably a part of the *ancien régime*, and when Louis XVI's brother, the Comte de Provence, who was passing incognito as the 'Comte de Lille', applied for refuge in Verona, the Doge's government could hardly refuse. De Lille lived for two years in the Venetian Republic, but was eventually asked to leave. He declared that he would not do so until he had expunged his family's name from the *Libro d'Oro* – the ancient register of the privileged classes in Venice – and until the armour donated by his ancestor, Henry IV, had been returned to him. The Republic of St Mark skilfully evaded these two embarrassing requests, and De Lille, to the immense relief of the Venetians, departed. The revolutionary government in Paris had been too irritated by De Lille's two years in Venice to be conciliated by his departure, and were much more antagonized by the fact that Austrian troops were allowed to move with impunity on Ventian soil. If the Directorate in Paris had been understanding of the plight of Venice, Napoleon was considerably less so. He threatened to burn down Verona and Venice. The Venetian Senate hastily agreed to provide him with a Danelaw to the value of a million francs a month, but this did not discourage him from invading Venetian territory. After his victorious campaign of 1796 he occupied Verona, and demanded an alliance with Venice. The Venetian government refused, still clinging to its neutral status. An anti-French rising in Verona in April 1797, and the sinking of a French ship, ironically called the *Libérateur d'Italie*, by guns in the Venetian fort on the Lido, brought matters to a head. By the Preliminaries of Leoben, which had just been signed, Napoleon had already promised most of the Venetian mainland to Austria. He now sent what was virtually an ultimatum to Venice, demanding the abolition of the ancient institutions of the Republic, the release of francophile political prisoners, and the breaking of diplomatic relations with Britain. On 1 May Napoleon declared war on Venice. The last act in the long life of the Senate was to issue orders for the defence of the city, and the withstanding of a siege, but the Doge, Ludovico Manin, and his ministers undermined the stand made by the Senate by a decision to come to terms with the French. The Grand Council was called to be told the government's decision. Only about a half of the members of the Council assembled – less than six hundred, and therefore not a legitimate quorum. Even so, the question was put as to whether Napoleon's demand for the abolition of the ancient constitution should be acceded to, and an overwhelming majority agreed to do so. On 16 May 1797 a proclamation announced the end of the old institutions, and the recognition of the people as sovereign, under a temporary emergency government. The hereditary rights of the nobility, and of the Grand Council, were thus surrendered. The French were to be asked to provide troops to guarantee law and order for a limited period.

These events were regarded by the people of Venice as a long-awaited revolution, to be accompanied by joyful demonstrations in the Piazza San Marco. A tree of liberty was planted in the centre of the Piazza, and the Libro d'Oro, with its names of the once-privileged families, was burnt. All prisoners were released, and the French tricolour was raised. Meanwhile the towns of the mainland – even places as near as Mestre and Chioggia, and the little island of Torcello – proclaimed their independence from Venice. On 17 October 1797 Napoleon signed the Treaty of Campo Formio with the Austrians, giving them Venice herself and her possessions across the Adriatic in Istria and Dalmatia. Before leaving the French helped themselves to Venetian ships, cash and many works of art, including the famous bronze horses which are today back in their places on the gallery in the front of San Marco. The French then departed, on 18 January 1798, the Austrians entering the same day. There was considerable irony in the fact that only six months before the people of Venice had been rejoicing at their new-found liberty. No one rejoiced at the arrival of the Austrians.

While he was betraying the Venetians Bonaparte continued to support and expand the Cisalpine Republic. On 19 May 1797 he decided to add to the Cisalpine not only Reggio and Modena, but also the mountainous country stretching across to Massa and Carrara. Ferrara and Bologna, which had briefly been united in the small Cispadane Republic, were annexed to the Cisalpine in July by a decree of the Directory in Paris. The Cisalpine Republic now included the ancient and considerable cities of Milan, Modena, Mantua, Bologna and Ferrara.

The Italian inhabitants of the Cisalpine Republic were not consulted over the drafting of its constitution, which was a copy of the French constitution of 1795. Both the Directors and the legislature were to be appointed by Napoleon himself. The five Directors – all Italians – were named with the publication of the constitution. The legislature was to have two chambers, the 'Council of Seniors', and the 'Grand Council'. Civil marriage was introduced, as were the inheritance laws adopted by the French Revolution, laws by which the right of primogeniture and deed of trust were abolished, and women given equal rights of succession to men. Although there were, then, some egalitarian features in Napoleon's creation of the Cisalpine Republic, the fact that they were all granted by his grace and favour – at a time when he was still merely a general in the French army – was offensive to the Milanese democrats. But it was precisely Napoleon's fear of this group which led him to act in so arbitrary a manner. He himself had no intention of bringing about a social revolution in Italy, and was merely concerned to appease the democrats so far as possible without giving them real power or allowing them basically to influence his policy. The Cisalpine Republic, with its three and a half million inhabitants, was more important for the national question than was any anticipation of social revolution. Austria was obliged by a term of the Treaty of Campo Formio to extend diplomatic recognition to the Cisalpine, but when Napoleon left Milan on 17 November 1797 the condition of the Republic as a neighbour to Austrian Venice was far from secure. Before his departure he had turned against the democrats, closing one of their clubs, the *Circolo costituzionale*, and curbing the press. After his departure the democrats reasserted some of their lost authority by reopening the Circolo costituzionale and re-assuming control of the police. Bonaparte's command of the French army in Italy passed to General Berthier, but from Paris Bonaparte tied the Cisalpine more closely to France by negotiating a treaty of alliance by which the Cisalpine was obliged to enter any war in which France was engaged as her ally. France was to leave an army of 25,000 men in the Cisalpine Republic, which was to pay the cost of the army, and the Cisalpine was itself to maintain an army of 30,000 men. These one-sided terms were forced upon the Cisalpine Republic by Talleyrand, Napoleon's foreign minister, but on protests from the Directors of the Cisalpine Republic they were appreciably modified: it was agreed that the Cisalpine need sustain an army of only 22,000 – even this figure being probably beyond its resources – and France was to guarantee the independence of the Republic and refer to it in future peace treaties. The Cisalpine Directory had not forgotten the fate of Venice. The treaty was signed finally on 22 February 1798, and was followed by a commercial treaty, limiting tariffs between the two states to 6 per cent. The conclusion of these negotiations suggest that the Cisalpine Republic had some claim to being regarded as an independent Italian sovereign state. To the French Directors and to French diplomats in Italy it seemed indeed that the Cisalpine Republic was becoming too independent, and that talk in Milan of uniting Italy into a single republic was becoming too uninhibited. Nor were the Lombard moderates less ambitious, in their way, than the democrats. At the Congress of Rastadt, which sat throughout 1798 to resolve Franco-Austrian problems, the Cisalpine Republic was represented by Melzi, who was pressing for the creation of an Italian kingdom to include the Cisalpine, Piedmont and Genoa. Not surprisingly, he had no success, and resigned office for the time being, withdrawing to the estates he owned in Spain. Meanwhile, on 13 April 1798, the French military authorities in Milan forced the resignation of the two most independently minded of the Directors. More drastic steps still were taken in the summer. A new constitution was introduced, making the legislative houses smaller and less influential. Thereafter continual changes were made, both in the constitution and the personnel of the Directorate, depending upon which French agent happened to be in Milan. The apparent independence achieved by the Cisalpine in 1797 was thus short-lived, nor did the desperate deficit revealed by the budget of September 1798 help things.

Yet the Grand Council of the Cisalpine was capable of debating basic issues in 1798 – a new code of laws, a new land settlement, and a new judicial system – but little could in practice be done in the uncertain international situation and the precarious financial state of the Republic. A sweeping plan to reform education was drawn up. Secondary education had under the Austrians been entirely in the hands of the Church. All education was now to be secularized, and science was to be given a predominant place. Latin, which was associated with the Church rather than with Renaissance scholarship, was no longer to be taught. Nothing was to come of the plan when Napoleon's enthusiasm for the ideas of the Revolution faded. But in other respects relations between Church and State in the Cisalpine Republic suffered a sharp change. The constitution promised absolute freedom of religion, except that the government was given the power to control the exercise of religious worship when it became harmful to the state. No one could 'be forced to contribute to the expenses of any cult'. By a law of October 1797 bishops were to be nominated by the Directors, and parish priests elected by their congregations, a practice which had previously been much more common than the Directorate probably realized. In 1798, after the Republic had appeared in Rome, monasteries in the Cisalpine Republic were dissolved.

All modernizing and secularizing activity in the Cisalpine Republic was cut short by the arrival of the Austro-Russian forces under Marshal Suvorov in the spring of 1799. The drift towards the War of the Second Coalition had originally seemed to strengthen the French position in Italy. The French had occupied Rome in February 1798, and the whole of Italy except Venice by March 1799. In April, however, the tide turned and with Suvorov's successful offensive – and with Napoleon in Egypt – the whole French position in Italy with its satellite republics collapsed. As the Austrians and Russians occupied Lombardy the rural population rose against both the French and the 'Jacobins' of the towns. The Austrians established in Milan a government under an Italian nobleman, Count Cocastelli, and made thousands of arrests and many deportations to Dalmatia. They were in occupation of Lombardy of thirteen months – from May 1799 to June 1800. For the inhabitants they were grim months. Anyone who had taken office, or played any public role, under the Cisalpine Republic was persecuted in a variety of ways, and the entire population suffered from the contributions they were forced to make to the war. Having contributed to Napoleon's war they were now contributing to the Habsburgs' war: the process must have seemed to them an unending and self-defeating one. The Austrians declared all the laws passed by the Cisalpine Republic to be null. While they had certainly been warmly greeted on their return, because it had meant the end of the period of ruthless looting by the French, when the Austrians in their turn departed in 1800 it was generally felt that the return of the French was the better of two evils.

Suvorov was defeated by the French in September 1799, but in a battle north of the Alps, at Zurich. Russia withdrew from the war, and the Austrian position in Italy became precarious in the extreme. Bonaparte, after the glories, follies and disasters of his Egyptian campaign, returned to France to make himself effectively the sole ruler by the *coup d'état* of 18 Brumaire (9 November 1799). Appointing himself once again commander of the army of Italy, he returned to the offensive, and by the victory of Marengo on 14 June 1800 he re-established his position in Lombardy. The second Cisalpine Republic had already been proclaimed nine days before Marengo. Once again its institutions were to come by the grace and favour of Napoleon. Executive power was given to nine men, for the time being, while legislative power was given to a body of fifty, whose main task was to prepare a constitution. The fifty-nine men concerned were all appointed by Bonaparte and were all moderates rather than democrats. The legislative body — the *Consulta* — was to be chaired by a Frenchman, Claude Petiet, who was commissioned to extract two million lire a month from the Cisalpine to pay for the French army in Lombardy. The men chosen for executive power by Napoleon were not calculated to give much confidence to the population, since they were pliable enough never to offend the French. The second Cisalpine Republic could hardly entertain the high hopes of the first. Three military occupations had taken their toll of civilized life. Administrative and financial chaos, underlined by an increasing number of deserters and outlaws prowling the countryside, gave the usual indications of the breakdown of an ordered society. Napoleon himself was preoccupied with diplomacy and could give little attention to the Cisalpine Republic until the spring of 1801. He negotiated with Austria the Peace of Lunéville, which was signed on 9 February 1801, allowed the Austrians to retain Venice, but deprived them of Verona, which was given to the Cisalpine Republic.

Finally Napoleon turned again to the internal organization of the Cisalpine. He recalled Melzi from Spain for discussions, but his conclusions were entirely his own. He decided to institute a virtual dictatorship in North Italy, as indeed he had done in France with the First Consulship. The dictatorship, however, as always, was concealed behind a complicated constitution, which allowed for electoral colleges, legislative houses, and a *Censura* of twenty-one men — bodies which were not elected by the public, but either appointed by Napoleon, or elected by each other in impotent vicious circles. In practice five or six hundred men — landowners, businessmen, or intellectuals sympathetic to the French — were nominated either directly or indirectly by Bonaparte. Of these bodies the only one that had any real significance was the Consulta di Stato, which was given, surprisingly, the right to elect the president and to advise the government. The president was the equivalent of the First Consul in France: that is, he was effectively a dictator, with the powers of appointing a vice-president and the ministers. Cynics must have assumed that Bonaparte intended from the start to fill this position himself, but he seems originally to have intended it for his brother Joseph, and to have been dissuaded from this idea by Melzi, who advised him that if the Italians of the Cisalpine were to have a foreign president it could only be Bonaparte himself, and that such a conclusion should be confirmed by the vote of a constitutional body of some kind. It was thus that the Consulta — a body of 441 men — was given the responsibility of electing the president. The thought of elections for a president being held in Milan was, however, more than Napoleon could stomach.

He therefore laid down that the Consulta should sit in Lyons, where it met at the end of 1801.

In January 1802 the Consulta began its work by approving the constitution which would provide the new régime with so elaborate a façade. It then proceeded to elect a president, by the indirect method of electing first a committee of thirty who would present nominations. The committee selected, by twenty-five votes to five, the name of Melzi, who promptly refused nomination. The committee then proposed another Italian moderate, Aldini, who also refused. The third choice, Villa, was not present to accept. Meanwhile Melzi had been trying to persuade the committee to face reality and nominate Bonaparte, which finally, by twenty-one votes to nine, they did. Even then, when the full Consulta met to confirm the election of Bonaparte, the courageous deputy for Monza, Bellani, spoke against the motion, saying it was offensive to Italian feelings, and infringed the independence of the Cisalpine Republic, which had been guaranteed by the Treaty of Lunéville.

Napoleon, already First Consul in France, had thus been treated as one among several possible candidates for office in Italy, and his election as president had been a somewhat grudging one. Even so his reaction was conciliatory rather than aggressive. He appointed an Italian, Melzi, as his vice-president, and in a speech delivered to the Consulta in Italian he took up a suggestion which was continually shouted at him by the deputies and announced that the Cisalpine Republic was henceforth to be known as the 'Italian Republic'. The two decisions were immensely popular, and did much to restore to Napoleon an enthusiastic following with the educated classes in Italy. His choice of vice-president recognized the unique position held by Melzi in the Republic. Although a nobleman, half Spanish, and the heir, from his mother's family, of huge estates in Spain, Melzi was immensely respected by most Milanese for his character and ability. Bonaparte shared this respect. Only a few critics, and some historians – among them, Thiers – considered Melzi lazy and ineffective.[3] The Austrian ambassador, Baron Sigismund de Moll, painted a glowing picture of Melzi as a man of dignity and honesty, with a profound knowledge of affairs of state. On the other hand, Joachim Murat, whom Napoleon was to make King of Naples in 1808, hated Melzi, who reciprocated the sentiment, although the two men put on a great show of mutual affection in public. Murat tried to blacken Melzi's name in Napoleon's eyes, but Napoleon was too shrewd to be influenced against Melzi. Charges made by Melzi's enemies were that he unjustly favoured Milanese in granting offices, and that he was generally weak, especially in his dealings with Napoleon. He was certainly careful to retain the favour of Napoleon, but that he survived during his first stormy period of office suggests that he was anything but weak. Moll believed that Melzi secured real autonomy for the Italian Republic, and gave its inhabitants a higher sense of liberty and honour; he prevented the disruption of the state by speculators or corruption; he went far towards destroying aristocratic privilege; he made finance and administration more honest; he revived commerce and cultural life.[4]

Melzi's sister had married Pietro Verri, who had been a considerable influence on him. Like Verri, Melzi as a young man had hoped for enlightened reforms in Lombardy from the Habsburgs, and had turned against the Austrians only in 1790. Although he served under the Cisalpine and Italian Republics, Melzi remained at heart a monarchist. He certainly did not believe in radical revolution, his ideal being a constitutional monarchy fortified by the support of the aristocracy and middle class. In helping to select ministers for the Italian Republic he found himself in complete agreement with Napoleon, who now looked for conservatively-minded men and found many of them in the Lombard nobility. The ministers, at least, were all Italians, and included among them one man of considerable ability – Giuseppe Prina, – who was made minister of finance and retained that post until 1814, when he was murdered by the Milanese crowd at the time of the collapse of the Italian Kingdom. A scrupulous and incorruptible financier, Prina became unpopular partly because of his cold, uncommunicative character, and partly because he ensured that Napoleon's financial demands were fully met before there was any expenditure domestically. He thus became, undeservedly, the scapegoat for the régime.

Melzi remained the predominant figure in the Italian Republic, but when, in 1805, the Kingdom of Italy was proclaimed, the vice-president did not become the viceroy, but was given the somewhat unimportant and decorative title of Grand Chancellor. Napoleon had assumed the title of Emperor in France in 1804. On 18 March 1805 he took the title of 'King of Italy', coming to Milan three months later for his coronation with the historic iron crown of Lombardy, today safely preserved in the cathedral at Monza. He nominated as Viceroy Prince Eugène de Beauharnais, a young man of twenty-four, the son of Napoleon's first wife, Josephine, and of General Alexandre de Beauharnais. Eugène was to remain viceroy until the French were driven out of Italy in 1814.

In September 1805 the war of the third coalition started, but before the end of the year Austria, devastatingly defeated at Austerlitz, was obliged to sign the Peace of Pressburg, by which she surrendered Venice to Napoleon and, with Venice, Istria and Dalmatia. These territories were added to the Kingdom of Italy, which thus possessed land on the eastern shore of the Adriatic that no united Italian state would ever possess again. In November 1807 the French occupied the Marches, which in April 1808 were also united to the Kingdom of Italy. Thus by the spring of 1808 the Kingdom of Italy included not only Milan, Venice and Bologna, but also the port of Ancona and coastline stretching for some fifty miles south of Ancona, down to the once Roman town of Fermo. Even Cavour, after the events of 1859, was not hoping to extend his Kingdom of Upper Italy beyond Ancona.

Under the monarchy of the Kingdom of Italy was a senate, appointed by Napoleon. Legislation, all main business of government, and treaties and declarations of war were submitted to the senate. Three electoral colleges, one representing landowners, one representing commerce, and the third representing the intelligentsia, together acted as a kind of constitutional court, which decided if the senate's decisions were constitutional, and were responsible for detecting corruption in officials. In the Kingdom of Italy, as in France, Napoleon inaugurated a Council of State to advise him directly on judicial and administrative matters. Day-to-day government was carried on by seven ministries – justice, foreign affairs, the interior, finance, war, the treasury, and religion. In other respects the French model was used. Old, historical, regional divisions were broken up and re-formed into twenty-four new departments, with names as soulless as the ones in France. Most of them were named after rivers – Mincio, Reno, Basso Po, etc. Only one of them, the Alto Adige, for rather special reasons, has remained in the public mind. The departments were placed firmly under centralized control by the appointment of prefects. The finances of the kingdom were put on a modern footing. Of the two ministries, finance and the treasury, the former was concerned with securing revenue, and the latter with public expenditure. An equally modern judicial system was introduced.

When Venice became part of Napoleon's Kingdom of Italy in January 1806 it was decided that Eugène de Beauharnais should reside alternately in Milan and Venice. Venice was declared a free port, to have free trade with all other countries except, of course, England. The King of Italy himself did not arrive in Venice until December 1807. When he finally arrived, however, he at once posed as the benevolent ruler, concerned with Venetian trade and commerce, with the care of the poor, and with public places – gardens, squares, and the like.

The closest approximation to a parliament provided by the constitution of the Italian Republic was the *Corpo legislativo*, though its powers were limited to the right to discuss proposed laws. When, soon after the proclamation of the Kingdom of Italy in 1805, it queried a new tax, Napoleon suspended its sessions and the régime began to appear in its true colours as an authoritarian one. Thus the Italian Republic copied the consulate in France, and the Italian Kingdom copied the First Empire in a negative sense, but also in the positive sense that codes of law were drawn up – civil, commercial and penal. A civil code, based on the Code Napoléon, was published in 1808, and a penal code in 1810. The only important divergence from the French pattern of codes was the omission of trial by jury from the code of penal procedure in Italy. The French system of universal conscription was also introduced, or, more precisely, from 13 August 1802 all young men over twenty who were fit, unmarried, and not ministers of religion, were called into the army for four years, unless they could afford a considerable tax which allowed them evasion.

The finances of the Italian Kingdom were complicated by the need to maintain both a French army and an Italian army subjected to the needs of France. Yet Giuseppe Prina struggled against fierce odds with some success, at least during the earlier part of his period of office. The land tax, on which the Austrian system had been based, was increased during the comparatively left-wing governments of the first Cisalpine Republic from 1796 to 1799. During the more conservative second Cisalpine the land tax was reduced and Prina, during the Italian Republic and Kingdom, reduced it yet further, partly substituting for it a personal tax on all males between the ages of fifteen and sixty. Only paupers, or the fathers of twelve or more children, were excluded. Prina also introduced indirect taxes on, for example, salt and tobacco. Although in some respects regressive, and inadequate in the last years of the Kingdom of Italy, Prina's taxes were effective in providing revenue in his first years of office, and were left largely intact by the Austrians after 1814.

Both trade and industry in Lombardy suffered from Napoleon's wars. When the three months' peace which followed the Treaty of Amiens between Napoleon and Britain in 1802 was ended, great efforts were made to keep British industrial goods out of the Italian market. A decree was issued in Milan in 1803, and revised in July 1805. Article I stated quite simply: 'English merchandize is prohibited in our Kingdom of Italy', and Article II added: 'All such merchandize presented at the customs will be confiscated, and from October 1 all goods found in the interior will be sequestrated as contraband.'[5] Italy was thus cut off from English wool and cotton, and obliged to buy it from France. It might have been thought that Italian industry could have developed more easily with British imports no longer arriving, but this was not the case. Napoleonic customs regulations ensured that industry in the Kingdom of Italy could not obtain the necessary raw materials. The Continental System was operated in such a way that the Kingdom of Italy became in effect an economic dependency of France. The woollen mills of Lombardy had previously obtained wool from the Papal States, but in 1809 the Papal States became part of the French empire, and so fell under the general ban which forbade the export of raw materials from France. In such a situation it is not surprising that a considerable contraband trade developed. Swiss companies were prepared to insure smugglers against being caught. Smugglers and insurers were equally threatened by the Napoleonic laws with ten years' hard labour if convicted, but the Italian tribunals were understandably reluctant to impose such punishment. In 1807 Beauharnais informed Napoleon that Italian industries could not find capital because 'not a single capitalist in Italy had the courage' to invest in such impossible conditions. Consequently Italian manufacturers could not buy the new machinery which was in use elsewhere in Western Europe.

In another respect the Italian Republic and Kingdom were less radical than the Cisalpine had been. The Catholic religion was declared the state religion, though religious toleration was still demanded. Bishops were to be appointed by the government; the state-controlled religion of Joseph II's day, and of Napoleon in France, was the pattern. Melzi, as a man of the Enlightenment, was eager that the Church should not be too independent of the state, but as a moderate he did not want the Church persecuted nor needlessly antagonized. The Catholic clergy in Lombardy had hoped that Napoleon, after becoming First Consul, would allow them more influence than they had enjoyed in the four or five previous years. They were soon disappointed, and during the life of the Italian Kingdom the priests became increasingly hostile to the régime, thus adding to its unpopularity among the peasants.

The classes which benefited most in the Italian Kingdom were certainly the richer ones – the landowners, and the rural middle classes, and especially those who had bought the Church lands sold by the government. The products of the land — wheat, rice, wine — were fetching far higher prices, and even the nobility, who had lost a few vestigial feudal privileges, were more secure and more prosperous: the incipient Jacobin movement of the years 1796 to 1799 had been suppressed, and the tax system did not weigh too heavily on the rich; it certainly weighed far more heavily on the poor.

So far as the urban middle classes went, there had been advantages and disadvantages in the Napoleonic régime. The Italian Republic and Kingdom had been a larger state than any previously existing in Italy, which had meant fewer customs barriers and more trade, at least within the area of the state. The introduction of single, rational systems of law, administration, currency, weights and measures, and the building of new roads, had given enormous advantages to merchants and businessmen. But if conditions for trade and commerce within the Italian Kingdom were favourable, Napoleon's European economic policy, as has been seen, was formulated for the interests of the French Empire proper rather than for Italy. But while the woollen industry of Lombardy was badly hit by its inability to import sufficient raw wool, those raw materials which were produced on a big scale in Lombardy — notably silk — could still be exported, with the result that the Kingdom of Italy managed to retain a slightly favourable balance of trade, even though her industries were declining.

Austria had declared war on France on 12 August 1813. In October an Austrian force entered Italy. By December they were in control of Venetia. When Eugène heard that Napoleon had abdicated, in April 1814, he signed an armistice with the Austrians — the Convention of Schiarino-Rizzino — and thereafter the Austrians occupied the whole of the former Kingdom of Italy, entering Milan already before the end of April. The Italian leader who emerged at this moment of crisis was the Lombard nobleman, Count Federico Confalonieri, who was still hoping to persuade the victorious powers to leave an independent Lombardy in existence, if necessary under an Austrian prince. He secured an interview with the British foreign secretary, Lord Castlereagh, but was told that his mission was a hopeless one. On 12 June 1814 the Habsburg government issued a proclamation that they had annexed Lombardy. Not all of the former Kingdom of Italy, however, did they retain. Of the twenty-four provinces into which the Kingdom had been divided fourteen now became part of the Austrian provinces of Lombardy and Venetia, one — the Alto Adige — became part of the Austrian Tyrol, but the remaining nine were partitioned between the Papal States, Modena and Piedmont.

The provinces of Lombardy and Venetia, which were to remain Austrian until 1859 and 1866 respectively, except for the short revolutionary interludes in 1848−9, had a population at the 1814 restoration of something over four million, slightly over half of them being in Lombardy. The new Lombardy, within the Habsburg Monarchy, included all the former Duchy of Milan, plus important territory which had belonged to the Republic of Venice before 1797 — Bergamo, Brescia and Cremona. The new Venetia, within the Habsburg Monarchy, consisted of that part of the ancient Republic that lay to the east of the Mincio. It was considerably poorer than Lombardy, simply because its land was less fertile.

After the fall of Napoleon the Austrians were in no hurry to dismantle the excellent administrative machinery he had left in the Kingdom of Italy, nor to sack the officials he had appointed. Paradoxically, a main grievance in Venice against the Austrians in 1814 was precisely that they had not dismissed all officials previously employed by the French, and had not wholly discarded the French administrative system as the King of Sardinia and the Pope had done. But the new rulers of Lombardy and Venetia had to move cautiously. Although most of the population, as always, would acquiesce silently in the change of régime, there is plenty of evidence of widespread hostility to the Austrians. A Habsburg official reported on 9 December 1814 that 'the public in general is discontented'.[6] There was a variety of reasons for Austrian unpopularity. Immediate ones were the Austrian ruthless requisitioning of food for the army – a policy moderated a little only through the intervention of the Emperor Francis himself, – and the widespread billeting of troops on Italian households. A more basic grievance which soon appeared in Venice concerned Austrian judicial practices. An account is given by an Englishwoman in the early 1820s – the Marchioness Catherine H. Govion Boglio Solari, who wrote under the pseudonym of 'A Lady of Rank'. According to her, all criminal proceedings in Venice were carried on in writing, with the accused never seeing a prosecutor. Many judges were 'Germans' (Austrians), Hungarians, or Bohemians, who knew nothing of Italy and could not speak Italian. The Court of Appeal invariably confirmed the first judgement.[7] A strong nucleus of unrest was provided by the disbanded officers and troops of the army of the Kingdom of Italy. There was resentment against the Austrian imposition of a censorship of a kind far more rigorous than anything Napoleon's officials had imposed.

Although the Austrians seemed prepared to spend money on an educational system for Lombardy and Venetia, their efforts were bound to produce a lopsided result since anything of a cultural or historical nature which might be taught to Italians was suspect for political reasons. They concentrated therefore on the sciences, even more than Napoleon's régime had done, with interesting long-term effects. In Milan the study of science and applied science – for example, engineering – acquired a social prestige scarcely even today equalled in Britain, whereas the study of the humanities came to be associated with secret and extremist political movements. Thus, still in the twentieth century a man who has been awarded a degree in engineering in Milan is as proud of his achievement as is a man awarded a degree in classics at Oxford, while the study of literature and history in Milan is still far more closely associated with a political consciousness than it is in any British university. Clearly the Austrian educational system in nineteenth-century Lombardy and Venice is only one factor explaining this contrast, but it is not a negligible one. Unfortunately for the Austrians, the educated classes in Italy were less likely to appreciate the positive features in the system than the negative ones. A scientific tradition developed slowly, but the Austrian attempt to stifle a national, historical, political consciousness was immediately apparent. The attempt was motivated by the great fear felt by Francis II and by officials in Vienna of the Italian secret societies, and especially of the Freemasons, though of others also – the *Illuminati*, the *Guelfi*, the *Adelfi*, and, of course, the *Carbonari*. Hostility to Austria led, late in 1814, to a conspiracy in Milan and Brescia, a conspiracy which the Austrians nipped in the bud in December. Just as feeling against Austria was generally much stronger in Lombardy than in Venetia, so was it much stronger on the Venetian mainland than in the city itself. In Venice the first winter after the return of the Austrians was a grim one, with an acute trade depression and a failure of the crop. The Venetians were mostly too wretched to think in political terms; in Lombardy, where social and economic conditions were much better, the inhabitants had time to concentrate on political grievances. The Austrians tried to treat the two provinces equally, considering them both to form a single 'Kingdom' of Lombardo-Venezia. In 1818 Francis II appointed his brother, the Archduke Renier, viceroy of Lombardo-Venezia, and Renier – aping Beauharnais – lived alternatively in Milan and Venice. Francis II had a personal preference for Venice, where he was often a visitor.

The history of the first Austrian restoration in Lombardo-Venezia, during the period 1814–48, is in political terms essentially part of the history of the Risorgimento, and so can be better treated in Part Three. In economic and social terms it has, however, a value of its own which should not be submerged in the history of Italy as a whole. The revolutions of 1848 briefly gave independence to Lombardy, and then, also briefly, union with Piedmont. They gave, too, a fresh short spell of life to the independent Republic of St Mark. Though an important chapter in the history of Milan and Venice, the story of 1848–9 is obviously also a part of the story of the emerging Italian nation and belongs also more properly to Part Three. The defeat of the revolutions in 1849 brought a restoration of Austrian power in Lombardy and Venetia, a restoration in most respects more heavy and oppressive than that of 1814.

The revolution of 1848 had established a constitution in Vienna, so that strictly speaking the régime restored in north-east Italy in 1849 was a constitutional one. In practice, however, the Austrian constitution of 4 March 1849 had never been operated, and in January 1852 it was declared abolished. The Habsburgs certainly had no intention of allowing their Italian subjects any form of representation. A large army of occupation was left in Lombardy and Venetia, so that Cavour was later able to say that Austria's rule in her Italian provinces was not that of a normal, responsible government – she was simply 'encamped' there. From 1849 to 1857 the governor-general of Lombardo-Venezia was a military man – the aged commander-in-chief, Radetzky. Not surprisingly, his rule was hated by the urban population of all classes. A very little support came from the peasants, who with some justification felt that their interests had been ignored by the revolutionary governments of 1848–9. But in the towns and among the rural upper classes there was resentment, as there had been before 1848, at the heavy taxes imposed by the Austrians, and at the knowledge that the Habsburgs extracted appreciably more in cash from Lombardo-Venezia than they ever put back in public works, administration or social services. In 1850 the land tax was increased by a third, and a tax on interest from capital, and a capital gains tax, were imposed. In the language of modern economies these were certainly 'progressive' taxes – taxes on the rich – but they antagonized a politically conscious section of the community.

A marked change came over Habsburg policy in Lombardo-Venezia after the Congress of Paris in 1856. Francis Joseph paid an official visit to the provinces, with the declared purpose of finding out their needs. An amnesty was issued for political offenders; subsidies were granted for flood victims; an indemnity of thirteen million lire which had been demanded from Venice for the revolution of 1848 was cancelled. A monument to Leonardo da Vinci was raised in Milan, and another one to Marco Polo in Venice. Radetzky, now ninety years old, was, a little belatedly, removed from Italy and replaced by Prince Maximilian as governor. Maximilian, Francis Joseph's brother, was the most liberal member of the family.. He started immediately to attempt to appease the Lombards and Venetians. He tried to liberalize trade, and he appointed more Italians to positions of responsibility than Radetzky had ever done. But Austria's change of heart came too late. After her defeat by the French and Piedmontese in the war of 1859, she was obliged to surrender Lombardy, though not yet Venice, and Lombardy was incorporated in the expanding Italian kingdom of Piedmont.

In human terms Lombardy had not fared so badly during the Austrian period from 1814 to 1859, though Venice had fared appreciably less well. But human well-being owes a great deal to social and economic conditions and to the effort and ability of the population itself – rather less, often, to the policy of the government. In the case of Austrian Italy in the first half of the nineteenth century the indigenous social and economic conditions provided well-being in spite of government policy, which was usually negative in its effect. It has been the fashion with English-speaking historians in the last twenty years or so to write of the comparatively advanced conditions of Lombardo-Venezia under the Austrians and to imply that because Lombardo-Venezia was in material terms better off than the rest of Italy it must have been better governed. A consideration of the economy and society of Lombardy and Venetia during the Austrian period suggests that their comparative well-being was due to factors quite other than the wisdom of the Habsburgs or their officials. There is, in fact, very little evidence of wisdom in that quarter.

The population of Lombardy put the various regions of the province to their best use. The mountainous regions and the foothills were in natural terms very poor, but were intensively cultivated by laboriously constructed terraces as in most hilly regions of Italy. Thus even in the hills, vines and mulberry trees were grown, and *mezzadria*, or share-farming, was practised. *Mezzadria*, however, was more common in Tuscany, and so will be discussed in Chapter Three. The proprietors were on the whole an energetic and responsible group. They often took considerable interest in their lands, even if they lived in Milan or other cities. It was fashionable for the rich Milanese to make trips to the hills, and to own villas there for short stays.

More than a third of Lombardy, however, is very flat plain, drained by the Po and its tributaries. Just as immense labour had gone into the construction of terraces in the hills, so in the plain immense labour had gone into the construction of irrigation canals. Some of the canals were an inheritance from the fifteenth century, or even earlier. On the plain the system of *mezzadria* did not prevail. Instead there were large estates, and a *rentier* class, who controlled labour in the interests of the proprietors. Rice and maize were grown, flax was produced and, as in the hills, mulberries were cultivated for the silkworm farms. There was also cattle farming, especially for the production of cheese, most famous of which was perhaps the product of Gorgonzola, not far from Milan. The proprietors were mostly absentees, the *rentier* class being powerful and rich, holding the large estates on lease from the proprietors, usually by paying a year's rent in advance. The noblemen, who often owned huge estates, usually lived in the towns. They were retrograde, in the sense that they were absentee landlords, yet from their ranks the liberal and nationalist movements drew much support. They were at least, then, less reactionary than their counterparts in the Kingdom of Naples. The proprietors who were not noble, and who sometimes lived on their estates, were in contrast more conservative politically, because they were more dependent on the Austrian régime, and could not easily, for example, go into exile in Piedmont, Switzerland or France; but they were open-minded and, when the crisis came, often ready for change. There was a tendency throughout the first half of the nineteenth century for the richer classes to settle more and more frequently in Milan, so that Milan became increasingly alive socially and conscious politically. The *rentier* class controlled considerable capital, and were rising in the social scale. In the 1840s most of them had been to secondary schools; their sons were to go to university. They themselves were probably more conservative in nationalist terms than the landowners, but at university their sons would come into contact with revolutionary ideas. But the familiar concept of a revolutionary 'rising middle class' is too simple to be applied to Lombard society in the 1840s. Nor was there the same vast number of unemployed lawyers that there was in the Kingdom of Naples, or had been in Paris in 1789. In Lombardy there were, however, numerous other professional groups – teachers, medical men, and the rather special group of engineers and maintenance officials, known as *compari d'acqua*, who kept the irrigation system working.

So far as the workers went, there was the skilled class of cheese-makers, who were comparatively well-off, but the greater number of agricultural workers on the plain were a prey to malaria, and had little independence, since their relationship with the *rentiers* and landowners was simply that of paid labourers, provided, it is true, with houses, but poorly paid and desperately insecure. An anonymous Lombard writer in 1846 depicted them vividly as being less well housed than the cattle and, although living surrounded by fat animals, unable themselves to afford meat.[8]

Against this must be set the knowledge that public services in Lombardy –

if not in Venice – were more advanced than elsewhere in Italy. The medical service in particular was a generous one. The rich Lombards had taken doctors with them when they stayed in their country villas, and had paid the doctors to attend poor peasants in the neighbourhood. The financing of this system was eventually taken over by local governments; vaccination was introduced earlier than elsewhere; and the Lombards became extremely proud of their health service – a service which was the work of the Italians themselves, and owed nothing to the Austrian imperial government, who had no parallel to offer elsewhere in the Habsburg Monarchy. The country priests, too, had a high reputation, acting often as teachers in the local schools, and usually on the side of enlightened change in social and economic matters. Carlo Cattaneo, by no means a conservative writer, praised the priests as warmly as he praised the doctors or the engineers who watched over the irrigation system. Reference has already been made to secondary and higher education; the Austrians also organized an advanced system of free and compulsory primary education, and if attendance in the mountains and the countryside, inevitably, was irregular, in the towns there is reason to believe that illiteracy was disappearing.

In the period between the restoration and 1848 there was considerable economic growth in Lombardy. Silk exports and agricultural production for home consumption both went up. The population of Lombardy in 1836 was nearly two and a half million,[9] which made it the most densely populated area of its size in Europe. Milan in 1836 had a population of 185,000, having risen by more than 50,000 since 1790. In three decades the population of Lombardy increased by nearly 400,000 – a rate which was greater than that of France, but which compared unfavourably with the rest of the Habsburg Monarchy, or with Britain, Prussia, or Russia. The economy generally was booming in Milan until the sharp depression of 1847 and 1848. More luxury goods – for example, carriages – were being sold, and there was much building activity. The export of silk to Britain, the rest of Europe and America was an important part of the economy, and if the Lombard silk industry was suffering from Indian competition by 1830 so far as the British market was concerned, sales to France and Germany continued to increase, and output increased generally at the remarkable rate – by Cattaneo's estimate – of 8 per cent per year. Another contemporary estimated that by 1859 Lombardy was producing as much silk as the whole of France. In the light of this fact there is no reason to be surprised at the dogged determination of Austria to retain Lombardy.

The number of landowners in Lombardy increased in the first half of the nineteenth century, not only in absolute terms, but as a percentage of the population. The process had started in the time of Joseph II with the dissolution of many monasteries. Ancient feudal rights to property had been suppressed also under the French occupation, and a certain amount of land had been nationalized or municipalized. Melzi in 1803, as Vice-President of the Italian Republic, had briefly reversed the process, by returning some land then in the hands of the state to its former owners. On the whole, then, land was passing into a greater number of hands, and a new rural middle class was appearing.

Merchants from the towns often bought land, and became farmers, mainly because of the high profits which could be earned in the production of silk. In Lombardy the usual tension between town and countryside, and the sharp distinction between townsman and countryman, was lacking. Silk, which was the preoccupation of both agriculture and industry, linked the two, brought prosperity, and made Lombardy economically a part of Western Europe beyond Italy and beyond the Habsburg Monarchy. On the whole the members of the ruling class who were most loyal to the Austrian régime were also the most retrograde in the use of new industrial and agricultural processes. On the other hand the aristocrats who were liberal and anti-Austrian politically were also liberal in their outlook on society and the economy. Thus Count Federico Confalonieri, a liberal and a Carbonaro, knew France and England well, recommended the introduction of gas lighting, the use of steamships on the Po, and greater public expenditure on education.

Commerce in Lombardy in the first half of the nineteenth century meant the sale and movement of agricultural rather than industrial products. And this meant on the whole the exchange of goods locally produced, locally purchased and locally consumed. A good deal of barter was still the order of the day. Milk was exchanged for grain. The women who wove linen took their pay in farm products or, on rare occasions, from traders, in finished cloth. There was much trade between the nine provinces of Lombardy, and each province had an economic character of its own.

In economic terms Lombardy was overpopulated. Although her agriculture was efficient and prosperous, it was insufficient for her dense population, so that cereals and even wine had to be imported. Fish, olive oil and the fruits of Southern Italy – the orange and lemon – had to be imported, and – since Lombardy herself had no port – passed through Genoa rather than Venice. But if Lombardy relied upon a great variety of imports, she could export silk, rice, paper and quite a number of luxury goods. Cattaneo – a reliable source – named silk and cheese as the two major exports in the 1830s, though silk was certainly the more important of the two. In Brescia firearms were manufactured and sold to Vienna and, in the early 1820, to the revolutionaries in Greece. The main market for Lombard silk, until at least the 1820s, was Britain, although towards the end of that decade the East India Company was providing Britain with silk from India and China. Soon afterwards, however, the French silk industry, centred on Lyons, developed to the extent that silk was needed from outside France, so that by 1829 Lombardy was exporting silk to France, and also to Germany and Russia as well as to England.

The success of the Lombard silk industry owed nothing to the Austrian rulers and everything to the industry, skill and intelligence of the Italian natives. Only now and then, by a fortunate chance circumstance, did the Austrians contribute something to Lombard prosperity. Thus the Habsburg government built a road to the Splügen Pass, to enable their armies to reach Italy more easily; the Lombards sensibly used the road to expand their commerce with Switzerland, Germany and the Netherlands. But even this unintended benefit from Austria was limited by the retrograde policy of the Austrians themselves: tariffs and transit dues slowed down trade over the Splügen and hampered the Lombards in their efforts to attract through trade from Genoa, which the Piedmontese tried, with some success, to direct through the St Gotthard. The Lombards did their best to cope with Piedmontese competition, which grew stronger in the railway age which started in the 1840s, but they had always to struggle against the hidebound authorities in Vienna.

The silk industry in Lombardy, in spite of the difficulties put in its way by Napoleon's commercial policy, had thrived under the Kingdom of Italy. In 1810 and 1812 silk goods had constituted half of the value of exports from the Kingdom, yet in 1812 the Chamber of Commerce in Milan had regretted the 'decline' of the silk industry, due to the falling off of trade generally. In Lombardy the silk industry was clearly the strongest part of a weak economy in the last years of the Napoleonic period, and after 1815 it recovered impressively. In Venetia on the other hand the silk industry declined after 1815, and the number of woollen mills operating was halved. Reliable statistics are not available; those that the Austrian régime preserved are probably unduly optimistic. But even they, as an eminent Italian economic historian, Rodolfo Morandi, expressed it, 'recognize the very sad extremes, the state of desolation, to which the Venetian provinces were reduced in these years of misfortune'.[10]

The Italian silk industry generally became painfully aware, about 1830, of competition from Asia. On the London silk market the imports from Bengal and China outstripped imports from Italy. Silk from Asia had acquired its importance for Britain during the Napoleonic wars. In the years after 1815, while British imports of Italian silk grew steadily, British imports of Chinese and Indian silk grew far more rapidly. The Asian silks were of a poorer quality than the Lombard silks, but France was by then producing silk which compared in quality with the Italian product. The Lombard silk producers were inclined to panic rather more than subsequent developments justified, but their alarm was understandable in view of their dependence on the London market. Much raw silk was exported to London and Lyons and, from about 1850, to Germany and Switzerland. The number of looms operating in Lombardy remained insufficient to exploit all the raw silk produced; there were only about a thousand looms in 1815, and even by 1850 not more than 4,400, all of them in the area of Como and Milan. The modern type of loom invented by J. M. Jacquard of Lyons, who died in 1834, replaced the older type only very slowly in Lombardy, only 20 per cent of the Lombard looms being of the Jacquard kind as late as 1850. By that time, however, the silk industry in Milan was the most modern in Italy, producing finished silks of high quality. The industry in Milan was centralized in the hands of three firms, one factory alone having thirty looms, which was large by Italian standards for that date. Silk products from Como, very highly valued at the start of the century, had lost their reputation by the 1830s, being replaced by those of Milan.

After silk the most important industry in Lombardo-Venezia was wool, more especially in Venezia – in Vicenza, Padua, and Verona – but also in

Lombardy – in Bergamo. Already in 1806 in the area of Vicenza there had been 169 woollen mills, giving work to 32,000 workers.[11] In Lombardy very fine cloths made from merino wool were produced in the neighbourhood of Como. These workers were not, of course, the kind of proletariat which was to emerge in Western Europe after the Industrial Revolution. They were peasants who worked in the factories only when they could take time off from their primary task, which was to work in the fields. In the general economic depression of the Napoleonic period, the Lombard and Venetian woollen industry had been partly saved by Napoleon's need for uniforms for his soldiers. But this need had been of use only to those mills which produced coarse cloths: the delicate products of Como were less in demand when politics and life were grimmer.

Some first, very small-scale, efforts had been made in the Napoleonic period to create an Italian cotton industry. Cotton was worked in these early days at Olona, just north-west of Milan, and at Cremona, but the Lombard factories were to a great extent employed only in finishing work on goods sent from Switzerland. After 1815 Lombardy was the first part of Italy in which the cotton industry was mechanized. The Lombard firms Ponti and Turati freed themselves from the control of London bankers by controlling the import of raw cotton from the USA themselves, and so dominating the internal Italian market in raw cotton. A more developed form of capitalism enabled the Lombard cotton industry to remain more powerful than the Piedmontese industry at least until the 1840s. Turati, in particular, were anticipating the growth of large-scale, highly financed, industry. Nine tenths of all the cotton looms in Lombardy were concentrated in the province of Milan, in the years 1845–55. Only one twentieth of the industry, however, owned by four firms only, was worked in modern factories in this period. The remaining nineteen twentieths was still of the 'cottage industry' type, with the looms functioning for only a part of the year when winter weather prevented the peasants from working on the land. The wages paid to the peasants for their part-time work in the textile industry were so pathetically small that the owners were not encouraged to adopt the more modern factory system. While they could secure easy profits from the old-style domestic industry there was little incentive for the owners to undergo the unknown risks of a new world, even though it might promise the possibility of great wealth.

Italian writers of the first decades of the century warned against the dangers of the new society centred on the factory, and pointed at what they believed to be the appalling and monstrous example of England. Giuseppe Sacchi, writing in 1842, declared that it was a mistake to underestimate the extent to which industry was already changing certain pockets of Lombard society. The good and the evil of industrialism already exists amongst us, and they exist with all their economic and moral consequences.' He supported his argument with horrific statistics relating to the district of Lecco in 1842. Out of a population of 9,133, as many as 4,603 worked in industry, most of them in the silk industry was already changing certain pockets of Lombard society. 'The good hours a day, and many of them fifteen hours, often right through the night.

Rickets, scrofula, and deformities of the bone structure were very common among the children, who often started work at the age of five. Many of them became simple-minded after working for a short while in the mills. The only redeeming feature was that work went on for only some three months a year.[12] The story of the human suffering endured during the early phase of industrialization, suffering caused by long hours of work, grim working conditions, and the illnesses which accompanied them is, of course, an old and familiar one. The historians who tried to refute the interpretation, during the lively debate of the 1950s, succeeded only in modifying it very slightly, and only so far as Britian was concerned. In the 1840s in Italy only small pockets — most of them in Lombardy — had so far experienced the impact even of the early phase of industrialization. With the depression of 1847–8 the whole Lombard economy started to stagnate, the reports of the Milan Chamber of Commerce acquiring a pessimism that had not been present before. The harvest failures in all crops all over Italy were exacerbated in Lombardy by a disease of the silkworm, defined in contemporary language as an 'atrophy of the cocoons'. Industry and agriculture, then, both suffered in Lombardy in the decade before independence.

As well as the textile industry in Lombardy — which included silk, wool, cotton, linen and hemp — there was a metallurgical industry — in iron, copper and bronze — which catered mainly for a very medieval market: monuments, ornaments and bells for churches. It was a declining industry in the first half of the nineteenth century, because of the shortage of fuel, which was to be a weakness of Italian industry until more than half-way through the twentieth century.

Concluding comments on industry in Lombardy before the unification of Italy can be left to two contemporary observers: Giuseppe Sacchi in *Annali di statistica* in 1842 estimated that the total population of Lombardy was 2,524,000, of whom 800,000 — nearly one third — were involved in some kind of manufacturing process, although the vast majority of these 800,000 were primarily concerned with agriculture. As the other contemporary observer, G. Frattini, observed in 1856: 'Lombardy is a predominantly agricultural country, but this does not prevent it from being also modestly industrial or from having the potentiality to become more industrialized.'[13]

The birthplace of banking in the late Middle Ages, Italy needed banks of the modern type for agriculture as well as industrial development. Milan was the first Italian city to have the benefit of a major savings bank — the Cassa di Risparmio, founded in 1823. Austrian Italy was also well served with insurance companies, founded early in the century — the Adriatico Banco di Assicurazioni, founded in 1826, the Assicurazioni Generali, founded in 1831 and, most important of all, the Lloyd Austriaco di Trieste, founded in 1833.

Few regions in Europe could have had better communications than Lombardo-Venezia. Both the Austrians and the French were good roadbuilders, and in addition to the roads there were in Lombardo-Venezia many smooth-flowing rivers, canals and lakes. In 1819 the important canal from Milan to Pavia was opened. Navigation on the Po itself, however, was in a less happy condition. At the Congress of Vienna in 1815 European statesmen had laid down regulations concerning navigation on international rivers – regulations which would introduce free trade on such rivers and ensure that no one state could limit such trade. Logically any river flowing through more than one state was clearly definable as an 'international river', but in 1815 only the Rhine was treated as such. In 1856 the Danube was the object of similar attention by the Congress of Paris. The river Po had Piedmont, Lombardo-Venezia, Parma, Modena and the Papal States all on its banks, yet it was never treated as an international river. Consequently the natural difficulties faced by navigators of the Po were greatly exacerbated by the numerous customs posts which slowed down and increased the cost of navigation. The Milanese protested at this state of affairs, without effect. Even so, before the railways came, communications were already good. Mail left Milan for Venice every day in 1830, and by 1839 a coach for passengers also left daily, taking thirty-six hours en route. Even more impressive was the service provided in 1834 by stagecoach, three times a week, to Turin and Paris. Milan was also linked in the 1830s by regular stagecoach services to Germany and, within Italy, to Rome and Genoa, though significantly there was no regular service to Florence or Naples. These trips by coach were still long and arduous. It took five days in the 1830s to travel from Milan to Vienna, so that it is not surprising that the seat of imperial government seemed a very remote and alien place.

Waste of time in travelling in the nineteenth century was irksome but unavoidable. More exasperating was the waste of time and expense occasioned by customs and tariff barriers. Lombard and Venetian merchants had long been impatient with the conservative tariff policy of the Austrian government. The belief in free trade which writers of the Enlightenment had sold to Joseph II had disappeared in the reign of Francis II. To the Chamber of Commerce in Milan Austrian commercial policy seemed mindlessly retrograde and oppressive. In particular Lombard transit trade suffered: Habsburg official policy prevented the Lombards from benefiting fully from their position astride the routes from the Mediterranean to Central Europe. In 1834 the Milan Chamber of Commerce recommended that the Habsburg Monarchy should join Prussia's *Zollverein*, not only for the sake of Milan, but for the good of the whole Monarchy. The Austrian government itself preferred to bypass Lombardy by using Trieste, which was built up in the restoration period to a position of rivalry with Genoa. Venice as a port was in the unhappy position of being regarded with hostility by the Milanese – since its use would deflect trade from the Genoa–Milan route to Western and Central Europe – and neglected by the Austrians in favour of Trieste. The belief of Milanese businessmen that their natural port was Genoa was to make the Piedmontese claim to be the leaders of Italy against Austria that much more convincing. In one respect the Milanese merchants were unenterprising: they made little effort to expand Lombard trade beyond Europe. The Italians of Trieste, encouraged by Austrian Lloyd and the Habsburg government, were more ambitious in capturing the route from London to India – first for mail and passengers, and in the 1840s for merchandise, especially tea and rice.

When the age of railways arrived a first line in Lombardo-Venezia was opened, in 1840, from Milan to Monza, and in 1846 a second from Milan to Treviglio – a first small section of the line to Venice. By 1849 there were still only three lines in existence. The line to Monza had been extended almost to Como, and a third line had been built, in Venetia – a much longer one from Venice through Padua and Vicenza to Verona. In 1854 the Venice–Verona line was extended to Brescia, and finally in 1857 the two systems in Lombardy and Venetia were linked by a line from Brescia through Bergamo to Treviglio. The Austrians had no intention of linking Lombardy and Piedmont by rail, in spite of the obvious economic reasons for lines between Milan and Turin, and Milan and Genoa. Venetia was certainly served rather better than Lombardy, but it was not difficult for the Italians to realize that this was conditioned by Austrian strategic needs. The Venice–Verona line was extended to Mantua in 1851, and before the war of 1859 the long distance from Verona up to Bolzano was linked by rail. After the war of 1859 the Austrians completed a line from Venice to Udine, and thereafter linked Venetia by rail firmly with the rest of the Monarchy. If the Austrian record in railway building in the 1850s was – not surprisingly, perhaps – better than that of the Papal States or the Kingdom of Naples, it was strikingly worse than the record of Cavour's Piedmont.[14]

Precisely because Lombardy was more advanced economically than the rest of Italy in the early nineteenth century many people in Milan already thought in terms of a widening economic unit throughout the peninsula. Without necessarily associating this concept with ideas of cultural nationalism, they nevertheless felt that the creation of the Napoleonic 'Italian' state – first as a republic, and then as a kingdom – had foreshadowed a larger Italian state, in a single market for trade. They had hoped that when Napoleon was defeated the crude exploitation of Italy by France would cease, but that the economic possibilities conceived in the Napoleonic period would become facts. Lombard disappointment at Austrian policy during the period 1814–48 was thus all the greater. No shadow of the forward-looking economic policy of Habsburg governments, in Vienna and in the Italian satellite governments, during the reigns of Maria Theresa, Joseph II and Leopold II, survived into the age of Metternich. The Austrian governments of the Restoration pursued an ecomic policy which was as bleakly conservative as their political policy. In so far as the Lombards enjoyed prosperity they did so in spite of, not because of, Vienna.

NOTES

There is a monumental history of the city of Milan: *Storia di Milano*, Milan, 1959. Volumes XIII, XIV and XV are the relevant ones for this book.

Venice has attracted rather more attention from historians than Lombardy. Jean Georgelin, *Venise au siècle des lumières*, Paris, 1978, gives a sympathetic impression of the Republic of St Mark before Napoleon I destroyed it, and another work on the last years of the Venetian Republic is M. Petrocchi, *Il tramonto della Repubblica di Venezia e l'assolutismo illuminato*, Venice, 1950, while for late eighteenth-century Venice there is also M. Berengo, *La società veneta alla fine del Settecento*, Florence, 1956.

A sharp focus on the Austrian political régime at the time of the 1815 restoration is provided by R. John Rath, *The Provisional Austrian Régime in Lombardo-Venetia 1814—1815*, Texas, 1969, a work based on thorough research, especially in the Vienna archives, and so written very much from an Austrian viewpoint. A volume of documents illustrating how justice was administered by the Habsburg régime after 1815 as Alfredo Grandi, *Processi politici del senato Lombardo-Veneto 1815—1851*, Rome, 1976.

K. R. Greenfield, *Economics and Liberalism in the Risorgimento*, Baltimore, rev. edn 1965, deals with the economics of Austrian Italy in a first part, and public opinion in a second part. It may be a slightly amorphous work, but it is immensely important, and the last section of this chapter leans heavily upon it. Walter Maturi, with his perceptive eye with regard to works of basic importance, gave it recognition in his *Interpretazioni del risorgimento*, mentioned in the previous notes. For the economics of Lombardy before the French Revolution one work is still interesting: C. A. Vianello, *L'industria, il commercio e l'agricoltura nello Stato di Milano nella seconda metà del secolo XVIII*, Milan, 1932. For a broad survey of Lombard agriculture, until the annexation by Piedmont in 1859, there is M. Romani, *L'agricoltura in Lombardia dal periodo delle riforme al 1859*, Milan, 1955. A good study of Venetian agriculture is M. Berengo, *L'agricoltura veneta dalla caduta della Repubblica all'Unità*, Milan, 1963. Finally, still valuable as a source book with many statistics for Lombardo-Venezia from 1815 to the second war of independence, is A. Sandonà, *Il Regno Lombardo-Veneto, 1814—1859. La costituzione e l'amministrazione*, Milan, 1912.

1. His account is in *La rivoluzione francese nel carteggio di un osservatore italiano*, Milan, 3 vols, 1900—4.
2. *Storia di Milano* (Fondazione Treccani degli Alfieri per la Storia di Milano), vol. XIII, *L'età Napoleonica (1796—1814)*, Milan 1959, p. 38
3. M. Roberti, 'Francesco Melzi d'Eril, vicepresidente della repubblica italiana (1802—5). Appunti dall'epistolario inedito', *Rivista di storia del diritto italiano* (1941—2), vol. 14—15.
4. Pietro Pedrotti, *Le vicende della prima Repubblica Italiana nei giudizi di un diplomatico austriaco*, Modena, 1953.
5. Quoted by Rodolfo Morandi, *Storia della grande industria in Italia*, Turin, 1966, p. 31.
6. R. John Rath, op. cit., p. 317.
7. *Venice under the yoke of France and Austria, with memoirs of the courts, governments, and people of Italy.* By a Lady of Rank. London, 1824, vol. I, p. 36.
8. Quoted by K. R. Greenfield, op. cit., p. 31.
9. *Annali di Statistica*, 1845, LXXXV, p. 14.
10. Morandi, op. cit. p. 55.
11. Ibid., p. 41.
12. G. Sacchi, 'Sullo stato dei fanciulli occupati nelle manifatture', in *Annali di statistica*, 1842, LXXIII, p. 248.
13. G. Frattini, *Storia e statistica delle industrie manifatturiere in Lombardia*, Milan, 1856. Both Sacchi and Frattini are quoted in Greenfield, op. cit., p. 81.
14. See Ch. 2, p. 63.

CHAPTER TWO

Sardinia-Piedmont

Frederick the Great said that Prussia was the work of man's hands: God had no part in it. The same might have been said of the Kingdom of Sardinia-Piedmont. More precisely, Piedmont was created by a tough, not over-civilized, dynasty – the House of Savoy, which had acquired sovereignty over a state by 1559 as the result of the linking of large feudal estates. The capital of their state, the city of Turin, lacked the historical dimension and architectural splendour of Rome, Florence, Milan, Venice or Naples, but in its quiet way it was a tasteful and beautiful city. Turin had missed out on the Renaissance, and by 1612 had fewer than 25,000 inhabitants. It nearly doubled its population in the course of the seventeenth century, and by 1790 had between 92,000 and 93,000 inhabitants. It had been growing in population more rapidly than Milan or Venice, but the 1790s was a decade of decline. By 1800 the population of Turin had fallen to about 80,700.[1] The country was a poor one, the bulk of its population being peasants living in little one-storey houses, each house occupied by a large, extended family, or often by two families. The birth-rate was high for Western Europe, but so was the death-rate, the average life-span in the 1830s being thirty-three to thirty-four years. About 24 per cent of births were illegitimate. Almost a third of the children born alive in the 1830s died before they were six, and in 1838 fifty-one children were found dead on the streets of Turin.[2]

The Dukes of Savoy, who governed this backward state of Piedmont, had acquired the island of Sardinia in 1720 and with it the title of 'King'. Henceforth the correct name of the state in diplomatic language was 'Kingdom of Sardinia' though, Sardinia itself being a little-populated and economically undeveloped island, the state was still referred to in everyday speech as 'Piedmont'. In the early eighteenth century a few reforms were made in the spirit of the times, reforms tending to limit feudal and ecclesiastical privileges, but under Vittorio Amedeo III (1773–96) reforms ceased, and military absolutism hardened. But Piedmont in the reign of Vittorio Amedeo III already possessed three attributes which were to survive – or to be retrieved – for the struggle of the mid nineteenth century. These were: first, the strongest army of an independent Italian state – though this army contained many foreign mercenaries; second, a good diplomatic service; and third, an effective bureaucracy. They were the typical attributes of an ancient, paternalist monarchy, and equally typical was the weak and antiquated economy on which the system was obliged to depend. The elements which favoured economic growth in Lombardy were lacking in Piedmont, where both agriculture and industry were starved of capital. While her army and diplomatic service might guarantee Piedmont independence in normal times, without a sound economy or dynamic social structure she was not in a fit state to face the abnormal times which were coming with the French Revolution and revolutionary wars.

Geographically a large part of the kingdom, but politically an insignificant one, was the island of Sardinia. It consisted mainly of hills on which sheep were pastured. There were very few roads, or towns, and very little commerce with the outside world. It was the one place in the whole of Italy where the links with Spain were still strong, stronger than in Naples or Sicily. The ruling class in Sardinia had relatives in Spain, and links of economic interest with Spain. The Piedmontese administered Sardinia through a resident viceroy, as the Spanish had done.

The city of Genoa was to be annexed to Piedmont for the greater part of the period covered by this book, but in 1790 she was still an independent republic, though a more decadent one even than the Republic of St Mark. The two republics had many points in common. As in Venice, so in Genoa, a privileged and carefully restricted circle of nobility filled all public offices of importance. There was in Genoa also a Libro d'Oro where the names of privileged families were recorded. The poorer classes bore the weight of taxation, which took the form mainly of indirect taxes on consumer goods. By 1790 the middle class was becoming impatient with the exclusiveness of the oligarchy. Genoa had been penetrated by the ideas of the Enlightenment. Even among the priesthood there were demands that the Republic should be reformed.

The King of Piedmont in 1790 was Vittorio Amedeo III, a cultured man who had already reached the age of forty-six before succeeding to the throne. He had spent a somewhat self-indulgent youth, and perhaps for this reason had been excluded from political affairs by his father. He had been on bad terms with his father and his father's ministers, whom he had removed from office on becoming king in 1773. He was an admirer of Frederick the Great, but copied him only to the extent of lavishing much attention on the army. He was, of course, not prepared for the shattering events in 1789 in France, but news of the French Revolution reached Piedmont very quickly since communications between the two countries were fast, and the Piedmontese upper class had no difficulty in reading French. Many recorded initial reactions were favourable. The dramatist, Vittorio Alfieri, who was later to write the bitter work, Il Misogallo, condemning the French for what they had done, in 1789 expressed approval when he heard of the fall of the Bastille. But publications, from cartoons to long articles, which ridiculed or attacked the Revolution were rather more numerous. The first wave of aristocratic emigrants to reach Turin from France arrived soon after the taking of the Bastille. Among them were the Count of Artois, younger brother of Louis XVI, and his Italian wife

Maria Teresa, daughter of Vittorio Amedeo III. They were initially received with some warmth by the Piedmontese court, but the Emperor Leopold II recommended caution, after which it was conveyed to the *émigrés* that the Piedmontese king would do nothing for them without the approval of the Emperor Leopold. With Louis XVI in difficulty with the new régime in Paris, Vittorio Amedeo became warmly aware of Piedmontese marriage links with the Bourbons. He determined to keep close links with the Habsburgs, but not to limit himself to this negative policy. He put forward a scheme originally suggested by the colourfully named Count Gian Francesco Galeani Napione di Cocconato in 1780 for a league of Italian states. In 1791 Napione again produced his scheme, by which all the Italian states would be linked in a loose confederation of which the Pope would be the nominal head. It was the first of several such proposals to be brought forward from 1790 to 1859, and it is interesting to note that the aims of the league in Napione's eyes were to liberalize and improve commerce in Italy, and 'to give re-birth to the ancient power and the ancient naval glory of Italy'. Napione's proposed league was no more successful than its more famous successors in the nineteenth century. Venice rejected the idea outright. Genoa and Tuscany, concerned for their trade with France, avoided giving a direct reply to the proposal. Austria and the Pope himself were unsympathetic. Only Bourbon Naples was seriously prepared to consider the proposal, which thus came to nothing.

Reactions to the French Revolution were rather more favourable in Genoa than in Turin. The middle class was more enlightened in Genoa than in most Italian cities. In 1796 Napoleon was to say of the Republic of Genoa: 'She has more genius and strength than is realized.' It was of course true that the ruling class was firmly wedded to the old régime and social system which gave them their authority and prestige, and the mass of the people – the workers in the port, the small merchants and shopkeepers – also remained loyal to the old order. But the richer middle class, who travelled in Western Europe and came into contact with new ideas, were beginning to think of change, while the very rich banking and commercial class no longer even wanted to attain the titles of the nobility. Writings from abroad, especially from France, were avidly read in the Masonic lodges, and even in public places. The Inquisition tried to enforce a censorship, but its task was more difficult in a large port than it would have been elsewhere. Even some of the nobility read the revolutionary writings from France, often simply because they were fashionable. When the Genoese ambassador in Paris, Cristoforo Spinola, reported in 1789 the opening events of the Revolution, the Genoese ruling class received them with only mild academic interest, believing that the movement could not possibly have implications for them. The first groups of Genoese to take the French Revolution seriously met in two or three offices of pharmacists, of whom the most active was Felice Morando, a fiery, imaginative, if ageing, Jacobin.

The Genoese régime, however, had by 1791 decided not to reject the events that had been taking place in Paris out of hand. Unlike the great monarchical powers, the Republic of Genoa extended recognition to the new constitutional régime in France. The conservative chief minister, the Marquis de Morteil, was replaced by Luca Nuguest de Sémonville, a friend of Mirabeau and of Lafayette. Salons, presided over by Genoese ladies in the Parisian style, adopted the literary tastes and social manners of the French Revolution, and discussed the new political ideas, if not always with great seriousness or depth. There were, however, those who thought seriously over political principles in Genoa; among them was Gian Carlo Serra, who led a group of noblemen who wanted a modernizing of the Genoese state. His younger brother, Gian Battista Serra, was more radical. In Paris during the revolution Gian Battista was considered a Jacobin, although he spoke against the motion to execute Marie Antoinette, and had to leave Paris for that reason. In Genoa he preached equality and the abolition of the oligarchic government, and hoped that the Genoese could provide a base for a French attack on Piedmont. Yet more revolutionary in spirit was Gaspare Sauli, a Freemason with contacts with left-wing republicans in Marseilles and Paris.

When war broke out between revolutionary France and Austria on 20 April 1792, Piedmont seemed one of the most natural allies Austria could find. Two of Vittorio Amedeo's daughters had married the two brothers of Louis XVI, the Count of Provence, who in 1814 was to become Louis XVIII, and the Count of Artois, who in 1824 was to become Charles X. One of Vittorio Amedeo's sons, who was himself to become Carlo Emanuele IV, was married to a sister of Louis XVI. The French king had not yet, of course, been guillotined, but real power had passed from his hands, and it was somewhat optimistic of the French government when, in the spring of 1792, it asked the Piedmontese government to join it in an alliance against Austria. The French offer included Milan, in exchange for Nice and Savoy. Vittorio Amedeo would not consider the proposals, but did not himself take the final step to war. Instead it was the French who, on 21 September 1792, went to war with Piedmont. They quickly occupied those parts of the Piedmontese state that were on their side of the mountains – Savoy, where the population welcomed them, and Nice. A revolutionary assembly at Chambéry proclaimed 'the decadence of the claims of the King of Turin to Savoy', the abolition of the titled hierarchy, the closing of monasteries and convents, and the annexation of Savoy to France. Nice too was annexed to what was now the French Republic. Faced with this emergency, Vittorio Amedeo signed an alliance with Austria in September 1792, and with Britain in 1793, the Austrians promising him armed assistance and the British promising him £200,000 a year in return for a Piedmontese promise to keep 50,000 men armed.

Meanwhile the Republic of Genoa was determined to maintain her traditional policy of neutrality. In the event neither France nor Austria was particularly eager for Genoese help in 1792. Genoa herself could hardly afford to go to war with Austria and Piedmont, nor would her commercial interests permit a break with France. French naval squadrons appeared frequently in the port of Genoa, and no protest was made by the Genoese government. Not only was Genoese commerce severely damaged, but in 1793 incidents between British and French ships were a serious infringement of Genoese neutrality.

There is an obvious parallel between Genoa's determination to remain neutral and that of Venice. Neither of the ancient Republics was to survive the Napoleonic wars.

In Turin, with the coming of the war, a Jacobin movement developed among the middle class and the poorer clergy. In the winter of 1792–3 a few people were arrested for being in correspondence with republicans in France. In 1793 three clubs demanding reforms – two of them republican – were opened in Turin. A member of the most moderate of the three clubs was a doctor, Carlo Botta, an early historian of the period. Doctors, or medical students, were often members of the clubs as were, inevitably, lawyers, but also merchants, priests, and a few noblemen. When the French military offensive of April 1794 started, a Piedmontese Jacobin conspiracy was discovered, a conspiracy which had been planned to coincide with the offensive. Some forty-eight men were arrested, three were executed, and many others escaped into exile. Since the French offensive was no more successful than the Jacobin conspiracy there were no further significant military developments on the Franco-Piedmontese border in 1794 or 1795. The 1794 spring offensive had necessitated a fresh Austro-Piedmontese Treaty by which it was agreed that in the event of victory Piedmont would either gain back from France the land she had recently lost and cede to Austria an equivalent extent of territory, or France would be permitted to keep Savoy and Nice, but would pay an indemnity to be divided between Piedmont and Austria. It was perhaps just as well for Piedmont that the French were not wholly defeated in 1794.

In neutral Genoa in 1794 a movement containing many shades of opinion, led by Gian Battista Serra and others, was energetically demanding a reform of the constitution and closer links with France. The ruling class in Genoa moved at first with great caution, arresting only a few of the more radical leaders, but then proceeded to deal with the more weighty ones. Serra was sentenced to five years in prison, but no heavier sentences were issued. Supported by French agents the conspiracy of 1794 against the oligarchy had no popular following, nor did its leaders want basic social changes.

A new military era started on 2 March 1796 with the appointment of Napoleon Bonaparte as commander of the Army of Italy. The French offensive was now renewed on a bigger scale. Vittorio Amedeo III had summoned a council of ministers in December 1795, and the majority of them had recommended that the war against France should continue. Only a few voices expressed some doubts about 'the blind horror of France, which had thrown Piedmont into the arms of Austria'[3], but they limited themselves to pressing that all considerations of war or peace should be made in a pragmatic and dispassionate manner. When the French offensive in April 1796 extended itself from the Alps to the Ligurian Apennines many of Vittorio Amedeo's ministers must have begun to wonder if their advice to the King had been sound. The French secured a minor victory at Montenotte, but the Piedmontese counter-attacked with some brilliance, and put up a fierce resistance. Even so, towards the end of April Napoleon could proclaim to his troops that they had occupied the richest part of Piedmont, taken 15,000 prisoners and killed 10,000 Piedmontese. As the Piedmontese army withdrew towards the Lombard frontier, Vittorio Amedeo's government decided to seek peace in spite of diplomatic pressure from Austria and Britain. The record of behaviour of the French army in this campaign was a poor one, in spite of ruthless attempts by Bonaparte to maintain discipline, including summary executions of the wilder troops. Towards the end of April Napoleon himself signed an armistice with Vittorio Amedeo's plenipotentiaries, and a definitive peace was signed at Paris on 15 May. Piedmont was obliged to cede Savoy and Nice to France. Savoy, although the province from which the Piedmontese reigning dynasty had come, was on the French side of the Alps, and so strategically a part of France, but Nice, although also separated from Italy by the formidable pass of the Grand Corniche, was nevertheless Italian in character. These two beautiful provinces were to remain hanging in the balance between France and Piedmont until 1860.

So far as the ideological struggle in Italy and Europe was concerned the fact that the French had granted terms to the Piedmontese monarchy – even though harsh terms – was a set-back for the forces of the revolution and for republicanism in Piedmont. A group of Piedmontese exiles in Nice had been in touch with Filippo Buonarroti, the Pisan revolutionary who had settled in Paris and become a friend of François-Noël Babeuf, who led the extreme left wing of the revolutionary movement in France. The Piedmontese exiles hoped to win the support of the Directory in Paris, but their contact with Buonarroti did them more harm than good. In March 1796, soon after Napoleon's appointment as commander of the army of Italy, but before the armistice of Cherasco, the Nice republicans drew up a 'Plan for a provisional revolutionary or republican government for Piedmont'. The document came to light only in 1949 when Armando Saitta found it in the archives at the Quai d'Orsay.[4] Containing eighty articles, it showed that these self-proclaimed 'revolutionaries' were prepared for no radical social revolution, but only very gradual change. They had none of the fire of Babeuf or Buonarroti. The leaders of the group at Nice were Ignazio Bonafous, a merchant, and Maurizio Pellisseri, a lawyer. When, two days before the armistice of Cherasco, a French army under Augereau entered the town of Alba, half-way between Turin and Genoa, Bonafous was made mayor of a distinctly Jacobin municipality, which promptly issued proclamations from 'the revolutionary heads of Piedmont' to 'the Piedmontese and Lombard people', 'the Piedmontese and Neapolitan army in Lombardy', and 'the priests of Piedmont and Lombardy'. The proclamations proposed a new flag for Piedmont – a tricolour of red, orange and blue, which was never to be adopted, a new constitution based on freedom and equality, and the abolition of 'feudal' weights and measures. 'Italian revolutionary legions' were to be set up, based on troops deserting from existing royal armies. The last proclamation was the most curious in that it appealed to the priests of Northern Italy to support the revolution as the early Christians had done. One of the leaders on the Alba town council was Professor Giovanni Ranza, who was a Jansenist. Probably the appeal to primitive Christianity was inspired by him. The leadership between Jansenism and Italian republicanism was to remain strong, and was to be an important influence on Mazzini, whose mother was a devout and puritanical Jansenist. The heady idealism of the Alba municipality was not given free rein for long. The French soon brought back several town councillors of the old régime, and Bonafous was left as mayor only on condition that the council should publicly recognize the sovereignty of the French Republic. Worse quickly followed. By the Peace of Paris Alba was handed back to the King of Piedmont, and on 19 June the old order was restored. From the point of view of Napoleon and the Directory in Paris the Piedmontese republicans were of use simply as a threat to the Savoy monarchy – and incitement to Vittorio Amedeo to come to terms with France.

After the Peace of Paris the Piedmontese republicans were no longer under the protection of the French. But the Jansenist, Ranza, continued to conspire, in touch with radicals in Milan, and in October 1796, working with Giuseppe Antonio Azari, shifted his operations to Pallanza on Lake Maggiore. Their plans on this occasion included the expropriation and redistribution of the lands and wealth of the nobility and the Crown. The conspiracy was unearthed. Azari was taken and shot. In this same month Carlo Emanuele IV succeeded to the throne on the death of his father, Vittorio Amedeo III. Carlo Emanuele was already forty-five. He had been given a more severely religious education than his father. Not an unintelligent man, he was weak physically and had a weak and bigoted personality. In January 1797 a plot to assassinate him was discovered. Four more men were shot. In June an attempt was made to kidnap the new king, and more people were executed. In the summer of 1797 several more risings broke out throughout Piedmont, one of them in Turin itself. In addition to men killed in the fighting, some ninety in all were executed. Many Piedmontese republicans escaped into exile to Lombardy or France, but Napoleon, disliking the social and anarchic character of the Piedmontese movement, was now opposed to it, and had Ranza imprisoned. After several hesitations he persuaded the Directory to sign a treaty of alliance with the King of Piedmont, which they did in October, though relations between Napoleon and the Piedmontese monarchy on the one hand, and Napoleon and the Piedmontese revolutionaries on the other, remained equally uncertain.

Meanwhile Napoleon had destroyed the old Genoese Republic, and on 6 June 1797 set up in its place the democratized 'Ligurian Republic', which was to last until 1805. As with the Cisalpine Republic, the Ligurian Republic had to survive in the face of the mass robbery organized by the French. It had come into existence after considerable internal troubles. In May 1797 there had been a radical rising against the rich bourgeoisie who ruled Genoa, followed by a backlash supported by the rural classes of the countryside outside Genoa. Napoleon restored order and a moderate régime. Inevitably a strong influence on the government of the Ligurian Republic was exerted from the French Legation, but until 1805 it was a recognizably Italian state. If most of the priests were hostile to the Ligurian Republic, the primate, Archbishop Giovanni Lercari, on 9 June 1797 announced his support for the new régime, which he believed would protect the Catholic religion and the prosperity of

49

Genoese commerce, and would bring peace. Initially the constitution was not typically Napoleonic but had an uncharacteristically archaic character, with its Doge and twelve senators. Such a constitution was clearly a temporary measure. It was followed by one modelled on that of the French Directorate of 1795: there were to be 5 directors, and 2 councils, one of 60 members, and one of 30. The constitution of the Ligurian Republic included, however, one radical document – a Declaration of Rights and Duties, which seemed to imply that among a citizen's rights was that to education. A plebiscite confirmed the constitution on 2 December 1797 by almost 100,000 votes to some 17,000. The five Directors appointed were all Italians, but moderate men who were not going to worry Napoleon by echoing the wish of the radicals and the radical press for union with the Cisalpine Republic.

That the Ligurian Republic had an element of real independence was illustrated, however, by the short war which was waged against Piedmont in June 1798. It was fought, of course, with the approval of the French, but the initiative came from the rulers of the Ligurian Republic, influenced, without doubt, by democratic exiles from Piedmont who had tried to start a rising in April. The various armed bands which had descended upon Piedmont in the spring of 1798 were all defeated, and over 100 prisoners were shot by the Piedmontese. The regular army of the Piedmontese monarchy had invaded the Ligurian Republic in pursuit of the irregular republicans, and it was then, in June, that the Republic had gone to war with Piedmont. French intervention to end the war followed at the beginning of July, and before the end of 1798 – in a sense as a result of the war – Piedmontese independence ended. General Joubert occupied Piedmont with his army without opposition. Carlo Emanuele IV, having reigned for less than two years, was obliged to recognize French authority. On 8 December 1798 he signed a document of abdication, ordering his people to recognize French laws, and his troops to obey the orders of the French High Command. Having signed this sad document, Carlo Emanuele went into exile, first to Parma, then to Tuscany, and finally to Cagliari on the island of Sardinia, where he could still feel that he had authority. From Cagliari he issued a protest against his treatment by the French, asserting that he had not abdicated of his own free will.

In February 1799 Piedmont was annexed to France. While those Piedmontese Jacobins who wanted union with the Ligurian or Cisalpine Republic, or who wanted the survival of an independent Piedmontese Republic, were obviously dismayed at this, there were some Italians – among them Ranza – who believed that they would fare better as citizens of the French Republic than as citizens of a satellite country occupied by foreign troops. However, a conspiracy against French annexation, probably organized by a very secret Jacobin society – the *Società dei Raggi* – was discovered, and several men were arrested and imprisoned.

Early in the spring of 1799 the Austrians and Russians were for the time being victorious against the French in Northern Italy. Suvorov, the brilliant Russian marshal, invaded Piedmont in May, entering Turin on 26 May. Risings in Piedmont against the French were on a considerable scale, but were rural and right-wing by nature — peasant movements led by priests or by former officers of Carlo Emanuele. Suvorov, however, refused to deal with these Piedmontese adventurers; instead he disbanded them and had their leaders arrested. He was inclined to restore Carlo Emanuele, but the Austrians were in no hurry to do so, since they wanted a free hand in making a territorial settlement in North Italy. In the event neither Suvorov nor the Austrians were to remain in Piedmont for long. Bonaparte returned in the spring of 1800, and after the victory of Marengo on 14 June could reoccupy not only Piedmont but the whole of North Italy to the Mincio. Once again Genoa received more favourable treatment than Piedmont: the Ligurian Republic was given a provisional government pending a final settlement. The final settlement when it came was a totally negative one: in September 1802 Piedmont was again annexed to France, where Napoleon was now First Consul and soon to be Emperor. The tragic legitimate King of Piedmont, Carlo Emanuele IV, in 1802 abdicated freely, and having no children declared his successor to be his brother, Vittorio Emanuele I. Carlo Emanuele himself went to Rome, and died there in 1819, having become a priest and joined the Jesuits.

During Napoleon's second Italian campaign in 1800 Genoa, occupied by a French army under Masséna, had been besieged by a large Austrian army and a British fleet. For two months Genoa underwent the ravages of famine and a typhus epidemic. A French general calculated that some 30,000 Genoese died in the siege, their bodies being piled high in the streets before being burnt in a huge communal cremation pile. The garrison capitulated on 2 June, only ten days before Marengo. The French relieving army arrived in Genoa on 24 June. The Ligurian republic which the French re-established had all the economic factors against it. Commerce and shipping were necessary for Genoese economic survival, since her mountainous narrow strip of territory could produce little but olives. But with the hostile British fleet destroying her commerce and shipping Genoa faced crisis, and could only place herself at the mercy of Napoleon. While the Ligurian Republic remained in theory an independent state, in 1804 two conventions were signed by which the French gained control of all the land and sea forces of the Ligurian Republic. In this situation the Genoese Senate, apparently with the approval of the people, sent a delegation, led by the Doge himself, to Milan to ask Napoleon to take over direct rule of Genoa as part of the French Empire. Napoleon graciously accepted their request. He believed that the acquisition was worth having for France, but in the event it was something of a diplomatic error, since it ensured the renewal of the war with England, and gave both Russia and Austria a stick with which to beat Napoleon.

That Napoleon regarded the acquisition of Genoa as an event of major importance is evident from the fact that he sent his Minister of the Interior, Champagny, to Genoa to inaugurate the new era by transferring French laws to the former Republic. Champagny promised the Genoese the revival of their glory and ancient wealth and the preservation of the Catholic religion. He divided the country into three departments, and introduced the French system of administration by prefects and sub-prefects. Genoa was to be a free port, not separated by customs barriers from the rest of the French Empire. There was to be a small legislative house, to which each of the three departments would elect nine deputies. Napoleon himself, with the Empress Josephine, arrived on 30 June, to an enthusiastic reception. When Champagny had completed his work of institutional construction he returned to Paris and Genoa fell under the administration of the French prefect. The institutions of the Revolution – not only new laws, but new regulations enforcing the decimal system for weights and measures, and the Revolutionary calendar – were introduced. The new regulations were all written in French, which favoured, although it often infuriated, the upper classes, but left the lower classes ignorant of the new laws and rules which were to control their lives.

The dissolution of religious houses under the French raised a storm of protests, and even the French prefects wrote to Paris in defence of the better of the institutions, especially those concerned with teaching. French taxes – direct ones, and indirect ones on salt and tobacco – were also inevitably unpopular, as was the thorough process of conscription to the French army in a country which had a strong naval, but no military, tradition, There were many cases of desertion, and even some of self-imposed mutilations. The material condition of Genoa during the French period was grim. The chief engineer in 1806 reported that there was a grave danger of the sewerage system overflowing and flooding the city. The breakwater and the equipment needed for the port were in a very bad state of repair. No works had been carried out in the port for ten years. The prisons in the town were inadequate and in an appalling condition.

As part of the French First Empire Piedmont too came under the sway of the Code Napoléon, of the French administrative system, with French prefects administering departments, and of the French judicial system. The schools in Piedmont were merged with the highly centralized French system. Piedmont was represented in the Senate and Assembly in Paris, and Piedmontese youths were conscripted into the French army. Prince Camillo Borghese, Napoleon's son-in-law – the husband of Pauline Bonaparte – was appointed governor of Piedmont, Liguria and Parma in 1808, but was allowed little real power. The French régime provided certain advantages to the Piedmontese middle class: it opened to them bureaucratic or military careers, formerly open only to the aristocracy. The poorer classes, subject to conscription and heavy taxes, had less to thank the French for, and many of them took to a life of brigandage. Napoleon's brutal treatment of Pope Pius VII[5] antagonized many of the peasants. There was, however, little organized resistance to the French. Only in the last few years before the fall of Napoleon in 1814 did secret societies of an anti-French type appear.

The island of Sardinia was never taken over by the French, but came under the influence of Britain after 1806, when the British were in control of the seas, although they never occupied this wild and inhospitable place. Vittorio Emanuele I, beginning his reign in June 1802 after his brother's abdication, had sense enough to keep on good terms with Britain and Russia, and so to ensure the restoration of the House of Savoy after Bonaparte's downfall.

On 25 April 1814 the Austrian Prince Schwarzenberg, commander-in-chief of the victorious allied army in Italy, announced: 'to the good and faithful subjects of the King of Sardinia that they would find themselves once more under the dominion of those beloved Princes who had brought them happiness and glory for so many centuries, that they would see again amongst them that august Family which had sustained the misfortunes of these last years with their customary courage and firmness'.[6] Vittorio Emanuele arrived back on 14 May, and tried to sweeten his restoration by abolishing conscription and several taxes, and saying that he forgave his oppressors. He was met by a group of men of the old régime, former courtiers and ministers, of whom the principal was Count Giuseppe Cerruti. They gave the returning monarch the absurd advice that he must destroy all evidence of the French period and return to the state of affairs that had existed before the Revolution. Unfortunately Vittorio Emanuele was only too ready to accept such advice. Like Cerruti he wanted to imagine that Piedmont was awakening from a long sleep of ugly dreams; he failed to understand that not everyone in Italy had been asleep. Cerruti became Minister of the Interior, and issued on 21 May 1814 a royal edict declaring that the legal constitution of Piedmont was that contained in a law of 1770, and amplified by provisions issued between 1770 and 1800. No subsequent laws could be held to modify these – which meant in effect that Piedmont became again a nakedly absolutist state. The Piedmontese Restoration was almost the classic one of the 1814–15 settlement. The Code Napoléon was repealed. The basic right of equality of all before the law was scrapped; patriarchal prerogatives in the family and ecclesiastical prerogatives in the state returned. The guarantee of a free and open trial for people charged with crime was withdrawn. A few small steps were taken by the king to modify the extent of the repression. Torture was never reintroduced, and by royal edicts in 1816 the civil restrictions placed on the Waldensians and on the Jews were lightened, although they could still not practise their religion publicly. Cerruti's 1814 edict meant that laws which had already been archaic and absurd in 1789, and which had somehow missed out on the Enlightenment, were brought back to this corner of nineteenth-century Italy. In practice it was impossible to enforce them. Vittorio Emanuele I had to resort to edicts and 'royal patents' to keep government operating.

From the Piedmontese point of view the most important step taken by the Great Powers at the Congress of Vienna was to hand Genoa to the House of Savoy, making the Kingdom of Sardinia/Piedmont into a state of three and a half million people. Piedmont became, by the acquisition of Genoa, a maritime and an Italian state – her centre of gravity moved away from the Alps towards the Mediterranean and into the Italian peninsula. Inevitably the preoccupations and sense of identity of the House of Savoy were to undergo a significant change. From the Genoese point of view the suppression of their ancient independent Republic was a savage and wholly unjustified step. The Great Powers tried to modify the severity of Piedmont's annexation of Genoa by laying down certain conditions which Vittorio Emanuele recognized in his patent of 30 December 1814, which, in annexing Genoa, established Provincial Councils to make recommendations to the royal Intendants. Each Council was to contain thirty local notables nominated by the king, and would have the power of blocking the imposition of any new tax of which it disapproved. The king further promised that Genoa would not be taxed more highly than other parts of the kingdom – another condition laid down by the Congress of Vienna. It was difficult for the Genoese to check the last point since the relevant figures were not published. The Provincial Councils were encouraged to discuss only their own, very local, affairs. Never did all the Councils meet together as a single body. The restored government was also ultra-conservative in its commercial policy. Internal customs barriers were re-erected between Liguria and Piedmont proper, and between Piedmont and Savoy. External tariff barriers were even more destructive of trade. Raw silk could not be exported until 1834. In particular the port of Genoa suffered from the quaint restrictions imposed, but for some years basic commercial advantages could not be wholly destroyed by government policy: the Continental System had ended; the British navy was dealing with piracy in the Mediterranean; Genoa was now part of a larger Italian state.

For some years Vittorio Emanuele I made no concessions to those members of the aristocracy and bougeoisie who recommended some degree of modernization. A half-hearted attempt to reform the administration in 1819 was abandoned when the revolution of July 1820 broke out in Naples. The revolutions of 1820 in Spain and Naples were reflected in Piedmont by an increase in the number of people inscribed in the secret societies. With the possibility in late 1820 and early 1821 of an Austrian intervention in Naples, the Piedmontese liberals – in touch with Lombard conspirators – hoped that they would have a freer hand in the North. They were ready to believe that Vittorio Emanuele I, hide-bound conservative though he had always been, would be ready to make war on Austria for the liberation of Lombardy and the expansion of Piedmont. They could have less hopes from his brother and heir-presumptive, Carlo Felice, but the second in line for the throne, Carlo Alberto, a young man of twenty-three, was regarded as a key figure. It was hoped that Carlo Alberto would either persuade the King to conduct a reforming and anti-Austrian movement, or else would lead such a movement himself.

Carlo Alberto's father, the Prince Carlo Emanuele of Carignan, had died when Carlo Alberto was only two, and the young prince had then gone into exile in France with his mother. He had grown up in difficult circumstances. His mother had been married again, to a French nobleman, with whom his relations were not good. Returning to Piedmont at the restoration, Carlo Alberto, as a boy of sixteen, was old enough to realize that the Piedmont of Vittorio Emanuele I was a primitive country indeed in contrast with the France of the First Empire. He was a more complex and a more tortured person than Vittorio Emanuele I, and already by 1821 the major influences on his character and philosophy – the more mystical ideas of the Catholic Church – had made their mark. Nevertheless he seemed to hold out some hope to the liberals. They must have realized that his personality was a solitary, remote and proud one, but he was at least young, and his attitude could be interpreted in a number of different ways. When, in January 1821, a group of revolutionary students occupied buildings of the University of Turin and the police dispersed them with a good deal of violence, wounding several of them, Carlo Alberto sent gifts to the injured students. More serious were his contacts with revolutionary officers in the army.

Among the leaders of the liberal conspiracy were Santorre di Santarosa and Carlo Asinari di San Marzano. These two men and three others visited Carlo Alberto on 6 March and appealed to him to lead the revolution, which he appeared to agree to do, though he was later to deny it. For several days Carlo Alberto kept in touch with the conspirators, following a line of action which was open to more than one interpretation: it is possible that he intended to lead the revolution and denied the fact only when the revolution had failed; it is possible, on the other hand, that he was simply collecting information which would enable the government to put down the revolution; again it is possible that he was simply keeping his options open.

The secret societies had always been strong at Alessandria, and it was here that, on 9–10 March, a group of officers and professional men seized possession of the fortress. A provisional government was established and the red, white and green tricolour was raised. This democratic, revolutionary government issued a manifesto 'in the name of the Italian Federation', proclaiming the Spanish Constitution of 1812, and declaring itself independent until the King should have assumed the title 'King of Italy'. The Spanish Constitution of 1812, which had granted universal manhood suffrage and a single assembly, had become enshrined in the mythology of the democratic revolution. On 11 March the 'Kingdom of Italy' was declared at Alessandria to be at war with Austria. In Turin there was considerable pressure on Vittorio Emanuele I to grant a constitution. For a moment he wavered, but then, having persuaded himself that Austrian and Russian intervention would not be slow in arriving, he decided to resist the liberal demands. However, when an army mutiny broke out in Turin – a day or two later than it had done in Alessandria – Vittorio Emanuele in some haste decided to abdicate. He had four daughters, but no son, so that his brother Carlo Felice was the legitimate heir, but his act of abdication was strangely silent about his successor, merely appointing Carlo Alberto as regent. Carlo Felice had left the country a week before on a brief visit to Modena. Vittorio Emanuele now departed for Nice; the hopes of the liberals that he might have accepted a constitution and led a movement against Austria had to be abandoned. The ministers of the old régime resigned office, and the young Carlo Alberto found himself – as so often in his life, either by fate or by temperament – wholly alone. The revolution, although without firm leadership, spread spontaneously in the towns around Turin. On 13 March Carlo Alberto produced a proclamation which was a masterpiece of ambiguity, even by his high standards. While declaring his 'submission to His Majesty Carlo Felice, to whom is owed the throne', he promulgated the 'Constitution of Spain' to be 'observed as law of the State', 'except for those modifications which by national Representation, in agreement with H.M. the King, will come to be deliberated'. Having, after a fashion, given Piedmont a constitution, Carlo Alberto appointed a new government and issued an amnesty to the troops who had mutinied provided that they immediately went back to their former command. The revolutionary troops in Alessandria, who had declared themselves to be the army of independent Italy, could hardly accept the terms of Carlo Alberto's amnesty, while the more conservative officers awaited orders from Carlo Felice. These were not slow in arriving. From Modena Carlo Felice declared that he would not recognize any change in 'the form of government' that existed before Vittorio Emanuele's abdication, and anyone who had declared a constitution would be recognized as a 'rebel'. After more vacillations and hesitations for two or three days Carlo Alberto escaped, with an armed force, from Turin to Novara, which was garrisoned by a force loyal to the old régime. Turin was left in the control of the moderate revolutionaries, among whom Santorre di Santarosa had emerged as the leading and most dynamic figure.

Carlo Felice meanwhile prepared to suppress the revolution. Metternich and the ministers of Prussia and Russia had met at the Congress of Laibach, primarily to deal with the revolution in Naples,[7] and were still in session there. Carlo Felice applied to them for help. Santarosa organized the troops loyal to the constitution sufficiently for them to fight an engagement against the troops loyal to Carlo Felice, supported by the Austrian army, at a point near Novara. The revolutionary forces were defeated, and the absolutist forces entered Turin. Hundreds of revolutionaries went into exile. No trace of the revolution remained.

Although Carlo Felice owed his throne to Austrian intervention, he asked at the Congress of Verona, which met in 1822, for a withdrawal of the Austrian occupying army from Piedmont, and with his request the Austrians complied in 1823. Carlo Felice asked also, at the Congress, for the exclusion of Carlo Alberto from the succession. The difficulty here was that Carlo Alberto's son, Vittorio Emanuele, who was one day to be King of Italy, was in 1822 a child of two. Metternich's attitude was all-important. In his eyes Carlo Alberto was the legitimate heir, and he was probably shrewd enough to realize that, from his point of view, Carlo Alberto, in the long run, was not a bad bet. The unhappy young man, however, had to perform a penance for his flirtations with dangerous men like Santarosa who actually imagined that kings should have some kind of limits imposed on their powers. Carlo Alberto's penance was that he should fight with the French army of Louis XVIII against the constitutional and legally established government of Spain, in 1823.

The reign of Carlo Felice, from 1821 to 1831, was a bleak one politically, and no less a bleak one economically. Even by 1830 Piedmont was still a very backward country in economic terms. She lacked a manufacturing tradition and no capital had been accumulated, either by trade or agriculture. Potentially, however, she had tremendous assets. The important port of Genoa was well placed geographically, near the passes which took routes from the Mediterranean to Western Europe. And above all Piedmont had national independence. Her lack of success from 1815 to 1848 was partly the result of her class structure. No commercial middle class of any size had emerged, and even the professional middle class was much smaller than that in Lombardy. Too many of the educated, or partly educated, class of Piedmontese lived unproductive lives as officers in the army. The paternalistic and militaristic governments of Piedmont pursued an even more protectionist commercial policy than did the Habsburgs.

On Carlo Felice's death in 1831 Carlo Alberto became king. For ten years he had been isolated and distrusted by Carlo Felice, and had become increasingly nervous and pessimistic. Having lost the liberal friends of his youth he had become by 1831 a solitary figure with a cadaverous face, a long, ungainly figure, and awkward manners. He came to the throne as a revolutionary movement was boiling up in Central Italy,[8] a movement which was kept at arm's length from Piedmont. As the 1830s progressed the Romantic revolutionary movement in Piedmont, as elsewhere in Italy, became increasingly dominated by the ideas of Giuseppe Mazzini and the conspiracies of his followers. To the Mazzinian movement Carlo Alberto was clearly seen as an enemy who had to be discredited and overthrown. In the 1840s a less revolutionary nationalist movement – the so-called 'neo-Guelph' movement – made its impact. In tne eyes of the neo-Guelphs Carlo Alberto had a more positive role to play, though a role always subordinate to that of the Pope. The Mazzinian and neo-Guelph movements constitute rather a part of the history of the Italian Risorgimento than of Piedmont, and will therefore be considered at some length in that context.[9] One aspect of the nationalist movement of the 1840s was, however, centred in Piedmont: it was in Piedmont that the scientific congresses, which played so important a role in spreading nationalist propaganda, found it most easy to meet. In September 1846 the *Associazione Agraria* organized a congress at Mortara, a town not far from the Lombard frontier, and representatives from Lombardy attended. The provocation to Austria was heightened when the radical Piedmontese political figure, Lorenzo Valerio, in an after-dinner speech at the close of the congress, referred to Carlo Alberto as the Italian leader who would drive out the foreigners. A few days later another congress, a *Congresso degli Scienziati*, opened in the more revolutionary atmosphere of Genoa, and was attended by subjects of Pius IX, whose initial acts in the Papal States had so significantly altered the political climate in Italy.[10] The Genoa Congress was used as an occasion for celebrating the centenary of the victory of the citizens over the Austrians in 1746. When Pius IX's reforming government in Rome proposed the formation of an Italian customs union the Piedmontese government could hardly refuse to take part in negotiations. In the event the governments of the Papal States, Piedmont and Tuscany signed a treaty establishing a customs union on 3 November 1847.

The treaty was signed, then, by three absolutist monarchies. Carlo Alberto had put his face firmly against any liberal reforms in a constitutional sense. Like the enlightened despots of the eighteenth century – though in a very different spirit – he wished to make the absolute monarchy more impregnable by buttressing it with a more efficient economy and administration. His problem was that men who – like Cavour – wanted to modernize the economy and administration, also wanted him to introduce a constitution. Such men would not have served an absolutist régime even if Carlo Alberto had been prepared to entrust them with office. He had, then, to depend upon the support of reactionaries, and in particular of the leader of the reactionaries, Count Solaro della Margarita, who was foreign minister. Yet Carlo Alberto seemed sincerely to believe that he was destined to lead a national movement against Austria, although by 1847 very few Italian nationalists would accept the leadership of an autocrat. One by one the King of Naples, the Grand Duke of Tuscany, and the Pope granted constitutions of one kind or another, while Piedmont remained an absolutist state.[11]

Born in 1792, Solaro della Margarita had been minister since 1835. A pious man, he had been alarmed at what he considered to be the highly dangerous steps taken by Pius IX, and especially by his amnesty by which hundreds of revolutionaries had been allowed to return to Italy from exile. Della Margarita visited Rome in August 1846, talked to the new Pope, and returned to Turin with his sense of alarm heightened. He was not alone in Turin in his stubborn opposition to any form of constitutional concession. The men around Carlo Alberto – both in his social circle and among his officials – had an outlook not unlike that of Della Margarita. If Carlo Alberto himself was a distant man without close friends, it is also true that he was deeply religious, and so influenced by the ultra-conservative Archbishop of Turin, Luigi Fransoni, and by the Jesuits. Solaro was unfortunate in the extent of the literary and political influence arrayed against him – Cesare Balbo, Massimo d'Azeglio and Cavour, all of whom, with many other enlightened members of the aristocracy, believed that some degree of liberalization of the régime was necessary. Less articulate than the aristocratic circle, but ultimately more important because of their numbers, were the urban and rural middle classes – bankers, merchants and small landowners. Connecting the two groups – in the sense that they were both articulate and numerous – were the professional men: lawyers, civil servants and teachers. All these bourgeois groups had come to realize that a constitution, at least, must be granted, while several of them believed that a continuous advance towards democracy must be made. Lorenzo Valerio was perhaps the best known of the democratic left, through his journal *Letture di famiglia*, which recommended a system of universal education. In May 1847 *Letture di famiglia* was suppressed for an assumed attack on the Jesuits, though the offending article had merely discussed with regret the transfer to the Jesuits of some members of the Barnabite Order, which it had praised. Another sin of omission of Valerio's journal had been its relentless refusal ever to mention the monarchy or royal family. Yet more radical than Valerio was Angelo Brofferio, a forty-five-year-old lawyer more typical of the revolutionary phases of the nineteenth century than Cavour. He had studied at the University of Turin, where he had been involved in student riots in January 1821, at least according to his own account although at the trial no evidence was found with which to convict him. While he was still a student, at the age of twenty-three, he wrote a tragedy, *Eudossia*, which was shown at Turin in 1825. But politics soon became his main passion, and in 1831 he was briefly imprisoned for having conspired against Carlo Felice. In 1834 he began to write for the *Messagiere Torinese*, contributing both political and literary articles. In 1844 he was again briefly imprisoned, this time for adultery, which under Piedmontese law was a criminal offence. Rather surprisingly, after the establishment of the Kingdom of Italy, Vittorio Emanuele II was to commission him to write the *Storia del parlamento subalpino*, of which six volumes appeared before his death in 1866.

If there was a growing demand for change in Turin in 1847, in Genoa the sentiment was often closer to revolution. Republicans in the great port were numerous, many of them Mazzinians. The Genoese did not need hints from Rome before they demanded freedom, but the people of Turin were more religious, and the impact of Pius IX's initial steps of reforming policy were for the Turinese little short of traumatic. There was a demonstration in Turin in honour of Pius IX on 1 October. Eight days later Carlo Alberto 'invited' Solaro della Margarita to resign as minister of foreign affairs, and on October 11 announced his successor – Count Ermolao Asinari di San Marzano. The fall of Solaro probably owed something to the visit of Lord Minto, British Lord Privy Seal, and a member of Lord John Russell's cabinet. But Carlo Alberto's conservative policy still did not change immediately, and when it did so, two or three weeks later, it was clearly only the result of several days of noisy demonstrations accompanied by numerous arrests. Count Ottavio di Revel, by no means a liberal, and a leader of the Right in later years, had been made minister of finance, and now advised the king that some reforms must be introduced. On 30 October the official *Gazzetta Torinese* at last announced reforms, though reforms which did not amount to a great deal. They tended to bureaucratize institutions formerly of a feudal, or royal, nature: thus the police were now to be controlled by the minister of the interior. Local government, however, was to be reorganized, and local councils elected. The most important of the reforms concerned press censorship: newspapers were now to be allowed to indulge in arguments concerning public administration, provided that they did so without offending the Crown, the Church, the government, or foreign monarchs. Cautious though this press reform was, it opened the door to demands for further reform, and the reforms as a whole encouraged popular demonstrations in Turin, Genoa and many other towns in the kingdom. The demonstrations were now sympathetic to Carlo Alberto, but included demands for more radical measures – for example, for the formation of a civic guard and the expulsion of the Jesuits. In Genoa the Mazzinians, prominent among whom were Nino Bixio and Goffredo Mameli, were concentrating on this kind of demand rather than one for a constitution. It was rather the moderates who returned to the question of the need for a constitution. Leaders of the two groups met in Turin on 7 January 1848. Valerio agreed with the Genoese that a petition should be presented to Carlo Alberto demanding a civic guard and the expulsion of the Jesuits. Cavour, who was also present, pointed out that a Catholic as pious as Carlo Alberto would be bitterly antagonized by a request for the expulsion of the Jesuits, and that a better policy would be to obtain a constitution as a necessary step to any programme of reforms. Paradoxically Valerio and most other democrats felt that to demand a constitution would be unrealistic and too drastic a step, while the moderates supported Cavour. Alone among the democrats, Brofferio felt that the time was ripe to press for a constitution.

For another month Carlo Alberto stubbornly refused to consider the possibility of a constitution. After the granting of one in Naples even Carlo Alberto's more conservative ministers tried to persuade him that it would be better to introduce one as an act of royal grace rather than submit, as the King of Naples had done, to revolution. Finally he gave way. A decree stating the principles on which the *Statuto* was to be based was announced on 8 February. The decree contained fourteen articles which were all short and some of which were very ambiguous. Article 1 was clear enough: the Catholic religion was to be the 'Religion of the State'. Other cults were to be granted toleration. By Article 2 the king's person was declared 'sacred and inviolable', and 'his Ministers are responsible'. This cryptic remark raised a big question: to whom were the ministers to be responsible? To the king, or to a parliament? Article 3 read: 'To the King belongs the executive power. He is the supreme Head of State. He commands the land and sea forces; he declares war; makes treaties of peace, of alliance and of commerce; he nominates all employees; and he gives all the orders necessary for the execution of the laws without suspending or dispensing with the observance of them.' Although the last phrase in Article 3 seemed to suggest that the king was beneath the law, and although even the most impotent constitutional monarch is always head of state, commander-in-chief of the army, and so on, it was nevertheless significant that Article 3 was the longest and most explicit article in the decree. Article 4 declared that 'the king alone sanctioned the laws and promulgated them.' The tone of the first ten articles suggested that the Statuto was to be as much a charter to protect the prerogative of the crown as to give some kind of representation to some of the people. But Article 6 allowed for the existence of two Chambers to co-operate with the king in exercising the legislative power. Article 7 laid down that the Upper Chamber would consist of members nominated by the king for life, while the Lower Chamber would be elected. Article 8 gave to the king and to each of the Chambers the right to introduce legislation, but reserved for the Lower Chamber the right to be the first to deal with financial measures.

The full Statuto was published on 5 March. The basic question which it left unanswered was: who was going to have the vote for members of the Lower Chamber? And this was to be answered in a very conservative sense in a later 'Electoral Law'.[12] But the Statuto itself contained important details which the decree of 8 February had not mentioned – such as freedom of association – and a clear statement that everyone, regardless of his religion, had equal rights of citizenship, including the right to public office.

Carlo Alberto's Statuto established a constitutional, but not a parliamentary, régime.[13] It was given as an act of grace by the king, not wrested from him by revolution – at least, so the legal fiction went. The historical truth was that Carlo Alberto granted it from fear of the revolution, but by the terms of the constitution retained as much of his prerogative as he could. The myth that the Statuto was simply granted by the king was to be exploded when Lombardy was annexed in June 1848, and received her free institutions not from the King's grace, but as the result of negotiation and plebiscite.

With the establishment of the constitution the old absolutist ministers resigned, and Count Cesare Balbo, whose name implied a moderately nationalist policy, was put at the head of a ministry.[14] The events in Turin which had led to the granting of the Statuto were soon set in a much broader perspective by the outbreak of revolutions all over Europe, and especially by the risings in Vienna, Milan and Venice. The vital question of whether, when, and how Carlo Alberto would go to war with Austria in support of the people of Milan and Venice is clearly not simply a matter of Piedmontese history, and must be considered in a later chapter. Carlo Alberto's Statuto was one day to be the basis of the constitution of united Italy. From its promulgation the political history of Piedmont was inextricably blended with the history of Italy, and will therefore be left for the central section of the book, along with a consideration of the brief but startlingly successful career of Cavour.[15]

The economy of Piedmont was in most respects very backward before 1848. It was based heavily on agriculture, and Piedmontese agriculture was in a primitive state – small-scale and dependent upon very local markets. Roads were poor, and trade was hampered by the conservative commercial policy. So far as Genoa and the Ligurian coastline were concerned there was definite economic decline at the start of the period. When the ancient Republic was finally snuffed out in 1814 Genoa was in an even greater state of economic depression than Venice, her trade having dwindled to a pathetic level. In Piedmont after 1814 there was a heavy duty on imported corn. Piedmont had to import corn except in years of exceptional harvests, the corn coming from France to Savoy, and from Lombardy to Piedmont proper. If the trade in corn were freed, the government feared that very cheap corn from the Black Sea coastal countries would be dumped in Italy. The idea of a sliding scale, like the one introduced in Britain by Peel and adopted in France and the Netherlands, was resisted by Piedmontese governments, though it had long before been recommended by Beccaria.

Banking had virtually been invented in Italy in the Middle Ages, but in spite of the long tradition of banking in Milan, Florence and Venice, there was no such tradition in Turin. A credit bank was founded in Genoa in 1844, but in Turin such an establishment was founded only on Cavour's initiative. On his two visits to London in 1835 and 1843 Cavour made a study of the banks, and especially examined the activities of the London and Westminster Bank, the Union Bank of London, and the London and County Bank. Negotiations for the creation of a bank of Turin entered their final phase at the beginning of 1847. Cavour had been trying to persuade his fellow-citizens that it was necessary to have a credit bank at Turin, but the minister of finance, Revel, was not happy with the proposal, since he was reluctant to leave it entirely in the hands of independent 'bankers'. Having secured the help of 'landowners' – one of whom was Cavour's friend, Count Ruggero di

Salmour – Revel allowed the project to go through. Ten directors were appointed, among them Cavour and Salmour, the other eight being 'bankers'.[16]

It was in the 1840s and 1850s that industrialization at any appreciable rate began in Piedmont. As in trade, so in industry, the Restoration period was a bleak one both in Liguria and Piedmont proper. In Liguria there had been marked industrial decline. The manufacturing districts which had once existed to the east and west of Genoa – along the Ligurian coast from Sestri to Noli, both today thriving tourist resorts – had almost ceased to exist before 1814. By 1830 only a little silk was worked, at Zoagli – perhaps not more than 5 per cent of what had once been produced. But if modern industry was very slow to come to Piedmont, some pioneering work had already been done very early in the nineteenth century. The introduction of machinery into the Piedmontese wool and cotton industries owed much to men from other countries. Jean-Paul Laclaire from Rheims brought machinery into his woollen mills in Turin, Casella and Rivoli (both places just outside Turin) in 1804. Laclaire dedicated a long life to building up a thriving business, and, as a believer in the necessity of protection in an undeveloped country like Piedmont, was still active enough to fight Cavour's free trade policies in the 1850s. From Zofingen in Switzerland John James Müller brought the first machines for the Piedmontese cotton industry to Intra on Lake Maggiore in 1810. These, and early industrialists among the Piedmontese themselves, were grim men, wholly devoted to their work, living austere lives with little cultural or social variety. Lacking the self-indulgences of ordinary people, they were not well placed to realize that to some extent their success was based on the misery of their employees.

The numbers employed in industry were of course small compared with those employed in agriculture. The ancient industry of mining employed perhaps 4,500 people by 1830. Lead, silver, iron ore, manganese, cobalt, even some gold, but very little coal, was mined. Much coal had to be imported, and a great deal of timber was used for fuel. More extensive than mining, as in all primitive economies, was the quarrying of stone for building. Even so, miners and quarrymen together numbered only some 22,000 in the 1830s. The three major industries were silk, wool and cotton. Figures existing for 1844 show that 43,924 workers were employed in the silk industry, most of them still in cottage industry, but some of them already in factories. The figure fluctuated drastically with the trade cycle, which brought its devastating alternations of hope and despair. 1844 was a comparatively bad year. People employed in the silk industry sometimes rose to 60,000, even in the 1840s. The woollen industry, as it had developed in England, needed coal. In Piedmont there was virtually no coal, so that hydraulic power instead of steam had to be used. This placed severe limitations on the choice of sites for woollen mills, and contributed to the backwardness of the industry. Compared with wool, on the other hand, cotton was an expanding industry, and had a great future. Industrial workers – most of them in textiles – numbered about 114,000 in 1844.[17]

The development of industry in the nineteenth century depended to a great extent on the building of railways. Long before he had made any impact on the political scene in Piedmont, Cavour had exerted an influence on the history of the railway. His interest in railways dated from his trip to Britain in 1835, when he visited the railway constructions in operation from London to Birmingham. In 1837 he was present at the opening of the line from Paris to Saint-Germain. He recorded in his diary his delight at riding on a railway train, and at once realized that railways would bring a 'revolution in the material world'. The first railway line in Piedmont was from Chambéry to the Lac du Bourget, in Savoy. In spite of its diminutive size, it ran into economic difficulties. In 1844 Cavour planned to form a company to build a line from Turin to Alessandria, and to co-operate in planning another line from Alessandria to Genoa. His plans were undermined by the government's decision to undertake the building of a Turin—Genoa line itself, but he certainly could not disapprove of that decision. As deputy in 1848 and afterwards he spoke in favour of rapid railway construction, and as minister he was from 1850 in a position to see his ideas put into practice. The decision by the old absolutist government of Piedmont in 1845 to embark on a fairly ambitious programme of railway building was greatly furthered some years later when Cavour, as minister of finance, negotiated a loan for the purpose from Hambro, the London bankers. As in other aspects of the economic history of Piedmont, development of the railways started late but, once started, in the 1850s moved rapidly.

The effect of industrialization and urbanization on the conditions of the people is always difficult to assess. It is no easier to assess with reference to Piedmont than with reference to Britain, France or Germany. The final assessment must be that rural conditions had always been extremely grim; urbanization usually mitigated the grimness to a slight extent in most cases, but in other cases it exacerbated it. In Piedmont before 1830 deformities and medical disabilities were much higher in the countryside than in the city, but this may have been due as much to in-breeding as to living or working conditions. When the workers arrived in the city there was no compensation for their lost sense of identity through any new sense of community. There were severe penal laws in Piedmont against collective action by workers. The appalling conditions of work were condemned by a few enlightened people – doctors, economists, some political commentators, among them the young Cavour, even some priests. The workers in the silk industry had a 17-hour day in the busiest season. One complaint not found in Britain was that workers had a long walk to get to work – sometimes of two hours if they worked in Turin – and so were tired before starting a very long day.

Piedmont was certainly slower than other states initiating social legislation. Carlo Petitti, Lorenzo Valerio and other political journalists recommended social reform by legislative measures. By twentieth-century standards these men were certainly moderates, but because they no longer thought of looking after the poor by works of charity, but instead proposed the passing of laws to grant some measure of social justice, they were regarded as 'revolutionaries'. And, in contrast to every opinion previously held, revolutionaries they were. Yet it must be added that the old standards of 'charity' in Piedmont were perhaps preferable to those in more 'developed' countries. Thus in a hospital for the poor in Turin in 1828 the menu for the day ran as follows: breakfast, at some time between 7 and 8 a.m., three ounces of bread; at 11 a.m. a full meal, consisting of nine ounces of bread, a main dish of vegetables, sometimes with meat, rice or *pasta*, and a quarter of a pint of wine mixed with water; at 6 p.m., six ounces of bread with soup or salad. In other words, Piedmontese paupers were given a meagre diet, but a more balanced one than that enjoyed by the average industrial worker throughout Europe. Wages for all workers in Piedmont were, of course, miserably low. Two cups of coffee in a fashionable coffee-house in Turin cost more than the average wage for the working day of a woman in a factory. There was much drunkenness among workers in Turin, but it was caused mainly by wine, which was not only less harmful than spirits, but perhaps a necessary stimulant, physically as well as psychologically, after the depressing experience of work in dirty and unhealthy surroundings. The pathetic attempts by the authorities to cure alcoholism – by temperance societies, Sunday schools, and the like – did not approach the root causes. The workers in Turin suffered as much as, perhaps more than, did those in Milan from the usual diseases associated with poverty and bad working conditions. Common diseases were typhus, which had always broken out periodically, and of which there was a particularly violent outbreak in the Val d'Aosta in 1844, scurvy, scrofula and pellagra, a horrible complaint whose early symptoms were a cracking of the skin and which often ended in insanity.

Epidemics affecting the whole population were not as common as they had been in earlier centuries, but Piedmont suffered severely from the cholera epidemic of 1831–2, and even more severely in 1835. In the summer of 1835 cholera raged particularly fiercely in Liguria, where for several weeks about three hundred people died every day. In Turin, where the 1835 epidemic was much milder than it was in Liguria, a working-class protest movement developed from the belief that the upper classes had deliberately spread the epidemic to get rid of unwanted surplus population.

Shortage of capital, both for industry and agriculture, meant that both were subject to sharp, recurring crises. Agricultural slumps in 1817, 1827 and 1842 brought famine conditions. The European economic crisis of 1845–7, whose most marked feature was the potato blight, did not bring to Piedmont tragedy on the scale experienced in Ireland or Germany, because the potato was not a prominent feature of the Piedmontese economy except in Savoy. But the secondary effects of the potato crisis – the shortage of food generally, and the consequent sharp rise in consumer prices – led to hunger and increased pauperism. A decree of 1836, coming just two years after the famous British Poor Law Act, dealt with pauperism in an authoritarian manner, regarding paupers as delinquents who would have to be forcibly enclosed in workhouses. The 1848 census estimated that paupers in Piedmont numbered over 30,000, and these were undoubtedly the more permanent and regular paupers, not poor people reduced to begging only during the slumps in the trade cycles.

Another estimate for the period 1845—9 puts the number at 33,000, of which 8,716 were accounted for in workhouses, while the great majority lived as tramps on the streets or in the countryside.[18] In Piedmont poverty was regarded, even by someone as enlightened as Lorenzo Valerio, as something which necessitated charity from above, not drastic social reorganization.

In another sphere, that of education, conditions in Piedmont were also primitive, probably more primitive than in Austrian Italy, but insufficient research has been carried out for such a judgement to be made with any certainty, and so far as educational standards and conditions elsewhere in the peninsula go, it would be misleading to make generalized statements. More work has been done on education in Piedmont than on education in the other Italian states before unification. The broad statement can be made that only about half of the population of Piedmont were literate. The contemporary official publication *Annuario economico politico* quoted the suspiciously precise figures for 1852 as being: out of a population of 4,916,087 there were 1,531,846 illiterate men, and 1,869,994 illiterate women.[19] In Turin the situation was a little better than elsewhere in Piedmont. In Turin 51 per cent of the total population (including small children) could read and write, and a further 8 per cent could read. The number of schools had increased sharply since 1847, there being 462 elementary schools in the province of Turin alone in 1852, and only 138 of these were private ones. The period of growth had been the revolutionary one between 1847 and 1850; some schools closed between 1850 and 1852, and the number of teachers in the state schools declined. But ever since the revolution of 1821 attempts had been made to expand education. A decree of 23 July 1822 had obliged town councils to establish primary schools, where children could be given free education in 'reading, writing, Christian doctrine, the elements of the Italian language, and arithmetic', but inadequate finance and, no doubt, other motives, had prevented this noble aim from being carried out. In so far as elementary education was introduced in this early period it was entirely the work of the Church. In the late 1830s there was renewed enthusiasm, stimulated by Valerio, Cavour, and others, for the establishment of secular elementary schools, especially for girls (who had received less attention in the past), Sunday schools, technical schools, and teachers' training colleges. The results of the movement were not immediately dramatic. In 1844, however, a teachers' training college, or 'school of method', as it was called, was opened in Turin, under the direction of the enlightened Abbot, Ferranti Aporti, in the teeth of opposition from the Archbishop, Luigi Fransoni. When Cavour created a Kingdom of Italy in 1861 he accepted the inheritance of all the Italian states with regard to education. It cannot be said that the inheritance from Piedmont was the most brilliant. The ancient traditions of Bologna, Ferrara and Padua, and the brilliant achievements of the University of Naples in the eighteenth century far outweighed anything that Turin could offer. Yet, at least, the bulk of the population of Piedmont were more literate than those of Naples or the Papal States. There had always been a respect for education in Piedmont, and only her economic backwardness had prevented that respect from being exploited.

To understand Piedmont's place in the history of Italy it is necessary to balance some very strong negatives against some very strong positives. So far this chapter has stressed the negatives, and, by halting the political history of the Kingdom in 1848, it has obscured the piling up of positives that occurred thereafter. For example, at the beginning of 1856 Piedmont experienced a considerable expansion of the press, nearly every newspaper either increasing its size, reducing its price, or doing both. The circulation of the papers was very small by English standards: very few of them sold more than a thousand copies, though this fact may give a false impression of the political dynamism of the small educated class, since the papers were taken by the coffee-shops and voraciously read there. Furthermore there was a great number of very small journals, not only in Turin, but in many small towns. The press was extremely lively, full of scurrilous satire of individuals, and charges and counter-charges of corruption between editors. The Left also held a great number of public meetings, which were well attended. The tradition of radical journalism from Carlo Alberto's reign had survived. Valerio's *Letture di famiglia*, suppressed in 1847, has already been mentioned. Later that year, when the censorship laws were at last lifted, a far more lively press had come into existence. Valerio himself founded the *Concordia*, which was ostensibly more loyal to the dynasty than his earlier journal, but was more extreme in condemning Austrian rule in Lombardo-Venezia, and soon in recommending war. Valerio's papers were certainly not the only ones to show great independence of spirit and democratic manners. With its many political exiles, immigrants from all over Italy, Piedmont by 1850 was an extremely dynamic world in the political, if not the social, sense. If the Piedmontese themselves seemed austere and unimaginative to the Neapolitans, they certainly did not give that impression to visitors from Victorian Britain. Mr Boyle St John, who was in Turin in 1856, was inclined to regard them as irresponsible, unstable pleasure-seekers. The Piedmontese institution which perhaps most impressed him was the state lottery. A Royal Lottery Office was established in every parish with more than 3,000 inhabitants, which meant that there were seventeen in Turin. All classes, and especially the very poorest, bought tickets for the lottery, and provided the Piedmontese government – especially in Cavour's day – with a considerable revenue. In effect the lottery supplied one of the instruments with which Piedmont was to secure the independence and unification of Italy – an instrument never mentioned in the heroic accounts of the Risorgimento.

NOTES

The history of Piedmont is so closely intertwined with both the national and the international history of Italy from 1790 to 1870 that many works relevant to Piedmont have already either been discussed in Part One, or will be mentioned in the notes to Chapters 8 and 9. In particular a selection from the extensive bibliography on Cavour is given in the notes to Chapter 8. But here a few books must be mentioned. A classic on Carlo Alberto is Adolfo Omodeo 'La Leggenda di Carlo Alberto nella recente storiografia' in *Difesa del risorgimento*, Turin, 1951. In recent times a short study of Carlo Alberto's reign is provided by Narciso Nada, *Dallo Stato assoluto allo Stato costituzionale. Storia del Regno di Carlo Alberto dal 1831 al 1848*, Turin, 1980. A paper read at a congress in 1958, illustrated by documents, gave a sharp focus on Piedmontese domestic politics after Carlo Alberto's defeat at Novara: Ennio di Nolfo, 'La crisi del partito moderato piemontese dopo Novara', in *Atti del XXXVII congresso di storia del risorgimento italiano*, Rome, 1961.

For the diplomatic history of Piedmont a massive work of 940 pages must be mentioned. Salvemini persuaded Nello Rosselli to undertake the task of making a detailed study of Anglo-Piedmontese relations over a period of thirty-two years. *Inghilterra e regno di Sardegna dal 1816 al 1847*, Turin, 1954, was published posthumously, seventeen years after Rosselli's murder by Fascists in France. It was perhaps sad that Rosselli spent so long on the research und writing of this book, since his other works, on Pisacane and on Mazzini and Bakunin, mentioned in Chapter 14, were so much more imaginative. But *Inghilterra e regno di Sardegna dal 1815 al 1847* will remain an important work of reference.

Genoa in the later modern period has perhaps not had the attention she deserves from historians. Bianca Montale is evidently preparing a full study, and as an *hors d'oeuvre* a collection of her articles was published in 1979: *Genova nel risorgimento. Dalle riforme all'unità*, Savona.

Important for the textile industry in its early days in Piedmont is Guido Quazza, *L'industria laniera e cotoniera in Piemonte dal 1831 al 1861*, Turin, 1961, while Gian Mario Bravo, *Torino Operaio. Mondo del lavoro e idee sociali nell'età di Carlo Alberto*, Turin, 1968, gives an impression of social conditions and ideas in Turin.

1. Giuseppe Melano, *La popolazione di Torino e del Piemonte nel secolo XIX*, Museo Nazionale del Risorgimento: Turin, 1961.
2. Gian Mario Bravo, *op. cit.*, pp. 17−19.
3. Quoted in Cesare Spellanzon, *Storia del Risorgimento e dell' unità d'Italia*, Milan, 1951, p. 131.
4. 'Struttura sociale e realtà politica nel progetto costituzionale dei giacobini piemontesi (1796)', in *Società*, V (1949), no. 3, pp. 436−55.
5. See Ch. 4 and 6.
6. Quoted in Federigo Sclopis, *Storia della legislazione negli stati del re di Sardegna dal 1814 al 1847*, Turin, 1860, p. 3.
7. See Ch. 5 and 7.
8. See Ch. 3, 4 and 7.
9. See Ch. 7 and 8.
10. See Ch. 4 and 8.
11. See Ch. 3, 4, 5 and 8.
12. See Ch. 8.
13. This argument was effectively put by Emanuele Flora in 'Lo statuto albertino L'avvento del regime parlamentare nel regno di Sardegna', *Rassegna storica del risorgimento*, XLV, i. Jan.−Mar. 1958.
14. For Balbo see Ch. 8.
15. Ch. 8 and 9.

16. The story is told in detail in Leopoldo Marchetti, *Cavour e la Banca di Torino* (*1847–1850*), Milan, 1952.
17. The figures in this paragraph have been taken from Gian Mario Bravo, *op. cit.*
18. *Ibid.*, pp. 131–2.
19. *Annuario economico politico*, Turin, 1852, pp. 60 and 207.

CHAPTER THREE

The Central Duchies – Tuscany, Parma and Modena

Tuscany had enjoyed the most splendid period of her history from the thirteenth to the sixteenth centuries, from the age of Dante to the age of Machiavelli. A considerable political and cultural decline had set in from the days of the High Renaissance, yet Florence had remained in many ways the most civilized of Italian cities. From the speech of her citizens was drawn the national language and, in spite of much 'reconstruction' in the nineteenth century much of the beauty of medieval and Renaissance Florence survived. In the early nineteenth century Florence was praised for being much cleaner than other Italian cities, in spite of the large number of open markets in the centre of the city, including for example a horse market in the Piazza degli Uffizi. There was a sharp contrast between Florence, the capital of the Grand Duchy, and Leghorn, its main port. While the Florentines prided themselves on their pacific, moderate and tolerant spirit, the citizens of Leghorn possessed a radical and dynamic outlook comparable to that of the Genoese.

The population of Tuscany in 1790 was estimated to be 1,058,000 – an increase of 113,000 since 1765.[1] It was thus by eighteenth-century standards thickly populated, its land in many areas intensively cultivated, and its towns growing.

Like Tuscany, the much smaller Duchies of Parma and Modena retained a political identity as independent states for the greater part of the period covered by this book. As satellites of Austria, Tuscany, Parma and Modena are usually considered together as the 'Central Duchies'. Yet geographically Parma and Modena were not related to Tuscany. They were on the other side of the Apennines and so, geographically, more closely related to the Papal Legations. They were a part, in other words, of the geographical region of Emilia, rightly known today as the source of the most sophisticated Italian cooking. But the policies of the Great Powers had dictated that the Duchies of Parma and Modena should retain nominal independence both from the Habsburg Monarchy and from the Papal States. The capital cities of the two Duchies, the cities of Parma and Modena, were smaller than many provincial cities in other Italian states. In 1790 both cities had populations of little more than 20,000.

In 1790 the House of Lorraine, a junior line of the Habsburgs, had been ruling Tuscany as Grand Dukes since 1737. From 1765 until 1790 the Grand Duke was Pietro Leopoldo, who became Emperor Leopold II in 1790. As ruler of Tuscany he was perhaps the most enlightened of all the enlightened despots. Both in a political and economic sense there was a nobility about Pietro Leopoldo's reign in Tuscany rarely equalled in the history of monarchy. Above all, in the field of penal law, he turned Tuscany into the most civilized corner of the world by putting into operation the ultra-enlightened reforms proposed by Cesare Beccaria in his *Dei delitti e delle pene*. When the more powerful enlightened despots of Prussia, Austria and Russia were busy abolishing torture, Pietro Leopoldo went one step further and abolished the death sentence – an astonishing achievement for the eighteenth century.

Pietro Leopoldo had not expected to become emperor. He had identified entirely with Tuscany, and on leaving for Vienna left power in the hands of a regency council whose president was an Italian, Antonio Serristori, and of whose other five members – the senators Gianni and Bartolini, and the councillors Schmidveiller, Ciani and Giusti – four were also Italian. But the Grand Duke was not leaving Tuscany in a settled state. His liberalizing of trade in foodstuffs, and the radical ecclesiastical reforms pushed through by Bishop Ricci, were unpopular. There were disturbances first at Pistoia and Prato, then at Leghorn, and finally in Florence itself. Pietro Leopoldo, alarmed by these disturbances, and still more by what was happening in Paris, withdrew his more radical criminal reforms, and on 30 June 1790 – a sad date in Tuscan history – brought back the death sentence.

On 21 July 1790 Pietro Leopoldo, now the Emperor Leopold II, renounced his sovereignty over Tuscany in favour of his second son, who thus became Grand Duke Ferdinando III. Leopold's elder son, Francis, was to become emperor. Ferdinando was still a minor, and was granted full powers as Grand Duke only in 1791, when he became twenty-one. He was of considerably less calibre than his father. When the Emperor Leopold died, on 29 February 1792, aged only forty-five, Austria lost an emperor who might well have become one of the greatest in her history, and whose balanced judgement was to be sorely needed in the dramatic years ahead. Francis now became emperor, and adopted a stance towards revolutionary France which was less tolerant than that which had been adopted by his brother in Florence. Ferdinando was by nature a hesitant youth, and was uncertain what policy to follow in the European crisis. He at first remained neutral, and entered the alliance against France only in 1793 when, on 28 October, pressure from the British forced him to sign a treaty of alliance with them. Tuscany was thus theoretically at war with France, but the civilized Tuscan tradition of existing virtually without an army ensured that the Grand Duke could play no part in the war. Tuscany was the first state to make peace with France – in February 1795 – but with the arrival of Napoleon in Italy in the spring of 1796 the Grand Duchy – in spite of being formally at peace with France – was invaded. The French army moved down the coast from Carrara to occupy Leghorn in June of 1796, but precisely because of the military weakness of Tuscany no French troops entered Florence until March 1799. Napoleon himself visited the city on 30 June 1796, and was warmly received by Ferdinando.

When the French army finally arrived in Florence in 1799, Ferdinando issued a proclamation recommending the citizens to 'maintain a perfect quiet'. He was subsequently informed by the Directory in Paris that he must leave Florence with his family within twenty-four hours. The Florentines were not elated at seeing the departure of the Grand Duke, and the French attempt to excite support by planting trees of liberty in the Piazza di Santa Croce and the Piazza di Santa Maria Novella also failed. The Florentines were more sceptical about the arrival of the French than were the citizens of other Italian cities. After the departure of Ferdinando the French set up a provisional government under their own diplomatic agent, instead of a fully fledged republic. When the French in their turn were defeated by the Russians and Austrians in Italy in the early summer of 1799 an ugly interim followed in Tuscany. A gang of religious fanatics from Arezzo, calling themselves the *Armata aretina*, and carrying out their bestialities with cries of 'Viva Maria', occupied Siena and subsequently Florence itself. They concentrated on the murder of Jews and suspected Jacobins. The numbers killed have never been properly assessed, but contemporary impressions suggest that they were considerable. The leaders of the gang were one of Ferdinando III's former officers, his wife, and her lover, the British minister at Florence, William Wyndham, who was officially on leave.[2] Their 'troops' consisted to a great extent of priests and monks. They ravaged Tuscany for some two months until the Austrians disbanded them in September, after which the Austrian occupation appeared a comparatively mild affair.

After Marengo the French returned in great force and re-entered Florence. Their settlement of Central Italy was for the moment a by-product of two Franco-Spanish treaties – those of 1 October 1800 and 21 March 1801. Lodovico, the Duke of Parma's son, and husband of the Spanish princess, Maria Luisa, was recognized as King of 'Etruria', a state which included Tuscany. The Duchy of Parma was annexed to the French Republic and ultimately, in May 1808, to the French Empire.

The territories annexed to the First French Empire were divided into departments under French prefects. Their conscripts went directly into the French army. French laws and codes were applied, as were the French administrative and educational systems. In 1809 Napoleon nominated his sister, Elisa Baciocchi Bonaparte, Grand Duchess of Tuscany, with the new administrative responsibilities attached to such a title. In reality Tuscany remained directly under the control of the Emperor himself. Conscription into the French army was particularly distasteful to the Tuscans with their long tradition of pacifism, but in other respects Tuscany was probably less influenced by the French occupation than was Piedmont.

With the restoration in 1814 Tuscany, as usual, avoided the more barbarous excesses practised in some other European states. The restored Grand Duke, Ferdinando III, was rather more enlightened and sensible than the other princes restored in Italy. During his years of exile he had been treated

71

gently by Napoleon, who had given him the principality of Salzburg in 1802, and the Grand Duchy of Würzburg in 1805. Salzburg was annexed to Austria in 1805, but even while he had been its prince Ferdinando had been unhappy, complaining of the climate and wishing that he was back in Florence. His return in 1814 pleased both the Tuscans and the Grand Duke and, if the institutions introduced by the French were mostly abolished, it is also true that there was no persecution of officials who had worked with the French. In short, Ferdinando was a moderate man, who had been born and educated in Florence, and whose identification with Florence was thus even stronger than Pietro Leopoldo's had been. He made himself very accessible to his subjects, holding regular audiences, appearing on social occasions with a minimum of pomp or measures of security, and walking the streets accompanied by a single servant. He would probably have been only too willing to grant a constitution if Metternich had permitted it. If he lacked the creative genius of Pietro Leopoldo he certainly brought with him the same civilized spirit.

His restoration at Florence was, however, interrupted by the Hundred Days, and Murat's short-lived bid to make himself King of Italy.[3] When Murat occupied Florence Ferdinando had to leave once more, but this time for a very brief spell. After the second restoration Tuscany was in all diplomatic senses treated as an independent state. The Grand Duke signed the Holy Alliance[4] as an independent sovereign on 27 January 1818, and foreign states opened or continued diplomatic relations with her as with a sovereign state.

The Grand Duke's government had an opportunity to display benevolence to the Tuscans just after the Restoration when, in 1815 and 1816, there was a general outbreak of typhus in Italy, as a result of the famine of those years. The very poor suffered most, but the government took immediate action to mitigate the suffering by subsidizing the import of foreign grain, and providing new hospitals for the victims of the multiple misfortunes.

The Restoration government also spent considerable sums on education. The Universities of Pisa and Siena were reorganized, and the scientific departments at Pisa were expanded, with a considerable enlargement of the library. The University of Pisa, founded in 1338, and turned into the centre of Tuscan scholarship by the patronage of Lorenzo the Magnificent in the fifteenth century, was to enjoy another period of academic distinction later in the nineteenth century. Restoration Tuscany also encouraged greater expenditure on the education of women, a project about which Pietro Leopoldo had always felt strongly. Ferdinando founded the Institute of Women's Education of the *Sacra Annunziata*, of which the director and teachers were all secular, in spite of its dedication. It was placed under the supervision of Ferdinando's wife, the Grand Duchess Maria, who for many years took a keen interest in the establishment.

Ferdinando appointed as his first minister (though nominally only 'minister of foreign affairs') a typical product of the Enlightenment – Vittorio Fossombroni, an engineer, tolerant, sceptical, and after the recent experiences of Europe a convinced conservative. He remained, like Metternich, an anti-clerical in a modified sense. The Jesuits were still forbidden to enter Tuscany, but much property which had been taken from other religious orders was restored to them.

The restored Grand Duchy of Tuscany acquired the island of Elba after Napoleon had been dispatched to St Helena. In his brief sovereignty of Elba, Napoleon had amused himself by having the roads improved, and even the local quarrying industry modernized. By a treaty in 1817 Tuscany was also to acquire the Duchy of Lucca, after the death of Marie-Louise, when the Bourbons would acquire Parma. Rather as the little Duchy of Lucca was dependent upon Tuscany, so was Tuscany itself, unavoidably, dependent in a military and diplomatic sense upon Austria. In the new atmosphere of repression in Italy it was clearly going to be difficult for Ferdinando III to avoid a degree of identification with Austrian policy. That he and his chief minister Fossombroni did in the event retain some of the progressive spirit for Tuscany that had never been lost since the days of Pietro Leopoldo was no small achievement. So tolerant was the atmosphere that the secret societies which appeared elsewhere in Italy had little *raison d'être* in Florence. What small influence was felt from the Carbonari and the other secret societies in Tuscany was treated with leniency and scepticism by Fossombroni. On one occasion, on being shown by his police correspondence between Tuscan and Neopolitan Carbonari, Fossombroni said with a laugh that all that need be done was to forward the letters to the addresses for which they were intended with the addition of a stamp reading 'Seen by the Police'.[5] Unfortunately one recipient of such a letter was so terrified that he killed himself – a consequence certainly not anticipated by Fossombroni. Only in Leghorn, with its maritime links with Naples, was there some clandestine revolutionary conspiracy, but the revolutions of 1820– 21 did not spread to Tuscany. Austrian troops crossed the Grand Duchy on their way to fight, but Tuscany remained neutral and provided no troops itself. On the contrary, Neapolitan refugees were usually welcomed in Florence, where they found that political discussion could be surprisingly uninhibited.

The tolerant attitude of the régime in Florence had one important consequence: Gian Pietro Vieusseux founded the *Antologia* in Florence in 1821. Vieusseux's parents had been Swiss, but he himself had been born, in 1779, at Oneglia on the Italian Riviera west of Genoa. Soon after the Restoration he settled in Florence, the obvious Italian city from which to pursue his journalistic and literary work. A man of considerable personal charm and diplomacy, Vieusseux managed to keep people of very varied opinions writing for the *Antologia*, even though he could not afford to pay them. The list of contributors included some of the great names of the Italian nineteenth century – Foscolo, Leopardi, Mazzini, Tommaseo. Vieusseux had preceded the work of the *Antologia* by founding a meeting-place for nationalist intellectuals from all over Italy – the *Gabinetto scientifico-letterario* – but it was the *Antologia* which made Florence the politico-cultural centre of Italy, until the Grand Duke's government was obliged by Vienna to suppress it in March 1833. Even when it took this step the government reimbursed Vieusseux with 3,369 lire, to cover the cost of copies seized by the police – a gentle hint of civilization in a dark age. But to give Vieusseux sole credit for the achievements of the *Antologia* would be unfair. He received enormous help from a younger man, Gino Capponi. Born in 1792, the Marchese Capponi was, like Vieusseux, a devout Catholic. If he knew less of the world than did Vieusseux, he was much more of a scholar. His knowledge of the classics, of French and English, and his stay in England, where he had contributed to the *Edinburgh Review*, did not make up for Vieusseux's long travels and experiences as a trans-continental commercial traveller, but made him appreciate the influence the *Antologia* could have. Without adding a word of overtly nationalist propaganda, the *Antologia*, by publishing distinguished literary and scientific works, written by the best minds in Italy, could not fail to give a sense of national identity to its readers. It was not surprising that Metternich should eventually decide that the *Antologia* must be suppressed.

The Restoration in Parma brought the moderate rule of Marie-Louise and her lover, the Austrian general Count Adarn Neipperg, who married her, morganatically, after Napoleon's death in 1821. In 1814 Marie-Louise had been Empress of the French for four years. Although she was a daughter of the Austrian Emperor Francis, her fortunes were inextricably linked with those of Napoleon, and since the victorious Allied Powers were determined never again to negotiate with Napoleon, but simply to overthrow him, it was extremely unlikely that Marie-Louise would remain on a French throne. Bernadotte, once a marshal of Napoleon, but in 1814 King of Sweden and an ally of Napoleon's enemies, wanted to make Marie-Louise regent during the minority of her son – Napoleon's son, the King of Rome. But Bernadotte's plan was opposed by Talleyrand, who persuaded the great powers that the Bourbons must be restored in France, an argument which the Austrian Emperor also accepted, although it involved the sacrifice of rights which might have been claimed by his daughter. Initially Czar Alexander I, perhaps the most powerful man in Europe in 1814, suggested that Marie-Louise should be given Tuscany, and that her son should succeed her, which would mean that she would be near Napoleon, who was to be given Elba. But the Austrians opposed the Czar's plan. Napoleon commented to Marie-Louise: 'It seems that your father is our most bitter enemy.' On 11 April 1814 he wrote to her from Fontainebleau, telling her of her fate:

To me they are giving the Island of Elba and to you and your son Parma, Piacenza and Guastalla. It is a place of four hundred thousand souls and an income of three or four million. You will at least have a house and beautiful countryside when your stay on the Island of Elba bores you and I become tiresome, which is bound to happen when I grow old and you are still young.[6]

In the event Napoleon was not to stay on Elba, nor was Marie-Louise ever to visit him there. Nor would Metternich allow the King of Rome to pass out of the safe-keeping of the Austrian government. Although the Emperor Francis had at first opposed the idea of his daughter occupying an Italian throne, and had wanted her to return to Vienna, once she was installed in Parma he became determined to uphold her rights there and her title as Archduchess.

For Talleyrand the establishment of Marie-Louise in Parma was an offence against the principle of legitimacy, involving as it did the ignoring of the rights of a branch of the Bourbons who had previously ruled Parma. Marie-Louise herself quickly adjusted to the idea of becoming the Duchess of Parma, and was no doubt encouraged in her enthusiasm by Neipperg. A cultured man, still in his thirties, Neipperg had lost his right eye as the result of a sword thrust. He and Marie-Louise were immensely happy together. A baby girl was born in 1817, and a boy in 1819. Neipperg died, at a comparatively early age, in 1829, after being secretly married to Marie-Louise for only eight years.

Not surprisingly, perhaps, Marie-Louise had no intention of scrapping all Napoleon's legislation in Parma. At first it was announced that the Code Napoléon and the French laws would be retained, and although the Code was eventually repealed in 1820, the one which replaced it retained unmistakable echoes. Marie-Louise's virtues as a ruler were all negative ones. She brought no original policies or reforms to Parma, but also she enforced no stupid or vindictive reaction. By the standards of Restoration Europe this makes her an enlightened ruler.

In the Duchy of Modena the Restoration meant the arrival of Francesco IV, a grandson of Maria-Theresa and a nephew of the Emperors Joseph II and Leopold II (Pietro Leopoldo). It meant also a far cleaner sweep of the Napoleonic regime than that carried out in Parma. The Italians who had held office in Napoleon's Kingdom of Italy were removed from office and were replaced by members of the nobility in Francesco's own circle of friends. The Jesuits acquired a commanding influence. Francesco IV had a considerable private fortune, and tended to see the Duchy of Modena as only a part of that fortune. In a sense, this was fortunate for the Modenese, since the Duke, by no means an incompetent administrator, was determined to run his Duchy as efficiently as possible. He realized that his sharp intelligence could be better employed in the running of a larger state, and he hoped that circumstances would permit him to acquire one. He had married Maria Beatrice, the daughter of Vittorio Emanuele I, in 1812 in Sardinia, where that King's court had been in virtual exile. Francesco's choice of wife had clearly been a political one: his succession to the Piedmontese throne was certainly on the cards. His strange behaviour in the crisis of 1830–31 was to be simply a sequel to these earlier ambitions. If he hated the liberals in Italy, he hated also Metternich and the godless Habsburg state, which had broken with the Jesuits in the days of Joseph II, and had prevented Francesco from acquiring a larger state in Italy than his diminutive Duchy of Modena. His friends were not only the Jesuits, but the ultra-right-wing *Concistoriali*, a clandestine Catholic sect. Francesco IV represented one of the most sinister and dangerous aspects of Restoration Italy.

There was, then, a marked contrast between the comparatively civilized régimes restored in Tuscany and Parma, and Francesco IV's restoration in Modena. Especially after the revolutionary movements of 1820–21 did Francesco step up the repression, acting through a hard-line chief of police, Giulio

Besini. After the arrest of some fifty people in 1822, Besini was assassinated – stabbed by a student, Antonio Morandi, who managed to evade the police and get out of the country. The use of a knife or a stiletto for an assassination attempt was feasible only if the crowd were known to be hostile to the victim. Otherwise it was a passport to martyrdom for the assassin: it may be more responsible than throwing a bomb in a crowded street, but it was certainly more risky. But if the crowd were known to be on the side of the assassin, as in Modena in 1822, and in Rome when Rossi was stabbed to death in 1848, then a stiletto could be effectively used. In Modena an unfortunate man, Antonio Ponzoni, who was almost certainly innocent, was charged with the crime by Besini before he died. Although the tribunal acquitted Ponzoni, Francesco IV, determined to have a vendetta against someone, kept him in prison for over eight years. A subsequent tribunal passed some further savage sentences – nine people condemned to death and forty-six to prison sentences. Of the nine condemned to death, seven had not been captured by the police, one had his sentence commuted to ten years' imprisonment, but one was beheaded – a priest, Giuseppe Andreoli.

In Tuscany Ferdinando III reigned until his death in 1824. A very favourable impression of his reign was given by a political émigré from the city of Piacenza in the Duchy of Parma, Pietro Giordani, who arrived in Florence in the year of Ferdinando's death. At the age of fifty, Giordani brought with him a considerable literary reputation. Eminent as a scholar in Greek, Latin and Dante studies, he was one of the most respected leaders of the classical movement in Italian literature, although today he is known mainly as the man who recognized and encouraged the genius of Leopardi. Giordani could hardly find words warm enough for the Tuscan government that received him in 1824. Far from being treated as a dangerous exile from a friendly country, he was lionized as a great literary figure by officials as well as by the world of the arts. He called Florence the 'Earthly Paradise', and in so doing attracted many more political exiles in the years ahead. But while exiles from the other Italian states found that they were not persecuted in Tuscany, the more politically-minded of them also found the country sadly lacking in political vitality.

When Ferdinando III died in 1824 he was succeeded as Grand Duke by his son, who became Leopoldo II and who retained Fossombroni, thus providing continuity between the two reigns. Leopoldo II was not less tolerant nor less remote than Ferdinando had been. A contemporary Tuscan, Alessandro D'Ancona, remembered having often heard the peasants speak of Leopoldo as 'Babbo' or 'Daddy'.[7] But the new Grand Duke's appearance did not help him. Thomas Adolphus Trollope, an older brother of the novelist, spent most of his life in Italy and knew Leopoldo II, of whom he noted that 'He was not such a fool as he looked, for his appearance was certainly not that of a wise, or even an intelligent man.'[8] But Leopoldo's rule was without doubt benevolent. Both the reduction of taxes and the draining of the Maremma – the marshlands near the coast south of Leghorn – were conducted under his initiative. For the greater part of his long reign – 1824–59 – he was immensely popular. He retained in office not only Fossombroni, but also Neri Corsini, a balanced and civilized man who never allowed the threat of revolution to frighten him into brutal acts. Neither minister believed that progress could be halted. As Fossombroni put it: 'Il mondo va da se' – 'The world progresses by its own momentum'. They were not great enthusiasts for change, but above all they believed in the spirit of tolerance, and this they would uphold in what they saw increasingly as a dark world of brooding passions. Leopoldo II's ministers refused to execute, or even to imprison, political offenders. The Piedmontese revolutionaries of 1821 who were sensible or fortunate enough to have escaped into Tuscany found, no less than did those from Naples, that they were safe from the vindictiveness of the authorities at home. But in the early 1830s the Tuscan government took a harsher line with working-class movements in Leghorn, where political offenders were frequently imprisoned.

The revolutions of 1831 affected primarily the Papal States, but also Modena and Parma, although not Tuscany. One of the most secret and obscure conspiracies of nineteenth-century Italy was that which centred on the figure of Francesco IV, the Duke of Modena. The conspiracy was the brain-child of a young subject of the Duke, Enrico Misley, whose family must evidently have been of English extraction, although there is no documentary evidence of the fact. Like Mazzini, Misley grew up in an academic circle, his father being a professor at Milan and Pavia. Enrico Misley himself studied law at these universities and at Modena. As early as 1823, at the age of twenty-two, Misley was in touch with a secret society – either the Carbonari or the Freemasons – on the one hand, but had also acquired the friendship of Francesco IV on the other hand. At about this time Misley conceived the bizarre idea of persuading Francesco IV – perhaps the least liberal of Italian princes – to put himself at the head of a movement to secure Italian freedom. Not surprisingly Misley's tortuous project gave him the reputation among some of his revolutionary associates of being a double agent. But, to his conspiratorial nature, the very improbability of the choice of Francesco IV as an Italian national hero seemed to make it proof against a premature Austrian intervention. Misley's immediate plan was to encourage Francesco to wrest from Carlo Alberto the Piedmontese succession. Misley believed that the Piedmontese liberals had been sufficiently alienated from Carlo Alberto by his betrayal of their cause in 1821 for them to be prepared to support Francesco IV in spite of that Duke's grisly political record. From 1826 to 1828 Misley built up a chain of contacts in Italy and France, including the elderly Lafayette, and the French banker, Laffitte, who was to play so large a role in the July Revolution in Paris and to be prime minister under his friend, Louis-Philippe. In 1829 Misley contacted the revolutionary exiles in London through an intermediary, Camillo Manzini, who was also from Modena. The group in London agreed to support Francesco IV provided that he led a genuinely nationalist movement – provided, that is, he was prepared to become king of a united Italy, not simply to lead a palace revolution in Turin. According to Manzini, when he returned to Modena and put this ambitious proposal to Francesco IV, the Duke agreed with it. In 1830 Misley returned to Paris and spoke to Louis-Philippe, so soon to be King of the French. Misley was in Paris for the July Revolution, and took pains to keep in touch with the men of the new government, though in the event he was to get little help from them. Although Misley spoke to Francesco again on his return to Modena in September 1830, the revolution in Paris had almost certainly made the Duke's position more difficult, since Metternich would now be more hostile than ever to any political change in Italy, and Louis-Philippe was unlikely to help. Evidently at this point Francesco IV decided to sever his fortunes from those of the Italian revolutionaries. He refused even to follow Metternich in recognizing the new régime in Paris. If he remained in touch with Misley it was almost certainly because he wished to keep himself informed of the conspiracy. But Misley returned to Paris in December, leaving control of the conspiracy in the hands of a Neapolitan, Ciro Menotti. Revolutionary leaders of these years usually came from the professions — especially from the army or the law — if they were not enlightened noblemen. Menotti, on the other hand, was a successful businessman, with commercial contacts in London. His liberal ideas had led to his arrest for a short while in 1821. In the last weeks of 1830 he established revolutionary cells in the Papal States, Tuscany and Parma. Menotti expressed his revolutionary aims as 'independence, union and liberty for all the towns of Italy', 'Representative Monarchy', whose king would be chosen by a 'National Congress', and whose capital would be Rome. He inherited Misley's links with Francesco IV, but did not trust him, while the Duke, for his part, enrolled volunteers and imported cannon from Piedmont to resist the conspirators.

In the Papal States there was forming a more significant conspiracy,[9] one fraction of which was centred in Rome around the Bonapartes. Louis-Napoleon Bonaparte, a young man of twenty-two, was so far only third in line for the succession as head of the House of Bonaparte. He had an elder brother, but the head of the house was Napoleon I's son, the Duke of Reichstadt, the 'little eagle', as he was called, who had, as has already been noted, remained a prisoner in Austria when his mother became Duchess of Parma. Louis-Napoleon, in spite of his youth, was nevertheless the most active and ambitious member of the family. When the future Lord Malmesbury met him, in 1829, in Rome, he found him to be 'a harum-scarum youth', but 'even then possessed with the conviction that he would some day rule over France'.[10] Expelled from Rome early in December 1830, Louis-Napoleon and his elder brother settled in Florence, and were there visited by Menotti. The Bonapartes planned to put the 'little eagle', whom they called 'Napoleon II', on the throne of a united Italy. It seems unlikely that Menotti would have approved of such an idea, but he probably did not take it seriously. It was anyhow unlikely that the Duke of Reichstadt could have been wrested from Metternich's charge. Menotti did, however, secure some cash from the Bonapartes, and a promise of help in the forthcoming rising. In Paris Misley was having less success. He found that most of the Italian exiles followed the aged Buonarroti in hoping for a far more radical programme for Italy, a programme which centred on the creation of a republic. Misley consequently kept himself somewhat aloof from Buonarroti's circle, but retained high hopes of success for a revolutionary movement in Central Italy. The new French government of the

July Monarchy openly gave its support to the principle of non-intervention in Italy and Misley was optimistic enough to believe that this would dissuade the Austrians from intervention. Menotti, at least, believed that the revolution in Modena should be synchronized with those being planned in the Papal States – in Bologna and the Romagna. A small arsenal had been collected in Menotti's house in Modena. The armed conspirators were initially to ensure that the Duke's palace – and the Duke himself – were under their control, before taking possession of the city. But Francesco IV already knew too much, and on 3 February, two days before the revolution was scheduled to start, Menotti's house was besieged by troops. Menotti and his friends put up some resistance, but were eventually seized, and their supporters from the outlying countryside failed to break into the city. Meanwhile, however, the revolution in Bologna had succeeded,[11] and the Grand Duke feared that a force might come from the Papal States to Menotti's help. Keeping Menotti with him, Francesco moved northwards to Mantua, where he hoped to receive supporting Austrian troops. The Austrian commander in Lombardy, however, refused to get involved, and the Duke decided to complete his flight by continuing to Vienna. In a very short time the revolutionaries were in control of the Duchy of Modena. A provisional government was formed under Biagio Nardi, a lawyer, and consisting of the usual social mixture – other lawyers, a military officer, and a liberal nobleman.

In Parma the lover of Marie-Louise, Neipperg, had been replaced by another Austrian, Baron Werklein, in 1829. As the virtual ruler of Parma, Werklein had come to be hated by the population. The news from Modena encouraged student riots in Parma, and demands for a constitution. The crowd distinguished between Marie-Louise herself who had never been unpopular, and Werklein, who was obliged to escape from the Duchy. Marie-Louise was begged by the crowd to remain, but eventually her nerve failed, and she moved to Piacenza where she was protected by an Austrian garrison. A provisional government was established also at Parma. The revolutionaries in Parma and Modena understandably hoped that help would come from the more important rising in the Papal States, but the revolutionary provisional government in Bologna took the extraordinary line that the French declaration against intervention in Italy ruled out any co-operative action between revolutionaries from the different states. Revolution spread throughout the Papal States in February 1831, though it stopped short of Rome itself. The French declaration in favour of non-intervention in Italy proved to be totally ineffective when Metternich decided that the time had come to smother the revolutions in the Duchies and the Papal States.

The revolutionary governments in the Duchies appointed a joint commander of their forces – General Carlo Zucchi, a subject of Modena who had taken part in the 1821 risings against the Austrians, and been arrested by them. He and his rather pathetic, but courageous, revolutionary forces made some show of resisting Francesco IV when the Duke returned with the troops which had remained loyal to him. On 9 March Francesco was back in Modena. Zucchi withdrew his army to the Papal States where the government at Bologna, pursuing its absurd fantasy of the principle of non-intervention, insisted that they should lay down their arms. Both Modena and Parma were reoccupied by the Austrians. Zucchi's role was a wholly honourable one, but it belongs more to the history of the Papal States than to that of the Duchies.[12] In Modena Francesco IV was again in control, and he was not the kind of man to welcome victory with magnanimity. Ciro Menotti was executed, many of his companions were imprisoned for several years, while the rest escaped into exile. Menotti became one of the most celebrated of Italian martyrs: Garibaldi was to name one of his sons after him.

A glimpse of the repressive atmosphere from 1831 to 1848 in Modena, where even the acquisition of a beard or a moustache made one suspect as a revolutionary, is provided by Mrs Frances Trollope, writing from Vicenza in October 1841: 'We have returned to pass through Modena, notwithstanding the notorious danger of being taken prisoners. Nay, we were bolder still; for we actually ventured to remain there for an hour or two. But the gentlemen of our party were very punctiliously shaved, and that gave us confidence . . .'[13]

The election of Pius IX in 1846 and the resulting spirit of change in the Papal States found echoes in Tuscany. On 3 November 1847 the Grand Duke's government signed a preliminary agreement with the Pope's and Carlo Alberto's governments for a customs union, an idea emanating from Rome. Already in August 1847 the growing revolutionary spirit had seized the people in Tuscany, though rather the crowds in Leghorn than in Florence herself. Leopoldo II reacted to the disturbances with conciliatory measures, giving a little more responsibility to his advisory council of ministers, the Consulta di Stato, and appointing to that body liberal-minded men – the lawyer, Vincenzo Giannini, as president, Cosimo Ridolfi, himself president of the much respected Academy of the *Georgofili*, an academy of economists and agriculturalists, and Gino Capponi. At the same time Leopoldo appointed as minister of foreign affairs and war Nero Corsini, who had held offices since 1831 and was at that time governor of Leghorn. Corsini had a reputation for civilized, if not permissive, administration. A civic guard was formed in September, an event loudly celebrated in Florence, but criticized in Leghorn where its limited character – its restriction to property owners – was noted. Radicals, especially in Leghorn, now began to demand a constitution, but many of the liberals felt this was going too far, and would be needlessly provocative of Austria. Corsini was braver than some of his younger colleagues and recommended Leopoldo to grant a constitution on the grounds that the immediate danger threatened from Leghorn rather than from Austria. Leopoldo was not yet ready to grant a constitution, but towards the end of September appointed a new ministry, with Leopoldo Cempini as its nominal head, but with Ridolfi in the key post as minister of the interior. Corsini was removed from office and replaced by Count Luigi Serristori as minister of foreign affairs and war. Serristori was not less courageous, in his way, than Corsini, but had different priorities, believing that the next step should be the levying of an independent armed force. Ridolfi, as virtual head of the government, agreed with Serristori that the country should be armed, and believed that the next step should be the completion of the customs union rather than the granting of a constitution.

The Grand Duke's new government achieved for him a small territorial gain early in October. It had been understood for some years that Tuscany might eventually acquire from the Bourbons the little Duchy of Lucca with its lovely capital city. In 1847 the reigning Bourbon Duke of Lucca, Carlo Ludovico, had, by his own extravagance, placed himself in a position not unlike that of the French court in 1789, though, of course, with rather smaller consequences for world history. A revolutionary movement in Lucca had persuaded the wretched man to make the usual concessions – a civic guard and a free press. Having made Lucca too hot for himself, Carlo Ludovico then escaped to Modena where he arranged for Lucca to be annexed by Tuscany, in return for a generous pension.

The most positive line of Italian policy pursued by the Grand Duke's government was the drawing up of the customs union. Tuscany had the most to gain from the customs union since her tariffs were appreciably lower than the Papal ones, and much lower than Piedmont's. To strengthen the Papal envoy's hand the Tuscan government had sent their own representative, Giulio Martini, to Turin, where the final discussions were taking place. Carlo Alberto's government had insisted that it could not be simply a question of a reduction of Piedmontese and Papal tariffs, but that the Tuscans must be prepared to raise theirs to conform more closely with the practice in the other two countries. To avoid a complete break the delegates at Turin had agreed to postpone decision on these difficult details, and had simply signed a declaration to the effect that agreement had been reached to form a customs union 'for the formation of a common tariff', which would be fixed at a Congress at which it was hoped Naples and Modena would also be represented. Francesco V of Modena, who had succeeded to the duchy on the death of his father, Francesco IV, in 1846, subsequently refused to join a customs union. Nothing in the end was to come from the proposal to form a customs union, but the failure was certainly not the fault of the Tuscan government, who could at least claim to have taken some practical, if very cautious, steps towards Italian unification. In the light of what was to follow the developments of 1847 in Tuscany do not seem particularly striking. Yet in contrast to the political stagnation of the previous three decades a strong ground-swell was apparent at the time. On 30 December 1847 an English-speaking newspaper, the *Tuscan Athenaeum*, was founded by the British colony in Florence. Its first number started with the observation that the previous six months in Florence seemed to have witnessed the events of a century.

In the last weeks of 1847 demonstrations of a democratic flavour took place in Leghorn, where revolutionary exiles from Naples – Nicola Fabrizi and Giovanni La Cecilia – led the agitation. It was rumoured in the first days of January 1848 that the Austrians were planning to invade the country, and this added fire to the democratic agitation. Emerging as the radical leader in Leghorn was the dour figure of Francesco Domenico Guerrazzi. With legal training at the University of Pisa, Guerrazzi had turned to literature, and had written his most famous novel, the *Assedio di Firenze*, in 1834.[14] Mazzini had met him in 1829 and been impressed by the strength of his personality, which he had nevertheless found chilling and terrifying. In 1848 Guerrazzi and the democrats of Leghorn were not at first aiming to overthrow the cautious Ridolfi ministry in Florence, but rather to put pressure on it to adopt more radical policies. In this they failed. The Ridolfi government had no intention of identifying itself with the poor people of the slums and docks of Leghorn. Guerrazzi was arrested, and La Cecilia sent to Elba.

Thus when the news of the Sicilian rising of January 1848 reached Tuscany Guerrazzi was in prison. A crowd at Leghorn demanded his release and the establishment of a constitution. The Grand Duke's government quickly responded by setting up a commission to consider a broadening of the Consulta di Stato and a reform of the laws on the press. The commission of five men, one of whom was Gino Capponi, interpreted its brief as including the planning of a constitution. It suggested a two-chamber legislature – a senate to be appointed by the Grand Duke, and a parliament elected on a very restricted suffrage. Neither Ridolfi nor the veteran politician, Giovanni Baldasseroni, who left his own account of these years,[15] believed the proposed constitution to be liberal enough for the spirit of the moment, though they too wanted to stop well short of universal suffrage. What resulted from the combined deliberations of the commission and Leopoldo's ministers was a constitution which left executive power in the hands of the Grand Duke, with a nominated senate, and an assembly elected by the richer taxpayers. All subjects of the Grand Duke were declared equal before the law, but Catholicism was declared 'the only state religion'. This constitution, cautious though it was, was greeted with public rejoicing.

There was a noticeable contrast between what was happening in Tuscany and the total lack of any similar developments in Parma and Modena which, although nominally independent states, were occupied by Austrian troops. But with the coming of war between Piedmont and Austria insurrection was to break out in the Duchies. The Austrians and their puppet rulers were driven out by revolutionary leaders who were inclined to seek union with Piedmont. On the death of Marie-Louise in 1847, the duchy of Parma had passed to Carlo II, son of another Marie-Louise – the Bourbon princess whose father was King of Spain. Carlo II, after changing his mind two or three times, finally decided on the more cautious course of handing government over to a regency council of Italians. The city of Piacenza, usually more forward in its policy than was its capital city of Parma, decided to secede from the duchy and unite with Piedmont, and confirmed its decision by a plebiscite. A few days later the conservative regency council in Parma was forced to resign by hostile demonstrations, and Carlo II escaped to Rome and exile. The new regime in Parma decided early in May 1848 to send troops to fight the Austrians, and finally to hold a plebiscite on the question of union with Piedmont. As with all other plebiscites conducted by Italian governments on the question – both in 1848 and 1859–60 – this one in Parma registered a big vote in favour of union with Piedmont.

In Modena Francesco V, like Carlo II, did not remain long after the departure of the Austrians. A moderate revolutionary government was formed also in Modena, which sent a somewhat larger force than Parma had done to fight the Austrians. Again the same pattern followed – the organization of a plebiscite, and a solid vote for union with Piedmont.

Far more important than the events of 1848 in the small duchies were developments in Florence. Demonstrations had greeted the news of the March revolutions in Milan and Venice and of the fall of Metternich in Vienna. The Tuscan government responded initially by allowing the enrolment of volunteers, but the military assistance Tuscany could provide against Austria seemed so slight as to be not worth the diplomatic consequences and risks involved. These had to be balanced, however, against the risks of alienating the demonstrators in Florence where, on 24 March, the Austrian legation was set on fire. The Tuscan government could at least display what might pass for nationalist enthusiasm by stepping up negotiations with the Pope and the Piedmontese and Neapolitan governments for some kind of league. Eventually popular pressure for at least a small army could no longer be resisted. A force, nearly half of which consisted of the recently enrolled volunteers, left on 5 April to fight the Austrians. Tuscany did not declare war on Austria, but the Tuscan foreign minister, adopting an apologetic tone, informed the Austrian *chargé d'affaires*, whose offices had already been burnt down, that Tuscan forces were moving to the assitance of the revolution in Lombardy.

Leopoldo Cempini remained chief minister until June 1848, when he was replaced by Ridolfi, who remained in office until August. Little enthusiasm for the war was displayed by Ridolfi's government. When the small Tuscan expeditionary force suffered casualties, no effort was made to replace them, partly because Ridolfi was a product of the long anti-militarist tradition of Tuscany, and partly because of the mutual jealousy between Tuscany and Piedmont. All the same, when the Pope made it clear, by his Allocution of 29 April, that he could take no part in the war,[16] and when the counter-revolution of 15 May succeeded in Naples and the new Neapolitan government withdrew from the war,[17] the Ridolfi government refused to follow suit in spite of its increasingly isolated position. More radical, popular movements began to make themselves felt in Tuscany, especially in Leghorn. Some of these movements were of a Luddite nature – protests against the introduction of machinery in industry; some were simply movements of protest at the high rate of unemployment; some were strikes for higher wages. Although they were not on a large scale, they give some indication that the preoccupations of the workers were not primarily with the war of liberation in the North, nor even with constitutional reform at home. The workers were more concerned with a concept they had already learnt from socialists in France – the 'right to work' – and with the right of labour to organize itself. But, as in Paris, so in Tuscany, the workers found no articulate leadership. At Leghorn Guerrazzi tried to use them as fuel for his assault on the moderate ministers, but he was really concerned with the interests of the radical middle class and disclaimed responsibility for industrial disturbances which might alarm even the poorer members of the bourgeoisie.

Before the elections for the Council the income qualification for the vote was halved. Elections were held on 15 June 1848. Even with the modification of the electoral law it was still the case that few people had the vote, and it was therefore not surprising that a conservative majority was returned. At the same time Leopoldo used his constitutional powers to nominate fresh senators. The newly elected men would clearly not represent the working-class unrest but, like the more democratic journals, were highly critical of the government for its half-hearted war effort. They were supported in their criticism of the government on this score by a man who was emerging as a significant Italian nationalist – Baron Bettino Ricasoli.

The Ricasoli family was already important in Tuscany in the eleventh century, and for Cosimo de' Medici in the mid fifteenth century the Ricasoli who owned the fortress of Brolio was to be treated as no ordinary citizen of the Republic. Bettino Ricasoli, born in 1809, was a man of strange contradictions. The history of his family in their feudal castle gave him the manner and the tastes of a patriarchal landowner with heavy responsibilities and great inherited power. His pride as an Italian, however, led him to approve the nineteenth-century doctrine of nationalism. A religious piety gave him a strong sense of the value of the individual, so that he could also accept that other typically nineteenth-century doctrine, the doctrine of liberalism. He was not a believer in democracy or equality, but the single-mindedness of his convictions as a nationalist and a liberal made him in some ways closer in spirit to Mazzini than to Cavour. He was the eldest son in a large family whose father died when he was only seven. His mother had sent him to a Catholic school where he was something of a rebel. Solitary and excessively serious, he rebelled not because he was idle or frivolous but because he felt that the standards of his teachers were inadequate. But Bettino had a worldly sense which he tried to conceal. At twenty-one he married a very rich girl, Anna Bonaccorsi, and thereby ensured that the somewhat dilapidated fortunes of the Brolio estate, where his father had lived rather too well, would be restored. Bettino himself worked with science and affection on the estate and in particular restored the vines, until Brolio became one of the best of the Chianti wines.

When the news of Carlo Alberto's defeat in July 1848 reached Florence, Ricasoli's journal, *Patria*, joined the democratic press in demanding the resignation of the Ridolfi government, and when, on the last day of the month, Ridolfi resigned, Ricasoli himself tried to form a government. On this occasion he failed, rather to the relief of the Grand Duke who rightly suspected Ricasoli of already looking for closer links with Piedmont. To be without an effective government at this moment – with Carlo Alberto's armies defeated and Austrian troops entering Parma and Modena – was dangerous for Tuscany. Through the mediation of Sir George Hamilton, British minister at Florence since 1846, a promise was extracted from the Austrians that their forces would not enter Tuscany, provided law and order was maintained there. Even before the Piedmontese signed the armistice of Salasco, an armistice between Tuscany and Austria was thus arranged. In Florence Gino Capponi, now almost blind, succeeded in forming a government at this unrewarding moment, August 1848. He made a realistic assessment of the military situation in Italy, decided that there was now no question of driving the Austrians out of Lombardy, and that the most which could be hoped for was some kind of Italian confederation. It was soon apparent that even a confederation or league could not include Naples, since Ferdinando II, now able to pursue a wholly conservative policy, vetoed the idea so far as he was concerned. Capponi was as eager as anyone for the formation of a loose Italian league, which would guarantee Tuscan independence, prevent domination by Piedmont, but provide a degree of economic unity between Tuscany, Piedmont and the Papal States. Such a programme was insufficient to satisfy the Tuscan democrats, who were also highly critical of the domestic policy of Capponi's caretaker government, which consequently survived for only two months. The Tuscan democrats still believed that the war against Austria could be successfully renewed, provided that a more popular government came to power, and the enthusiasm of the whole people could be harnessed. But democratic-nationalist enthusiasm was still not linked with republicanism, nor with the genuinely working-class movement in Leghorn. The democratic-nationalist movement in the summer of 1848 was most coherently expressed in the press, rather less coherently in the activities of the clubs, and very ambivalently in street demonstrations, where the various forms of democratic sentiment – nationalist, republican and socialist – were all inevitably present. The democratic wing of the nationalists was still led by Mazzinians demanding a constituent assembly, elected by universal suffrage, and ultimately representing the whole peninsula.[18]

The already inflammatory situation in Leghorn was agitated still further in August when Father Alessandro Gavazzi arrived. Gavazzi was a Barnabite from Bologna with strong nationalist sentiments, a highly demonstrative orator who had already been driven out of more than one Italian state. He asked permission to cross Tuscany on his way to the Papal States, but the government refused to grant it. Their refusal was the signal for a great popular uproar, while the crowd escorted the friar in triumph to a hotel in Leghorn. The government promptly reversed its decision, now declaring that Gavazzi could leave Tuscany for Bologna. But the friar, clearly enjoying his success, insisted on staying longer to address a few more popular gatherings. To seek permission to do so he left for Florence by train, but was arrested *en route*, and taken to the frontier. The government had not handled the matter well. When the news of Gavazzi's arrest and expulsion reached Leghorn the crowd broke into open revolt, captured the Palazzo Communale, and for a day took the governor into custody, before repenting of their hasty action and releasing him. The city remained, however, in the possession of an insurrectionary and armed crowd. Gino Capponi's government, still in office in Florence, had to take some steps to deal with the revolt in Leghorn. It therefore sent some thousand troops, escorting an Extraordinary Commission and under the command of Colonel Leonetto Cipriani, who had fought against the Austrians and might therefore, it was vainly hoped, be well received. He had, in the event, to fight his way into the city and to take possession of the palace by force. Although he appeared at first to have accomplished that task with comparative ease, the appearance was deceptive. On 2 September there was a general rising, the troops from Florence were forced to surrender, and Cipriani somewhat ignominiously fled. The initiative was then taken by a group of businessmen in Leghorn, who wisely decided that they needed to find a new temporary authority in the grim but impressive person of Guerrazzi, who would be accepted by great numbers of democrats in his native city of Leghorn, but would be opposed to any socialist tendencies. Guerrazzi, who was at the time in Florence, was thus invited to return to Leghorn and take over power. He agreed, was accepted by revolutionaries in control in the port and succeeded in setting up a provisional government commission. He established a municipal guard and brought a degree of order to Leghorn, but Capponi unwisely refused to make him governor, so that a revolutionary atmosphere persisted.

Meanwhile another potential leader had returned to the Tuscan scene. Giuseppe Montanelli, born in 1813, had graduated in law in the University of Pisa, where he had played a big rôle in founding a socialist group dedicated to the study of the writings of Saint-Simon. From 1840 he was teaching law at the University and giving his teaching a strongly socialist slant. He had founded a secret society called the *Fratelli italiani* in 1844, and the journal *Italia* in 1847. He had fought in the 'Five Days' in Milan, and was wounded at the battle of Curtatone. He was taken as a prisoner-of-war to Innsbruck, but was released and now returned to Florence towards the end of 1848, having been elected in his absence to the new Tuscan assembly. Received with great popular rejoicing in Florence, Montanelli succeeded in persuading the reluctant Capponi to reopen negotiations with Leghorn – which now meant, in effect, with Guerrazzi. Montanelli believed that Guerrazzi must be appointed governor of Leghorn without delay, and to prevent further agitation elsewhere in Tuscany the government should take the initiative in the national question. He proposed the election of a *Costituente*. The Mazzinian concept of a Costituente which Montanelli accepted was more than a simple constituent assembly elected by universal manhood suffrage, more, that is, than a piece of constitutional machinery. It was to have a Messianic purpose – to prepare the way for the voice of God speaking through the voice of the people. From Leghorn, Guerrazzi, however, suggested that Montanelli himself should be made governor, a solution which pleased the people of Leghorn. On arriving in Leghorn early in October, Montanelli created a considerable stir by making a passionate, but closely argued, speech in defence of his ideas of a Costituente. In the mounting excitement it was no longer possible for the cautious ministers of Leopoldo II to remain in office. A few days after Montanelli's speech Capponi and his colleagues resigned. In the resulting uproar all over Tuscany the Grand Duke bowed to democratic pressure and appointed to be his ministers men who were at heart republicans. Montanelli became prime minister and minister for foreign affairs, Guerrazzi minister of the interior, and Giuseppe Mazzoni, an industrialist from Prato, minister of finance and public works. Montanelli addressed the assembly in terms carefully chosen to please his admirers without frightening Leopoldo II. But while the public cheered him, and the Grand Duke approved, the deputies gave him a sullen reception. It was clearly imperative to obtain a new assembly. The house was therefore dissolved and elections fixed for 20 November. The newly elected house was not much further to the left than the previous one, with the difference that the conservatives and moderates now lacked enthusiasm, and there was no longer any question of restoring a government of the Capponi tendency. Montanelli and Guerrazzi remained in office, but Guerrazzi, once regarded as a demagogue supported by the poor of Leghorn, was now basing his strength rather on the middle-class revolutionaries of the clubs, and was alarmed lest Montanelli's more democratic stance should stir up a social revolution. Montanelli had certainly been influenced by the writings of Saint-Simon, but this was true also of Mazzini, and did not make either of the two men socialists. On the contrary, Montanelli's preoccupations – again like Mazzini's – were not with social questions, but with the extreme nationalist aim of calling an Italian Costituente. Guerrazzi was perhaps influenced by his office: as minister of the interior he had to deal with popular disturbances, and as a minister of Leopoldo II he seemed more concerned for the well-being of the sovereign than did Montanelli.

Meanwhile in Rome the Pope had fled, the Roman Republic had come into being, the first representatives of an Italian Costituente had been elected, and a decree of 16 January 1849 invited other regions of Italy to elect representatives by universal suffrage.[19] After all Montanelli's preaching about the Costituente, and attempts he had been making to interest the Piedmontese in the idea, it was not surprising that the crowds both in Leghorn and Florence itself demonstrated in favour of taking up the offer. On 22 January the Tuscan government proposed to the chamber that thirty-seven deputies should be elected, by universal suffrage, to represent Tuscany in the Costituente in Rome. Leopoldo II agreed with the proposal only because Montanelli had threatened to resign – a step which would probably have led to violent revolution. Montanelli told the house that if the Costituente at Rome, after the arrival of the thirty-seven deputies from Tuscany, decided to end Tuscan independence and dethrone the Grand Duke, the decision of the 'Italian people' would have to be respected. Guerrazzi was hoping that this would not be necessary, but that Leopoldo could be bribed into accepting the Costituente by the offer of an enlarged state of Central Italy, presumably within an Italian federation. Montanelli's speech to the house, however, and the unanimous acceptance of his proposal by the house, were more than the Grand Duke could take. Perhaps the surprising feature is that he had remained in Florence so long. On 30 January 1849 he moved to Siena, and on the night of 7–8 February went secretly to the coast, where he boarded a British ship which took him to Gaeta in the Kingdom of Naples. Hearing of Leopoldo's departure the chamber elected Montanelli, Guerrazzi and Mazzoni as triumvirs in a provisional government; the chamber was then dissolved and elections, by universal suffrage, fixed for 12 March – elections, that is, for a new assembly of 120, and for the 37 deputies to go to Rome. Mazzini had arrived in Florence on 14 February, and he and Montanelli wanted to take the revolution a big step further by declaring the Republic and fusing it with the Roman Republic in a single state. Guerrazzi successfully opposed both proposals throughout March, arguing that they would merely invite armed intervention by Piedmont, or Austria, or both, and that Tuscany, in her traditional state of being without an army, would have been unable to do anything about such an intervention.

Guerrazzi's attitude of caution, if not defeatism, confused the issues, and when elections were held for the assembly on 12 March there was a general air of disenchantment. The social policy of the provisional government, however, had some positive features: taxes on the working class had been eased in an attempt to placate left-wing circles in Leghorn, and public works had been organized to provide jobs. But the fate of Tuscany depended on the fortunes of the renewed war between Piedmont and Austria, not on the success or failure of the government in Florence. The Austrian victory at Novara on 23 March encouraged the Tuscan government to take emergency measures. On 27 March Guerrazzi was made dictator, and promptly sent Montanelli to Paris, ostensibly to negotiate with the French government, but more probably to get him out of the way. In the event Montanelli was to remain in exile for the next decade. Guerrazzi himself, although now ready to receive back the Grand Duke provided he could remain in office, was thrown from power, after being dictator for only a fortnight, by the combined action of moderates in Florence and conservative opinion led by the priests in the countryside. On 12 April the city government of Florence seized control of the situation, and had Guerrazzi arrested. Democratic clubs and newspapers were closed. The counter-revolution was accompanied by some disturbances across the country and rejected by Leghorn. Moderate hopes that the Grand Duke might return, but would leave the constitution intact, were soon disappointed. Leopoldo II accepted Austrian advice to remain in exile in Naples until the Austrians had occupied Tuscany. In May the Austrian army moved in, meeting stiff resistance from the people of Leghorn. That the Grand Duke was being restored by Austrian armed strength, rather than by the will of the people of Tuscany, was painfully apparent. So far as the Austrians went, however, it was still to be proved true that 'he who lives by the sword, must perish by the sword'.

Like Leopoldo II the rulers of Parma and Modena owed their restoration to Austrian arms. In Parma Carlo II had been forced to recognize the truth, and had abdicated in March 1849. His son, Carlo III, succeeded him, and reigned for the next five years, by his worthless and arbitrary rule effectively destroying any affection that still remained for this branch of the Bourbons. In 1854 he was assassinated by a fine and brave man, the saddle-maker Antonio Carra. Carlo III's son, who was a minor, succeeded to the Duchy, with his mother, Marie-Louise, as Regent. Maria-Louise was a sister of the Comte de Chambord, whose chances of becoming King of France remained strong for many years. Inevitably Parma moved steadily away from the sphere of the reactionary policy of Austria into that of the ultra-reactionary policy of the

French Bourbons. Parma abandoned the customs union with Austria and Modena when it came up for renewal.

In Modena the situation was less complicated. Francesco V was quite simply an Austrian archduke, ready to do what Vienna told him. In the event this led to administrative and legal reforms which, if limited, were not negligible. Even so, the dependence in the last resort of both Parma and Modena upon Austria was inescapable, whereas Tuscany, with her long traditions of cultural independence and her robust sense of identity, appeared too big for Austria completely to swallow. The 1849 restoration in Tuscany was clearly modified by Leopoldo II and his Italian advisers, and so was milder than the restorations elsewhere in Italy. The trial of Guerrazzi, which lasted until 1853, shocked Tuscan liberals, but was in its way an indication that the conscience of the restored régime was far from dead. Guerrazzi's prison sentence was commuted by the Grand Duke to one of exile. Although the death sentence was restored on paper, this civilized people did not resort to its use, even after so considerable a crisis. But the tragedy of 1848–9 could not be annulled even in Tuscany. No one could suppose that the Grand Duchy had been permanently restored. No one could fail to remember that Leopoldo II had been restored by Austrian arms. In April 1850 he agreed – unavoidably, of course – that the Austrians should leave an occupying army which, in the event, stayed until the spring of 1855. By a decree of 21 September 1850 the House of Deputies, which had anyhow not met since February 1849, was declared permanently dissolved. Nor was it simply a restoration to the situation of 1847. Even the freedom of the press of the pre-revolutionary years was no longer permitted. On 6 May 1852 a decree from the Grand Duke annulled the constitution. Leopoldo himself sincerely believed that the experiments of 1848 must be abandoned, but he was reluctant to appoint ministers eager to carry out a black reaction. In May of 1849 he had appointed a liberal ministry, but they found it impossible to pursue a policy which would satisfy Vienna, and remained in office for only a year. In their place Leopoldo appointed two men of a more conservative bent: Landucci and Baldasseroni. Leonida Landucci, who was minister of the interior from 1850 until 1859, had been a liberal in 1848, but had become disillusioned, and was now prepared to impose the absolutist régime. Giovanni Baldasseroni, who was minister of finance for this last decade of independent history, was one of history's survivors, and like most survivors, remained tolerant to the end. He agreed on a Concordat with the Pope in 1851, giving a few additional privileges to the Church in Tuscany – for example the right of bishops to exercise a censorship on religious writings, – but the Concordat surrendered rather fewer powers to the Pope than had first been expected. It was in line with the policy of the Emperor Francis Joseph in Vienna, where a similar retreat from an independent state policy with regard to the Church – or 'Josephism' as it was called, after Joseph II, who had inaugurated it – was in progress. Baldasseroni's Concordat, as a compromise, pleased neither the clericals nor the liberals but, in the reactionary atmosphere of the day, must be considered a moderate step of policy. A grave economic situation, caused mainly by the Austrian occupation, did not prevent him from making material improvements – draining marshland, enlarging the port of Leghorn, and encouraging a continuation of railway building. But the grim fact of the Austrian occupation remained. The presence of an Austrian army for seven years was disastrous for the Tuscan economy. The Grand Duke's government had to pay a sixth of its income to Austria for the cost of the occupation and private Tuscan citizens had to provide billets and transport for the Austrian army.[20]

The second restoration in the Central Duchies can be said to have ended their independent histories. The events of 1859–60, which were to merge the three Duchies in a united Italy, are essentially part of that history of Italian unification and must be considered in a later chapter.[21]

Just as the political history of Tuscany during the last half century of her independent existence was by no means a wholly black one, so her economic history had several points of strength. In the first place she maintained her free-trading tradition for much of the period, and in the second place there was some vitality in her manufactures. To suggest that a policy of free trade in Tuscany was wholly beneficial to her economy would, however, be misleading. The policy adopted during the reign of Pietro Leopoldo, a policy essentially of free trade, had probably favoured foreign interests – British, French and Dutch – rather than Tuscan interests. Tuscan industry was not sufficiently developed to face foreign – particularly British – competition. A free trade policy was abandoned during the Napoleonic period, but reaffirmed in 1814. If its effect on industry was unfortunate, its effect on agriculture was more varied. The issue of free trade was hotly debated at the time, especially during the period of the first restoration, by the Georgofili and in the columns of the *Antologia*. The point was made that if free trade was not harmful to Tuscan agriculture as a whole, it was certainly harmful to the poorer peasants with small holdings. Yet the export of some agricultural products – especially olive oil and wine – was encouraged, and by the 1850s the free trade policy of Leopoldo II had led to a considerable increase both of exports and imports. The impact on Tuscan society was considerable: in Leghorn a commercial middle class and a dockyard working class had grown up – classes quite alien to the old-world society of Florence.

So far as the scale of foreign trade went, Tuscany by the 1850s was on a par with Lombardy and Venice rather than with the Papal States and Naples with their more retrograde economies. In 1858 the value of foreign trade in Piedmontese lire per head of population was 73 in Tuscany, 73 also in Modena, and 64 in Parma – figures comparing well with those for Lombardy (78) and for Venetia (65), and very well with those for the Papal States (42) and Naples (27).[22] The figures reflect, among other things, the comparatively lively condition of the port of Leghorn, as opposed to the stagnation of Naples or Palermo. The population of Leghorn had in fact increased from 48,293 in 1814 to 91,321 in 1855.

Tuscany was a country of small-scale industry, though there was an element of industrial growth from the end of the eighteenth century, and more diversification than in other Italian states. The textile industries had been important in Tuscany since the Middle Ages. Throughout the eighteenth century they had been declining, and Pietro Leopoldo's liberalization of trade had not helped sickly, small-scale industries. In 1790 there were riots of artisans in the silk industry. With the single exception of a new firm producing ceramics – which in the Renaissance had been an important Florentine product – Tuscan industry at the start of the nineteenth century was stagnant. But by 1830 the silk industry, while not comparing in scale with that of Lombardy, had doubled its output, and was to double it again between 1830 and 1859. Some mills were in Florence itself, where the Matteoni firm had as many as 800 looms; other mills were in Lucca, Siena, Pisa, Pistoia and Prato; while some looms were worked in cottages in the country. But the evidence of industrial growth is apparent only in contrast with the economic stagnation of the eighteenth century. Although raw silk and finished products were both being exported by the 1840s, the silk industry was in great need of modernization.

The woollen industry was only a little more modern in its methods. Some 9,000 people were employed in the woollen industry in the 1850s, mainly in Prato. It was still, however, partly a cottage industry, although Giambattista Mazzoni had bought a few pieces of modern machinery in the 1820s. One exotic product emanating from the Tuscan woollen mills was the fez, exported in considerable quantities to the Middle East. Another peasant industry which produced goods for export was the straw hat industry, and unworked straw was also exported. Surprisingly, straw accounted for one quarter of the total exports from Tuscany in 1841. The paper industry, too, had 143 efficient, if small, factories in the 1850s.[23] Paper was exported from Tuscany to America.

The Tuscan iron industry, in which the young Vilfredo Pareto was to play a not very successful managerial role in the 1880s, originated with the acquisition of Elba and Piombino, a port on the mainland opposite Elba. From 1815 until 1832 the extraction of pig iron was a state monopoly, but the monopoly was abandoned in 1832 and pig iron could thereafter be imported free of custom duty. The Tuscan iron industry was soon to account for a third of the total Italian production. Linked to it was the shipbuilding industry at Leghorn where both merchant ships and warships for foreign governments were constructed.

But the diversification of industry in Tuscany must not be allowed to conceal its smallness of scale. Expansion was very slow because there was too little investment for the purchase of new machines, and no technical education or training. Technical advance depended on the imaginative initiative of a few untrained individuals, much as it had done in Britain earlier.

The economic backwardness of Tuscany was viewed with some complacency by opinion in the Grand Duchy, where it was believed that Tuscany was an island of well-being in a sea of Italian and European states which were experiencing the horrors caused by rapid and unplanned industrialization. There was, of course, an element of truth in this message, which was repeated not only by conservative writers, but by at least one avowed democrat – P. Giachi, who published his *Catechismo al popolo* in Florence in 1847. The argument that the Grand Duchy was wise to discourage investment in industry, and encourage comparatively high investment in agriculture, was thus a familiar and officially accepted one, and one adopted by most of the economists of the Accademia dei Georgofili. There was, however, one early exception among the Georgofili – Vincenzo Salvagnoli, in the 1830s, was already protesting that, in the context of the European economic development of the day, Tuscany would have to start a more intensive form of industrialization. After all, he argued, in earlier centuries Tuscany had led Europe in manufacturing, banking and commerce; these activities had certainly not failed to bring her prosperity. Why, now, should she depend so heavily on agriculture? Indeed agriculture itself would gain new life as the result of industrialization. But the arguments of the more conservative writers – Lambruschini and Capponi – were not without point. If industry produced a more highly mechanized agriculture there would be unemployment among the peasants. It was not an argument which bothered Cavour in Piedmont, but Lambruschini and Capponi were more humanitarian in their outlook than Cavour. They did not want economic advance for the majority of the population if it meant yet greater impoverishment for an unemployed class on the land. They were also, it is true, afraid of marauding gangs of unemployed tramping the countryside. Most of the writers of the Accademia dei Georgofili were essentially paternalistic in their outlook, and tended to complain of the crudely materialistic outlook of the age, as older people in any generation are apt to do. Lambruschini in 1843 adopted such a tone: 'Most people', he wrote,

complain because the net income of the landowner is small. And the landowners are not the only ones to complain: the merchant, the artisan, the employee complain. . . . And why? Because a secret longing to be rich consumes them all. . . . Virile and noble pleasures of the spirit, genial but pure pleasures of the imagination, gentle and spiritual pleasures of the heart, are considered follies, are sneered at as 'poetry'. Money and power, that is all they want. . . .[24]

Ridolfi was rather more ready than Lambruschini for economic change, but Ridolfi, too, believed that the change should be limited to the field of agriculture. It would, for example, be foolish, he believed, to imagine that the textile industry, which in Renaissance days had been so prosperous, could be revived under modern conditions. All that could be hoped for so far as industry was concerned was to exploit Tuscany's mineral wealth a little more. And Ridolfi, also, was afraid, by 1842, of the 'threat' to civilization if 'the social question' were not solved.

A measure of economic development in Western Europe in the early nineteenth century was the extent to which the railways had been built. In Tuscany they were constructed comparatively early. The first line connected Leghorn and Pisa. By 1848 a line connected Leghorn to Florence, and another line from Florence to Pisa, via Pistoia and Lucca, was almost completed. But though important within Tuscany, these lines were not a great source of wealth, because they did not connect with other lines in Italy. On the eve of Italian unification, in 1859, Tuscany had 266 kilometres of railway lines, which did not compare well with the 850 in Piedmont, nor with the 524 in

Lombardo–Venezia, but compared strikingly well with the 100 in Naples, and the 96 in the Papal States.

The basic element in the economy of the Central Duchies was, inevitably, agriculture. The economies of the Duchies of Parma and Modena were more exclusively agricultural than was that of Tuscany. Although predominantly arable, the agriculture of the two small Duchies included also the raising of cattle and pigs, the sale of dairy products and – more especially in Modena – of wine. In Parma, on the other hand, the potato was grown rather earlier than in other parts of Italy. The productive lands of the two Duchies were in the Po plain. Those parts of the Duchies on the slopes of the Apennines defied economic development. But even on the plain the irrigation system of the Duchies was less developed than that of Lombardy, partly because graver technical problems were posed by the proximity of the Apennines and the dramatic seasonal variations of water levels caused by the mountain streams.

That the landscape of Tuscany has a striking beauty of its own has been recognized by generations of visitors from all over the world. But in strictly agricultural terms much of the countryside was unproductive in the nineteenth century. Only one tenth of the land is flat, three tenths consist of quite rugged mountains, and much of the country to the west was, in the nineteenth century, undrained and malarial: especially was the dramatic country between Volterra and the sea unfit for cultivation. Tuscan agriculture was also under-financed, in sharp contrast with Lombard agriculture. The agricultural land of Tuscany was mainly the property of large landowners, but, in contrast with the situation in the Kingdom of Naples, where the owners held their land in the form of single huge estates, the Tuscan landowners held many small farms, each with a varied production of wine, grapes, olives, other fruit and corn. From 1815 until 1860 the number of landowners was increasing.

The relationship between the peasants and the landowners was perhaps less unhappy than in most parts of Europe, but to decide whether the peasant enjoyed tolerable conditions or extreme poverty depends upon an analysis of the system of *mezzadria*, on which cultivation of the land was largely based. By the institution of the *mezzadria* the peasant retained a portion of the produce of his labour himself. The landowner supplied implements, manure and drainage, so that the *colono*, as the agricultural labourer was called, was in one sense, in Marxist terminology, a 'proletarian', since he often did not own even the instruments of his labour. Yet his position was somewhat more dignified and less wretched than was that of a landless farm worker in, say, Britain or the Kingdom of Naples. The Tuscan *colono* had certain responsibilities which they did not have: for example, he had to provide some of the seed, usually half. But he had a clear-cut right of great importance – the right to half of the produce of his labour. To pass judgement on the system of *mezzadria*, then, is difficult, and is not unlike the issue of the bottle which the optimist considers half full and the pessimist considers half empty. It can be argued that by the *mezzadria* the peasant had an element of freedom mixed with an element of security, that it was therefore a not unhappy compromise between feudalism and capitalism – a system typical of Tuscany, a land of compromise and toleration. The Tuscan peasant was also comparatively well housed, judging from surviving nineteenth-century cottages, and if, like peasants elsewhere, he ate meat only on special occasions, he yet had a balanced diet – of bread, olive oil and wine, with beans providing protein.

But the system of *mezzadria* was a static one in that it did not lead to economic growth. In Western Europe in the nineteenth century, when everyone believed in growth and expansion, it seemed archaic. However, not all Tuscan peasants were included in the system of *mezzadria*, and it seems undisputed that those who were outside the system suffered greater hardships.

The question of the *mezzadria* was hotly debated from the 1830s until unification and beyond, but certain points were generally accepted – that, for example, it was preferable to any form of serfdom, and something which could well be defined as 'serfdom' still survived in certain parts of the Habsburg Monarchy (though not in the Italian parts) until 1848, and something which was unmistakably and brutally 'serfdom' survived in Russia until 1861. But in the more advanced agricultural communities of Western Europe – for example, in France – the peasants were more liberated and more productive than under the system of *mezzadria* in that, even if they did not own their land, they simply paid rent for their cottages and their land. A system of rented land, perhaps with a tied cottage, was recommended for Tuscany at first, in the 1830s, by Leonida Landucci, and then, more emphatically, by Vincenzo Salvagnoli. But men who might be defined as 'liberal conservatives' – Lambruschini and Capponi – continued to defend the system of *mezzadria*. The fact remained that the *mezzadria* was not a highly productive system, and the *mezzadri* themselves were usually in debt. But since the big proprietors, and the government, continued to approve of the *mezzadria* – mainly because it preserved a stable and conservative society – it survived. The big landowners remained in control.

NOTES

For studies of the ruling dynasties in Tuscany, Parma, Modena and Lucca, Antonio Archi, *Gli ultimi Asburgo e gli ultimi Borboni in Italia (1814–1861)*, Rocca and San Casciano, 1965, is useful. As a study of the press in Tuscany there is Ilaria Porciana, *L''Archivio Storico Italiano'. Organizzazione della ricerca ed egemonia moderata nel risorgimento*, Florence, 1979. Leghorn, a place very distinct from the rest of Tuscany, has had a work dedicated to it: L. Bortolotti, *Livorno dal 1748–1958*, Florence, 1970.

An early life of Guerrazzi which concentrates more on his writings than on his political activity is Furio Lopez-Celly, *Francesco Domenico Guerrazzi nell'arte e nella vita*, Milan, 1918. A short life of Montanelli which includes some of his sonnets and letters is Assunta Maradi, *Giuseppe Montanelli e la Toscana dal 1815 al 1862*, Rome, 1909. A more recent, short work on Montanelli, also with a few of his letters, is Giovanni Spadolini, *Un dissidente del risorgimento (Giuseppe Montanelli)*, Florence, 1962. Montanelli wrote his own account after the events of 1848–9: *Memorie sull'Italia e special-*

mente sulla Toscana dal 1814 al 1850, Turin, 1853. Ricasoli's papers are being edited by Giulia Camerani and Clementina Rotondi – *Carteggi di Bettino Ricasoli*, Rome. The latest volume, XXVIII, published in 1978, covers the period January 1873–March 1876. In other words the volumes which concern Ricasoli's role before 1870 are already in print.

A charming impression of the English colony in Florence is provided by Giuliana Artom Treves, *Anglo-Fiorentini di cento anni fa*, Florence, 1953.

For the economic history of Tuscany there is L. Dal Pane, *Industria e commercio nel Granducato di Toscana nell'età del risorgimento*, Bologna, 1971, and C. Pazzagli, *L'agricoltura toscana nella prima metà dell'800*, Florence, 1973, and, more briefly, Pazzagli's *Per la storia dell'agricoltura toscana nei secoli XIX e XX – Dal catasto particellare lorenese al catasto agrario del 1929*, Turin, 1979.

1. Giovanni Baldasseroni, *Leopoldo II Granduca di Toscana e i suoi tempi. Memorie*, Florence, 1871, p. 31.
2. S. T. Bindoff, E. F. Malcolm Smith and C. K. Webster, eds, *British Diplomatic Representatives 1789–1852*, Camden Series, 1934, p. 172.
3. See Ch. 6, p. 170.
4. See Ch. 7, p. 174.
5. G. Stiavelli, *Antonio Guadagnoli e la Toscana dei suoi tempi*, Turin, 1907, p. 193; quoted by Giuliana Artom Treves, op. cit.
6. Marianna Prompolini, *La Duchessa Maria Luigia. Vita familiare alla corte di Parma*, Bergamo, 1942, p. 78.
7. Alessandro D'Ancona, *Ricordi ed affetti*, Milan, 1908.
8. *What I Remember*, London, 1973 (1st edn 1887), p. 147.
9. See Ch. 4, p. 105.
10. *Memoirs of an ex-Minister*, London, 1885, p. 26.
11. See Ch. 4, p. 106.
12. See Ch. 4, p. 108.
13. *A visit to Italy*, London, 1842, vol. 2, p. 156.
14. See Ch. 11, p. 265.
15. Baldasseroni, op. cit.
16. See Ch. 4, p. 115, and Ch. 8, p. 203.
17. See Ch. 5, p. 146, and Ch. 8, p. 203.
18. For Mazzini's idea of a constituent assembly see Ch. 7.
19. See Ch. 4, p. 116–17.
20. Domenico Demarco, 'L'economia degli Stati italiani prima dell' unità', *Rassegna storica del risorgimento*, XLIV, April–Sept. 1957.
21. Ch. 9.
22. Giorgio Candeloro, *Storia dell'Italia moderna*, vol. IV, Milan, 1964, p. 211.
23. Most of the statistics in these paragraphs come from Domenico Demarco, op. cit.
24. 'Sulle cautele che vogliono aversi nel tentare novità in Agricoltura. Lettura di turno del Socio ordinario R. Lambruschini, nella domenica 13 febbraio 1842', in *Atti dell' Accademia*, vol. XX, 1843, pp. 182–97. Quoted by Carla Ronchi, 'Liberismo e protezionismo in Toscana prima dell 1848', *Studi storici*, 1959–60, 1 no. 2, Istituto Gramsci, pp. 249–50.

CHAPTER FOUR

The Papal States

The Papal States in the eighteenth century consisted of Lazio (the antique world around Rome), Umbria (the very beautiful hilly province immediately to the north of Rome), the Marches (the district to the east of Umbria), the Legations (which included the cities of Bologna and Ferrara, across the Apennines to the north), and two isolated towns to the south — Benevento and Pontecorvo, wholly surrounded by Neapolitan territory. The important division in political terms was that between the area to the west of the Apennines, an area whose centre, the city of Rome, had been the heart of a world empire and a medieval theocracy, and the area to the east and north, which had a less glamorous past, but had developed its own traditions of protest and independence. In the eighteenth century the part of the Papal States centred on Rome looked to the south, towards Naples, the part centred on Bologna, Ferrara and Ancona looked to the north, towards Europe. The area centred on Rome was commercially backward. Lazio was a region whose land was divided between very large landowners, some of them ecclesiastics, some of them of the ancient feudal nobility. The economy of Rome herself was pre-industrial and, in that she depended to a great extent on the flocks of pilgrims who visited her from all over the world, the same as it had been in the Middle Ages. With a population of about 163,000 in 1790, she was second in size only to Naples among Italian cities. It was, of course, a city under the régime of priests, although there had always been a rich lay aristocracy, most of whom — like the Colonna and Orsini — had survived from the Middle Ages. Another section of the aristocracy were the descendants of families of former popes or cardinals — the Barberini, the Odescalchi, the Chigi.

Bologna was easily the second largest city in the Papal States, with a population of 70,000 in 1790. Ferrara, a university city second only to Bologna, contrasted with Bologna in that she had declined economically since being part of the Papal States. In 1792 the population of Ferrara numbered some 27,000 — appreciably less than it had done in the seventeenth century.

Throughout the eighteenth century the papacy had been losing influence as an international force. Not only had the Enlightenment led to a decline in the intellectual and spiritual authority of the popes, but the great Catholic powers themselves had been shaking off the influence of Rome. Mainly on the insistence of the Spanish government, but also with the approval of France and Austria, Clement XIV in 1773 had suppressed the Jesuit order, the order which had successfully upheld the authority of the pope in Catholic Europe for over two hundred years. The Jesuits were not to be recognized again by the papacy until after the Napoleonic period.

In 1790 the reigning pope was Pius VI, who had been elected in 1775. His own name had been Giannangelo Braschi, and he had been born in 1717, in Cesena, into a family of the nobility of the Romagna. He had been made a cardinal less than two years before becoming pope. Intellectually superior to most of his successors, he had been educated by the Jesuits from the age of ten, and had graduated in law at the age of seventeen, in 1735. He had then served in various diplomatic and administrative offices, eventually under Benedict XIV (1740–58), and in the great struggle over the Jesuits during the pontificate of Clement XIII (1758–69) he had been careful not to be aligned with either side. He had at that time been secretary to Cardinal Rezzonico, a member of a congregation charged by the pope with the task of looking into the question of the Jesuits, who had been expelled from France and other European states. When asked his opinion on the grave matter of the Jesuits, Braschi modestly – and shrewdly – refused to give it. In 1766 he had been placed in control of the papal treasury.

In spite of the sickeningly pious expression on his face in the sculptured portrait by Canova in St Peter's, Pius VI was not a pious man. He was a great nepotist in the most literal sense of the word. His nephew, Luigi Onesti, was given a splendid wedding in the Sistine Chapel, an extravagant wedding present, and a duchy. As ruler of the Papal States, however, there is little doubt that Pius tried to improve the well-being of his subjects. In particular he tried – as other popes had done before him, and as other rulers were to do after him, with rather more success – to drain the Pontine marshes, the unhealthy stretch of coast to the south of Rome, between Cisterna and Terracina. If the scheme was ultimately a failure, it at least gave work to some 3,500 men. The main reason for its failure seems to have been that no arrangements were made to settle farmers on the drained land, with the result that even the minimal achievements gained were not exploited, and soon lapsed. The water oozed back. But Pius VI also built roads, dredged the Tiber, and encouraged archaeological excavations. During his pontificate Rome became a popular resort of the European nobility, writers and artists. As well as Canova, Goethe and the French artist, David, lived in Rome.

However, the finances of the Papal States were in a bad way, and were certainly not helped by the extravagances of Onesti. It was a low ebb in the history of the Church. Pius VI probably felt sympathy for the Jesuits, but in the international ethos was too weak to restore them. Joseph II had virtually nationalized the Church in Austria, and the French Revolution soon went much further by introducing the Civil Constitution of the Clergy. Even so, Pius VI was eager to avoid a break with the revolutionary government in Paris, and did not condemn the Civil Constitution of the Clergy until 1791, by which time the French government had already annexed Avignon. On 31 May 1791 the pope withdrew his nuncio from Paris, but this break in diplomatic relations did not discourage the French minister at Naples, in November 1792, from sending a French representative to Rome – a journalist, Hugou de Bassville, who at once started to collect around himself a revolutionary and pro-French circle. The pope's officials reacted by stirring up anti-French sentiment, and on 13 January 1793 Bassville was murdered. Relations between the revolutionary government in Paris and the papacy were not exactly improved by the murder. The papal government had been arresting 'Jacobins' since 1792, and these 'Jacobins' were mostly respectable members of a middle class who were happy to find support from outside the papal states. But an obscure conspiracy which was unearthed in Bologna in that year included members of the working class who were motivated simply by their poverty.

Not until 1796, however, did French armies invade the papal states, after Napoleon had announced in May that the Roman people were to be liberated from their long servitude. After losing Bologna, Ferrara and Ravenna, Pius VI secured an armistice but it was only after negotiations had failed and a new outbreak of fighting had ensued that, in February 1797, the pope accepted the terms of the Treaty of Tolentino, in so doing surrendering Avignon and the Legations of Bologna, Ferrara and the Romagna. The invasion had not only ended any pretence of papal independence, but had imposed severe financial burdens on the papacy, so that, in the course of 1797, papal finances collapsed. In that year the harvest failed, and Rome experienced a grave food shortage. In the summer a republican conspiracy was uncovered, one of the revolutionary leaders being a member of the large Jewish minority in Rome, a certain Ascarelli. Napoleon had appointed his brother Joseph as his agent in Rome, and Joseph Bonaparte succeeded in getting Ascarelli and the other republican conspirators released from prison in November 1797. The position in Rome, however, moved rapidly towards a crisis. A reactionary party, violently hostile to the French, was led by Cardinal Zelada. At first, even so, the French armies did not occupy Rome, but at the same time the French did not prevent the republic from being declared in Ancona on 19 November. In disturbances in Rome on 28 December a French general, Duphot, was shot dead by papal forces. Joseph Bonaparte delivered a strong protest and left Rome, and shortly afterwards the French forces moved in to establish a Roman Republic on 15 February 1798. Pius VI was declared to be deposed as temporal sovereign. A government of seven consuls was provisionally established. The inevitable tree of liberty was planted on the Campidoglio, and a republican flag was raised, a flag of white, red and black, a flag without a future.

Pius VI responded to these colourful events by declaring that he could not give up an authority which had been invested in him by God. On 20 February the French informed the pope that he must leave Rome within two days, whereupon he left immediately for Tuscany. Not since the 'Babylonian Captivity' of the Avignon period in the fourteenth century had the pope been obliged by an outside power to leave Rome. Pius stayed in Siena for three months, and then travelled to Valence, where he died in August 1799.

The French themselves prepared a constitution for the Roman Republic, and based it on their own conservative constitution of 1795. There was to be an executive government like the French Directory, of five members, and there were to be two legislative chambers, both very small. Generally speaking, in nineteenth-century Europe, authoritarian regimes kept their legislative chambers very small, while more democratic ones went in for large assemblies. The Roman Republic was to have a 'Tribune' of 72 members, and a 'Senate' of 32. For the time being the constitution stated bluntly that the French commander-in-chief should nominate the five 'consuls', or members of the executive government – a clause which effectively made a mockery of the whole constitution. This first Roman Republic, anyhow, was to last for only eighteen months. The second Roman Republic, that of 1849, which was to last for an even shorter period, was, deservedly, to earn a more noble place in the corridors of history.

The first Roman Republic was significant, however, in one sense: for the first time the middle class in Rome had got the upper hand over the aristocracy and the higher priesthood. Positions of responsibility were held by professional people – lawyers, doctors, or by the poorer clergy. Social groups which had been suppressed for so long – including even the Jews, who had been persecuted by the Catholic Church for centuries – supported the Republic. It is difficult to know what the poorer people in Rome felt, but what evidence there is suggests that they were not hostile to the Republic, nor to the French. The Italians are an optimistic race: they always assume – against all the evidence – that the incoming régime will be better than the outgoing one. There was only one ugly, counter-revolutionary rising in Rome, on 25 February 1798. The priests stirred up anti-semitic sentiments in the Trastevere, the poorest quarter of Rome, a rabbit-warren of narrow streets on the Vatican side of the Tiber, but fortunately the French had little difficulty in suppressing the revolt. More serious opposition to the Republic developed in the provinces. A revolt in Umbria in April 1798 took several days to suppress. In 1799 a more general movement against the Republic spread.

The short-lived first Roman Republic experienced an element of journalistic activity, and political clubs were founded; both of these developments were to set a pattern for the second Roman Republic of 1849. On the negative side, the Republic faced a grave financial crisis: the French made outrageous demands, and inflation soared. But in defence of the policy of the French in Rome it must be said that Paris had abandoned them, financially, with the result that in February 1798 a group of officers and troops mutinied, because they had not been paid for some months. As a prelude to the War of the Second Coalition a Neapolitan army drove the French out of Rome in November 1798, but a few weeks later the Neapolitans were defeated and the French returned. The Roman Republic survived until September 1799.

On the death of Pius VI, Cardinal Gregorio Chiaramonti was elected, and took the title of Pope Pius VII. Chiaramonti had been born in 1742, at Cesena, the birthplace of Pius VI. A Benedictine monk, he had become bishop of Tivoli at the age of forty and, after being made a cardinal, bishop of Imola at the age of forty-three. His reaction to the French Revolution had been a far more open and generous one than that of most priests throughout Europe. He found it hard to believe that the principles of liberty, equality and fraternity could be opposed to the teaching of Jesus of Nazareth. At Christmas 1796, as Bishop of Imola, he had made his famous statement to the effect that it was possible to reconcile democracy and Christianity. The conclave of cardinals who elected Chiaramonti pope met, from force of circumstances, in Venice, but a few months later he could return to Rome. He inherited Pius VI's Secretary of State, a man of great distinction – Cardinal Consalvi. Under Pius VI the papacy had fallen into bad times, but under Pius VII and Consalvi – after a period of acute crisis – the papacy was to recover prestige.

Two of the leading artists of his day – David and Lawrence – have left us visual impressions of Pius VII. Sir Thomas Lawrence's portrait in Windsor Castle gives perhaps the more vivid character sketch of the two. Lawrence's Pius has a fatalistic expression, a slightly sardonic smile as he peers out at the follies of the world. Certainly there was a fatalistic element to his pontificate. A pope who had once sympathized with the ideals of the French Revolution, he was to suffer imprisonment and acute physical hardship under the man who claimed to be fighting for those ideals, but who in truth represented a cynical materialism as much opposed to the ideas of 1789 as it was to the spirituality of the Catholic Church. Yet Pius VII was one of the survivors of history, and was still to be pope when Napoleon was no longer emperor of the French.

The new pope in 1800 was immediately involved in difficult negotiations with Napoleon, negotiations which resulted in the Concordat of 1801 between France and the papacy. It marked a restoration of the Catholic Church in France, but a restoration giving strong powers to the French state. The French government retained the right to appoint archbishops and bishops, but with the pope exercising a veto. Priests were to be paid by the French government. So far as the Papal States were concerned, Pius VII remained sovereign, but lost Bologna, Ferrara and the Romagna. The Concordat was not a success. Relations between Napoleon and the new pope quickly deteriorated. Even so, when, in 1804, Napoleon invited Pius to Paris to crown him Emperor, the pope, after painful deliberations, accepted the invitation. With six cardinals and more than a hundred other attendants, the Pope left for Paris on 2 November 1804. One cardinal died on the way, but the rest of the party was met in the forest of Fontainebleau by Napoleon. The coronation ceremony itself was something of a farce. Napoleon kept the pope waiting in Notre Dame for an hour before he arrived himself, and took the imperial crown from the pope's hands to place it aggressively on his own head. Yet the pope seemed in no hurry to leave Paris, remaining until the spring of 1805, even after Napoleon himself had left for Milan, where he was to make himself 'King of Italy'.

That Napoleon was in a sense the restorer of the Catholic Church in Europe, and that, in his ill-mannered, uncouth way, he showed some recognition of the pope's position, is undeniable. He could not, however, believe that the pope's sovereignty over the Papal States was a vital element of Catholicism, and in this the future was to prove him right. But Pius VII, like all the other popes before 1870, believed that the Papal States were 'the seamless garment of Christ', without which the Church would lose her independence. He was thus bitterly offended when Napoleon occupied Ancona, on 18 October 1805, for purely military reasons. In April 1806 Napoleon occupied Civitavecchia, but did not move further into the Papal States until the summer of 1807 when French forces occupied most of the Marches and Umbria.

On 2 February 1808 a French army marched into Rome. Napoleon had moved very very slowly; he realized that to destroy the temporal power was not a step to be taken lightly. He was no Jacobin and did not want to repeat the events of 1798. Paradoxically his caution did not endear him to the Roman crowds. They would have responded to a dramatically democratic appeal, as they had done before, and would do again in 1848. But a mere gnawing away of papal power did not please them. In 1808 they demonstrated their hostility to the French by boycotting the carnival, the annual event which few Romans would normally miss. But by the winter of 1808–9 the pope was virtually a prisoner in the Quirinale. On 17 May 1809 Napoleon published a decree declaring that Rome had become 'a Free Imperial City', and that the Papal States were now a part of the French Empire. Pius VII managed to have a bill excommunicating Napleon and his minions posted on the walls of the main churches of Rome. In June the pope himself was arrested in the early hours of the morning. He was bundled into a coach and taken on a nightmarish ride, first of all into Provence, and then back to Savona, on the Ligurian coast.

On 17 February 1810 Rome was incorporated into the French Empire, with the mollifying declaration that she was the 'Second City of the Empire'. For administrative purposes the Papal States were now divided into prefectures precisely as France herself had been. They also elected representatives in the French assembly and senate. A less cheerful aspect of the arrangement was that conscripts from the Papal States went straight into the French army. But Jews and Freemasons were given civil rights, and the Code Napoléon was introduced. Meanwhile the pope remained a prisoner in Savona, deprived of contact with his advisers or the outside world. In 1812 Pius was removed from Savona to Fontainebleau, on a long, cruel and painful journey. He was ill, and the trip was hurried because Napoleon was afraid of popular manifestations in the pope's favour. He was kept a prisoner in the palace of Fontainebleau, and when Cardinal Pacca met him there on 18 February 1813 he found the pope 'bent, pale, emaciated, with his eyes sunk deep into his head, and motionless as though he were dazed'. Napoleon, unwittingly, had succeeded in creating a Catholic martyr, and after his cosmic defeat at Leipzig there was little he could do about it.

At the restoration Pius VII's reputation was high. It was felt by most Italians that he had been treated brutally by Napoleon, but that he had suffered with courage and had remained a moderate and balanced person. At the moment of the restoration the Catholic Church was at a low ebb. An Orthodox

Christian power, Russia, and two Protestant powers, Prussia and Britain, were in dominant positions, while Metternich, so far as his religious convictions went, had inherited the sceptical outlook of the Enlightenment. It was only after the restoration of 1815 that a strong Catholic revival developed as an aspect of the Romantic movement.

Pius VII's Secretary of State, at this critical moment in the history of the papacy, was Cardinal Ercole Consalvi. At the Congress of Vienna Metternich hoped to secure papal territory from the Po valley, arguing that geographically Bologna and Ferrara belonged rather to the Austrian north of Italy than to the papal centre. Consalvi, although not formally a delegate of the Congress, since the Papal States were not formally represented, was in Vienna, and was successful in persuading the representatives of the Powers that the territory of the Papal States should remain intact. So far as the régime in the Papal States was concerned, Consalvi at first gave the impression that he believed that some lay element should be present in the administration, that what had happened in the Napoleonic era could not be entirely disregarded nor reversed. But with the *Motu proprio* of 6 July 1816 Consalvi dropped his liberal façade. It may be that Pius VII and Consalvi, although reasonable and moderate men, were surrounded – as Farini says – by clerical fanatics, and that their every move was watched and to some extent undermined, by their colleagues in the papal court.[1] But the *Motu proprio* went far towards integrating the different parts of the Papal States under a predominantly clerical administration. The state was divided into seventeen provinces of which five – those beyond the Apennines – were to be under the authority of a legate (hence the term Legations), who was in each case a cardinal. The twelve provinces nearer Rome were to be more directly governed, but through the authority of delegates, who were also priests. Advisory bodies, termed 'congregations', were appointed by the government and these, at least, included some lay members. The legates and delegates had the same kind of authority as the prefects of Napoleon's day and, although they were clerics, the fact that a standardized system was introduced constituted a degree of modernization. The anachronism of baronial jurisdiction which had lasted until Consalvi's day was at last abolished in the Legations and the Marches. It had been restored in 1814, and even the *Motu proprio* of 1816 did not abolish it in the rest of the Papal States unless the barons themselves wished to delegate their judicial powers to officials recognized by the state. The considerable number of dues originally paid to the barons, and hunting and fishing rights outside their own lands, were all now abolished, without compensation. All lands and property of the Church taken over by the State in the revolutionary and Napoleonic era were retained by the State, but in this case indemnities were paid to the ecclesiastical or monastic bodies concerned. Papal state finances were far from healthy in spite of the immense wealth of the Papal court. Some reform of the tax system was carried out, though the most unpopular taxes – the *macinato*, or tax on the grinding of corn, and the stamp tax on published material – remained intact. Internal customs were standardized throughout the State, as were the State monopolies on salt and tobacco. The Code Napoléon was abolished at the restoration, but in 1817 a new code of civil procedure was introduced. The other papal codes which had been in force before the French period were reintroduced, except that torture and flogging were now abolished from the penal code. The French Revolution, even in Rome, had secured a few small strides forward. The *Motu proprio* could hardly be considered a triumph of enlightenment, yet it was disliked by the majority of cardinals, who considered Consalvi a dangerous innovator. Their opposition prevented him from introducing any lay element into central government. Even the moderate reforms of 1816 were not going to survive the death of Pius VII, when Consalvi was dismissed from office. There remained the framework of a police state, a state in which the judiciary had no independence from the government, a state in which all publications were censored, and which was itself considered as the private property of the papacy.

The years of the first Restoration were ones of great hardship, approaching famine, for the pope's subjects. Unemployment and begging were widespread and endemic, with great numbers of people wholly dependent upon the charitable institutions of the Church. Brigandage was common in the countryside, and petty theft a feature of everyday life in town and country alike. Many of the priests and bishops, and even some of the cardinals, were without doubt kind and generous men, but kindness and generosity are unfortunately no substitute for employment and plentiful food. Change, however, was inevitably coming. The sale of Church lands and property in the Napoleonic period had given birth to a new middle class, more particularly in the cities of the Legations — Bologna, Ferrara, Ravenna, Forli, and Pesaro. Professional and commercial classes who had previously been landless had acquired land, while artisans who had previously been independent were ruined by the beginnings of the Industrial Revolution in England, the Low Countries and France and the overwhelming competition which this represented. Political danger to the régime came, however — as usual — from the rising class rather than the declining one, though the crowds who were to demonstrate on the streets of Bologna in 1831, and of Rome in 1848, and eventually to stage insurrections, were composed of both groups. The radical enemies of the papal régime were not so closely identified with the secret societies as were the revolutionary groups in Naples. The Carbonari, the most famous and influential of the secret societies, had been founded in Naples, and began to penetrate the Papal States only very slowly after the Restoration. In particular the Carbonari were not active in Rome itself, but rather in pockets in the Marches, the part of the Papal States closest in spirit and character to the Kingdom of Naples. Another secret society, the *Società Guelfa*, had cells in the Legations and was probably founded in Bologna rather than in Naples. The two societies were in close touch in 1815, and finally in 1818 joined forces. The Carbonari managed to publish two or three secret and illegal newspapers in the Papal States. Their plans for furthering the cause of Italian nationalism were not clear-cut, but were certainly one aspect of their policy. Other aspects were concerned with internal matters of the Papal States: they wanted a lay administration, and some wanted to break with the pope altogether and encouraged Tuscany to annex the northern parts of the Papal States.

Pius VII, who was in the event to live until 1823, appeared to be dying in 1817. The death of a pope always meant a moment of danger for the régime, before a new pope was elected. The conspiracies and revolution of 1831 followed the deaths, in quick succession, of Leo XII and Pius VIII. In 1817 there was an attempted rising, planned by the Carbonari, at Macerata. The date fixed was 23 June, but before the rising could take place the police had acquired information and made arrests. Eleven men were condemned to death, but their sentences were eventually changed to life imprisonment.[2]

A large body of popular opinion in the Papal States was bitterly opposed to the secret societies. An extreme Catholic sect called the *Sanfedisti*, patronized by the papal government and dedicated to rooting out revolutionary or liberal sympathies, had appeared in the Napoleonic period. In spite of the fanaticism of the Sanfedisti, even Cardinal Consalvi, in other ways so civilized a statesman, found them a useful weapon against the Carbonari. In Consalvi's day, however, they were less influential than they were to become in the 1820s during the pontificate of Leo XII.

The revolution of 1820 had no counterpart in the Papal States, but was bound to have repercussions.[3] Consalvi was still in office. While sympathizing with the Neapolitan Bourbons in their hour of need, Consalvi remained cold in his attitude to Austria. There was some violence, and a number of murders in the Romagna in fights between Carbonari and Sanfedisti, and many people were inevitably arrested. It was the last major crisis which Consalvi had to face, and his handling of it showed great wisdom. Instead of reacting in panic, Consalvi ordered that the administration should function with greater than customary mildness. He could not control the fanaticism of the Sanfedisti who tried to terrorize known liberals, but his posture of moderation and conciliation almost certainly contributed to the lack of revolution in the Papal States. When the Austrians intervened in Italy in 1821 Consalvi commented that 'the remedy is perhaps worse than the disease'.[4] Unfortunately he could not control the Cardinal Legates across the Apennines, who arrested many liberals and exiled them. In particular the Legate in Ravenna, Cardinal Rusconi, Bishop of Imola, whom Farini described as 'a person both incapable and superstitious', and the Legate of Forli, Cardinal Sanseverino, described by Farini as 'a man of southern temperament and prone to excess', seized the opportunity to exile liberals from the Papal States. The last years of the pontificate of Pius VII, who died on 20 August 1823, were thus blemished by the acts of his minions in the Legations.

The comparative enlightenment of Pius VII's pontificate disappeared abruptly with his death and the election of Cardinal Annibale Delle Genga as Pope Leo XII on 27 September 1823. Della Genga had been the private secretary of Pius VI, and had held diplomatic posts in Switzerland and Germany. Pius VII had used his diplomatic services in negotiations with Napoleon, and the Emperor's brutal treatment of the pope partly explains Della Genga's violent hatred of the ideas of revolutionary and Napoleonic France. His relations with Consalvi had been very bad, but Pius VII had made him a cardinal in 1816. On his election as pope he was sixty-four — not a great age so far as popes go — but he was frail, and declared that if they elected him they would be electing a corpse. He was elected by a combination of the enemies of Consalvi, and immediately on becoming pope he vindictively deprived Consalvi of his office. Far from being a corpse he then displayed considerable energy, not only in performing ceremonial functions, like visiting monasteries and prisons, but in returning the Papal States into a wholly clerical regime. He also inaugurated a grim repression in the Romagna. Cardinal Rivarola was sent there, with full powers. He sat in judgement on a great number of political offenders. On one day alone — 31 August 1825 — he passed sentences, mostly of varying lengths of imprisonment, on 508 people. Seven were condemned to death, but in the event not executed. Rivarola became a much hated figure, and in July 1826 an unsuccessful attempt was made on his life by a baker, Angelo Ortolani. The head of police in Ravenna was killed shortly afterwards, and in May 1828 four men were executed for these crimes. In spite of the repression the Carbonari extended their links in the Papal States, and already in 1825 had cells in Rome itself. In that year a cook, Angelo Targhini, and a medical doctor, Leonida Montanari, were condemned to death and beheaded.

The repression of Leo XII also took institutional forms. The bull *Quod divina sapientia* placed education entirely under the priesthood, and brought back many clerical privileges which had in recent times been eroded. The Jews were no longer allowed to hold property, and were forced to sell any houses or land they possessed within a given period; those who had left the ghetto were to return to it; deprived of civil rights the Jews were to be the responsibility of the Holy Office. Those Jews who could afford to do so now wisely left the Papal States for Tuscany or Austrian Italy, where some of the rudiments of civilization still existed. Leo XII brought back other less vicious, but equally quaint, rules, as, for example, that teaching in the universities should be exclusively in Latin.

If Leo XII was a reactionary in almost every sense, it does not follow that he was a friend of Metternich's Austria. On the contrary, like his predecessors Pius VII and Pius VI, and his successors, Gregory XVI and Pius IX, he was determined to keep the Papal States as far as possible free of Austrian influence. Only his immediate successor, Pius VIII, who was pope for less than a year, was a real friend of Austria. Leo XII died early in 1829. Pius VIII, who had been Cardinal Castiglione, was the Austrian candidate, a man of sixty-eight, who had been a cardinal since 1816, described by Farini as having 'a reputation for piety and devotion, with some propensity to superstition'.[5] The Sanfedisti became even more influential during the short pontificate of Pius VIII than during the long one of Leo XII.

An account has already been given of the revolutionary movement of 1830–31 in the Duchies of Modena and Parma.[6] Already in December of 1830 Ciro Menotti had established a revolutionary cell in Bologna as well as those in the Central Duchies. Menotti was thinking in terms of a united Italian monarchy whose capital would be Rome.

After the death of Pius VIII on 30 November 1830 the papacy remained vacant for more than two months. Not only Menotti but conspirators in Rome regarded these two months as a golden opportunity. The Bonaparte family, expelled from France by the Vienna Settlement of 1814–15, had made a habit of wintering in Rome. Charles Louis-Napoleon Bonaparte, one day to become the Emperor Napoleon III, was at this time a wholly inexperienced and somewhat foolish young man of twenty-two. He led a hare-brained conspiracy to capture the papal castle of Sant'Angelo, in the heart of Rome, on the Vatican side of the Tiber. From there he planned to declare his cousin, the 'Aiglon', Napoleon I's only legitimate son who was a prisoner of the Austrians, 'King of Italy'. Louis-Napoleon himself, for the time being, would rule in Rome as regent. As with all Louis-Napoleon's conspiracies from 1830 to 1848, there was a mixture of magnificence and folly in this one. Unfortunately the authorities in Rome had little difficulty in uncovering the conspiracy and arresting the conspirators. Louis-Napoleon was expelled from Rome and hastened to Florence where his mother and elder brother were staying. In Florence the Bonapartes were contacted by Menotti, who persuaded them to take part in the rather more serious rising which Menotti was planning in the Duchies and the Legations.[7] A revolution in the Papal States was likely to be a more significant proposition than risings in Parma and Modena, but the inspiring figure was without doubt Menotti. The Papal States produced no great revolutionary leader at this moment. A lawyer, Filippo Canuti, was a useful contact for Menotti, but can hardly be considered a leader of the revolution, which was a spontaneous rising of the discontented professional classes. At first these classes collaborated with the old papal authorities, but as the papal authorities, frightened out of their wits, withdrew from Bologna, something approximating to a revolutionary provisional government took over. A non-violent revolution had taken place. Canuti was realistic enough to suggest that the revolutionary government in Bologna should give some support to Menotti in Modena, but his colleagues felt – with the blindness of the innocent – that the principle of non-intervention proclaimed by the July Monarchy in Paris excluded such a policy.

To Menotti it seemed that his vision of a great revolutionary nationalist movement was being betrayed by small-minded men in Bologna, but these men themselves were merely concerned with removing the corruption and incompetence of clerical rule and returning to the secular administration of Napoleonic days.

Even with an apparent shortage of leadership the revolutionary movement in the Legations spread quickly, and overlapped into the Marches. The papal authorities put up little resistance, and papal forces sometimes went over quickly to the revolution. The secular middle class was opposed solidly to the pope's temporal power, and was supported by the politically conscious artisans. The papal authorities tried to rally the peasants to their cause, but with little success. The local provisional revolutionary governments which came into existence in the Legations and the Marches tried to attract peasant support by reducing the price of salt and local taxes but, since many of the revolutionary, anti-clerical leaders were themselves landowners, they were re-luctant to introduce any genuinely radical social reforms.

One leader, at least, emerged in the Marches. Colonel Giuseppe Sercognani had been an officer under Napoleon, and was now appointed by the provision-al government of Pesaro, on the coast of the Marches, to be commander of their civic guard. Collecting an appreciable force around him, Sercognani mar-ched south to the papal port of Ancona and accepted the surrender of this considerable town on 17 February 1831. The fall of Ancona encouraged the spread of the revolution not only throughout the Marches, but in Umbria. Perugia, the provincial capital of Umbria, fell to the revolution on 14 Febru-ary even before the final capitulation of Ancona.

Cardinal Cappellari was elected pope on 2 February 1831, taking the name of Gregory XVI. A monk and an intellectual, the new pope had had no experience of politics, and had not even been a bishop. He had to be conse-crated Bishop of Rome on becoming pope. His election at this moment of crisis was clearly not calculated to make him the most liberal of popes. The revolutionary forces, however, had not passed into Lazio, the province of Rome itself, nor had there been any outbreak in the city since the initial farcical attempt of the Bonapartes. What demonstrations occurred in Rome were more often than not demonstrations in favour of the new pope. Sercogna-ni himself was quite prepared for a march on Rome, but his forces amounted to only some 3,000 and were poorly equipped. The revolutionary provisional government at Bologna seemed nervous at Sercognani's success. They feared that an attack on Rome itself would encourage intervention by the great Catholic powers. But they were under pressure from more forward-looking groups in Bologna, and on 8 February published a decree which 'declared broken every link which made us subject to the Roman pontiff'. The decree continued to declare that 'general Committees of the people will be convoked to select deputies, who will constitute the new government'.

After the initial decree the revolutionary government in Bologna went on to reorganize the finances, reduce customs duties, and create an independent and less arbitrary judicial system. The model they worked on was almost inevit-ably taken from the Napoleonic period – the only period in which they had experienced a modern and more regular system of finance and justice. The leader of the revolutionary group in Bologna, Giovanni Vicini, was in his sixties, and had been a deputy in the Cispadane Republic. On 26 February he arranged for an 'Assembly of Notables' to meet in Bologna. They numbered fifty-four, and were far from being violent radicals. Vicini was elected presi-dent, and so in effect remained the leader of this very cautious revolution. The Assembly, as was expected of it, pronounced, as its first decree, that the temporal power of the pope had ended. On 4 March 1831 it declared a pro-visional constitution. There were to be a president and seven ministers, and a consultative body elected by the existing assembly. The government was to be called the 'Government of the united Italian Provinces' and for the time being it would meet in Bologna. Vicini was to be president and Terenzio Mamiani, who was to play a bigger role in 1848, was to be minister of the interior.

Meanwhile the Austrians had decided to intervene. On 6 March they occupied Ferrara, but then paused for a fortnight, showing at least some respect for the forces which the 'United Provinces' at Bologna had put in the field. But the provisional government at Bologna was not ready for a heroic resistance against the Austrians. Vicini, not the most courageous revolutionary leader of all times, resigned as president, but in the event had to remain in office as there was no one to replace him. However, a new and more representative assembly was elected although it never had the opportunity of meeting. Perhaps its greatest claim to fame was that the poet Giacomo Leopardi was elected as deputy for Recanati. On 20 March the Austrians finally marched upon Bologna, and the revolutionary government withdrew to Ancona. A new general, Carlo Zucchi from Modena, had been placed in command of the army of the United Provinces. Like Sercognani, who had been – probably wrongly – suspected of treachery, Zucchi proved an efficient military commander. His army fought a courageous rearguard action against the Austrians outside Rimini, and he still had plans for marching on Rome. Zucchi was by no means completely defeated when news reached him that his political bosses in Ancona had surrendered to the papal authorities. The papal legate, Cardinal Benvenuti, who had been a prisoner of the revolutionary government, was released and given back executive power in return for the promise of an amnesty. His promise was honoured neither by the Austrians nor by Gregory XVI.

The Austrians were to remain in occupation of Bologna until 1838. Louis-Philippe's government had meanwhile sent a force to occupy Ancona and it, too, was to remain until 1838.[8] It might have been expected that the Austrian and French forces would have exercised a little civilized control over the irregular papal forces who returned in their full savagery. This, unfortunately, was not the case. The *Centurioni* behaved with their accustomed barbarism throughout the Romagna and the Marches, and thereby prepared the way not only for the revolutions of 1848, but also for the ultimate extinction of the temporal power.

Revolutionaries in the Papal States did not accept their failure of 1831 lightly. Discontent and conspiracies, especially in the Legations, persisted throughout the pontificate of Gregory XVI. A considerable plot was unearthed by the police in 1844. Among four men tried and condemned to life imprisonment were two whose names were later to be central to Italian history: Giuseppe Galletti, from Bologna, who was to be given office by Pius IX in 1848, and Felice Orsini, whose attempted assassination of Napoleon III fourteen years later was to move the Italian question into a new phase. But the 1844 conspiracy is a part rather of the history of the Risorgimento, and must be considered in that context.[9]

On 16 June 1846 Cardinal Giovanni Maria Mastai-Ferretti, Bishop of Imola, was elected pope and took as his name Pius IX. His was to be the longest pontificate in the whole history of the Catholic Church. It was also to be one of the most eventful. He had been born in 1792 in Senigallia, a little town in the Marches, not far from Ancona. His family was part of the local aristocracy.

His father had been *gonfaloniere* (or mayor) of Senigallia; and one of his uncles had been the bishop of Pesaro. At the age of eleven, in 1803, he was sent to the College of San Michele in the dramatic hill town of Volterra. His school companions were thus for the most part children of subjects of the Grand Duke of Tuscany, a fact which may well have given him a broader view of Italian affairs than a school in the Papal States would have done. His best subjects were apparently mathematics and the sciences. He had at first been intended by his parents for a military career, but the idea had to be abandoned because of the weakness of his health. At school he had a particularly bad first attack of what was diagnosed as epilepsy in 1809. He was taken home to Senigallia in the belief that he could not be given adequate care and treatment at school. Any medical diagnosis of the early nineteenth century is, of course, open to question, and the symptoms of Mastai-Ferretti's illness – whatever it was – seem to have disappeared by 1818. All that can with certainty be said is that he was a highly-strung person, who suffered from acute fits of nerves. The reports of a continual trembling of his lip merely confirm that he was ultra-sensitive, not that he was epileptic.

Mastai-Ferretti's experiences before being elected pope had been varied. He had been a missionary in South America, president of the administrative Commission of San Michele at Rome, and was finally made a cardinal in 1839. His election to the papacy, however, was a surprise to the outside world. It had been assumed either that Metternich would secure the election of a conservative or that, if a liberal were to be elected, it would be Cardinal Gizzi, whom Pius IX was to appoint as his secretary of state.

Pius IX started his pontificate with a dramatic gesture of conciliation to the liberals. On 17 July 1846, barely a month after his election, he granted an amnesty to all people imprisoned or exiled for political offences. Provided they took an oath of loyalty to the pope they would be allowed to live as free men in the Papal States. Something like 2,000 potential revolutionaries were thus once more walking the streets of Rome, Bologna and the rest of the state. Many of the men who returned to Rome were received in audience, with great kindness, by the pope. The amnesty was greeted by wild demonstrations of excitement and affection for the pope, not only in Rome itself, where there was usually a reservoir of enthusiasm for any pope, even when he was singularly undeserving, but also in the cities of the Legations and the Adriatic, where the fashionable outlook was a strongly anti-papal one. Among those in Rome who cheered the pope most loudly at this stage were the figures who would lead the revolution late in 1848. The most colourful of them was Angelo Brunetti, affectionately called 'Ciceruacchio'. Born in the heart of Rome in 1800, he had at first earned a living with a handcart, but had then managed to buy himself a small wine business. Immensely popular with the teeming masses of the Trastevere, he enchanted them with his revolutionary oratory, though whether he had ever actually joined either the Carbonari or Mazzini's *Giovine Italia* is by no means sure. Even the very conservative Frenchman, Alphonse Balleydier, who was a witness of the Roman events of these years, gave a sympathetic picture of this large, generous-hearted demagogue. Ciceruacchio was an active and hard-working man, says Balleydier, and had only two faults – his pride and his weakness for wine.[10] The enthusiasm for Pius IX which Ciceruacchio expressed after the announcement of the amnesty was probably sincere, but he certainly hoped to pressurize the pope towards a broad programme of democratic reform. His unique position was that of a worker who became a revolutionary leader: the other revolutionary leaders in Rome were to be from the usual social circles – eccentric noblemen and members of the professional classes: lawyers, teachers and medical doctors. A doctor who was to play a prominent rôle was Pietro Sterbini, six years younger than Ciceruacchio. Sterbini had been a member of the Carbonari, and then of the Giovine Italia, and his political stance was identical to that of Ciceruacchio in spite of their very different social backgrounds. Sterbini had written appalling plays, and worse poetry, but was a sincere democrat, if not a great revolutionary leader. Another interesting figure who emerged in Rome in these months was Carlo Luciano Bonaparte, Prince of Canino. A son of Napoleon's brother Lucien, Canino was something of a freak in the extravagance of his oratory, and contrasted sharply with another revolutionary figure of the moment, a quiet lawyer, Carlo Armellini, who was to be, with Mazzini, one of the triumvirs of the Roman Republic.

The enthusiastic demonstrations which greeted the amnesty in Rome in 1846 were peaceful and good-natured ones, but in the Romagna, where the secret societies were more influential on the one hand, and the Sanfedisti on the other, there was a considerable amount of violence, and even some deaths. The Sanfedisti and the Centurioni were without doubt appalled at the pope's liberal start to his pontificate, and made no secret of their hostile feelings towards him.

When on 8 August 1846 Pius IX appointed Cardinal Gizzi as his secretary of state, liberals in the Papal States were again favourably impressed. Gizzi had been the great white hope of the liberals before the obscure and modest Mastai-Ferretti had emerged as pope. Yet one observer in Rome, Luigi Carlo Farini, described Gizzi as 'a weak and hesitating person, whom some even suspected of duplicity'.[11] Events were certainly to show that Gizzi was less liberal, or at least more cautious, than Pius himself. But something at this point should be said of Farini, whose record of these years of papal history is one of the fullest we have. Born at Russi in the province of Ravenna in 1812, Farini was educated to be a medical practitioner. He became involved in liberal-minded conspiracies and was exiled by Gregory XVI. Pius IX's amnesty allowed him to return. He was to play a varied role in the revolutionary period, holding posts during Pius IX's liberal phase in 1848, but being removed from office by the Roman Republic in 1849. The extent to which he had moved to the right was illustrated by his acceptance of office under the French occupation in 1849. One day he was to be prime minister of united Italy, but his importance for 1848 lies primarily in his full account, from his own peculiar, passionate and opinionated standpoint, of the events in Rome in that year – an account translated immediately into English by the young William Ewart Gladstone and published by John Murray in 1851.

110

Gizzi did not deserve Farini's censure, but he was frightened at the way things were going, and one of his first acts as secretary of state was to circulate the provinces with recommendations that public demonstrations should be discouraged. On the other hand he appointed commissions of enquiry into the building of railways, reform of the administration, and possible establishment of an advisory council of ministers for the pope. Gizzi no doubt imagined that he was following a policy along a knife-edge – trying to keep the movement of popular enthusiasm under control, while promising reform and moderniza-tion. As so often happens with this kind of attempt, it antagonized rather than conciliated both radicals and conservatives alike. Already on one occa-sion, in November 1846, the pope was met by a rather sullen crowd in the Corso. But the Roman crowd was a volatile one, and would soon return to rapturous applause when fresh reforms were announced. In quick succession new commissions were appointed: to prepare a reform of civil and penal law, to take care of the paupers, to improve education and find work for unemployed youth; and on these commissions some lay members were given places. Promptly, once again, Pius IX became a hero in the eyes of the Roman crowd, although the appointment of numerous commissions did not necessarily mean that substantial reforms would follow, and the presence of lay members on the commissions certainly did not mean that laymen were to be given important posts in the administration.

Meanwhile Pius himself was careful to discount any suggestion that his policy marked a break with that of his predecessors. In the preambles to his decrees Pius modestly protested that he was simply carrying forward reforms which Gregory XVI would have introduced had he lived longer. Only the most devout subject of the pope could have believed that Gregory, who had been pope from the age of sixty-six to the age of eighty-one without bringing in reforms in spite of pressure from the Great Powers, had really intended to do so at the end of his pontificate.

After the amnesty of 1846 Pius IX's next important step in unwittingly preparing the way for the revolution of 1848 was to permit the existence of an independent press. Gizzi issued a law on 15 March 1847 ending censorship of publications by the Church, and handing it over instead to a committee of five men, of whom four were laymen. The committee could exercise censorship only if they gave a written explanation of their reasons for doing so. Much depended upon the extent to which the new form of censorship would be enforced. A few newspapers were certainly condemned, but that the cen-sorship of the majority of publications was a lenient one is apparent from the fact that over a hundred independent newspapers existed in the Papal States at the start of 1848. Already before Gizzi's press law an influential newspaper had been founded in Rome – *Il Contemporaneo* – by which the people could learn where and when popular demonstrations, torchlight processions, and the like were being held. In its original form *Il Contemporaneo* was a comparatively moderate paper, but after Gizzi's press law Pietro Sterbini became the editor and it acquired a strongly revolutionary flavour. Alongside the growth of an inflammatory press, political clubs also started to appear and quickly acquired a large membership. The most influential club was the Circolo Popolare, where Sterbini also had a leading role.

The coming revolution thus had potential leaders as the result of the amnesty of 1846. It had an active propaganda conducted by the press and the clubs. That it should also be provided with arms by the pope was more than even the most sanguine radical could have hoped. Needless to say, the pope did not intend to create an armed revolutionary force, but demands for a 'civic guard' came from varying quarters. Ciceruacchio and his friends saw the civic guard as the 'people in arms', but others saw the need for some kind of armed force which would prevent violent action by the crowd and protect property. Yet other people — Gizzi among them — feared that a 'civic guard' would pass out of the control of the papal government, and that the hope should therefore not yield to demands for its creation. Gizzi's advice was disregarded, and the formation of the civic guard was the occasion of his resignation. From its very foundation it had a popular character, and Ciceruacchio subsequently became its commander. There can be little doubt that the granting of the amnesty, the relaxation of the press censorship, and the formation of a civic guard were more important elements in the prelude to the revolution of 1848 in Rome than was the creation of the *Consulta* by Pius IX in 1847. The Consulta was simply another body whose function was to advise the pope, but it was an elected — if an indirectly elected — body, and it was not restricted to the clergy.

By July 1847 Metternich was sufficiently alarmed at what was going on in Rome to take a step which turned Pius IX's reforms into a decisive chapter in the history of the Risorgimento, and a not insignificant chapter in international history. Ferrara although since the Vienna settlement a city under papal sovereignty, had an Austrian military force to garrison the magnificent castle in the city's heart. On 17 July the Austrians issued orders that their troops should — in spite of the Treaty of Vienna, and thus in the teeth of international law — occupy the entire city of Ferrara. Pius IX was, with good cause, outraged, and lodged a strong formal protest. Once again the pope became a hero in the eyes of Italian nationalists. From South America Garibaldi offered the services of his Italian Legion should the pope need them.

Pius IX's Consulta met on 15 November 1847. It consisted of twenty-four members, four for Rome, two for Bologna, and one for each of the other provinces of the Papal States. Marco Minghetti, one day to be prime minister of united Italy, was one of the twenty-four. The president was Cardinal Giacomo Antonelli, who was to have a rather different role in the future history of Italy. In addressing the newly appointed Consulta, Pius IX gave little encouragement to the liberals among them. He told them bluntly that his sovereignty had come from God, and that the existence of the Consulta could in no way diminish this fact. They would be very mistaken, he said, if they saw some Utopia of their own, 'or the seeds of an institution incompatible with papal sovereignty' in the Consulta. The Consulta — and more particularly Minghetti — were not to be subdued by the pope's harangue. In recording their 'thanks' to the pope they pointed out the need for financial reform, including a reduction of taxes on the poor; administrative reform, which would allow a normal civil service to come into being; and an educational reform. Few sovereigns have been 'thanked' in more explicit terms. The Consulta went on to decide that its debates should be published, though this was against the advice of Cardinal Antonelli and proved to be difficult in practice, since the papal bureaucracy was not accustomed to publishing official documents.

The year of revolutions, 1848, began in January with the rising in Sicily, which provided Pius IX with an opportunity to have his revenge on Metternich for the outrageous occupation of Ferrara in July 1847. When Metternich requested permission to send troops across the Papal States to suppress revolution in the Kingdom of Naples – as he had done in 1821 – the pope sent an abrupt refusal. It was perhaps the last genuinely heroic act of this remarkable and sad man. It was followed by extraordinary demonstrations in his favour and these demonstrations without doubt went to his head. In a *motu proprio* he asked God to bless 'Italy', and in the age of Metternich 'Italy' was a dangerous hypothesis. However, on 10 February 1848 he issued a proclamation to the effect that the reforms already received by the people of the Papal States were entirely through his grace and favour. Any further reforms would also depend upon his judgement, and he would do nothing which 'did not conform to his duty', a formula generally regarded as meaning that he was under no obligation to introduce a constitution. To the outside world, however, he was regarded as the pope who had blessed 'Italy'. On 4 March Cavour wrote in *Il Risorgimento*: 'the great reconciliation of the priesthood with the cause of progress, with the principles which inform and dominate modern society, wonderfully prepared by Vincenzo Gioberti, has been fulfilled and blessed by the most high Pius'. The pope himself, on 11 February, when reviewing the officers of the civic guard, had announced that he had appointed a commission to consider all the reforms so far accomplished, to see how they could be extended 'in harmony with needs, and with the present desires'. He was ready to carry out what he had promised so long as it was not contrary to the principles of the Church and of religion (a statement which must have raised a few eyebrows among the more exacting of logicians). Rather than abandon the principles of the Church, Pius said, he would throw himself 'into the arms of Providence' – a phrase which was a euphemism for his departing from Rome. He went on to put across the interesting, if dubious, argument that states which had introduced constitutions had copied the idea from the papacy. 'We have had the chamber of deputies . . . and the chamber of peers in the Sacred College of Cardinals since the age of Sixtus V.'[12]

Later in February 1848 Pius IX came to realize that a constitution of some kind would have to be granted. News reached Rome of the revolution in Paris, and of the granting of constitutions in Florence and Turin. But Rome could not be compared with Paris, Florence or Turin. Rome was the centre of a world religion, and the pope was the spiritual head of a great congregation. To grant a constitution to his temporal subjects, while retaining full sovereignty over his spiritual subjects, would present certain difficulties. Not all issues could be neatly pigeon-holed as 'temporal' or 'spiritual'. Education and marriage were two aspects of life over which the Church felt responsibility, yet they were aspects of the life of the citizen over which the State would be reluctant to give up responsibility. Pius IX did not fully understand the meaning of the word 'constitution' but thought always in terms of a more broadly based consultative body. When he finally decided to allow a 'Council of Deputies', he justified it with these words: 'Since our neighbours have judged their people sufficiently mature to be allowed the benefit of a representation not only consultative, but deliberative, we do not wish to show less respect to Our own people.'[13] Rather pathetically the pope was saying that he had to emulate the King of Naples, the Grand Duke of Tuscany and the King of Piedmont. His constitution was introduced on 14 March 1848. It set up a parliament of two houses. The conservative cardinals had hoped that the College of Cardinals could form the upper house of any parliament which the pope would be rash enough to introduce, but Pius was clear that the upper house in his constitution must be a body distinct from the College of Cardinals, though nominated by him. The lower house was to be elected on a severely restricted franchise. The College of Cardinals, as well as the pope, retained a veto on the findings of the parliament. Whether this was really a 'constitution', in the English or French sense of the word, is open to argument, especially when one considers Article 25, which allowed civil rights only to Catholics. Even if one overlooks the small Protestant minority in Rome at this time, one can hardly forget the twelve thousand people of the Jewish ghetto[14] who were explicitly excluded from citizenship by this constitution. Usually basic constitutions proclaim certain liberties – for example, liberty of conscience. The assumption is that no one should be forced to pretend that he or she believes what he or she does not believe. Even the greatest coward cannot change his belief because of the threat of physical burning (adopted by the Catholic world some centuries earlier), or by theoretical burning in some supposed after-life (adopted by the Catholic Church in more recent centuries). To most right-thinking people in the nineteenth century liberty of conscience was a basic human right. Montanelli was surely not mistaken in seeing the reluctance of the papacy to grant liberty of conscience as the fundamental difference between Pius IX's 'constitution' and the genuine constitutions which regulate the lives of free men.[15]

The assembly elected under the constitution of 1848 was moderate in character. The hundred people elected included 3 princes, of whom one was the Bonaparte Prince of Canino, who was more radical than most of his commoner colleagues, a duke, 5 marquises, 24 counts, 19 lawyers, 9 doctors, 6 professors, 3 engineers – all of them property owners.[16] In social terms, then, they were not exactly revolutionary in character, but they included highly intelligent and distinguished people. And in its historical context Pius IX's constitution had one great element of novelty – it allowed a secular body to be elected and to introduce legislation. It was not a novel element which appealed particularly to the clubs or the crowd, who were deeply disappointed at the limitations of the constitution.

The attitude of Pius IX to the war between Austria and Piedmont is essentially a feature in the history of the Risorgimento, and must be dealt with later.[17] But his Allocution of 29 April 1848, by which he renounced any idea of fighting against Austria, had profound effects on his position in the Papal States. The lay ministers resigned from his government, and the Civic Guard made a dramatic gesture of independence by moving into the Castel Sant'Angelo, which was still a formidable fortress in Roman terms. In a sense the revolution had already begun. Of the two major political clubs even the more moderate one, the Circolo Romano, announced that it would remain in permanent session, as did, inevitably, the more radical one, the Circolo Popolare. Faced with this kind of popular protest the pope made a striking concession when, on 4 May 1848, he appointed Count Terenzio Mamiani minister of the interior. Mamiani is a key figure in the story. When Pius had issued his amnesty in 1846, Mamiani had refused to take the oath of loyalty to the pope which would have allowed him to return from exile. Instead he had proposed his own terms – that he should simply obey the laws of the state – and on those terms he had been allowed to return. In a sense he had obtained over the pope a moral victory which lesser revolutionary mortals had failed to obtain. Mamiani thus had a reputation for honesty and integrity which was by no means undeserved. For three months he remained the pope's chief minister – a good record by the standards of 1848. Inevitably he was accused by his enemies on the right of being a tool of the revolutionary clubs. The truth is that he maintained an independent policy in a moment of acute crisis. The pope underestimated the value of Mamiani, just as he was to overestimate the value of Pellegrino Rossi.

Mamiani's position thus became impossible. He himself wished to preserve papal sovereignty – in other words to preserve the Papal States – but under a responsible lay government, at least for the time being. But many of his colleagues in the council of deputies, among them Sterbini and the Prince of Canino, would have preferred to act without the co-operation of the pope, if not in the teeth of his opposition. Pius himself, in the event, took advice from other, reactionary, associates, and asked the Habsburg government to accept his mediation in the war between, as he put it, 'the German nation' and 'the Italian nation'. The offer was a curious one. The phrasing seemed to accept an understanding of the assumptions of nineteenth-century nationalism, but was unacceptable both to the Austrian authorities and to Italian nationalists. The defeat of the Piedmontese in July 1848 rendered both the pope's ill-judged iniatiative and Mamiani's policy ineffective.

The ending of the war meant that many of the former soldiers of the pope's army who had fought illegally in the north under Giacomo Durando now returned to Rome, and brought their arms with them.[18] Their presence in Rome certainly heightened the temperature, though the evidence that they themselves frequently resorted to violence is prejudiced and unconvincing. There is no doubt, however, that their arrival terrified Pius IX, who now decided to appoint as his chief minister the proverbial 'strong man', an embittered academic, Count Pellegrino Rossi. The new minister was a cultured and highly intelligent man, who had been professor of law at Bologna and had subsequently gone to France as a political exile in the days of Gregory XVI. He had then returned to Rome as Louis-Philippe's ambassador, and had subsequently secured the confidence of Pius IX. He was a tall, thin, austere figure, and the Roman crowds took an instant dislike to him. He felt, and was not shy of expressing, a profound contempt for Mazzinian ideals, and for the cherished dreams of the clubs in Rome. He forbade the carrying of arms in Rome, and recalled many of the semi-military *carabinieri* who were loyal to the pope. He was widely believed to be preparing a *coup d'état*, by which the pope would be enabled to abolish the constitution.

On 15 November Rossi was murdered in the midst of a great hostile crowd as he entered the assembly. His murder was probably planned by the Circolo Popolare. Subsequent tribunals had difficulty in establishing the guilt of any single individual, but this did not deter the Austrians, after the so-called 'Second Restoration', from executing Ciceruacchio and two of his sons, the younger of whom was only thirteen. On 16 November an unplanned, but effective, insurrection against the pope took place. The Civic Guard, supported by armed members of the crowd, fired on the pope's palace, the Quirinale. One shot passed through a window and killed a bishop inside the palace. Some people still wanted the return of Mamiani; others wanted Sterbini; yet others wanted the mild-mannered Mazzinian, Giuseppe Galletti. Unknown to most people in the crowd, Pius had already made Galletti minister of the interior. The pope's policy had therefore become somewhat ambiguous, but on 24 November he left Rome secretly, to accept refuge in the Kingdom of Naples at Gaeta. He left in the company of the beautiful and talented Countess Spaur who had, at the age of sixteen, married an English archaeologist, Dodwell, and, after Dodwell's death, the Bavarian prime minister, Count Spaur. Countess Spaur's influence over the pope was believed to be considerable, and it is highly probable that it was she who persuaded him to leave Rome and to seek the protection of Ferdinand II, yet she has escaped mention by most historians.

Galletti's government tried, rather pathetically, to pretend that it was still the legitimate government appointed by the pope, but since the pope himself denounced it, and since Mazzini, from Switzerland, poured ridicule on the attempt,[19] Galletti soon had to admit, reluctantly, that he was leading a revolution. On 18 November he announced his programme, which included the election of a Costituente for the whole of Italy, but went on to say that 'a federative act . . . would respect the existence of the single states, and leave intact their form of government'. The relationship between events in Rome and the national question must be considered in another context[20] but, so far as the well-being of the people of Rome was concerned, the record of Galletti's government was not wholly negative. Sterbini had been appointed minister of public works, and had discovered that a fund already existed for maintaining public works of art. He used this fund to give employment to the building trade, which probably accounted for the largest single body of workers in this pre-industrial city. It is a little ironic that the first revolutionary government in Rome in the nineteenth century should have embarked on a programme of reconstruction of churches, but the most numerous of public buildings in Rome were undeniably the churches, and builders would prefer to build anything rather than nothing. Nor was the building activity directed only at churches. A new, broad road – still an important thoroughfare – was built along the Tiber embankment by these previously idle men. On 3 January 1849 the revolutionary government abolished the most hated of all the taxes on the peasants – the *macinato*, a tax on the grinding of corn. To abolish this tax, which was very easy to impose, brought a considerable revenue but hit the poorest and most helpless of the population, was an act of considerable courage.

The constitutional position in Rome was that the Council of Deputies, elected under Pius IX's measure of 1848, was still in existence. This body happily now handed over power to a *Giunta di Stato*, consisting of three men, who were to organize the election of the Costituente. In what must to many people have seemed a power vacuum in Rome, the population remained calm, non-violent, but excited at the prospect of a Costituente meeting in Rome, as they were equally excited at the showing of the premier of a Verdi opera, the *Battaglia di Legnano*, which coincided with these dramatic political events. The Costituente met on 5 February 1849. One of its deputies was a sailor-and-soldier of adventure whose fame was yet far from its peak – Giuseppe Garibaldi. Four days later it declared the end of the temporal power and the birth of the Roman Republic. On 12 February it proclaimed that its legislation would be in the name of 'God and the People', and that the author of this phrase, Giuseppe Mazzini, should be granted citizenship of the Republic.

Mazzini himself reached Rome from Florence on 5 March. Received with immense sympathy, he behaved with quiet dignity and was at once recognized as the natural leader of the Roman Republic. A week after his arrival Piedmont went to war, for the second time, against Austria, but was defeated in less than three weeks. The pope at Gaeta was meanwhile collecting together a sufficient number of cardinals to hold a consistory on 20 April. He announced to the consistory that he had asked for the help of France, Spain and Naples against 'the enemies of our most holy religion and civil society'. The armies of the reactionary powers would now be pouring into Italy, and in this atmosphere of crisis the Roman Costituente elected a triumvirate – Mazzini, Carlo Armellini, a lawyer, and Aurelio Saffi, a young aristocratic scholar and friend of Mazzini. The triumvirate – and in effect Mazzini – ruled Rome for just over three months. In England during his exile Mazzini had seemed to friends and enemies alike to be an unrealistic visionary. Yet his rule of the Roman Republic was not only tolerant and enlightened but – for its brief, tormented spell of life – effective and successful. In Rome, it is true, he inherited a full democracy, in the sense that the sovereign body was already an assembly elected by universal suffrage. Previous ministers – Mamiani, Galletti, Sterbini – had already introduced forward-looking social policies, and if their records have been ignored by historians this is the fault of the historians rather than of the protagonists of 1848. But it is yet true that a man of total integrity was still

117

needed in Rome, and few figures in history have had quite the integrity of Mazzini. Robespierre certainly had integrity of a kind, but it was related to violence and intolerance. Mazzini, on the other hand, in his brief period of office in Rome, managed to be at once a strong, and a tolerant, leader. He did not draw on his salary, which he had, anyhow, fixed at a very low sum, but preferred to eat in a workers' restaurant and to occupy for his office a small, accessible room in the Quirinale.

His attempts to grapple with the forces which destroyed the Roman Republic are a part of the history of the Risorgimento, and must be dealt with in a later chapter.[21] So far as the history of the Republic herself goes, it must be said here that a French expeditionary force under General Oudinot disembarked at Civitavecchia on 25 April 1849. The mayor of Civitavecchia, Achille Mannucci, who had been in office for only a month, protested somewhat weakly, and there was no obstacle to prevent the French army setting out immediately for Rome. The Assembly in Rome, however, voted for the defence of the Republic and 'the resistance of force by force'. Garibaldi was placed in command of the army in the field, and in the general enthusiasm even women and children took up arms. The first encounter between the armies of the French and the Roman Republics took place on 30 April. The French were driven back, and Nino Bixio's legion took an entire French battalion prisoner. Meanwhile an army of some 12,000 to 15,000 Neapolitans advanced on Rome from the south, while a Spanish force disembarked at Fiumicino, opposite Elba. Garibaldi was now needed to command the Roman forces against the Neapolitans. Mazzini could not believe that the French Second Republic would continue its aggression. Hoping for a negotiated peace, therefore, he received Ferdinand de Lesseps, French consul at Madrid, in Rome, and a convention was signed on 31 May. Garibaldi defeated the Neapolitans – not for the last time – at Velletri. The Austrians meanwhile had invaded with an army of some 16,000, and besieged Ancona, which resisted for twenty-five days. On 3 June Oudinot announced his refusal to ratify the pact signed by Mazzini and Lesseps, and renewed his attack. Meanwhile the Spanish expeditionary force had been increased to 9,000 men and 400 horses, but carefully refrained from any warlike encounters. According to one Italian observer the Spaniards made a bad impression on the Italian population by their habit of 'swearing like Turks', and bathing in the nude in public fountains.[22] They embarked at Terracina, having done nothing to help the pope. June 3 was a day of desperate fighting between the French and the troops of the Roman Republic. Since the French army was one of the best trained and the best equipped in Europe, the achievements of Garibaldi's men were almost unbelievable. The Italians depended to a great extent on the bayonet, that terrible weapon which necessitated immense physical courage to use.

Meanwhile, during the grimmest moments of the siege of Rome, public order in the streets remained good. Arthur Henry Clough, the English poet, was in Rome at the time, and noted that the Italian soldiers were behaving rather better than British soldiers normally behaved. Mazzini proclaimed the abolition of the death sentence, and would have recoiled from the idea of executing any potential traitor. There were to be no September Massacres nor Reign of Terror in Rome. French priests who had been imprisoned were released by Mazzini's orders. Prostitutes who had been imprisoned were not only released but offered jobs as nurses in the hospitals, much to the disgust of the hypocrites who are present in any society. There was also a creative element to Mazzini's policy. The clearing of the Roman slums, already started by his immediate predecessors, was intensified by Mazzini. In the countryside the poorest peasants were given land, taken from the religious orders, who were certainly not thereby impoverished. Few rulers have tried, as Mazzini did, to reconcile freedom, social order and social justice.

The destruction of the Roman Republic is, again, part of the history of the Risorgimento.[23] When the pope returned to Rome, on the afternoon of 12 April 1850, he was cheered by the crowds. He never went back to his old home in the Quirinale Palace, where Mazzini had conducted his quiet and civilized administration. Pius instead established himself in the magnificence of the Vatican, where the popes have remained ever since. Pius IX himself was disillusioned with politics, which he was now to leave, with disastrous consequences, to his secretary of state. The pope himself returned to his old love, theology, or to be more accurate, medieval mythology. In particular he was interested in Mary, the mother of God, who does not play a very prominent role in the Gospels, and played no role at all in the scholarly debates of theologians in the nineteenth century. But she had mitigated the grimness of the Middle Ages with a spirit of gentleness and humanity, and it would he wrong to dismiss Pius IX's preoccupation with this figure of mythology as the superstition of a simple and elderly man. It could well be that he was right in thinking that her influence in the nineteenth century was by no means a bad one. The question, however, belongs rather to a later chapter of this book than to the history of the Papal States.[24]

Antonelli, who had been pro-secretary of state when Pius was in exile in Gaeta, was made secretary of state when the pope returned to Rome, and remained secretary of state until his death in 1876 – only two years before that of his master. The new minister became a *bête noire* of English and German Protestants. Gregorovius referred to his jaw – 'a jaw that is thousands of years old and belonged to the creatures of the mud who devoured, devoured'.[25] Certainly Antonelli was a corrupt and brutal man, but his jaw – judging from his portraits – was very much the jaw of any middle-aged, rather self-indulgent, person. More to the point, Antonelli's brother was allowed to run a rich bank, and Antonelli himself left a considerable fortune to his relatives. If Pius IX seemed reminiscent of the Counter-Reformation and the age of Tiepolo, Antonelli was an equally anachronistic reminder of the age of the Borgias.

On 12 June 1855 an attempt was made on the life of Cardinal Antonelli. The attempt was not successful, and the man responsible, a certain De Felici, was arrested. On 30 June he was condemned to death. There is evidence that Antonelli himself would have preferred the sentence to be mitigated to one of life imprisonment, but that Pius IX was so appalled at the attempt that he insisted that the death sentence must be carried out.[26] At this time the pope's dominions still practised the barbarity of public executions. On this occasion however the papal government did not want to draw too much attention to what was obviously a political crime. It was therefore announced that the scaffold, on which was constructed a guillotine, would be moved to an un-accustomed place, though in the event the execution took place at the normal site, in the Bocca della Verita. De Felici's death was one of considerable hero-ism, and deserves the attention of historians. In the presence of the priests who were sent to him he repeatedly sang an aria from *Il Trovatore*: 'Oh how slow is death to come to the man who wishes death'. He showed no glimmer of fear on the scaffold, but simply looked around very slowly to see if there was anyone he knew in the crowd. In a sense the tragedy came after his execution. His wife had a total and irreversible mental breakdown; one of his brothers drowned himself in the Tiber. De Felici was the fifteenth person to be beheaded in the course of one month in the Papal States, and it must be remembered that his crime was that of attempted murder, not of murder. Catholic historians, whether Italian, British or American, have tended to keep quiet about the bloodshed, and the tumbling heads, in this, the period of the second restoration of the popes.

The political history of the Papal States had shown signs of sweetness and light before the trauma of 1848. The social and economic history of the region remained uncompromisingly bleak throughout the period covered by this book. A Frenchman writing in 1859 commented:

The immoral concentration of all wealth in the hands of a small number of parasites . . . the violence committed against natural economic justice, in favour of the privileged classes, leaving to agriculture neither freedom nor protection have reduced it [the Papal States], especially in the areas around the capital, to the most deplorable condition.[27]

But if this was the condition of the wretchedly poor provinces around Rome, it was less true of the Marches, Northern Umbria, or the provinces of Bologna and Ferrara. In these parts of the Papal States the very fertile land was ex-ploited by the growing of corn, rice, vines and fruit. Even in the hilly parts of Umbria and the Romagna olives, fruit and vines were grown. Only the dis-trict around Rome itself was wholly and miserably depressed, and infected by malaria. Very little of the land was cultivated; much of it was used as pasture for sheep. In the simplest terms of an agricultural economy the Papal States could not feed themselves. The production of tobacco, in the province of Ancona, could well have provided a profitable export, but tobacco was a gov-ernment monopoly and the accounts of the industry were shrouded in secre-cy. A very considerable number of cattle, horses, donkeys, sheep, goats and pigs were bred, but they were not well cared for and the breeding was disorgan-ized. An immense amount of effort at grass-roots level was squandered. If the Legations were economically advanced in contrast with the rest of the Papal States, they were backward compared with Lombardy, and perhaps even with Tuscany.

The great Roman aristocratic or ecclesiastical families who owned the land of Lazio were absentee landlords, who often also owned land in other Italian states and especially in Naples. Their estates were usually rented by another rich class, who had varying contractual relations with the peasants who actually worked the land, relations which sometimes approached the system of *mezzadria*. Umbria claimed, with some justice, to be 'the garden of Italy', on the grounds of its natural beauty rather than because of any horticulture produced by man. The land was owned ultimately by a very limited number of people, if less limited than the number who owned land in Lazio. The manner in which it was farmed in Umbria lay somewhere between the confused tenantships of Lazio and the comparatively orderly system of *mezzadria* in Tuscany. The hilly and mountainous regions of Umbria provided very little livelihood for anyone, and those who managed to scrape an existence from the steep slopes and rocky soil had to migrate in the winter to the estates on the low ground of Lazio. The Marches — the southern parts of the eastern coast of the Papal States — were marginally less impoverished. Here the system of *mezzadria* was practised on the land and there was a not unhealthy fishing industry in the small towns of the coast. The largest port of the Marches, Ancona, still traded with the Eastern Mediterranean countries, but had if anything declined during the eighteenth century.

If the Legations, centred around Bologna and Ferrara, were the least backward part of the Papal States, here, too, there were very poor hilly regions and marshland along the coast, but the flatter and better drained central region grew enough agricultural products for small-scale exporting.

Bologna, where silk and hemp were produced, was the only genuine industrial centre in the Papal States. Before 1848 what industry there was was stagnant and corrupt. The policy of the papal government which imposed interminable customs dues and sold concessions of monopolies to single manufacturers sapped any incentive there might have been. Roads, especially over the Apennines, were very primitive. Industry was therefore in the hands of small artisans with only local markets. In the Romagna sulphur was mined and exported, and a paper industry existed in the Marches. But more goods were imported than exported from the two main ports of Ancona and Civitavecchia, the balance being made up by the invisible exports of tourism and pilgrimages. There was little scope for investment. The middle classes tended to put their surplus profits into savings banks, one of which was founded in Rome in 1836 and others in Bologna and Spoleto in 1837. Such banks were not a novelty in Italy, since they had already existed during the Renaissance. During the pontificate of Gregory XVI papal finances went heavily into the red, and the papal government had to borrow large sums from banks in Rome and Genoa, and from the Paris branch of Rothschild.

But even in periods when the government was less embarrassed the people of the Papal States remained desperately poor. Mrs Trollope, visiting the Papal States in 1841, found the people suffering from 'dirt and melancholy neglect', which contrasted sharply with the conditions she had found in Lombardy and Tuscany. One of her comments is doubly revealing: she refers to the 'picture of human misery, ignorance and destitution . . . sadder . . . than I have ever witnessed . . . except perhaps among the manufacturing population of Manchester and its neighbourhood'.[28] It was almost certainly less terrible to be destitute in the hills of Umbria than in the slums of Manchester, but the choice was clearly one between two evils. The conditions of the peasants in the regions near the west coast — the far north, the Maremma, and, nearer to Rome, the *Agro romano* — were wretched, in the sense that they had been deteriorating since the sixteenth century, and the population had actually declined. While the price of corn increased, the income of agricultural workers remained the same. The middlemen could grow richer and buy their own land, yet there was no large-scale capital investment in land of the type experienced in Lombardy.

In the city of Rome itself the lower classes did not, of course, constitute a modern proletariat. They consisted, in the higher strata, of independent artisans, linked in medieval-type corporations. There were a large number of builders, a vast number of domestic servants, and the unemployed and beggars. There was the Jewish ghetto, whose people had been confined in the dark days of the Counter-Reformation, and since then their conditions had steadily deteriorated as crushing penal taxes had been imposed upon them. In 1790 it was calculated that more than one in six of the population of the Papal States depended on poor relief of some kind from the Church. Nor did things improve thereafter. Poverty was more acute and the lumpenproletariat larger in the Papal States than anywhere else in Italy, except for the Kingdom of Naples, where the concept of 'poverty' reached new dimensions of horror.

NOTES

The English liberal Catholic historian, E. E. Y. Hales, has written two books of significance: *Revolution and Papacy 1769–1846*, London, 1960, and *Pio Nono*, London, 1954. There are two thorough studies of papal administration at the beginning of the nineteenth century by Dante Cecchi — *L'amministrazione pontifica nella prima Restaurazione (1800–1809)*, Macerata, 1975, and *L'amministrazione pontifica nella seconda Restaurazione (1814–1823)*, Macerata, 1978. The latter, dealing with the work of Consalvi, is perhaps the more important. A recent work by an Austrian Catholic historian deals with relations between Austria and the papacy in the early nineteenth century — Alan J. Reinermann, *Austria and the Papacy in the Age of Metternich, (1809–1830)*, Washington, 1979, of which only the first volume has so far appeared. Luigi Carlo Farini's passionate denunciation of his enemies must still rank as a significant piece of historical writing. Translated by Gladstone as *The Roman State from 1815 to 1850* in three volumes it was published in London in 1851. For the pontificate of Gregory XVI there is D. Demarco, *Il tramonto dello stato pontificio. Il papato di Gregorio XVI*, Turin, 1949. Two works by Piero Zama cover in some detail the risings in the Papal States in 1831, and — the much less serious one — in 1845; *La marcia su Roma del 1831*, Rome, 1976, and *La rivolta in Romagna fra il 1831 e il 1845. I giudizi dell'Azeglio, Mazzini, Farini, Capponi, Montanelli ed altri*, Faenza, 1978. A splendid collection of articles by Alberto M. Ghisalberti relate to the history of Rome in the period: *Momenti e figure del risorgimento romano*, Milan, 1965, while two classics in French on the Roman Question deserve to be mentioned: E. About, *La Question romaine*, Brussels, 1859, and Emile Bourgeois and E. Clermont, *Rome et Napoléon III (1849–1870)*, Paris, 1907.

L. Dal Pane, whose work on the economic history of Tuscany has been mentioned in the notes to the previous chapter, has also written on Bologna: *Economia e società a Bologna nell'età del Risorgimento*, Bologna, 1969, while important for an understanding of rural society in the Papal States is a study of the Borghese family's policy with regard to their vast estates and their adjustment to changing conditions – Guido Pescosolido, *Terra e nobiltà: i Borghesi, secoli XVIII e XIX*, Rome, 1979.

Other works which are in varying degrees relevant to this chapter will be mentioned in the notes to Chapter 13.

1. Luigi Carlo Farini, *The Roman State from 1815 to 1850*, trans. W. E. Gladstone, London, 3 vols, 1851.
2. With regard to this and other political trials in the Papal States in the nineteenth century, English-speaking historians have often misled their readers by writing of political offenders being 'sent to the galleys'. Whether the writers themselves really imagine that in the mid nineteenth century the pope had a fleet of galley-ships propelled by prisoners with oars is an open question, but some of their more innocent readers have probably been deceived into thinking that such was the case. The confusion has been caused by the use of the Italian term 'galere', which originally meant 'galleys', but which in modern times came to mean simply 'prison', since the galleries of nineteenth-century prisons resembled the decks of a ship.
3. See Ch. 7, pp. 178–9.
4. Farini, op. cit., vol. I, p. 15.
5. *Ibid.*, p. 31.
6. See Ch. 3.
7. See Ch. 3, pp. 78–9.
8. See Ch. 7, p. 180.
9. See Ch. 8, p. 198.
10. *Histoire de la révolution de Rome. Tableau religieux, politique et militaire des années 1846, 1847, 1848, 1849, et 1850 en Italie*, 1851, vol. I, p. 25.
11. Farini, *op. cit.*, vol. I, p. 221.
12. G. Spada, *Storia della rivoluzione di Roma*, vol. II, pp. 45–6, Florence, 1868.
13. Alberto M. Ghisalberti, *Momenti e figure del risorgimento romano*, Rome, 1965 p. 39.
14. Domenico Demarco, *Una rivoluzione sociale. La repubblica romana del 1849* Milan, 1944, p. 17.
15. For a detailed discussion of Pius IX's constitution, see Ghisalberti, *op. cit.*, pp. 41–7.
16. *Ibid.*, p. 48.
17. See Ch. 8.
18. For Durando's part in the war see Chapter 8.
19. Letter to Giuseppe Lamberti, 4 December 1848, *Scritti editi ed inediti di Giuseppe Mazzini*, ed. M. Menghini, vol. 37, Imola, pp. 174–83.
20. See Ch. 8.
21. See Ch. 8.

22. Temistocle Mariotti, *La difesa di Roma nel 1849*, Rome, 1902.
23. See Ch. 8, p. 207.
24. See Ch. 13, p. 287.
25. Quoted by E. L. Woodward, *Three Studies in European Conservatism*, London, 1929, p. 296.
26. The whole grisly story is told, with his usual eloquence, by Ghisalberti, op. cit., pp. 242–3.
27. C. de La Varenne, *L'Italie Centrale*, Neuilly, 1859, p. 356, quoted by Domenico Demarco, 'L'economia degli stati italiani prima dell'unità', *Rassegna storica del risorgimento*, XLIV, April–Sept., 1957.
28. Mrs Trollope, *A Visit to Italy*, 2 vols, London, 1842.

CHAPTER FIVE

The Two Sicilies

The foreigners who come to our country seeing the serene beauty of our sky and the fertility of the fields, reading the codes of our laws and hearing talk of progress, of civilization and of religion, might believe that the Italians of the Two Sicilies enjoy an enviable happiness. And yet no state in Europe is in a worse condition than ours, not excepting even the Turks. . . . In the Kingdom of the Two Sicilies, in the country which is said to be the garden of Europe, the people die of hunger, are in a state worse than beasts, the only law is caprice. . .[1]

Luigi Settembrini, writing in 1847 – admittedly a grim moment in Italian and European history – well expresses the paradox of the history of Naples in modern times.

The sovereign in the eighteenth century was known as the 'King of the Two Sicilies', although it was not until the nineteenth century that reference was made to a 'Kingdom of the Two Sicilies'. The two regions were administered separately, under separate laws, in the eighteenth century. Even so, Italian historians have usually referred to the state as the 'Kingdom of Naples', and this practice will be followed in this book. The royal court remained, of course, normally, at Naples, but a viceroy was appointed for Sicily and had his court at Palermo. The two peoples have always been recognized as being completely distinct in character. The national stereotype given to the Italians by other Europeans – that of a volatile, quick-witted, passionate, but somewhat disorganized people – has also been given to Sicilians by Continental Italians. Continental Naples had been a united kingdom for some six centuries.

The most remarkable fact about the Kingdom of Naples was the immense size of its capital city, in view of the small extent of the state and its great poverty. There is reason to suppose that Naples was the largest city in Europe – perhaps in the world – in the sixteenth century, and perhaps already in the fifteenth century. The seventeenth and eighteenth centuries witnessed further great population growth, but in the first half of the nineteenth century the population remained static. In 1791 when the total population of the Continental kingdom was assessed as being about five million, that of the city of Naples was thought to be over 400,000. This meant that the city's population was well over twice that of Rome, three times that of Milan, and four times that of Turin or Florence. The figure for 1791 in Naples must, however, be regarded as only an approximate one. Only from the French period – or, to be precise, from 1809 – were accurate statistics kept. Two censuses made in 1807, one by the army and one by the police, suggest that the population was declining quite rapidly at that time, no doubt because of the wars and the social upheavals of the period. The provincial council of Naples in 1808 recorded grimly that times were bad, 'subsistence difficult, marriages rare, and the present generation lean and unhealthy'. But the two censuses of 1807 did not agree on the rate of population decline, and so are not reliable. Many people may have falsified the returns to avoid conscription of themselves or their sons. The first reasonably reliable census was made in 1813, under Murat, and returned a figure of 326,130. Thereafter the population of the city fluctuated, but did not show a marked growth or decline over-all. There were sharp falls during the cholera epidemics of 1836–7 and 1854–5, and in 1848, for economic rather than political reasons. But the figure quickly recovered after the crisis had passed.[2] By the middle of the nineteenth century Naples was still the third largest city in Europe, after London and Paris, larger, that is, than Vienna, Berlin or St Petersburg.

Yet Naples was not an industrialized city. Rather she was a grotesque parasite, many of whose inhabitants were royal employees, priests, domestic servants, and beggars. She lived on the back of a desperately overworked, desperately poor, peasantry, who were given no civic rights.

The island of Sicily had a quite separate history from that of the mainland, and had fused a greater variety of cultures – classical Greek, Roman, Arabic, Norman, Spanish – with the peasant masses retaining their own, easily identifiable, Sicilian ethnic and cultural character. The nobility, descended in part from Norman or Spanish families, were more mixed in their origins than the peasants. The island's capital, Palermo, with an estimated population of about 140,000 in 1798, was the third largest city in Italy – larger than Milan or Turin.

In spite of the reforming activity of Naples during the Enlightenment, the basic fact of absolutism, with its inevitable weaknesses, remained: no political or administrative initiative could be taken without the king's approval. The king in 1790 was Ferdinando IV who had succeeded to the throne in 1759, when he had been a child of eight. His father, Carlo III, had become king of Spain in 1759, but his previous ministers had continued to rule Naples during the minority of Ferdinand, even though they had moved to Madrid. The education of Ferdinand himself was neglected, probably deliberately, so that he would remain under the thumb of the government in Spain. Consequently the only skills he acquired in his youth were to shoot accurately at game, to fish and to row. Several witnesses commented, however, that he was an honest, open man, and not unintelligent considering he was so ignorant. But the traumatic events of his reign were to alter his personality fundamentally, and few would have called him honest by the end. At the age of seventeen he was married to an Austrian princess, Maria Carolina, a daughter of Maria Theresa, and sister of the Emperor Joseph II, Pietro Leopoldo of Tuscany, and Marie

Antoinette of France. Maria Carolina was also in her teens, but had a stronger personality. They had seventeen children, but the marriage was not a happy one. Ferdinand was dominated by his wife in political, as in domestic, affairs.

Before 1780 the ideas of the Enlightenment, although strongly anti-clerical and anti-feudal, had had no practical effect on the feudal economy. On the whole the island of Sicily had been provided with rather more enlightened ministers, in the years before the French Revolution, than had mainland Naples. Domenico Caracciolo, Marquis of Villamarina, viceroy of Sicily in the 1780s, had done more than anyone else to introduce the ideas of the Enlightenment to the island. But he had realized the immensity of his task, and in 1774 had complained that the lack of a middle class in Sicily undermined any attempts at reform. 'Sicily is inhabited', he wrote, 'by great lords and wretchedly poor people.'[3] The professional class – which meant, primarily, lawyers – were closely linked to the barons, and so were opposed to reform. Where Caracciolo's reforms had had practical results had been in his dealings with the Church. He had abolished the Inquisition, suppressed some convents, obliged some monasteries to open schools, and laid down that legal cases against the Church should be tried by lay courts. In 1790 Caracciolo's successor, the Prince of Caramanico, had been viceroy of Sicily for four years, and was to be viceroy for a further four. Like Caracciolo, Caramanico was a product of the Enlightenment, but was more sceptical, less idealistic, and his relations with the Sicilian nobility were far better. He managed to pass through a few minor reforms, as, for example, making illegal the few remaining instances of personal servitude.

The French Revolution destroyed the alliance between the aristocratic intellectuals of Naples and the absolute monarchy. The Neapolitan monarchy had not been unsympathetic to many of the ideas of the Enlightenment. The Queen, Maria Carolina, in her earlier days had worked for an independent foreign policy for Naples and had certainly not suppressed enlightened ideas. By the time of the death of Caracciolo in 1789 she had, however, moved to a more authoritarian stance, exemplified by the appointment of her favourite, the Englishman John Acton, as chief minister in that year. Events in France from 1789 to 1794 soured her attitude to any further reforms. The preoccupation of the Queen and Acton was now to oppose any revolutionary idea. The intellectuals, for their part, turned against the monarchy, believing that the austrophile inclinations of the Queen and the anglophile inclinations of her minister were not in the best interests of the kingdom. The French Revolutionary government infiltrated their agents into the kingdom, where they easily made contacts with the masonic lodges. The clubs enrolled noblemen, priests and intellectuals. The term Jacobin was, rightly or wrongly, already being applied to them in 1792. Certainly they read the French newspapers and enthused over the news from Paris. From the Neapolitan point of view there was much to be said against Acton's policy. The execution of Louis XVI enabled Acton to persuade Maria Carolina to sign a treaty with Britain in 1793 which involved Naples in war with France, a war which protected British naval interests but which led twice to the invasion of Naples by foreign armies.

In the War of the First Coalition the Neapolitan record was at first a good one. Neapolitan cavalry, serving on the flank of the Austrian army in Lombardy, were praised by allies and enemy alike, and the Neapolitan fleet served effectively alongside the British. But a fifth column was forming inside the kingdom. In 1794 a conspiracy was discovered against the monarchy – in a sense the first revolutionary conspiracy of the entire Risorgimento. It was the work of a group of nobles and professional people who had been influenced by the ideas of the Enlightenment, but it found support also with some of the poorer priests. Many of the conspirators escaped but many were arrested. Three of them were executed. One of them, Emanuele De Deo, was only twenty-one years old, and died with great dignity.

It is surprising that subsequent romantic myth-makers of the Risorgimento did not make more of his death. Many other people convicted of conspiracy were imprisoned or deported. In the following year a conspiracy which may well have had contacts with French Jacobinism was discovered in Sicily. Its leader, Francesco Di Blasi, was arrested, tortured and hanged. Others were hanged, and many others imprisoned. The monarchy was over-reacting to these conspiracies: over the years 1795–7 a savage police activity was conducted.

For a year or two from 1796 Naples stood on the sidelines, while the emergence of Napoleon Bonaparte transformed the life of northern and central Italy. The French moved ever closer towards Naples, and after they had occupied Rome the Neapolitan government signed a treaty of alliance with Austria. Nelson arrived in Naples after his victory in Egypt, and was received as a hero by Maria Carolina and her royal appendage. Nelson had a personal link with the queen, through his love affair with the British ambassador's wife, Emma Hamilton, who was a close friend of Maria Carolina.

In December 1798 Ferdinand IV was partly responsible for the outbreak of the War of the Second Coalition, though the first war had never been formally ended. Bolstered up by English, Austrian and Russian support, the Neapolitan government moved against the French, and their army succeeded in occupying Rome. But their triumph was brief. Defeated in several encounters, the Neapolitan army evacuated Rome, and the French entered the kingdom of Naples. Ferdinand and Maria Carolina were grateful to utilize Nelson's ship to escape to Palermo. Before the French could enter Naples they had to fight a bloody battle against the *lazzaroni*. The term *lazzaroni* was not coined by academic sociologists, and so is not very precise in its application. It certainly includes Marx's lumpenproletariat – the beggars and the unemployed, – but it includes also a host of people who were actively employed, if only as casual labour, as fishermen or dock workers. The *lazzaroni* played an important role in Neapolitan history, and will crop up again in the chapter.

On 22 January 1799 the Neapolitan liberals proclaimed the Republic to be known as the Parthenopean Republic, using the classical name for Naples. Championnet, the French commander, was, however, in real control – a fact clearly recognized by the Neapolitan republicans. On 24 January he appointed a provisional government under Carlo Lauberg. Although Championnet retained a veto on any measures taken by the government, his relations with Lauberg remained good, and he allowed a free press to come into existence, and clubs to be founded. These aspects of the French regime could, without stretching the term too far, be called 'Jacobin'. Championnet, a civilized man, resisted the outrageous demands of the Directory in Paris that he should secure an immense amount of loot – art treasures in royal and private hands – and he was therefore recalled to France.

The Neapolitan Republic of 1799 was very slow to recognize the claims of the peasants, who wanted a formal declaration ending feudalism and a radical resettlement of the land. For this reason, and because the French troops were looting and brutalizing them, the peasants quickly turned against the Republic and followed the advice of the priests that they should work for a Bourbon restoration. Counter-revolutionary armed forces thus began to form among the peasants, led by brigands or priests,and were soon in control of several towns and large tracts of territory. At first consisting only of scattered and disorganized bands, the movement was united by the sinister figure of Cardinal Fabrizio Ruffo , who prevailed upon the king at Palermo to let him go to Calabria and organize a force. With only eight companions he sailed on 7 February and quickly established in Calabria what he called the 'Christian and Royal Army', which in the course of March occupied the main towns of the province. Early in May the greater part of the French army marched away from Naples to the north where they were needed against the Austrians. On 13 June Ruffo's barbaric hordes entered Naples; for some days appalling acts of murder and horror were committed in the streets of the vast, tragic city. The men guilty of the atrocities were partly Ruffo's followers, and partly the desperately deprived and wretched *lazzaroni* of Naples, who were reacting to long and unnoticed social neglect by murdering, raping, looting and destroying on a scale which no one had anticipated. The intelligent and civilized leaders of the Republic had certainly never anticipated such savagery. Many of them continued to resist in the two fortresses of Castel Nuovo and Castel dell'Uovo, until Ruffo agreed to guarantee them a free passage to Toulon, or a free existence in Naples, in return for their surrender. But on 24 June Nelson arrived with the British fleet and the British minister, Sir William Hamilton, and Lady Emma. Nelson and Hamilton insisted that the republican leaders must be treated as traitors and Ferdinand, who arrived back in Naples on 8 July, agreed. The king's return was thus the signal for another massacre, this time conducted by the restored monarchy. More than a hundred republicans were hanged or beheaded.

The middle-class 'Jacobin' revolutionaries had wanted a democratic regime like that in France in 1792–3, but they had been nervous about the social consequences of such a regime and certainly had not wanted a social upheaval. Some of them had not considered the landless peasants as forming part of 'the people' at all, but there were others with more generous, even socialist, ideas. Thus Vincenzo Russo had wanted to abolish property, and most of the 'Jacobins' had been genuinely concerned to relieve the suffering of the poor. But the leaders of the Republic of 1799 had never exerted authority in the provinces, although the provincial bourgeoisie had been prepared to back them.

Benedetto Croce, perhaps the most famous of Neapolitan historians (although he was many other things besides), provided a Hegelian interpretation of the revolution of 1799. His theory was that there was an educated minority who had absorbed the ideas of the Enlightenment and the French Revolution, and who 'abominated the memory of a Nelson, who came to protect the worst and the most outworn of our institutions and to drown in blood every noble and generous effort'. The educated minority, in spite of being a minority, represented the true spirit of Naples: 'it pursued an ideal that was contrary to reality, but because the reality had no ethical basis it was powerless to prevail'. In Hegelian terms, 'the real' would have to correspond to 'the ideal' in the long run. It was an attractive and optimistic doctrine, but in applying it to nineteenth-century Naples one has to assume that the creation of a united Italy was ideally good, and that it marked a step forward for the Neapolitans. The cynic might well comment that it would have been difficult for Naples to take a step backwards. But it is not difficult to sympathize with Croce's verdict on the leaders of the 1799 revolution: 'The idealists were a small group of standard-bearers among an ignorant crowd which threatened to, and nearly did, overwhelm them, which sent them to prison, death, and exile and inflicted great moral suffering'. As Croce said, 'the monarchy, which had been at the centre or in the forefront of political progress, took fright and had recourse to desperate means of resistance. It did not simply sink to a secondary progressive role, but went over to the opposition, and became definitely negative and reactionary.'[4]

The peasant armies which had enabled Ruffo to restore the Bourbons in 1799 realized, over the seven years from 1799 to 1806, the mistake they had made. Ruffo had promised them that their tax burden would be lightened, but his promise was, of course, broken by the Bourbons and nothing was done to satisfy their need for land. The most that could be said for this first Bourbon restoration is that it brought four or five years of peace. But after the breaking of the Peace of Amiens in 1803,[5] and the occupation of Apulia by the French, the Bourbons had again to seek the help of the English. After Austerlitz, on 2 December 1805, Napoleon declared that the Bourbon dynasty no longer reigned. Thus in February 1806 the French were again in occupation of Naples and Ferdinand IV and Maria Carolina in exile in Sicily. Napoleon gave the throne of Naples to his brother Joseph, who remained king for two years until he was transferred to the throne of Spain. After the arrival of the French in 1806 there was no general peasant rising on the scale of 1799, although the Bourbons, helped by British forces, managed to stir up a restricted rising in Calabria, but this was — though with some difficulty — suppressed by the French.

Joseph Bonaparte, as King of Naples, gave some ministerial posts to Frenchmen, but many to Neapolitan noblemen. He had a consultative Council of State of thirty-six, the majority of whom were Italians. The Napoleonic institution of the *Conseil d'Etat*, which has worked well in France, has always seemed strange to British constitutional notions. It is in effect a central body of technical and legal experts, with considerable powers both of an administrative and a judicial nature. The Neapolitan historian Vincenzo Cuoco, author of the *Saggio storico sulla rivoluzione napoletana del 1799*, the first attempt to analyse the revolution of 1799 (see Ch. 6, p. 167), was a member of the Neapolitan Council of State in the French period, and had considerable respect for Joseph Bonaparte, who was certainly a good choice as king of Naples. A more cultured man than Napoleon himself, he had studied at the University of Pisa, and had thus a more intimate link with Italy than had the emperor. He was not, however, eager for political power, but was content to carry out Napoleon's policy, which included one dramatic and significant step: on 2 August 1806 feudalism was declared abolished. The barons were no longer to have their own judicial courts, nor their own military establishments, nor certain tax privileges. They were, however, confirmed in their property rights, but immense efforts were made to sort out precisely what these rights, and what the communal rights, really were. Commissions were appointed, and numerous decrees published, but the Bourbons were to inherit a totally confused situation in 1815. Ironically the attempts of the governments in the French period to have a fairer distribution of land had the reverse effect. Some of the barons, and many of the middle class acquired more land; the peasants remained with little or none.

Joachim Murat, who succeeded Joseph Bonaparte as king of Naples in 1808, was a more active and ambitious man. He was quickly recognized by many of the Neapolitan upper classes as a genuinely national, and therefore legitimate, monarch. His inclination to be independent of Napoleon culminated in 1814, in his joining the alliance against him. Like Joseph Bonaparte, Murat could not rule in Sicily. From the time when the Bourbons arrived in Sicily, at the end of 1805, until 1811, the island was occupied by British troops, but its internal rule was not a preoccupation of the British government in London. The British who were in Sicily, however, had to deal with the Bourbons, and relations were not good. But the people of Sicily, under the English from 1806 to 1815, enjoyed certain advantages. The Continental System imposed by Napoleon, to exclude British exports from Europe, gave considerable benefits to the Sicilian economy, which remained in touch with the advanced British economy. Whereas the citizens of Continental Naples were conscripted into Napoleon's armies and taken away to remote and horrific campaigns, the inhabitants of Sicily were left in peace – a hungry peace, perhaps, but still peace. Nor did foreign armies bring desolation to the towns and countryside of Sicily.

The British did not interfere in internal Sicilian affairs until 1811. In July of that year Lord William Bentinck arrived in Palermo as minister at the Neapolitan court and commander of the British navy and army in the Mediterranean – a not insignificant appointment. The Bourbons were in theory still sovereign in Sicily, but Bentinck was in fact in control. The so-called 'revolution' of 1812 in Sicily was largely his work, with the help of

Sicilian noblemen, lawyers and priests. Most nineteenth-century revolutions have lawyers among their leaders, but the Sicilian movement of 1812 was more predominantly an aristocratic one, based on a defence of ancient feudal privileges. It was analogous to the 'revolt of the Notables' in France in the years 1787—9, not to the great Revolution of 1789. The parliamentary tradition in Sicily was a strong one, but it was also a conservative one, linked to feudal traditions. As in 1787 in France, so in 1812 in Sicily, the nobility struggled to preserve their privileged institutions, but above all their exclusion from being taxed. The Sicilian barons themselves, however, did not look to any analogy in French history, but rather to British history. The English, like the Sicilians, had had a Norman conquest, and the English parliament had enabled an aristocratic class to resist being taxed arbitrarily by the crown. When Bentinck arrived he was only thirty-six, yet had already been Governor of Madras for four years. He had served as an officer in several military campaigns. He was no orthodox British diplomatic agent, but a man with idiosyncratic ideas and considerable moral courage. In London the opposition party was demanding a break with the Bourbons, and the *Morning Post* was insisting that Sicily should be annexed to the British Empire. Bentinck himself was quickly convinced of the need for Britain to intervene in Sicilian affairs, not so much for Britain's sake as for the well-being of the Sicilians. If Britain secured reforms in Sicily the effect would be 'to place the King safely on his throne, to give happiness to an oppressed people, to make their island forever independent of French invasion, and to exalt the British character'. The British government in London was a little sceptical of embarking on basic reforms in Italy, but instructed Bentinck to say, in general terms, to the Bourbons, that the British Government was prepared to continue supporting them only if the Bourbons, for their part, were prepared to give the Sicilians a greater share in running their own affairs, specifically by respecting the expressions of grievances by the Sicilian parliament.

After his arrival in Sicily Bentinck soon discovered that his main opponent was the queen, Maria Carolina, who believed that Britain was planning to annex Sicily. He himself had rather more interesting plans. The Archduke Francesco of Este, in exile in Sardinia, had volunteered to lead a national Italian rising, with the help of Austrian officers and British money, with the aim of establishing an Italian Kingdom free of French influence. Bentinck pressed this plan on the government in London, explaining that the Italians could act as the Spanish had done, being 'a people equally brave with the Spaniards, and equally enthusiastic in the cause of liberty, but much more intelligent and more tractable'. Perhaps surprisingly the British government eventually accepted his suggestion and allowed him £100,000 for planning such a rising. Needless to say, nothing came of it. Bentinck's more realistic plan was to establish a constitution in Sicily, a plan resisted by Maria Carolina and, less effectively, by Ferdinand. In January 1812 Ferdinand handed over power to his son and heir, who was to become Francis I, and who now took the title of Vicar. Francis was less opposed to the idea of a constitution and, unlike the king, not suspected of treachery, but he was extremely weak, and to what extent he had been delegated responsibility by the king was not clear. The strongest, if not the most balanced, personality in the Bourbon court was Maria Carolina. She referred to Bentinck as the *bestia feroce*, and he came to believe that she was at the root of his difficulties in getting a parliamentary constitution for Sicily. In March 1812 it was discovered that she had been in secret negotiations with Murat, and Bentinck now insisted that she should be sent into semi-exile twenty-five miles away from Palermo, where she could not influence the ministers nor her son Francis. Meanwhile Bentinck was virtually ruling Sicily himself in the interim before a constitution could be drawn up. It was decided that a parliament should be elected as a constituent assembly to draw up a constitution which would be on the lines of the English Constitution. As Sir Charles Webster commented in his study of Castlereagh's foreign policy, for the first time the English Constitution was to be written down.

The old Sicilian parliament was thus called in June 1812, and in one month drew up fifteen articles on which the constitution of 1812 was to be based. There was to be a parliament with the power to legislate and to impose taxes, subject to the king's veto; the king was to retain executive power, but his ministers were to be responsible to parliament – presumably as well as to the king. The parliament was to consist of two houses, having a remarkable resemblance in their forms and powers to the English parliament. One of the fifteen bases bore an equally remarkable resemblance to Magna Carta though, of course, in a modernized form. The abolition of feudalism was confirmed by articles 12 and 13, although the House of Peers, where hereditary barons and upper clergy sat by right of birth, was an essentially feudal element of the constitution, as it still is in the United Kingdom in 1983. The constitution which was drawn up on the basis of the fifteen articles allowed for a lower house of 155 deputies, elected by a minority of the male population who earned a certain income. The upper house consisted of 185 members, a third of them priests. If the king were to reacquire Naples, his eldest son was to become king of Sicily, since 'from today henceforth the said kingdom of Sicily is independent from Naples or from any other kingdom or province'. Maria Carolina was eventually thrown out by Bentinck in June 1813. She sailed to Constantinople and Odessa, and then journeyed to her home in Vienna where she died in September 1814. Her reign, which had started so favourably, had embraced a dramatic period of European history, and it would be ungenerous not to see in it an element of tragedy.

With the defeat of Napoleon at Leipzig in October 1813 the British government no longer felt the need to encourage parliamentary movements in Europe. Bentinck was told by Castlereagh that the constitutional experiment in Sicily was over. The experiment had always been accepted by Castlereagh in a cynical spirit. Bentinck left Sicily in July 1814. The Bourbons returned to Naples after the Hundred Days.[6] A decree of 8 December 1816 suppressed the Sicilian constitution of 1812 and declared Sicily reunited with Naples. But Sicily had been a constitutional state, if a very disturbed one, for four years. Those years were not to be forgotten.

On his restoration in 1815 Ferdinand took the new title of 'Ferdinand I' to mark a break with the past and the inauguration of what was to be called 'the Kingdom of the Two Sicilies'. His restoration after the defeat of Murat had been very much a product of Austrian policy. Metternich and Castlereagh were in close agreement on the nature of that restoration: there was to be no vindictive repression of people who had served under Murat, but equally there were to be no liberal institutions. Ferdinand's task was not an enviable one. Apart from the growing poverty of the country, there was now the added difficulty that Sicily had enjoyed *de facto* independence from the mainland for a decade, and was not likely to take kindly to being again under the rule of Naples.

The Neapolitan minister who was to dominate the first five years of the Restoration was Luigi de' Medici, who in many respects played the same enlightened role in Naples as that played by Cardinal Consalvi in the Papal States. Medici made no secret of his belief that the French Revolution, and the French period in Naples, had brought many advantages. Like Louis XVIII in France he decided not to antagonize the bureaucracy which had existed in the Napoleonic period, but rather to work with it and through it. Medici, after all, was a product of the Enlightenment, and hoped to remove the more archaic features of Neapolitan society, provided there was no talk of constitutions or civil rights. At the same time he could not betray the people who had worked with the Bourbons during the exile in Sicily. Rather he hoped for a general reconciliation. He intended to keep many of the institutions Naples had acquired in the French period, and to extend them to Sicily, which would thus become, in his words, 'a posthumous conquest of the French Revolution'. But the liberals – and especially the members of the secret societies – were not happy with Medici's policy either in Sicily or on the mainland. They were, however, optimistic. They believed that it would take very little pressure to persuade Ferdinand I to move towards a constitution. What they did not know was that a secret treaty existed between Naples and Austria, signed on 12 June 1815, by which Ferdinand promised to withhold a constitution. The Carbonari had briefly supported the restoration of the Bourbons in this vain hope that they would accept a political programme leading to a constitutional regime. The Prince of Canosa, who was made minister of the police early in 1816, believed that, since the Carbonari could not be reconciled, they must be quickly suppressed by the police. Canosa was even prepared to work with a reactionary sect, the *Calderari*, who were the equivalent of the Centurioni in the Papal States, and for whom Medici felt considerable distaste. Even the Austrian and Russian ambassadors in Naples believed that Canosa was a dangerous man, and gave their sympathies to Medici, with the result that Ferdinand I was persuaded to sack Canosa in June 1816.

Medici was now determined to disband both the Calderari and the Carbonari. On 8 August 1816 a law proclaimed that all secret societies were forbidden. It was much more effective against the Calderari than against the Carbonari, who were better organized and had, after all, a forward-looking policy. Medici was also determined to integrate Sicily into the Kingdom of Naples, and to eliminate from everyone's memory the British period in Sicily and the constitution of 1812. Since the autonomy, and the constitution, of Sicily under the British had been the work of Bentinck rather than of the government in London, Medici's task was not so difficult. The unification of the Two Sicilies was accompanied by mild reforms in some respects so far as the island of Sicily was concerned. The local administration introduced in Continental Naples in the Napoleonic period was not only retained, but was now extended to Sicily. In the same way a new judicial system and a modified version of the Code Napoléon, already operative in Continental Naples, marked a break with the past when they were extended to Sicily. But for Sicily none of this was a substitute for the constitution they had lost.

If Medici was enlightened in some of his attitudes and policies, he was reactionary in giving sharply increased authority to the Church. On 16 February 1818 he and Consalvi signed a Concordat after long negotiations. It restored ecclesiastical courts to deal with offences by priests, placed censorship in the hands of the bishops, and re-established many monasteries. Although it left property taken from the Church by the state in the days of the Enlightenment, of Joseph Bonaparte, and of Murat, in the hands of the state, it laid down that the king could not dispose of this property without the pope's permission. The king, however, retained the right to appoint bishops, but the pope had the right subsequently to approve their consecration. The bishops were then to be obliged to swear an oath of loyalty to the king – which they would certainly not be reluctant to do. To the Neapolitan professional classes the most objectionable part of the Concordat was that which gave the Church the power to suppress any books or journals – a stranglehold on freedom of thought in the kingdom.

The restored Kingdom of Naples faced a grave financial situation. The Austrians imposed a heavy indemnity on Naples for her defeat in the brief war of 1815. In other words, the restored Bourbon government had to pay for the failure of Murat's gamble, and understandably felt that this was a little hard on them. Another sum – not much less considerable – had to be found to keep the Austrian army of occupation supplied. Smaller sums in bribes had to be paid by the Bourbons for the diplomatic support they had received from Talleyrand and Metternich at the Congress of Vienna. The final outrage from the point of view of Ferdinand I was that he was obliged by Czar Alexander I to pay a large sum to Eugene de Beauharnais in compensation for his loss of the viceregency of the Kingdom of Italy. To face these extraordinary expenses Medici inherited a sound financial condition from Murat's administration. Even so, he felt it necessary to follow a policy of retrenchment. Projects of public works, drainage, and improving the harbours were halted, and there were severe cuts in expenditure on education. In so doing Medici could avoid increasing taxes or customs dues, but without doubt halted the material progress which had been a characteristic of the French period. His halting of material progress would have mattered less if he had granted some kind of constitution. This failure the liberals could not forgive him. They had worked towards the restoration of the Bourbons precisely because they believed that the French system had been too centralized and had denied individual liberties. But in a sense Medici was still too French.

In Sicily the years between 1815 and 1820 produced many grievances: the centralizing administrative reforms had been applied by the government in Naples in an insensitive manner which had taken no account of local feeling and tradition in Sicily; not only had the island been gravely affected by the collapse of prices for its agricultural products since 1815, but Palermo had lost its position as a free port. The revolutionaly movement in Sicily in these years was based essentially on Palermo, which had been given a favoured position during the British occupation. Messina and the other cities in the east of the island had always been jealous of Palermo's predominance and were, if anything, more prepared to accept that of Naples. The particularism of Italian cities in the nineteenth century – *campanilismo*, as it is sometimes called – is often seen by English-speaking histories as an indication that Italy was not yet ready for unity. But the reverse is true. Precisely because Palermo was reluctant to be ruled from Naples, and Messina was reluctant to be ruled from Palermo, the citizens of the three places could the more readily become part of a united Italy, where the ancient rivalries would assume a purely cultural rather than a political significance.

The initial success of the Spanish revolution of January 1820 encouraged liberals in Naples to consider action. The outbreak started on 1 July, and was the work of a mere thirty Carbonari led initially by a priest, Luigi Minichini. They were supported, however, by over a hundred non-commissioned officers and soldiers of the cavalry. They advanced from a little place called Nola to the town of Avellino, and were joined by other members of the secret societies, but not by any mass following. The officers in command of the royal forces in Avellino were men who had served Murat, and although they were not members of the Carbonari, their attitude to the rising was somewhat ambivalent. Their hesitant reactions enabled the leaders of the rising to declare that the officers were in agreement with them, which compromised the officers and perhaps encouraged them to believe that such was indeed the case. Meanwhile the supreme commander of the Neapolitan forces, the Austrian General Nugent, ordered three separate columns to advance on Avellino. They were, however, prevented from reaching Avellino by the revolutionary forces, and the movement began to become a general uprising, as it became apparent that the population was generally sympathetic. The troops and some of the officers who were supposed to be suppressing the revolution had been thoroughly imbued with Carbonari ideas, and were less than half-hearted in obeying Nugent's orders. What clinched the success of the revolution, however, was the action of a divisional commander, Guglielmo Pepe, who was to become one of the heroes of the Risorgimento, both in 1820 and 1848. An Englishman, Thomas Trollope, knew Pepe, and gave a rather devastating impression of him as a person: 'He was a remarkably handsome man, but not a brilliant or amusing companion. . . . He had a kind of simple, dignified, placid manner of enunciating the most astounding platitudes, and replying to the laughter they sometimes produced by a calm., gentle smile which showed how impossible it was for his gentle soul to imagine that his hearers were otherwise than

136

delighted with his wit and wisdom.'[7] But whatever impression Pepe might have made on English society, he played a controlling role in the revolution of 1820 in Naples. On 5 July he led two regiments of cavalry and one of infantry in support of the insurrection, and acquired command of all of the revolutionary forces. On 6 July Ferdinand I published an edict promising a constitution within eight days. But the period of eight days seemed suspiciously short for the drawing up of a constitution, and the revolutionaries rightly believed that they could not trust the king to grant an adequate constitution off his own bat in so brief a period. The Carbonari now began to demand the Spanish Constitution of 1812, which granted universal male suffrage, direct elections and a single-chamber legislature. The government therefore published on 7 July a decree promising the 1812 constitution, subject to certain modifications which Neapolitan circumstances would demand, and which would be decided by a 'constitutionally convoked' assembly. The revolutionary forces then entered Naples without resistance. Pepe was received by the king. The revolution seemed to have succeeded.

A new government was appointed composed of men who had served under Murat. Pepe was placed in command of the army. The king swore an oath to defend the constitution. No one had been killed or even wounded in this revolution, and yet no mass movement developed to defend it when Metternich decided to suppress it, nor had the king the slightest intention of keeping his oath. The Carbonari, no longer a secret society, increased their numbers enormously, and wild rumours spread that they planned to give the land to the peasants and dissolve or radically reform the Church. The rumours were in sharp contrast to the mild measures taken by the government. Parliament, elected according to the new constitution, met on 1 October, when the revolutionary government had already been in existence for three months.

Meanwhile the Sicilian question had reached a crisis. The Sicilians had never adjusted happily to their loss of home rule in 1816. The economy had deteriorated sharply since the end of the British occupation, mainly because of the disastrous fall in agricultural prices coupled to the conservative customs policy. A Sicilian revolutionary movement was growing, not yet linked to any Italian nationalist sentiment, but based to a great extent on the seventy-two guilds, or *maestranze*, which had existed for centuries. When news of the July rising in Continental Naples reached Palermo, riots broke out in the streets. Demands were made for the 'Constitution of 1812', by which some meant the radical Spanish constitution of 1812, some the English-type Sicilian constitution of that year, and some, no doubt, were not too clear of the distinctions between them. Naselli, the lieutenant-general of the island, hastily announced that the Spanish constitution would be adopted and a governing body formed of men from the English period. The crowd, however, was now quite out of control; offices of the government were burnt and prisoners were released. By 17 July the revolutionaries, led by the *maestranze*, had established themselves in power, and General Naselli left by boat for Naples.

The split between the revolutionaries in Sicily was now complete. Two of the barons who had held office in Bentinck's constitutional government of

1812 were killed and then beheaded by the *maestranze*. One of them, the Prince of Aci, had been thought by Bemtinck to be a somewhat erratic lightweight, but by most people he had been considered the most radical member of the government of 1812. The people now in control in Palermo were a strange mixture of political extremists and medievalists — terrorists from a medieval society. There has been much discussion as to whether the term 'Jacobin', applied to the Neapolitan revolutionaries of 1799, is a misnomer. At least it can be said that there is a more genuinely 'Jacobin' character in the Sicilian revolutionaries of 1820. But in the original Jacobin revolution in Paris from 1792–4 there had been close contact between the radical middle class and the *sansculottes*. This, as Antonio Gramsci so vividly explained, was lacking throughout the entire Risorgimento, and in Sicily in 1820 no less than in other places and at other times. The *maestranze* in Sicily in July 1820 did not trust the bourgeoisie, but preferred to accept a provisional government headed at first by a cardinal — no less — and then by a prince — the Prince of Villafranca. The group of seventy-two *maestranze*, however, were to have a veto on any act of this provisional government. A weakness of the revolutionary movement was that it was confined to Palermo: in most other parts of the island there was a reluctance to break completely with Naples. A small civil war was even fought between the forces of Palermo and those in other Sicilian cities. The Carbonari in Naples had no sympathy with the revolutionaries of Palermo, who seemed to them to be merely confusing the real issues of the revolution. The nobility and middle classes in Palermo kept up the pretence of forming part of a united revolutionary movement, but were in reality alarmed at the predominance of the *maestraze* and at the extent to which the crowds in the streets had armed themselves. The upper classes therefore secured the formation of a civic guard, which they hoped would be able to protect property and ultimately wrest control from the urban workers. Meanwhile a Neapolitan army was mopping up resistance of armed groups in the interior of the island, and moving uncomfortably close to Palermo. The revolutionary ruling group in Palermo therefore decided again to enter into negotiations with the Neapolitan government. Their decision led to a direct class struggle in Palermo. An armed crowd attacked and defeated the civic guard, and prepared to resist the Neapolitan army. The attack on Palermo inevitably came, on 26 September, but was savagely resisted. Neither side could impose its will on the other, with the result that again negotiations were started and a temporary armistice reached.

In Naples the Carbonari had been the spearhead of the revolutionary movement, but they reaped few gains from its success. They could not provide men who were responsible enought to take office after the revolution had succeeded, and their strength lay in the provinces rather than in Naples itself. The revolutionary initiative in Naples was therefore grabbed from the hands of the Carbonari by more cautious men, who looked for a restoration of something like the régime of Murat, and who were convinced monarchists. In this sense the revolution of 1820 in Naples anticipated the July Revolution of 1830 in Paris: the insurrection had been the work of radicals and republicans, but the fruits of victory were enjoyed by politically shrewd monarchists, though in Naples they were perhaps less shrewd than they were to be in Paris, and were not to enjoy success for long.

The newly elected parliament met in Naples on 1 October, with the Sicilian question still hanging fire. The deputies were mostly middle-class, professional people, but with a few noblemen and priests. They decided to reinforce the army in Sicily and to undermine the revolutionary movement in Palermo by working closely with the Carbonari in Messina, where Palermo was so heartily disliked. But in broad terms their policy towards Sicily was to be one of repression, and they were even prepared to deplete their forces on the Continent – where they were soon to face an Austrian attack – by sending troops to Sicily.

Metternich saw the success of the moderate revolutionaries in Naples as a threat to the whole Austrian position in Italy. The international aspects of the 1820 revolution will be dealt with in greater detail in a later chapter.[8] Suffice it to say here that Metternich decided to use the Congress System – the international arrangement by which the Great Powers had agreed to meet from time to time to discuss the political situation in Europe, especially when revolution seemed to threaten a change in the *status quo* – to secure the consent of the other Powers for Austrian intervention in Naples. He therefore arranged for a Congress of the Powers to meet in Troppau in October, resulting in the declaration by the rulers of Austria, Prussia and Russia of what became known as the Troppau Doctrine, which stated that international intervention would have to be conducted in the event of illegal institutions being introduced in a European state. At Troppau no arrangements had been made specifically to deal immediately with the Neapolitan situation. Ferdinand however had secretly conveyed to Metternich his desire to escape from Naples, and the decision was therefore made to hold another Congress, which Ferdinand would be invited to attend. The congress was held at Laibach in January 1821. It seemed to the government in Naples that to refuse the king the right to accept the invitation of the Powers would be tantamount to a declaration of war against them. The king promised to preserve the constitution, and not to accept any modifications of it without the consent of parliament. Yet no sooner had Ferdinand escaped from Naples than he shamelessly declared that he had been constrained by force to grant the constitution, and he immediately asked for Austrian intervention. Metternich had not been prepared for quite such a precipitate request, since he knew that some of the other Great Powers were by no means happy with the idea, but he decided that his best policy was to comply with such an explicit request from a friendly government.

The ministry in Naples was morally bound to resist Austrian intervention, although its military position was obviously a hopeless one. An army under Guglielmo Pepe put up a brave and spirited resistance, but could not prevent the Austrians from entering Naples on 23 March 1821.

In the repression which followed Ferdinand I made no distinction between those moderates who had wanted a constitution but had been prepared to remain loyal to the dynasty, and the genuine revolutionaries. He reappointed as minister of police the savagely reactionary Prince of Canosa, who conducted a terrible policy of retribution. He was particularly brutal towards the Carbonari, several of whom were executed publicly. Even Metternich protested and secured the dismissal of Canosa. But arrests, executions, and long terms of imprisonment continued for several years, as did conspiracies and unsuccessful risings.

At this point it will be perhaps worth considering an intelligent, enlightened and significant Neapolitan, whose life bridged the years 1790–1848. Luigi Settembrini is best remembered for his pamphlet of 1847, entitled 'A protest of the people of the kingdom of the two Sicilies', but his autobiography was a *tour de force* which gave a vivid picture of life in prison for a political offender, and which should certainly have attracted as much recognition as Silvio Pellico's *Le Mie Prigioni*. Pellico's book, published in 1832, was pious, innocent; Settembrini's was honest, extrovert, generous. Inexplicably, it has hardly been noticed by historians. Luigi Settembrini was a typical nineteenth-century revolutionary. The son of a lawyer, and the grandson of two lawyers, Luigi was seven when the revolution of 1820 struck Naples. On their way to church Luigi and his father were offered a tricolour cockade. His father refused it, but Luigi took it and so, as he says, 'at the age of seven I was a Carbonaro'. But Luigi's father had joined the national guard during the revolution of 1799, and during the reactionary persecutions by the *lazzaroni* had seen many naked corpses – 'very white', because they were the corpses of 'gentlemen'. Luigi himself was sent to Naples to study law at the age of sixteen in 1828. An impression of his generation of students at Naples comes from a passage in his *Ricordanze*, written when he was sixty-two: 'the young, except for a very few, are all good, with open hearts; they have every beautiful and generous action; they have an instinct for good, and I found them all liberals'. But as they grew older the young were corrupted by the world of officialdom. Only a very few retained their youthful purity of enthusiasim. But they were enough to keep a liberal movement alive in the dark days of the 1820s and 1830s. Settembrini was typical of a generation of revolutionaries who had been attracted to the liberal movement through their familiarity with the literature of Romanticism – in particular, the writings of Alfieri and Foscolo.

A small attempt at revolution in the province of Salerno in 1828, recorded by Settembrini, has largely escaped the attention of modern historians, and never received the canonization given to the Bandiera brothers some years later. Three brothers, the Capozzoli, who lived in the village of Bosco in the province of Salerno, and who were believed to be members of the Carbonari, started an agitation for a constitution. A royal army of several hundred men moved in and destroyed the village of Bosco with artillery. Fortunately the inhabitants had already fled. A military court condemned twenty-two people to death, and some sixty to prison. Another seven people in Naples itself were condemned to death as accomplices, and eighty imprisoned. A priest, De Luca, who was eighty years old, was beheaded.

Ferdinand I died in 1825. His son, Francis I, continued the Bourbon tyranny for five years. He had a court favourite, Michelangelo Viglia, who took bribes on a considerable scale from the relatives of people condemned to death, and from men who wanted civil, ecclesiastical or military posts. Camillo Caropreso gave him a great sum, and was made minister of finance. Francis I died in Spain in 1830. Throughout his reign, and into the reign of his successor, Ferdinand II, the risings continued. Many death sentences were passed and some, though not all were carried out.

Ferdinand II had seemed, at first, to promise better things. He granted an amnesty, which released many political prisoners, and allowed many political exiles to return. Some army officers who had been cashiered in 1821 were given back their commissions. But there was a mean streak in the character of Ferdinand II. He had a sharp distrust of other people, and a reluctance to spend money on anything but the Church and the army. The ministers he appointed to the central government were the most reactionary he could find. He gave Sicily the semblance of autonomy by sending them a viceroy in the person of his brother Leopold, Count of Siracuse. The minister of police, Nicola Intonti, who had shown no liberal sentiments in the past, decided to cash in on what appeared to be a new spirit in the monarchy, and recommended the introduction of some mild constitutional measures. Ferdinand's response was to have Intonti arrested and exiled. Intonti's successor, Francesco Delcarretto, imposed a yet more brutal prison régime than the previous one. But at the end of 1832 Maria Cristina of Savoy was married to Ferdinand II, and her influence mitigated the severity of the criminal code. She persuaded the king to call a halt to the executions, and during her short life (she was queen from 1832 until her death in 1836) no capital sentence was carried out. Ferdinand himself was an ignorant man, who never read a book, could not spell, and despised intellectuals. One of his main pleasures consisted in playing childish pranks on his courtiers.

Delcarretto, the minister of police, was allowed immense powers, quite beyond his office. A complete sceptic politically, he made contacts with the Carbonari, partly to secure spies, and partly to safeguard himself against a successful revolution. However, rather surpisingly, he formed a civic guard, but one composed only of people from the upper classes. They were given a fine green uniform but had to hand in their rifles after each exercise.

From the autumn of 1836 an appalling epidemic of cholera raged in the kingdom for a year. In the island of Sicily 65,256 people died – a tenth of the population. The toll was less terrible on the mainland, but in the area of Naples some 14,000 people died. The epidemic was accompanied by numerous risings, all unsuccessful, inspired by the belief that the government, or government agents, for a variety of different reasons, had deliberately spread the epidemic.

By turning again to the evidence from Settembrini, an impression of the prison life which so many Neapolitans had to endure in the reign of Ferdinand II can be obtained. In 1841 there were about 1,500 people in the terrible prison of the Vicaria in Naples. The cells were dark, damp and had a permanently nauseating smell. In the winter the prisoners were bitterly cold; in the summer they felt they were in an oven. Their sleep was disturbed by the need to drive away the rats. There was a subtle class distinction, in that one part of the prison was called 'the prison of the noblemen', although it was not a particularly privileged place. It contained

about four hundred men tormented by the stench, by the darkness, by the insects, never comforted by sunshine or clean air . . . those who were yet to be tried mixed with those who had already been sentenced, political offenders mixed with murderers, the student who had been late in submitting his documents alongside the man who had cut his wife into small pieces. . .[9]

By 1848 the contrast between the Kingdom of the Two Sicilies and the rest of Italy was acute. In Piedmont and Tuscany there was much open political debate, and even in the Austrian provinces civil, criminal and administrative justice was conducted according to known rules. In the Papal States Pius IX had altered the whole political climate. Only in the Kingdom of Naples did an arbitrary and brutal tyranny offer no hope for the future, and it was therefore not surprising that the Kingdom formed the setting for the very first European revolution of 1848. On 9 January in Palermo a manifesto was circulated, calling the people to arms: 'Dawn on 12 January 1848 will mark the glorious epoch of universal regeneration.' But property, the manifesto declared, will be respected. A revolutionary of 1820, Francesco Bagnasco, had written the manifesto and had it printed. Inevitably the authorities obtained copies, but could hardly believe that a genuine revolution would be announced three days in advance. Even so, eleven suspects were arrested on 10 January. The manifesto had promised that anyone who came into the main *piazza* on the morning of 12 January would be provided with arms, but no one had taken steps to secure arms on the scale which would be needed.

On 12 January the streets of Palermo were more crowded than usual, though whether with people who genuinely wanted to take part in a revolution, or with curious sightseers, there is, of course, no way of knowing. There was no organized leadership, but arms began to be circulated, and clashes with the troops and police began to occur. A few deaths resulted from the disturbances of 12 January, and in the poorest quarter – the Fieravecchia – barricades began to go up. Finally a leader emerged in the person of Giuseppe La Masa, who formed an organizing committee in Fieravecchia. By 13 January peasants from the countryside had joined the rising. In these first days the number who were prepared to fight was very small – though it included some women. Their arms were pathetic – a few shotguns, some pistols, and knives. Against them was a royal army of 5,000 or 6,000 men, with artillery and cavalry, but with the disadvantages of a sullen and hostile population, and the tortuous network of medieval streets which made up Palermo. The Neapolitan army reacted by shelling the city from the fortress of Castellammare. To this point it had been an essentially popular rising, with the potential bourgeois leaders waiting on events. Another 5,000 royal troops arrived at Palermo by sea on 15 January, but by this time the revolutionaries were in control of the city. Another leader of the Sicilian revolution was emerging – Rosalino Pilo, a Sicilian nobleman who was to play a decisive and tragic role in 1860.[10] He, La

Masa and the rest of the revolutionary committee were demanding the restoration of the 1812 Constitution. The appeal to a constitution which had already been in operation without doubt attracted members of the upper class to the revolution, but even without such an appeal Sicilian opposition to the Bourbons was probably solid. On 18 January Ferdinand II offered a degree of institutional autonomy to Sicily but his offer was rejected. The royal troops left Palermo on 27 January and much of the rest of the island was fairly easily captured by the Sicilians, so that already by the middle of February the royal troops held out only in Syracuse and the fortress of Messina. Syracuse was to fall to the revolutionaries in April, but the fortress of Messina held out.

The revolution of 1848 in Sicily brought social upheaval of a complex kind. Members of the upper classes – noblemen and bourgeoisie – formed revolutionary committees to exercise government in the towns, but a lower stratum also became militant. Peasants in the countryside marched on the small town and village centres to destroy the local records, and in particular those relating to payments of the tax which bore most heavily upon them – the *macinato*, or tax on the grinding of corn. Prisons were opened and thousands of inmates were released. On 28 January the revolutionary provisional government in Palermo decided to form a national guard with the conservative objective of controlling the masses. A banker, Baron Pietro, was placed in command. The revolutionary government controlling Palermo was a committee under the chairmanship of Ruggero Settimo, an elderly retired naval officer, who had been minister of war in the constitutional government of Bentinck's time, and vice-president of the revolutionary government of 1820. On 2 February Settimo's government announced that it had taken over the government of the whole of Sicily until the election of a parliament which would 'adapt the Constitution of 1812 to the present'.

Meanwhile in Naples news of the revolution of 12 January in Palermo had arrived surprisingly quickly considering the communications available. The feeling against the Bourbons in Naples was less solid. There was the traditional middle-class group in opposition, and many among the urban workers had developed liberal ideas, but the great mass of paupers still looked affectionately to the Bourbons for their livelihood. In the provinces of Continental Naples, however, there was the same spirit of revolt that there had been in 1820. In particular the province of Salerno, not so far south of Naples, and suffering from famine, seemed a likely spot from which revolution might spread. On 17 January, in this area, the secret societies started a rising. Archives in the town halls were burnt and a few Bourbon officials were executed for past acts of repression. The rising in the province of Salerno added to the fears of Ferdinand II, who allowed an independent press to come into being. On 20 January an amnesty was granted to political offenders awaiting trial – who were not negligible in number – and on 23 January it was announced that all political offenders were to be released from prison but detained on an unspecified island for the time being. Ferdinand's concessions were treated by the revolutionaries with the contempt they deserved. Carlo Poerio and others, in Naples herself, prepared a petition demanding the constitution of 1820, mod-

143

ified by the addition of a second chamber. Poerio had been imprisoned several times since 1837, and it was he who was to be visited in prison by Gladstone in 1851, before Gladstone's publication of the famous *Two Letters to the Earl of Aberdeen*, which exposed the full horrors of Neapolitan prisons. On 27 January 1848 a massive demonstration in the streets of Naples demanded a constitution. The king decided to yield, accepted the resignation of his existing ministers, whose leader was the Marquis of Pietracatella, and appointed in their places a more liberal ministry under Nicola Maresca, the Duke of Serracapriola. On 29 January the new government published a decree promising a constitution with a chamber of peers and a chamber of deputies, but in other respects strongly monarchical. There were, however, to be a national guard and a free press. The announcement of a constitution was greeted by great displays of public enthusiasm in Continental Naples, most of them, though not all, sympathetic to the king. In Sicily the attitude was very different: in Palermo the revolutionary government declared that only a parliament elected under the Constitution of 1812 could modify that constitution; in other words, Sicilian resistance would continue. In Naples Serracapriola, the new prime minister, was thus placed in a difficult position, which he decided to handle by turning the Neapolitan question into an international one – by asking the British minister and the French *chargé d'affaires* to mediate between his government and the revolutionary one in Sicily. The latter were also prepared for British intervention, so that when Lord Minto arrived in Naples shortly afterwards, his position seemed to be a strong one. But the British attempt at mediation was to fail, after long negotiations.

The details of the promised constitution were published on 11 February 1848, and were seen closely to resemble the very conservative constitution of the July Monarchy in France – a constitution which was about to be thrown overboard by revolution in Paris. The king was to retain a real veto of all laws, and a law which he did not approve could not be discussed again during the same session of parliament. He was to nominate all members of the upper chamber, and – more important – a consultative council of state. He was to be commander of the armed forces but, while he could change the composition of the national guard, he could not dissolve it altogether. The national guard, whose junior officers were to be elected, was clearly intended to represent the revolution, but to represent its conservative features as well as its novel ones. No right of association nor public meetings were granted, and not only was the Catholic religion to remain the established one, but no other religion was to be practised. The lower chamber was to be directly elected – this at least was an advance on the constitution of 1820 – but the vote was to be limited according to an income to be decided later.

Throughout February negotiations over Sicily continued, with mediation in the hands of Lord Minto, the French not having been invited to take part by the Sicilians. The English were wrongly suspected of harbouring the design of annexing Sicily, and were certainly not indifferent to Sicily's fate. No agreement, however, was reached, and on 1 March Serracapriola's government resigned, though Serracapriola himself returned to the premiership a few days later with a different group of ministers, including Carlo Poerio as minister of education. Minto and the new government drew up provisions for Sicily, according to which Ferdinand II agreed to legalize the parliament which the Sicilians had decided to elect, provided they adapted their Constitution of 1812 to the changed circumstances, and remained subjects of the king. Ruggero Settimo was appointed as lieutenant or viceroy in the island, and Sicily was to have her own foreign ministry under a Sicilian. Further details were to be settled by the parliaments of Naples and Sicily, and in the event of disagreement the newly elected parliaments in Turin and Florence were to be asked to mediate or, failing them, Pius IX. Minto went personally to Palermo with the terms, but was simply informed that they were unacceptable. He finally succeeded in extracting counter-proposals, the main point of which was that the royal Neapolitan troops should be withdrawn from the island. Naples refused to accept the counter-proposals, and a decree was now published declaring that the measures passed in Palermo were null and void. Popular pressure in Naples, however obliged the government to expel the Jesuits before the end of March and, with the revolution in Milan and the war in the north, to break off diplomatic relations with Austria on 20 April. Meanwhile Neapolitan volunteers to fight against Austria were assembling. On 3 April a moderate government under Carlo Troya had been formed, and this government succeeded in persuading the king to accept a modification of the constitution by which elections were soon to be held with a slightly less limiting franchise. The king was still to nominate the senators, but now from a list presented to him by electoral colleges, and the Italian tricolour was to be the flag of the kingdom.

The Sicilian revolution was one step ahead. Already on 25 March a parliament had met, elected by all literate male adults – in effect, a small minority of the population but at least not limited by income. The Sicilian parliament decided that they should elect a president, who would then nominate six ministers to form with him a provisional government. As the result of this decision Ruggero Settimo was elected president. Neither Settimo nor the ministers he appointed were particularly radical figures. Both the Neapolitan and Sicilian governments decided to take part in the proposed Italian league, and Settimo's government decided to embark a hundred volunteers – not a vast force – under the command of Giuseppe La Masa, for Leghorn, to fight in the war in the north. On 13 April it declared that Ferdinand II was no longer King of Sicily, that the Bourbons would never again occupy the Sicilian throne, and that another Italian prince would ultimately be invited to become king. Republicanism, then, was not regarded as an alternative to the Bourbons. Only Giuseppe La Farina, still in 1848 a republican, later to be devoted to Cavour and the Piedmontese monarchy, spoke in opposition to the motion concerning an Italian prince. He was warmly applauded, but the new government was afraid, in particular, that if they did not opt for a monarchy they would antagonize Britain, who was believed to be their only friend among the Great Powers. Ferdinand had declared the Sicilian decree of 13 April illegal and 'of no value', but withdrew his forces from Sicily apart from a garrison in the citadel of Messina. Spasmodic artillery exchanges took place between the royal force in Messina and Sicilian troops.

In Naples it was decided to take part in the war against Austria and to send an expeditionary force under the command of Guglielmo Pepe, but not until the beginning of May did the expedition set off. Throughout April the peasant movement of unrest, incensed by the injustice of the usurpation of common land, spread throughout Continental Naples. The peasants stopped paying taxes and sometimes forcibly occupied land. Some radical middle-class leaders of this movement had picked up some of the socialist ideas which were now current in France. The word 'communist' had been used previously to mean a person with a right to the use of land held in common. Now that it was acquiring the modern ideological meaning, it was beginning to strike terror into the hearts of the richer classes. The so-called 'moderates' who had gained power by the revolution showed no inclination to join forces with the peasant rising, but were, if anything, less sympathetic to the peasants' needs than the absolutist Bourbon government had been. The *lazzari* or lumpen-proletariat in Naples lived on charity from the Church or the court, and were therefore supporters of Bourbon absolutism, and were disappointed that the moderate revolutionaries had done nothing for them. A few radical working-class leaders agitated for 'the right to work', which they were clearly not going to be granted. Deputies elected in April according to the constitution were now hoping to broaden it, and perhaps change the nature of the upper house, if not abolish it altogether. The king however insisted that they should swear an oath to the constitution that he had granted: in other words, that the newly elected lower house should not turn itself into a constituent assembly. The chief minister, Troya, and his colleagues decided at this point to resign as a protest against the role the king was playing. The population of Naples was swollen by crowds from the provinces, some of whom had come to the capital with their deputies for the opening of parliament, and many to sign up for the war. Hearing ugly if unsubstantiated rumours that the king was preparing a *coup d'état* against parliament, the crowds called for an insurrection, and the barricades began to go up. Early on the morning of 15 May royal troops – mostly Swiss mercenaries – took up strategic positions in the city. Bitter fighting soon broke out and lasted for some hours. A few hundred of the national guard fought on the side of the popular insurrection, while the *lazzari* helped the royal troops. About one hundred and fifty people were killed – twice as many among the insurgents, who were vastly outnumbered, as among the troops, who used artillery. The assembly had remained sitting, somewhat ineffectively, throughout 15 May, but in the evening was dissolved by royal troops. On 16 May the king called a new government of men appreciably to the right, and on the 17th both the lower house and the national guard were declared dissolved, and on the 18th Pepe's army in the north was recalled. The king and his new government were thus acting with great speed, but to dismiss Ferdinand's action as simply a *coup d'état* against the constitution would be to over-simplify. The new ministry of 16 May, though comparatively conservative, was not opposed to a constitution of some kind, and a new

146

parliament was in the event elected in July and sat until the following March. It was not, however, an effective body, so far as the limiting of the king's authority was concerned. The most likely explanation of the king's policy in the light of Neapolitan history of the 1850s is that he was hoping to be able to destroy the constitution – the events of 15 May gave him the opportunity, eventually, to do so – but he felt obliged to maintain the facade of a constitution until the revolutions of 1848 had failed elsewhere. His break with the radicals and even with the liberal moderates was now complete; the former henceforth looked to the formation of a republic – and preferably an Italian republic; the latter placed their faith in Piedmont, and many of them escaped to Turin, where they were to play a big part in the politics of the 1850s. In Calabria the radicals stirred up a popular rising which survived for two months of guerrilla fighting, but by the middle of July the royal troops were in control. That the peasants, led by a few radicals, were far more determined to resist reaction than the urban middle class is a strong point in defence of Gramsci's thesis of the Risorgimento as an agrarian revolution *manqué*. Among the few radical members of the middle-class revolutionaries who tried to give the peasants leadership, one or two, like Benedetto Musolino (who should not be confused with a much smaller and more miserable figure – Benito Mussolini) were courageous and popular. Other radicals were pathetically ineffective.

In Sicily the class struggle was if anything more clear-cut. The peasants and urban workers found leaders with socialist ideas and, in particular, a woman, Teresa Testa di Lana. But the upper classes became more united to face this threat and had the national guard to defend them. By September the Bourbon government in Naples felt strong enough to move against Sicily. An army of some twenty thousand was sent to take Messina, which underwent a savage bombardment for three days. The Sicilians, with strong civilian support but with an army of only some six thousand, resisted courageously, but could not prevent the Neapolitans from taking the city. To stop further bloodshed the commanders of the French and British Mediterranean fleets persuaded both sides to accept a truce, followed by an armistice on 8 October. The armistice, however, did not lead to permanent peace. In the spring of 1849 fighting again broke out in Sicily, and it was not until May of 1849 that the Sicilians were finally defeated and had to abandon hopes of autonomy. In their resistance to tyranny the Sicilians were thus roughly on a par with the Venetians and the Hungarians.

On 13 March 1849 Ferdinand II decreed the end of parliament but did not yet dare to proclaim the abrogation of the constitution. He had made the Prince of Cariati chief minister after his coup of 15 May 1848, and Cariati's government remained in force until 6 August 1849. The king then felt safe enough to dispense with Cariati's ministry, which had yet a few ministers sympathetic to the constitution, and to appoint Giustino Fortunato as chief minister and minister of foreign affairs. Fortunato had been a republican in 1799, and had managed to retain minor public offices during both the Napoleonic and Restoration periods. An unscrupulous opportunist, he was by 1849 bitterly opposed to a constitution. Ferdinand II was to sack him in

January 1852, and already in 1849 was treating his ministers with scant respect. He had decided to rule the kingdom personally and arbitrarily and in so doing had helped to seal its fate. A police state was created and a bitter repression was enforced. Endless trials and prison sentences followed. Silvio Spaventa, Luigi Settembrini and Carlo Poerio were sentenced to imprisonment, as were hundreds of others. If the bloodshed and horrors which accompanied the restoration after the revolution of 1799 were in 1849 avoided, it is yet true that the educated class, who had wanted reasonable change, were imprisoned or exiled. But it was too late to stem the tide of nineteenth-century thought. Revolutionary groups still met secretly. On the other hand the trauma Ferdinand II had experienced in 1848 had been too great for him even to consider changes, even when his cautious ministers recommended them. Nor did his ministers want change in economic policy: virtually nothing was to be spent on public works or education; it was for the Church to provide the social services which were already being provided, to some extent, by the state, in other countries. Of state expenditure in 1854 nearly a half was devoted to the army, roughly the same as that devoted to education. Even in 1858, when efforts had been made to improve the public image of the régime, five times as much was being spent on the army as on public works. There is a sad irony in these statistics, when the poor showing of the army against Garibaldi in 1860 is remembered.

In 1849 Ferdinand II had given the commanding officer of his troops, General Filangieri, full powers in Sicily. He occupied Palermo in May and tried to conciliate as many of the upper class as he could. There had been a general exodus of revolutionary leaders in April, and this saved Filangieri the embarrassment of conducting savage reprisals. In the event he felt safe in issuing an amnesty to all of the revolutionaries except a few specified leaders – some forty of them – who had all made their get-away. Filangieri would have been inclined to give the Sicilians a degree of administrative independence, but Ferdinand II was now determined to put them under a police state. In the autumn of 1849 decrees were published appointing a Sicilian, Giovanni Cassisi, minister of Sicilian affairs, though his office was to be in Naples, but the internal affairs – administrative, judicial, ecclesiastical, etc. – though under the authority of Naples, were to be separate for Sicily. A quarter of the central expenses of the Kingdom was to be borne by Sicily, though administered, of course, in Naples. Authority in Sicily itself was to be vested in a 'lieutenant general' who was to be supported by advisory councils but who was to be appointed by the king and totally under his authority.

The economy of the Kingdom of Naples was the most primitive in Italy, in the the sense that much of the land was in the hands of a few absentee landlords, who still retained considerable feudal privileges – mostly in the shape of taxes, in spite of all the talk of 'abolishing feudalism' in the eighteenth century. There is an irony in the fact that the school of economics in the University of Naples was the most advanced in Europe, but the economy of the kingdom was among the most retrograde. Other symptoms of feudalism were the large size of the royal army and the great numbers of priests, monks and nuns – about

82,000 in 1792, or one in sixty-four of the whole population.[11] The Church in the Kingdom had an enormous income, much of it from land, but much of it also from voluntary contributions. Three quarters of the land in the kingdom was in the hands of either the nobility or the Church. Much of this land was uncultivated, because prices of farm products were so low. Yet the pasturing of sheep, far from producing a great woollen industry, gave very small returns. Internal customs and bad communications prevented the movement of agricultural goods, so that markets remained purely local.

The middle class which emerged in the Kingdom of Naples was not a commercial nor industrial one, but a professional one, and more specifically a huge horde of lawyers, fastening like vultures on to the legal confusion which the kingdom had inherited from its various régimes. It was not difficult to become a lawyer in the Kingdom of Naples: no one demanded high academic qualifications. In the city of Naples alone there were 3,600 lawyers in 1792. The more successful of them earned very good salaries.[12]

A lower stratum of the middle class were the artisans, protected by guilds which had existed since the Middle Ages, protected, that is, from intrusion by workers outside the guilds, and against any form of trade unionism which might encourage the poorest workers to co-operate. But just as the feudal regulations protected the richer artisans from the poorer workers, so did they prevent the richer artisans from becoming modern capitalists by the system of internal customs and taxes.

But if these conditions had prevailed in the 1790s, with the arrival of the French new principles were adopted – the 'abolition of feudalism', equality of all before the law, the removal of much clerical power and influence, an attempt to expand education; these were principles which had repercussions on the economy. The laws passed under Joseph Bonaparte in 1806 'abolishing feudalism' and subsequent laws in the French period defined the precise rights of the barons. Those lands which they had inherited from remote ages, or from the pragmatic law of 1536, were recognized as theirs, but common lands subsequently usurped were to be taken back by the state. In Sicily the Constitution of 1812 also declared feudalism abolished, but the terms of the constitution did nothing to further the principle. On the contrary they did more to help than to harm the 'feudal' barons in economic terms.

The restored Bourbon government after 1815 faced difficulties in its economic policy which were by no means its own fault. It could not be blamed for the catastrophic fall in agricultural prices which followed the end of the Napoleonic wars. When the Bourbons attempted to modernize and bureaucratize the state and the economy, they found that their attempts conflicted with the private interests of Neapolitan entrepreneurs. As we have seen, the number of entrepreneurs in Naples was very limited – certainly in comparison with economically more advanced countries. In 1844 only three hundred people – 0.07 per cent of the population, or 2 per cent of property owners – were merchants or businessmen, while 25 per cent of the property owners were lawyers or doctors. Furthermore this limited circle of entrepreneurs remained remarkably closed; very few new names appeared among them over the years after 1815. In other words the commercial life of Naples was dominated by a restricted and unchanging elite, who did not depend only on commercial profits for their income, but on other sources, primarily land.

The fall in prices during the first half of the nineteenth century — both of cereals and olive oil, and textile products — crippled the Neapolitan economy. Another sign of economic decline was the bad state of the ports. Manfredonia, the chief exporting port for the cereals of Apulia, was in a dangerous condition, and other ports, chief of which were Bari and Brindisi, were badly silted up.

The small circle of entrepreneurs not only had great weight in the economy as traders and financiers, but were also rich landowners and speculators in land. Their economic base, in fact, was land, and they usually converted profits from their other activities into the land in the end. A few very rich entrepreneurs married or bought their way into the nobility in the first half of the nineteenth century. The cash which they invested in land seems, however, to have brought no agricultural improvements. The rich simply bought more land, rather than improving the land they already had. The peasants remained impoverished and deeply in debt, often paying 15 per cent interest on loans.[13]

It is an open question whether the peasants of Sicily or of the mainland were the poorer. The Sicilian peasants had always been desperately poor, but their poverty from the fifteenth to the eighteenth century had given the island the appearance of prosperity in that the grain produced was more than they could afford to consume themselves, and was thus exported on a considerable scale. Even this superficial prosperity which benefited only a small part of the population was disappearing in the course of the eighteenth century, and in the nineteenth century economic decline was affecting all classes. And from the end of the eighteenth century the peasants had one clear-cut specific grievance: much land which had formerly been held in common had been usurped or enclosed by the great landowners. It was sometimes estimated that this was the case with a third of the entire land in the kingdom. It was a constant source of grievance, but without a government prepared to conduct a very radical agrarian policy nothing could be done about it. The middle-class revolutionaries who came to power briefly in 1799 and 1820 were not going to concern themselves with this peasant matter. Typical of their attitude was that of Vincenzo Cuoco, the Neapolitan historian and politician who, in his famous firsthand commentary on the revolution of 1799, which has already been mentioned, argued that nothing should be done about the enclosed lands. With the ending of feudalism, he believed, there was no longer a function for common land. To the argument that, even so, there should nevertheless be a redistribution by which what had once been common land should be given to the poorer peasants, he protested that this would mean taking land from able and successful peasants and giving it to those who were too poor or too incompetent to cultivate it properly. It would mean, Cuoco said, expropriating those who were cultivating land which was 'still bathed in the sweat of their fathers'. He overlooked the fact that much of the former common land had become part of vast estates owned by absentee noblemen, whose sweat had certainly never watered their lands.

Only for one brief moment in the nineteenth century did the Neapolitan economy seem to be recovering. Immediately after Ferdinand II came to the throne in 1830 there was a startling increase in commerce and investment. But the boom lasted only until 1836, and from that year until the very grim economic crisis of 1847–8 there was a sharp decline, with many bankruptcies and the projects of the 1830s being abandoned. Nor, of course, did the boom of the early 1830s bring much in the way of relief to the peasants. It so happens that for 1835 we have a vivid contemporary impression of the largest town in Calabria – Catanzaro, a town with about 20,000 inhabitants, who still spoke a dialect full of Greek words. According to Luigi Settembrini, who was living there at the time, there were two great scourges – earthquakes and brigands. The town had little life of its own: the ancient silk industry had long since declined, and all manufactured goods came from Naples. The first paved road linking Catanzaro to the rest of the world came only in 1838; in 1835 there was still only a dirt-track, which even the mules found difficult to negotiate. No one left the town without a gun, for fear of the brigands. Property owners were permitted by the government to keep an armed force of servants to protect them. A man who had once committed a crime of some kind tended to become a brigand, and anyone seen armed in his company was declared to be an outlaw by the government. The tragedy of Calabria, as of Sicily, was that an inherently intelligent people were led by poverty and the primitive nature of their institutions to use their intelligence in crime and violence.

Cereals, of course, constituted the basic agricultural product of the kingdom. Only in some of the less poverty-stricken parts, usually near the coast, were there more specialized agricultural products. Of these, olive oil was the most important, and already in the early nineteenth century constituted almost a third of the value of all exports. The number of vineyards also increased after 1815, but little wine was exported. With one or two exceptions the wines of the south were less well known than the wines of Tuscany, Umbria, Piedmont or the Veneto.

Little need be said about industry in the Kingdom of Naples because there was little. The Bourbon administrations always made the mistake of concentrating industry in or near Naples itself, and consequently of spending money on public works only in that area. In the years before Naples became part of the Kingdom of Italy the metallurgical and textile industries – the only major industries – were established near Naples or outside Salerno. The Banco di Napoli limited its operations strictly to the capital until 1857, when a branch was opened in Bari. Inevitably, also, railways radiated from Naples. That the very first railway in Italy should run from Naples to the very poor suburb of Portici was surprising since there had not even been a decent road before. The opening was understandably the scene of great festivities. The line was extended, through Torre Annunziata, to Castellammare and, later, a little inland, to Nocera. Another line, at the same time, was built from Naples to the royal palace at Caserta, and then on to Capua. The main purpose of these very early railways was partly to give the Bourbon monarchy some prestige, and partly perhaps also to enable the movement of troops for the defence of the capital. They attracted foreign, not Neapolitan, investment. A French company, Armand Bayard, and a French engineer, Verges, constructed the first Neapolitan railway line, using French capital. Bayard was granted generous concessions by the Neapolitan government. No customs duties were charged on the material which had to be imported from France, and the profits of the company were not taxed. The project was praised by the French press, who commented on the enlightened policy of the Neapolitan Bourbons, and expressed the view that Naples was a safe place for French investment. By 1843 there were eight railway engines, bought in Newcastle from Stephenson and Longridge Starbuck, running on the short line from Naples to Caserta. British and French companies pressed the Neapolitan government to build more lines, but Ferdinand II had lost his initial enthusiasm, and Naples rapidly fell behind other Italian states in railway building.[14] As an indication of this it must be recorded that the line which had so soon been constructed from Naples to Nocera was only very slowly extended to Salerno, to be opened in August 1860, very shortly before the arrival of Garibaldi. Yet another, much longer, stretch was being built from Capua to Ceprano, nearly half way to Rome, but this was completed only after the Kingdom of Naples had ceased to be. There was little excuse for limiting the building of railways to the region around the capital. The province of Apulia, away in the heel of Italy, was densely populated and could claim to be economically active, to be, indeed, the main source of exports for the kingdom. If olive oil constituted about a third of the exports of the kingdom in the early years of the century, by 1858 it was accounting for two thirds of the exports, and most of the olive oil was produced in Apulia. In the last, sad days of the Neapolitan kingdom the people of Apulia were still showing considerable signs of life. They had made technical improvements in the production of olives, and were protesting that the government denied them railways or decent roads and persecuted them with an archaic commercial policy.

The bulk of the population in the kingdom were victims of acute poverty and brutal corruption. Many peasants lived in miserable huts and slept under straw like animals. In periods of famine they ate grass and seeds which sometimes killed them more quickly than starvation would have done. The city of Naples had the distinction of having the largest poorhouse in Europe: in 1835 it housed 6,000 paupers. The poor outside the capital survived mainly on maize and beans; bread was too expensive. In Naples itself a black bread made from a very poor quality flour was eaten. The people who sold the bread would increase its weight by adding stone dust. Wine was controlled by a small monopoly of merchants, who often adulterated it with a variety of additives, turning it, as one witness reported, into 'a slow and powerful poison'.[15]

NOTES

A great deal has been written on nineteenth-century Naples, and here only a small selection of writings can be mentioned. Basic works are Domenico Demarco, *Il crollo del regno delle Due Sicilie*, Naples, 1960, and R. Moscati, *Il Mezzogiorno d'Italia nel risorgimento*, Messina, 1953. In English, Harold Acton wrote two idiosyncratic works which looked at the Bourbons with exaggerated sympathy, but were certainly imbued with a rich understanding of Naples – *The Bourbons of Naples, 1734–1825*, London, 1956, and *The Last Bourbons of Naples, 1825–1861*, London 1961. A. Lepre has written three important books: *Contadini, borghesi ed operai nel tramonto del feudalismo napoletano*, Milan, 1963; *La rivoluzione napoletana del 1820–21*, Rome, 1967; and *Storia del Mezzogiorno nel risorgimento*, Rome, 1969. Another important work deals with a period of Neapolitan history which has been rather overshadowed by the revolutionary phases: G. Cingari, *Mezzogiorno e risorgimento. La Restaurazione a Napoli dal 1821 al 1830*, Bari, 1970.

Because of the grave social problems of the South throughout modern times, much scholarship has been lavished on the economic and social history of the Kingdom of Naples. Demarco's basic work of 1960 has already been mentioned. More recently – in 1979 – two works deserve mention, and one of them is later referred to more specifically in the footnotes: John Davis, *Società e imprenditori nel regno borbonico 1815/1860*, Bari, 1979, which makes an important study of continental Naples in these years; the other, Stefania Martuscelli, *La popolazione del Mezzogiorno nella statistica di Re Murat*, Naples, gives a sharp focus on the population of Murat's Kingdom of Naples.

Specifically for the history of Sicily other works will be cited in later chapters, but here it seems appropriate to mention Rosario Romeo's first important work, *Il risorgimento in Sicilia*, Bari, 1950 (paperback edn 1973), and the second of Denis Mack Smith's volumes on the history of Sicily, *Modern Sicily after 1713*, London, 1968, a brilliant narrative.

1. Luigi Settembrini, *Una protesta del popolo del regno delle Due Sicilie*, Naples: Morano, 1847.
2. Claudia Petraccone, *Napoli dal '500 all''800. Problemi di storia demografica e sociale*, Naples: Guida, 1974.
3. Rosario Romeo, op. cit., 1973, p. 54.
4. Benedetto Croce, *History of the Kingdom of Naples*, ed. H. Stuart Hughes, Chicago, 1965, pp. 196–202.
5. See Ch. 6, p. 166.
6. See Ch. 6, p. 170.
7. *What I Remember*, London: Kimber, 1973.
8. See Ch. 7, pp. 178–9.
9. *Ricordanze della mia vita*, ed. Adolfo Omodeo, Bari: Laterza, 1934.
10. See Ch. 9. His name has usually been rendered in the past as 'Rosolino' Pilo, but it now seems established that he signed himself 'Rosalino' Pilo.
11. Domenico Demarco, op. cit., vol. I, p. 3.
12. Ibid., p. 4.
13. These three paragraphs are based on a recent work by a British scholar: John Davis (op. cit.), a highly important work of economic history.
14. Ibid., pp. 143–6.
15. S. de Renzi, *Topografia e statistica medica della Città di Napoli*, Naples, 1845, quoted by John Davis, op. cit., p. 317.

PART THREE

The creation of the nation-state

The Origins of the Risorgimento: Italy in the era of the French Revolution and Napoleon (1790–1815)

That Metternich called Italy 'a geographical expression' is repeated *ad nauseam* by candidates for examination, probably all over Western Europe. More often than not the expression is assigned to 1815, although it was really coined shortly before the revolution of 1848 and Metternich's own fall from power. The date of the expression's origin, however, is unimportant, since it would have been equally untrue at any moment of Metternich's life. The 'Atlantic Ocean' or the 'Alps' are geographical expressions, as is 'Africa', since there is no ethnic, cultural nor historical link between, say, Egypt and Liberia. 'Europe' is more than a geographical expression since it has the cultural and historical dimension.[1] In the nineteenth century 'Italy' was also much more than a geographical expression, and had been for many centuries.

The Romans had united Italy into a confederation in the third century BC, at least up to the Arno, and when Cicero wrote of 'Italy' he meant precisely what we mean today. The concept of 'Italy', then, is a great deal more ancient than that of 'England' or France'. Political unity did not, of course, survive the fall of the Roman Empire, but the idea, and the memories attached to it, lived throughout the Middle Ages. Dante had a clear concept of a place which he called 'Italy', which corresponded to no existing political entity but which already had many of the characteristics which were to justify the movement of Italian nationalism in modern times. Dante recognized that Italy enjoyed a common culture and customs, and he defined her geographical boundaries precisely. He could personify her, both to bless, or – as in some famous lines from Canto VI of *Il Purgatorio* – to curse her:

Ahi serva Italia, di dolore ostello, nave sanza nocchiere in gran tempesta, non donna di provincie, ma bordello!
(Oh servile Italy, house of suffering, a ship without a pilot in a great tempest, not mistress of provinces, but a brothel!)

Dante, more than any other single man, had contributed to the creation of the Italian language, and had defended it in *De Vulgari Eloquentia*.[2] That he lived in Italy and spoke and wrote what was to become recognized as the Italian language was clearly a basic part of his identity. He also hoped that the Emperor would come from Germany to conquer Italy, and here his political hopes were obviously distinct and disconnected from his instinctive sense of the cultural unity of Italy. As A.P. d'Entrèves argued, Dante's wish that the Emperor should extend his control over Italy was motivated mainly by his ideal of the establishment of universal peace, and partly by his conviction that his beloved Florence, which had exiled him, should be punished.[3] It was of course impossible in the high Middle Ages to conceive of the modern notion of a 'nation-state' or of 'nationality' in the nineteenth-century sense of the term. Yet the writers of the Risorgimento can perhaps be forgiven for thinking of Dante as a precursor. His impression of Italy as a country united not only by a great and civilized language, but also by social customs and traditions, was one which was to give cohesion to the making of the nation-state more than half a millennium later. It also illustrated the emptiness of Metternich's characterization of Italy as 'a geographical expression'.

Another figure from Italy's past who was venerated by the writers of the Risorgimento was Niccolò Machiavelli. Their treatment of Machiavelli was no less anachronistic than their treatment of Dante, yet here, too, their patriotic instincts were not without justification. Of all the secularizing thinkers of the Renaissance, the one who seemed most emancipated from ecclesiastical or theological authority was Machiavelli. In so far as nineteenth-century Italian nationalism was a movement against the Papacy, it could well look on Machiavelli as a founding father. Yet Machiavelli's concept of the Italian nation is still much closer to that of Dante than to that of Mazzini. In the first place Machiavelli's idea of a nation was an extremely vague one. He used the word *nazione* a few times, but he sometimes wrote of Italy, France or Spain as *provincie*.[4] He used the word *patria* far more frequently than *nazione*. None of these three words, *provincie*, *nazione*, or *patria*, did he use in a very consistent or specific sense. Federico Chabod demonstrated that Machiavelli used the word *provincie* when referring to a people or tribe on one occasion, but when referring to a politico-territorial unit on other occasions; and that he used the word *nazione* of Florence rather than of Italy.[5] Until the eighteenth century Italian writers continued to use the word 'nation' with careless imprecision, writing of a Piedmontese 'nation', but also of an Italian 'nation'. Machiavelli, then, with his very clear conception of the rights of the state, and of the obligations of the citizens to the state, never imagined that state sovereignty should correspond with a 'nation', a 'nation' clearly defined by cultural or linguistic homogeneity. Like Dante and the generations between them, he loved both Florence and Italy, but whereas he recognized that Florence was, and must remain, an organized and independent social and political unit, he thought of Italy only as a country in which one people possessed one language and had inherited a single set of customs and traditions. But this was enough to give Machiavelli tremendous potency as a myth for Italian nationalists of the nineteenth century: and if the myth did not correspond with the historical figure, yet it was not unrelated to it. While Machiavelli became almost an incarnation of the devil in the eyes of Shakespeare and his English contemporaries, for Italians he quickly became, and remained, a national hero. To some extent the Italian nationalist interpretation of Machiavelli was justified by the last short chapter of *The Prince*, which has often weighed more with Italians than all the rest of the book – one might almost say, than all the rest of his writings – put together. This last chapter constituted his reaction to the events of 1494, when a large French army had invaded Italy. As for most Italians of the Renaissance, Italy was for Machiavelli the only wholly civilized part of Europe, yet after 1494 she was to be occupied by, and under the domination of, barbarian foreigners. The waves of foreign invasions from 1494 to 1513, when Machiavelli wrote *The Prince*, convinced him that Italy needed a strong leader who would drive away the barbarians. In the last chapter of *The Prince* he advised Giuliano dei Medici, the ruler of Florence, to undertake this task of national salvation. His concern was clearly not with any institutional unity of Italy, but rather with a diplomatic and military unity of the Italian states, a unity expressed in particular through a citizen army, rather than by disinterested mercenaries. His intention was not to integrate Italy into a single state, certainly not to submerge the Florentine Republic into a greater Italy in any political sense. He was not thinking of a doctrine of nationality, since no such doctrine had been conceived. Nevertheless Machiavelli did envisage some unity of action of the Italian states, a unity of action which should be directed and inspired by an Italian prince. There had, at least, been one significant change since the Middle Ages. Whereas Dante had dreamed of a German emperor imposing peace between the Italian states, Machiavelli looked for salvation from a native prince. To this extent Machiavelli's outlook had moved closer to modern ideas of nationalism, but the change had been rather a reflection of the growth of self-sufficient, secular states in Italy than an original intellectual approach on Machiavelli's part. For Dante the German emperor had not seemed a foreign authority, an authority from 'outside', as Maximilian II or Charles V seemed to be to Machiavelli. For Dante the Emperor had still been a universal figure, whose centre of power happened to be in another part of the Christian commonwealth. For Machiavelli even the Pope had lost much of his universal character, and if Machiavelli did not envisage the possibility of a 'state' or a 'kingdom' of Italy, he was yet already contrasting Italian disunity with the strong, united kingdoms to the north. A prince should imitate both the lion and the fox. 'Those who act only like lions are foolish.' But an Italian prince could compensate for the greater physical strength of the kingdoms to the north by employing the tactics of a fox. Many Italians from the Renaissance to the Risorgimento accepted this theme, believing that they would have to employ their higher civilization and more refined intelligence to overcome the brute force of the barbarian nations beyond the Alps. In particular the House of Savoy was to try in the seventeenth and eighteenth centuries, with increasing success, to play the barbarian powers off against each other, and it was this tradition that Cavour was to continue in the nineteenth century. Oddly enough, German writers, from Luther in Machiavelli's day to Treitschke in the nineteenth century, repeated the theme of the greater, if more devious, diplomatic skill of the Italians. Luther had written that 'the German people, with its noble nature, is praised for its constancy and faithfulness thoughout history', but that it had been tricked by 'Italian' cunning and deceitfulness. And Treitschke believed that the Germans, in contrast to the Latins, had a primordial innocence.

A sense of national identity, which seemed to be emerging in sixteenth-century Europe, was to suffer severe setbacks. The scientific revolution of the late seventeenth century seemed to establish universal, immutable truths, and the cultural fashions of the eighteenth century became increasingly international and standardized throughout Europe, not least in Italy. The strong and so-called 'enlightened' monarchs of the eighteenth century, Frederick the Great of Prussia or Catherine the Great of Russia, spoke French, and patronized a cosmopolitan, gallicized, culture. Yet before the end of the eighteenth century a few writers in Europe, and especially in Germany, had taken a fresh interest in the *Volk* cultures of the nations, and their work was to have great influence on nineteenth-century Italy, especially via the writings of Mazzini, who had been influenced in particular by the writings of the German philosopher Herder.[6] While the term 'nation' had originated at a remote period, the term 'nationalism' seems to have been first used by Herder.[7] While Dante and Machiavelli had identified themselves as Italians, because of the language they spoke and the culture they had inherited, this kind of national self-consciousness became politically significant only with the nineteenth century. Of the nationalist movements of the nineteenth century a common language was an important element for the Germans, the Poles, the Hungarians, the Czechs, the Romanians, the Greeks and, of course, the Italians. Ultimately not one of these nationality groups was to fail to create an independent state, even if the independent states created themselves contained minorities speaking other languages. Language-nationalism was certainly one of the most powerful and tangible categories of nationalism, but it is important to realize that it is a category which has subsequently been identified and defined by political scientists and historians: it was rarely a self-conscious political movement in itself. Certainly before 1848 very few Italians would have said: 'Italy should be liberated from the Austrians and united into a single state, because Italians have a common language.' The movement was more spontaneous, more instinctive and less explicit in its reasoning. Even politically active Italian nationalists initially felt themselves to be Italians instinctively and only on further reflection would justify that feeling by specific references to their language, culture, traditions or social customs. It was in this instinctive sense of belonging to a nation which had not yet been allowed political expression that Italians of the Risorgimento were clearly a part of the Romantic movement. And the Romantic movement in its political form owed much to the impassioned and brilliant writings of Jean-Jacques Rousseau. In his *Considerations on the Government of Poland* Rousseau clearly anticipated the sentiments of ninetenth-century nationalists and the spirit of Mazzini. Arguing that Poland's anarchy and the sparseness of her population made her especially vulnerable to attack from the more powerful states around her – Russia, Prussia and Austria – Rousseau declared:

I can see only one means of giving her the solidarity that she lacks: that is, as it were, to infuse the soul of the parts throughout the whole of the nation; to establish the republic so strongly in the hearts of the Poles that she may survive in spite of all the efforts of her oppressors: there it seems to me is the only asylum that force can neither reach nor destroy. We have just seen a proof which we will always remember: Poland was imprisoned by Russia, but the Poles remained free.[8]

It was this spirit of Romantic nationalism which was to give the Risorgimento its impetus, but which was also to make it a clear reaction against the Enlightenment.

Yet, whether they realized it or not, the binding force of a common language gave to nineteenth-century nationalists a novel and dynamic characteristic, and the importance of language in the life and sense of identity of a nation was first fully realized not by Rousseau, but by Johann Gottfried Herder. Herder's ideas about language and the *Volk* were the seeds from which the earliest version of nineteenth-century nationalism was to grow. He believed that language had developed historically with the growth of human reason, and that it was therefore an intrinsic and organic part of a people or a *Volk*. It expressed their very essence, and was a projection of their total intellectual life and social behaviour. The language of a people is also its main link with the past, and so gives continuity to the life of the *Volk*. Herder believed that the state should be based on this single *Volk* or nation, but should be organized by spontaneous and *ad hoc* institutions. It should be a natural, organic growth, not the result of military conquest or political pressures. A nation of this pure and spontaneous kind would have no aggressions, no reason nor desire to make war on its neighbours. Thus would emerge an international community of free, peace-loving nations. Herder's approach, then, was a pacific and humanist one. While he endorsed the respect for the concept of 'Humanity' which was common to the French writers of the Enlightenment, he meant by the term rather more than they did. For him Humanity, or *Humanität*, embraced not only all human creatures alive at that moment, from the German peasant to the African negro, living as yet undisturbed by Europeans in his tropical jungle; it included also the dead and the unborn. Love of humanity involved an understanding of the origins and history of all the diverse groups of mankind, and a concern for their posterity. The nation, cemented by a common language, thus had the added dimension of time, projected as it was in Herder's thought into the past and the future. In contrast, a large empire including many conquered nations was bound to lack stability.

A kingdom consisting of a single nation is a family, a well regulated household: it reposes on itself, for it is founded by Nature, and stands and falls by time alone. An empire formed by forcing together a hundred nations, and a hundred-and-fifty provinces is no body politic, but a monster.[9]

Mazzini was to read Herder in French translation, and many of Herder's ideas are echoed in Mazzini's writings. The Risorgimento, then, must be seen as a part of the European movement of Romantic nationalism, a movement heralded by a Frenchman, Rousseau, and a German, Herder, but brought perhaps to its purest point by the Italian, Mazzini.

The writers of the Italian Enlightenment, however, had been little concerned with thoughts of nationalism, or even of Italian independence. Perhaps the most influential and in a sense the most 'modern' of them were Pietro Verri and Cesare Beccaria. They were both concerned with economic and humanizing reforms in Lombardy under the Habsburgs; the idea of fighting for a united, or even an independent, Italy was quite alien to them. Where, then, did the idea of a Risorgimento, an Italian resurgence, originate?

The nationalist movement in Italy, as in Germany, had its roots in the eighteenth century. But whereas the national consciousness of the Germans was emerging from a *Volk* culture with feudal origins and in a predominantly rural setting, that of the Italians was essentially the property of those educated classes in the cities who had abandoned, or were beginning to abandon, the use of local dialects. Thus it was in the literature written primarily for the upper classes – tragic drama or the novel – that early hints of nationalist sentiment in Italy can be found, and it was the Piedmontese dramatist, Vittorio Alfieri (1749–1803), who first used the term *Risorgimento* in demanding a politico-ethical revival in Italy. In 1775 Alfieri had experienced an emotional crisis in which he discovered the emptiness and futility of his life as a young nobleman in Turin. In writing his first tragedy, *Cleopatra*, the performance of which brought him success, he realized that he knew the Italian language inadequately. Since the Renaissance the Tuscan form of Italian had been accepted as the correct national language, and it was to Tuscany that Alfieri had gone in 1777 with the explicit purpose of learning pure Italian. In that same year he had written a political tract, *Della tirannide*, a bitter denunciation of tyranny in all its forms, which yet makes no distinction between foreign and native tyrants. Except for a brief attack on foreign mercenaries, in the tradition of Machiavelli, there is no trace in *Della tirannide* of Italian nationalism. Many years later, however, Alfieri was to raise a first cry for 'national freedom'. For him 'nationality' had become a characteristic of importance of the future of a people, rather than for its past, and Mazzini was to inherit this attitude. What gave a people a sense of 'nationality' was not so much the geographical or material conditions they had experienced in common with the past, but the political programme – the dream of liberty – which they shared for the future.

Another eighteenth-century figure who seems, if in a very vague sense, to be anticipating the Risorgimento is the Piedmontese historian Carlo Denina. Born in 1731, Denina had published a comparative study of Italian, French, English and German literature in 1760, the first attempt to do anything of the kind in Italy. In it he made the acute observation that the unique character of English literature in his day owed a great deal to the freedom of the press – in other words to a purely political factor. In 1769–70 he published the three volumes of his *Revolutions of Italy*. The third volume of this work was charged by a Jesuit priest with having seventeen heretical propositions, but Denina survived the attack. In 1782 he went to Berlin and was presented to

Frederick the Great, whose conversation impressed him by its 'depth and the breadth of his historical understanding'. When the French revolutionary wars broke out, Denina added a book to his *Revolutions of Italy*, which took the story from 1713 to 1792 and showed that he was hostile to revolutionary France. But after the triumph of Napoleon Denina meekly accepted the post of imperial librarian in 1804. In 1803 he had written a dissertation encouraging the Piedmontese to accept the French language as their own, and for this later Italian nationalists would never forgive him. Yet he himself continued to write in Italian. He died in 1813.

His life, then, was not a heroic one, nor one calculated to make him a prophet of the Risorgimento. Yet Carducci called his *Revolutions of Italy* 'the first general history of our people'. Although written in the tradition of the Enlightenment, and consciously and deliberately in the spirit of Montesquieu and Voltaire, the great work was to have considerable significance for the history of Italian nationalism. Denina imagined that he was writing, as he put it, 'to further the advantage of the human race', but for many Italians the importance of the book was to lie in the fact that it dealt with Italy as a whole. There had been many historians of Florence or Venice: to take the history of Italy as a study was more original, and Denina himself was aware that it presented difficulties which were not present in the writing of a history of England or Spain. However he believed – as did Herder and other writers of the Enlightenment – that the character of a people was the product of factors of physical geography – climate or soil – and consequently the Italian people had an identifiable character which did not depend upon political institutions. It was therefore possible, if difficult, to write a history of Italy, since the Italian national character had not changed since pre-Roman days. In the last book of the *Revolutions of Italy*, the one written in 1792, Denina noted the apparent lack of patriotism among the Italians. The explanation for this lack, he believed, was the absence of a united government and a united set of laws. 'But if there should ever be a war between one of the nations beyond the Alps and Italy, patriotism and the much-sung virtue of the ancients would certainly rise again . . .' *Risorgerebbe* is the word he uses; in this passage he is not far from a dream of a Risorgimento. 'Certainly patriotism would be more general in Italy if she were animated by an identity of interests, and if there were a centre for a union, which would perhaps not be difficult to find, precisely there where it had once existed', concluded Denina, the last somewhat obscure phrase presumably referring to Rome.[10]

Italians of the eighteenth century certainly did not formulate a clear programme for securing the independence and unity of Italy. All that can be said is that there was a faint stirring of patriotic sentiment, a gentle whisper of a coming *Risorgimento*. But political events, in the dramatic years from 1792 to 1815, were to be more important for Italian history than the speculations of Italian writers, although in the long run those speculations, also, were to have their influence.

The war which started in 1792 between revolutionary France and the old monarchies was in a sense the first ideological war of modern times. Although

France was still technically a monarchy, she was fighting for the doctrine of popular sovereignty, and although Austria and Prussia were highly civilized and enlightened states, they were still fighting for the doctrine of monarchial legitimacy. Nor was Austria quite so civilized a state as she had recently been. The Emperor Leopold II, who had once been the Grand Duke Pietro Leopoldo of Tuscany, had died early in 1792. He would certainly not have gone to war to save his foolish sister, the French queen, Marie Antoinette, from a fate which she had seemed to invite. Even so, it was not the new Austrian emperor, Francis II, who declared war, but the revolutionary French assembly. By November 1792, after an uncertain beginning, the French revolutionary army could win victories and pass to the offensive. By December the Austrians and Prussians were retreating across the Rhine. Already in September Italy had become involved in the wars, in that the French revolutionary government had ordered the occupation of Savoy and Nice without declaring war on Piedmont. The repercussions of this act of aggression have already been noted in Chapter 2. The Italian states, then, entered this long period of warfare as enemies of France, and in the War of the First Coalition a Neapolitan army and navy both fought against France with considerable credit.

In 1795 the government of the Directory took over in Paris, a government whose policies were to have considerable importance in Italy. The step which was to have greatest significance for Italy – as for Europe and the world – was the Directory's appointment of a very young officer to command the French army in Italy for the Great campaign of 1796 – a certain Napoleon Bonaparte. At the age of twenty-seven this raw Corsican found himself in command of a large, enthusiastic, revolutionary army. He had left Corsica as a small boy of ten to study at the military academy at Brienne. He was commissioned in 1785, and in 1793, after several uncertain years, was made captain of artillery, with the immediate task of destroying a rebellion in Toulon. The rebellion he destroyed with little effort, and was promptly made a brigadier general. His fortunes originally, however, were linked to those of Robespierre, and when Robespierre was guillotined Napoleon was imprisoned for a month, but then immediately pardoned. The fate of the House of Bonaparte was to be closely tied to that of Italy until 1870, and perhaps the most astonishing career of modern times was to shape Italian history for the next twenty years. It is open to argument whether the Bonapartes should be considered an Italian family. Until 1796 Napoleon spelt his name in the Italian form 'Buonaparte'. The Buonapartes had been settled in Tuscany from the eleventh to the sixteenth century, when they had emigrated to Corsica. Napoleon's mother's family, the Ramolino, had also been Italian in its remote origins, but had emigrated to Corsica even earlier than had the Buonapartes. Napoleon had been born in 1769, little more than a year after his birthplace had passed from the sovereignty of the Republic of Genoa to that of the French monarchy. Legally, then, he was born a subject of Louis XV, but that has not prevented Italians from claiming him as a fellow-countryman. A popular series of biographies, published in Fascist days and entitled 'Great Italians', included both Julius Caesar and Napoleon Buonaparte. The main difficulty with the theory is that Napoleon was always relentlessly determined to consider himself a Frenchman. If he came to feel a special relationship for Italy it was less because of his family background than because of his own first brilliant achievements in Italy in 1796.

The French defeat of Piedmont in the spring of 1796 has already been noted in Chapter 1. Napoleon's first substantial victory against the Austrians was the battle of Lodi in May 1796. It is interesting that at this point the government of the Directory in Paris were more interested in Italy and Napoleon was more interested in the defeat of Austria. The Directory in Paris were thinking of an occupation of Rome, and perhaps of Naples, but Napoleon had his sights set on Vienna. Five days after Lodi Napoleon entered Milan and then proceeded to conquer much of Lombardy. He was halted, however, at Mantua, which fought a stubborn siege until February 1797. In that same month, as the result of his invasion of the Papal States, for which he had shown no great relish, Bonaparte secured the Treaty of Tolentino, by which the Pope surrendered Bologna and the Romagna. On 18 April he forced the Austrians to accept an armistice – the preliminary Peace of Leoben. The central points of the peace did not concern Italy – Austria gave up her Belgian lands to France, but a congress was to meet to arrange a definitive peace between the two great powers. Austria was to recognize the Cisalpine Republic, but France was to recognize Austrian conquests of Venetian territory, supposing that such conquests were ever made. The Peace of Leoben, then, did not immediately betray Venice to the Austrians, but it contained strong hints of what was to come. In May 1797 Napoleon went to war with the Venetian Republic in one of the most cynical moments in the career of this totally amoral man. French troops occupied Venice even before the formal proclamation of the Cisalpine Republic in July.

The ambiguity of Napoleon's policy in Italy was now becoming apparent. At almost the same moment that he was creating an Italian state – the Cisalpine Republic – including the cities of Milan, Bologna and Ferrara, he was planning to hand over Venice to the Austrians. By the Treaty of Campo Formio Venice was ceded to the Habsburgs. The Peace of Leoben was confirmed in that the Belgian provinces were now to be definitively part of France. Campo Formio, then, set a pattern which Metternich was later to follow. In 1815 Metternich was only too glad to be rid of Belgium, provided that the Habsburgs could retain their Italian provinces. The awkward, nostalgic desire of the Habsburgs to retain north-eastern Italy was to be one of the basic causes of the Risorgimento, and so of the creation of modern Italy.

Even the peace of Campo Formio could not be considered definitive, since it was a treaty only between France and Austria, not with the Holy Roman Empire. A congress was therefore to meet at Rastadt to discuss the peace of central Europe. But this congress, which sat for over a year, reached no agreement. The issues involved were not Italian ones, but the simple question of whether there was to be war or peace certainly concerned Italy, who has always suffered from the tendency of the European peoples to murder each other, and to do so, if possible, on Italian territory. In February 1798 the French occu-

pied Rome, the Roman Republic was proclaimed, and Pope Pius VI was
kidnapped. Meanwhile General Bonaparte had washed his hands of Italy and
Europe and set out on his glamorous Egyptian campaign. He occupied Malta
en route, and landed in Egypt on 1 July, taking possession of Alexandria the
next day. Three weeks later he defeated the Egyptian army in the Battle of the
Pyramids. It would, of course, have been surprising if the French army had
failed to defeat these primitive forces. Napoleon was simply carrying out a
public relations operation, but so adept was he in this particular technique
that even when his fleet was destroyed by Nelson in the Battle of the Nile in
August Napoleon continued with his campaign as though nothing had
happened.

In Napoleon's absence the War of the Second Coalition broke out in
Europe, and this was essentially an Italian affair.[11] It brought great tragedy to
Naples, tragedy for which Napoleon, stranded, even if triumphant, in the
Middle East, was by no means to be blamed. Initially an alliance was signed
between Britain and Russia on Christmas Eve, 1798. Naples, along with Austria, Portugal and Turkey, soon joined the coalition. Napoleon's somewhat
casual occupation of Malta had brought the coalition into being, in that the
Russian Czar, Paul I, was the Grand Master of the Knights of Malta and,
through his bemused and unstable view of the world, detected that Napoleon
had committed an offence against him. On these remote causes did the
Neapolitan revolution of 1799, which created the Parthenopean Republic as it
was called, depend for its survival. Meanwhile Napoleon had invaded Syria in
February 1799 but, finding his army dying of the plague, had withdrawn to
Egypt. In July, with one of his more dramatic generals, Murat, who was later
to play a considerable role in Italian history, Napoleon defeated the Turks and
the British in the Battle of Abukir. But the public relations operation had
now served its purpose. On 24 August Napoleon left Egypt for France, where
he rightly guessed that more promising developments were taking place.

In the spring of 1799 the War of the Second Coalition had led to the arrival
in Northern Italy of Austro-Russian forces under Marshal Suvorov.[12] The Russian marshal himself crossed the St Gotthard Pass back into Switzerland in
August. Russian forces seemed to be dominant in Western Europe. But, even
in the absence of Napoleon, the genius of one of his marshals, Massena,
halted the Russo-Austrian forces. The unstable Paul I suddenly decided to
abandon his allies and the war against France. The Second Coalition dissolved
as rapidly as it had been formed. Its most tragic victims had been the intelligentsia of Naples, victims at the same time of the social outcasts of the city
and the brutality of Nelson.

Napoleon was now First Consul of France, but by no means had all his
ambitions been fulfilled. The Rastadt Congress had failed, which meant that a
hostile Holy Roman Empire still existed. However, he was now undeniably
the head of government in France for a term of ten years. On 24 December
1799 the Constitution of the Year VIII, as it was called, was introduced. A
plebiscite recorded an overwhelming majority in its favour. It gave full executive powers to Napoleon, but bolstered these up with a complex constitutional

facade, which in practice was to mean very little. The effect on Italy of all the movement and drama of 1799 could not at the end of the year be predicted. The Neapolitan liberal historian, Vincenzo Cuoco, wrote, at that moment.

What will be the destiny of Naples, of Italy, of Europe? I do not know: a profound night surrounds and covers everything in an impenetrable shade. It seems that the fates are not favourable to Italian liberty, but that, on the other hand, with the new and better order of things, they may not withhold some hope of it . . .[13]

Cuoco's 'new and better order of things' meant the success of Napoleon yet, while Napoleon was succeeding in France, he was suffering setbacks in Europe. In April 1800 there was a successful Austrian offensive against his general, Masséna, whose army in Italy was split in two, one part falling back towards Southern France while the other was besieged in Genoa.[14] There is no evidence that the appalling human suffering experienced in the siege of Genoa had any impact on the sensibility of Napoleon. To suggest that this automaton of a man had any sensibility would perhaps be an extravagance. He was, however, preparing a new offensive, which was to be as brilliant as that of 1796. An army under General Moreau was despatched into Southern Germany, which it succeeded in occupying without fighting a spectacular battle. Napoleon himself showed his predilection for Italy by leading a great army over the Great St Bernard Pass in May 1800. He entered Milan on 2 June and re-established the Cisalpine Republic.[15] But the real test came after his entry into Milan. As Franklin Ford has suggested: 'It is conceivable that no other battle, until Waterloo, was so crucial for Bonaparte's career as that which decided this second Italian campaign.'[16] If the First Consul had lost the Battle of Marengo his name would probably be no better known than those of a dozen other French generals of the eighteenth and nineteenth centuries. But Marengo was won by the French against a very much larger Austrian army, and Napoleon became the undisputed hero and leader of the French people. The Austrians agreed to an armistice, by which all fortresses to the west of the River Mincio, the river which flows out of Lake Garda and on which stands Mantua – in other words a river very far to the east of Milan – and all fortresses south of the Po, were to be occupied by the French. The Treaty of Lunéville on 9 February 1801 virtually confirmed the terms of the armistice. The French were back in Northern Italy.

Napoleon's position in Italy seemed to be fortified when, in March 1802, he signed with the British the Treaty of Amiens, a treaty by which he was at peace with every European state. The British gave up several extra-European conquests by the Peace of Amiens, but the French agreed to evacuate the Papal States and the Kingdom of Naples: Napoleon seemed, after all, firmly established in Northern Italy. But the Peace of Amiens did not last; Britain and France were at war with each other again in 1803. Napoleon made himself Emperor in May 1804.[17] At once the manner of his rule changed. He assembled around him a court peopled by a new nobility, but a nobility based on meritocracy rather than aristocracy. Democracy had disappeared in France and could now hardly hope to appear in Italy. In 1805 Napoleon proclaimed himself 'King of Italy'.[18] In that same year a coalition of Powers formed again against France, and the War of the Third Coalition began. On 11 April the Russian government signed the Treaty of St Petersburg with England, and on 9 August Austria joined the coalition. In deciding to renew war with Napoleon the Habsburg government was certainly influenced by his policy in Italy — his assumption of the crown of the Kingdom of Italy and his outright annexation of the Ligurian Republic to France. Sweden also joined the Third Coalition, but Prussia remained neutral: one constant factor in Napoleon's success until 1813 was that the other Powers never acted in complete unison against him.

When England had been his only enemy Napoleon had built up a considerable army at Boulogne. Whether he ever intended an invasion of Britain has been debated, but it seems improbable that so large an army could have been solely an instrument of psychological warfare. It seems more likely that Austria, and her concern to retain territory and influence in Italy, saved Britain from a French attempt at invasion. Instead of moving against Britain Napoleon marched his army of Boulogne towards Germany, and soon took command of it himself. The main Austrian army was still operating in Italy, where Napoleon left Masséna in command. The Emperor's personal involvement in Italy seemed to be diminishing. Instead he secured an appreciable victory over the Austrians at Ulm on 17 October, when an Austrian army of some 30,000 surrendered.

The war at sea was as vital for Italy as the war in Central Europe. On October 21 the Battle of Trafalgar ensured British naval supremacy both in the Atlantic and the Mediterranean. Nelson was killed in the battle; he was unlikely to find many mourners in Italy. Trafalgar was a solitary victory for the Third Coalition. After the Battle of Ulm Napoleon entered Vienna in November, and in Italy Massena's successes forced the large Austrian army under the Archduke Charles to retreat over the Alps. But by far the most shattering battle of 1805 was Napoleon's victory at Austerlitz on 2 December. The combined Austro-Russian army was totally defeated, suffering the appalling loss of 25,000 casualties. Austerlitz was of immediate significance for Italy, in that Austria promptly signed the Peace of Pressburg with France, surrendering Venice and the Dalmatian coastline. Less immediate but no less real was the consequence for Naples, where the French were in occupation by February 1806, and Napoleon's brother Joseph was king. Napoleon now dominated the mainland of Western, Central and Southern Europe; Britain dominated the Mediterranean. For Italy this meant regimes controlled by France throughout the mainland peninsula, but a régime controlled from London on the island of Sicily. The political condition of Italy had a certain crude simplicity about it.

On 12 July 1806 Napoleon founded the Confederation of the Rhine, a union of German states which was to become, briefly, the successor to the Holy Roman Empire. That ancient institution, which had once been of such significance for Italy, was dissolved on 6 August 1806. The last Holy Roman Emperor, Francis II, abandoned the title and called himself instead 'Emperor of Austria'. His new title gave him less claim, in an age of nascent nationalism, to possession of Italian territory. While Austria, in the last days of 1805, had abandoned the war against Napoleon, Prussia in 1806 re-entered it. Rarely has a country embarked upon a war in a less secure position than that occupied by Prussia in 1806. Her only allies were England, who could do little to help her and with whom relations were anyhow far from happy, and Russia. Inevitably, on 14 October the Prussians suffered total defeat at Jena, and a few days later Napoleon entered Berlin. The Russians were not to be so easily defeated. From the terrible battle of Eylau on 7−8 February 1807 neither the Russians and Prussians on the one hand, nor the French on the other, could claim a victory. Even Napoleon now paused for some months, but in May occupied Danzig and then moved eastwards. The centre of the European war was moving away from Italy, where benevolent régimes established by Napoleon were in power. For once the European peoples had decided to kill each other in some other corner of the continent. In May 1807 the Battle of Friedland was fought between the French and the Russians, who still had some Prussian support. Friedland was as bloody and terrible as Eylau, but Napoleon secured from it a more clear-cut victory. On 25 June he met Czar Alexander I on a raft in the middle of the River Niemen, and there composed with him the Treaty of Tilsit. The significance of Tilsit so far as Italy was concerned was that Russia recognized Joseph Bonaparte as King of Naples. Russian recognition may have pleased Napoleon, but it meant little in Italy, where the French occupation of Rome on 2 February 1808 was considerably more important. Joseph anyhow was shortly afterwards, in 1808, transferred to the throne of Spain, without any reference to the wishes of the people of Naples, whose upper class had acquired respect and affection for the Emperor's intelligent brother.

Decisions for the future of Europe were now being made at a point far removed from Italy. At Erfurt in September 1808 Napoleon, Alexander I, and something approaching forty German sovereigns met in the kind of congress that only Napoleon could organize. The ostensible purpose of the congress was to establish friendship between France and Russia. This it singularly failed to do. Nor did it prevent a bitter war from breaking out in April 1809, when the Austrian Archduke Charles invaded Bavaria with an army of some 170,000. It may not have been immediately apparent, but it is clear in retrospect that this was the beginning of the War of German Liberation. Henceforth the new ideology of nationalism was more likely to work against Napoleon than for him. It did not, however, prevent him from winning the Battle of Wagram against the Austrians in July 1809. As a result of Wagram the Austrians were obliged to sign the disastrous treaty of Schönbrunn with the French. By it the Austrians ceded huge territories and some three and a half million subjects. They also agreed to join Napoleon's Continental System, which forbade the import of British products, and to break off all relations with Britain.

In 1809 Napoleon's dominance of Central Europe seemed the major factor in world affairs. But already his control of Europe was being threatened at the fringes. An English force had established itself in Portugal, and from October 1810 were holding the lines of Torres Vedras in defence of Lisbon. Such remote concerns, however, did not bother Napoleon. In April 1810 he had married Marie-Louise, the daughter of the Habsburg emperor, partly because the Austrian foreign minister, Metternich, had decided that his country could survive only by a temporary alliance with Napoleon. In March 1811 a male child was born from the marriage, and given the title of 'King of Rome'. Traditionally the first son of the Holy Roman Emperor had been crowned as King of Rome. By claiming the title for his infant son Napoleon was thus asserting his succession from the Holy Roman Emperors, but also linking his fate, once more, with Italy.

In the next year, 1812, Napoleon made mistakes on a massive scale – on a scale proportionate to his genius. So far as Italy was concerned, his treatment of Pope Pius VII was as ill-judged as it was brutal.[19] More important for the fate of Europe was Napoleon's invasion of Russia in June. A vast army of about 430,000 men crossed the frontier into Russia. Without experiencing Russian resistance they reached the city of Smolensk by mid August, and destroyed it. On 7 September they fought the terrible battle of Borodino, inflicting and receiving dreadful losses. Napoleon's army by no means consisted only of Frenchmen. As well as Austrians and Germans, there were very many Italians. At Borodino the Russian general, Kutusov, immortalized and rightly praised in Tolstoy's *War and Peace*, resisted the French, but at the cost of appalling casualties. Perhaps a third of the Russian army, but also a quarter of the French army, was lost. Many Italians died at Borodino, to little purpose. Thereafter Kutusov, by a stroke of the kind of imagination usually denied to military men, decided to defeat Napoleon by avoiding him. Moscow was abandoned, the empty city being occupied by the French only nine days after Borodino. Less than twenty-four hours later the fire started and the city was largely destroyed.

In 1812, then, the war had moved very far away from Italy. With the Grand Army went Joachim Murat, the King of Naples, and Eugène de Beauharnais, the Viceroy of the Kingdom of Italy. In their absence the majority of Italians enjoyed a comparatively enlightened administration under the ministers they had left behind in Naples and Milan. For once, at least, there was peace in Italy. Only the wretched Italians who had been conscripted into Napoleon's army, and who were said to have fought well at Borodino, suffered the horrors of the long retreat from Moscow which started in mid October. Less than one in eight of them survived, the number of those dying from exposure, starvation or its attendant diseases being roughly equal to those killed in battle. Murat was in command of the cavalry of the Grand Army. Initially he played an inspiring role during the retreat, but relations with Napoleon became increasingly strained. Like Napoleon, Murat was a self-made man. The son of an innkeeper, he had climbed to success by his personal magnetism. But he lacked Napoleon's penetrating intelligence, and had played too independent a role as King of Naples for Napoleon's taste. In December he resigned his commission and returned to Naples, fearing that Napoleon was planning to replace him on the Neapolitan throne. He suspected even that Napoleon was plotting to this end with Caroline, Murat's own wife, Napoleon's sister.

In March 1813 Prussia went to war with France, and on 12 August Austria too entered the war. Once again Italy was to be a battlefield. An Austrian army invaded Italy in October and had conquered Venetia by December. But the fate of Italy, as of Europe, was settled in Germany. The four-day Battle of Leipzig, from 16 to 19 October, virtually brought to a close the Napoleonic wars. A bigger and even more terrible battle than Waterloo, which was really only an appendix to the wars, Leipzig has always figured less prominently in English textbooks, simply because the British were not present. But it was at Leipzig that the defeat of Napoleon was ensured. With the remnant of his army the Emperor retreated into France where, at Fontainebleau, on 11 April 1814, he abdicated. The repercussions of his abdication for Northern Italy have already been considered.[20] For Southern Italy the situation was complicated by the ambiguous position of Murat, and his dramatic role during the Hundred Days. The decision to send Napoleon to the island of Elba, and to leave him there virtually unguarded, was not the wisest of those made by the victorious Powers. Learning that the peace-makers at the Congress of Vienna were disagreeing almost to the point of war with each other, and that the restoration of the Bourbon king, Louis XVIII, was far from popular in France, Napoleon decided on one last throw of the dice. He landed at Cannes on 1 March 1815 and, gathering a considerable army around him, marched on Paris, which he entered triumphantly on 20 March. The Austrian, Prussian, Russian and British governments somewhat slowly and hesitantly decided to build up a joint army to resist this unexpected threat and the Duke of Wellington was placed in command. In spite of the astonishing speed with which Napoleon had assembled an army of some 150,000 men, he was yet hopelessly outnumbered. His only ally outside France was the man with whom his relations had been so ambivalent – Joachim Murat. Murat decided that he would join Napoleon in this last desperate struggle against despotism and reaction, and that in the process he would unite the whole Italian peninsula into a single kingdom. His forces entered Rome and Bologna, but then his military skill, which in the past had been unquestioned, deserted him. At Tolentino, on 3 May, he was defeated by the Austrians. He escaped to France, and offered his services to Napoleon, who somewhat ungratefully rejected them. In August Murat was in Corsica, and at the end of September sailed for Calabria, with a pathetically small force of followers, intending to secure once more his kingdom of Naples, where the Bourbons had been reinstated. He was taken prisoner, and, on 13 October, shot. His life had had all the elements of Italian opera, part-comic, part-tragic. But he had been the first man to attempt, in hard political terms, to unite Italy. Meanwhile Napoleon met his enemies at Waterloo, and the Napoleonic era, for Italy and for Europe, was over.

NOTES

An English historian who has comparatively recently carved out a unique place for himself in the historiography of eighteenth-century Italy is Stuart Woolf. His first service to English-speaking readers was to translate and edit the brilliant works of Franco Venturi. More recently he has published two impressive works of his own: 'La storia politica sociale' in Volume III of the Einaudi *Storia d'Italia*, Turin, 1973, and a version revised for English-speaking readers: *A History of Italy 1700–1860*, London, 1979.

Relevant for the opening of the period covered by this chapter is C. Zaghi, *La rivoluzione francese e l'Italia*, Naples, 1966. For the so-called Jacobin *triennio* three books deserve mention: G. Vaccarino, *I patrioti 'anarchistes' e l'idea dell'unità italiana (1796–1799)*, Turin, 1955; for the Neapolitan revolution, as well as Cuoco's classic study which is discussed in the text, there is G. Cingari, *Giacobini e sanfedisti in Calabria nel 1799*, Messina, 1977; and Carlo Ghisalberti, following the traditions of his father as a historian of the Risorgimento, has specialized in constitutional history and written, among much else, *Le costituzioni giacobine del triennio 1797–99*, Milan, 1959.

For the Napoleonic period there are C. Zaghi, *Napoleone e l'Italia*, Naples, 1966, and Pasquale Villani, *Italia napoleonica*, Naples, 1978. A vital documentary collection for the Cisalpine Republic is C. Montalcini and A. Alberti, *Assemblee della Repubblica Cisalpina*, II volumes, Bologna, 1917–48. Melzi's papers have been published in 8 volumes: *I carteggi di Francesco Melzi, duca di Lodi*, Milan, 1958–65. The South in the later Napoleonic period is treated in U. Caldora, *Calabria napoleonica (1806–1815)*, Naples, 1960, and, even more specifically, by A. Valente, *Gioacchino Murat e l'Italia meridionale*, Turin, 1965.

1. The emergence of the idea of Europe has been explored by Denys Hay, *Europe: the Emergence of an Idea*, Edinburgh, 1957, 2nd revised edn 1968.
2. See Vol. II of this History, *Italy in the Age of Dante and Petrarch 1216–1380*, by John Larner.
3. *Dante as a Political Thinker*, Clarendon Press, Oxford, 1952.
4. As in Ch. 55 of the *Discorsi*.
5. Federico Chabod, *L'idea di nazione*, Laterza Bari, 1962.
6. For Mazzini's political ideas and their origins see Ch. 7.
7. Chabod, op. cit., p. 36.
8. *Gouvernement de Pologne*, Garnier edn: Paris, 1962, p. 346.
9. J.G. von Herder, *Reflections on the Philosophy of the History of Mankind*, University of Chicago Press edn, 1968, p. 130.
10. *Delle rivoluzioni d'Italia*, Venice, 5 vols, 1792–3, III, p. 461.
11. See Ch. 5, p. 128.
12. For the impact of Suvorov's arrival in Northern Italy, see Ch. 1, p. 24, and Ch. 2, pp. 50–1.
13. Vincenzo Cuoco, *Saggio storico sulla rivoluzione napoletana del 1799*, ed. Pasquale Villani, 1801, rpr. Bari, 1980, p. 211.
14. See Ch. 2, p. 51.
15. See Ch. 1, p. 25.
16. Franklin J. Ford, *Europe 1780–1830*, Longman, London, 1970, p. 192.
17. See Ch. 4, p. 100.
18. See Ch. 1, p. 27.
19. See Ch. 4, p. 101.
20. See Ch. 1, p. 31.

CHAPTER SEVEN

Revolutionary creeds in an age of political stagnation (1815–40)

The 1815 settlement, incorporated in two Treaties of Paris and the Treaty of Vienna, shaped a map of Europe which was not greatly changed for several decades. Since it brought Austrian sovereignty firmly into north-eastern Italy, and Austrian influence into much of the rest of Italy, it has never found great favour with Italian historians. With English-speaking historians its reputation has fluctuated. The Victorians on the whole regarded it as bleak and reactionary, but the Victorians were accustomed to comparative peace in international terms, and could see only that the 1815 settlement propped up a world of régimes which were reactionary in domestic terms. After the sobering experience of the First World War, and the doubts about the wisdom of the Peace of Versailles, English-speaking historians – and especially Charles Webster and Harold Nicolson – began to suggest that perhaps the 1815 settlement had been more successful than the 1919 settlement. Their argument was carried to extremes in the 1950s in the USA during the Cold War. American historians – chief among them being Peter Viereck and Henry Kissinger – tried to present Metternich as a statesman of great wisdom who had kept the peace of Europe for some thirty years, while making desperate, if unsuccessful, attempts to reform the Habsburg Monarchy. Their interpretation could be accepted only by historians who closed their eyes to the documentary evidence, and in particular to Metternich's own letters. Even so, the 1815 settlement was not an entirely negative one, and at least it brought peace, if an unhappy peace. It brought, also, many enemies: the intellectuals and the professional men resented the renewed influence of the aristocracy and the priests. But these enemies of the settlement were for the time being unimportant. More important in 1815 was the concept of a 'Great Power', a term which was first used during the Vienna Settlement. The 'Great Powers' at Vienna in 1815 were Russia, Austria, Britain and Prussia. It was they who decided the terms both of the peace with France and the more general territorial settlement. One of their decisions, after some hesitation, was to restore the Bourbons to the French throne in the person of Louis XVIII. The Bourbon monarchy in France was to last until 1830. Its policy towards Italy was never a very positive one; it merely acquiesced in Metternich's policy of repression.

Whereas the Bourbons followed a policy of active intervention in Spain in the 1820s, they made little attempt to exert influence over the neighbouring state of Piedmont.

The First Treaty of Paris, signed on 30 May 1814, gave France back her boundaries of 1792, and imposed no indemnity – generous features granted in an attempt to make the restored Bourbons more popular. Even the works of art looted from other parts of Europe – and on a grand scale from Italy – were not to be returned. This meant the condoning of a primitive act of theft, yet it must be admitted that since 1814 many more people have enjoyed art treasures which were on public exhibition in the Louvre than would have been the case if they had remained in comparatively obscure churches and palaces in Italy. France was, of course, to give up all her conquests in Europe beyond her 1792 boundaries. The territorial settlement of Europe as a whole was referred to a congress which was to meet at Vienna. The deliberations of the congress were interrupted by the Hundred Days, which necessitated the signing of a Second Treaty of Paris, by which an indemnity was now imposed, some – but not all – of the looted art treasures were to be restored, and a few border districts were to be taken from France. One such border district was given to Piedmont – that part of Savoy which is on the French side of the Alps, and which stretches down to the shores of Lake Geneva.

Before the signing of the Second Treaty of Paris on 20 November 1815 the final act of the Treaty of Vienna had been signed, on 9 June 1815, and that treaty contained the core of the 1815 Settlement. In many ways the settlement recognized that to bring back the world of the *ancien régime* was impossible. Over three hundred German states had been rationalized by Napoleon into thirty-nine. The Treaty of Vienna left them at thirty-one. Henry Kissinger's phrase, 'A world restored', is very wide of the mark. The doctrine of 'legitimacy' had been pressed on the other plenipotentiaries by Talleyrand, the representative of Bourbon France. Logically, of course, no régime is 'legitimate': it is necessary only to trace its origins to find a usurper or a conqueror. And if the 'right of conquest' is to be accepted, then Louis XVIII should certainly have been called Louis XVII. But the peacemakers of 1815 did not really believe in 'legitimacy'; they accepted it merely because Talleyrand – in an attempt to bolster up the claims of the Bourbons – persuaded them that there should be some 'principle' behind the settlement. But the principle was extended only to dynasties and to dynasties not even always. The King of Saxony had been Napoleon's last ally, and was therefore to be deprived of half his kingdom, without any reference to the 'principle of legitimacy'. So far as Italy was concerned, the republics of Venice and Genoa were not to be restored, even though they had existed for very much longer than most European monarchies, had followed for many decades a respected set of laws, and so were 'legitimate' by any standard of logic. But republics were out of fashion, and so far as they were concerned the 'principle of legitimacy' had to be forgotten.

The other Italian aspects of the Vienna Settlement concerned Piedmont and Lombardo-Venezia. The British plenipotentiary, Lord Castlereagh, was particularly concerned that states neighbouring France should be strenghtened as much as possible. His preoccupation told in favour of Piedmont who, as has been seen in Chapter 2, gained the great port of Genoa and the Ligurian coastline.

Metternich was quite prepared for the North Rhinelands to be given to Prussia, and seemed unaware of the strategic significance of this decision; he was also not at all distressed at losing the former Austrian Netherlands, which were before long to become Belgium, but which in 1815 were to become part of the United Netherlands under the Dutch king, William. What seemed to concern Metternich much more than Germany or the Netherlands was Italy, which he desperately wanted to make a sphere of Austrian influence. The Treaty of Vienna went a long way towards fulfilling his wishes: Lombardy and Venetia were placed under the sovereignty of the Habsburgs, and relatives of the Habsburgs were recognized as sovereigns of Tuscany and Modena. Metternich had even wanted to go further and to grab from the Pope the great city of Bologna and the fine city of Ferrara. This was denied him, although he was allowed to place an Austrian garrison in the castle in the centre of Ferrara.

Besides Metternich the other dominant figure on the continent of Europe in 1815 was Czar Alexander I. Originally attracted by the ideas of the French Revolution, Alexander I had by 1815 become a Christian mystic, and believed that if the sovereigns of Europe could love each other and their subjects in a Christian spirit there would be an end of wars and political disturbances. With this warm-hearted, if naive, aim, he invited all Christian sovereigns to sign a Holy Alliance. Only three European sovereigns failed to sign: the Ottoman Sultan was clearly excluded on grounds of religion; the King of England, George III, had suffered a complete mental breakdown, but his Prince Regent anyhow could not sign since his signature would have no validity without the sanction of parliament; and the Pope refused to recognize a higher Christian authority than his own. But the other sovereigns of Italian territory signed. There was considerable irony in the fact that the term 'Holy Alliance', originally intended by the Czar to suffuse a spirit of Christian love over Europe in the place of the brutal materialism of Napoleon, came to be associated with the dominance of the autocratic Powers, Russia, Austria and Prussia. To Italians the 'Holy Alliance' certainly meant simply an alliance of three unholy tyrants.

More significant in political terms than the Holy Alliance was the Quadruple Alliance of the four victorious Great Powers. The Quadruple Alliance was the brain-child of Castlereagh, who persuaded the other three governments that they must all keep in close personal contact. It was agreed, then, that periodical meetings should be held between high representatives of the four governments – heads of state, heads of government, or, at least, foreign ministers – with two clear purposes in mind. The first was to administer the peace terms with France – to ensure that she paid her indemnity, and to arrange for the control and ultimate withdrawal of the Allied army of occupation. The second, more interestingly, was to survey the condition of Europe, and to ensure that she was not threatened by any sudden or revolutionary changes. Out of the Quadruple Alliance came what was to be known as the 'Congress System', a system by which Metternich sought to stamp out revolution in Europe – and especially in Italy – while keeping the other Powers informed of his policy, if not in full agreement with him. Metternich had thus turned a mystical dream of the Czar, and a pragmatic device of Castlereagh, into a powerful instrument for keeping the peace, but a peace which was politically and socially stagnant. The rulers of the Great Powers, then, held certain assumptions in common – that the world needed a long peace after the long period of warfare, that the only way of ensuring peace was to consider the 1815 Settlement sacrosanct, and that even a modification of a domestic régime of a European country would endanger that settlement. For example, while it might seem on the surface innocuous for Piedmont or Naples to become a constitutional monarchy instead of remaining an absolute monarchy, the resultant parliament from such a constitution might give expression to desires to liberate Lombardy and Venice from Austrian rule. Castlereagh, no less than Metternich, and – increasingly from 1818 onwards – Alexander I also, were acutely aware of such possibilities. But Metternich was the most directly concerned, and his career from 1815 to 1848 was to be a central factor in the history of the Risorgimento.

Prince Clemens Wenzel Nepomuk Lothar Metternich-Winneburg had been born in 1773 at Coblenz on the Rhine. His father had been in the diplomatic service of the Archbishop-Elector of Trier, but had then acquired a post in the Habsburg's diplomatic service. This did not mean that the Metternich family moved to Vienna, since Metternich's father was made the Austrian representative to the three Rhenish electors, so that Metternich grew up in the Rhineland, a corner of Europe which was part-provincial, part-cosmopolitan, but which had very little, if any, sense of 'national' identity. Metternich was to become a minister of the Emperor, a kind of international civil servant, who rarely thought of himself as either a 'German' or an 'Austrian'. In 1788 he was enrolled in the University of Strassburg as a student of constitutional law. At Strassburg, at the age of sixteen in 1789, he watched demonstrations by a violent liberal crowd, and was later to account for his hatred of liberalism to this youthful experience. Because of the French Revolution he was obliged to leave Strassburg and move to the University of Mainz, where he met many French émigrés who no doubt fortified his aversion for the ideas of 1789. But the young Clemens Metternich was by no means a straightforward reactionary. In 1794 in Brussels, where his father had been made Austrian minister, Metternich wrote his first published work, a pamphlet declaring that the methods of the *ancien régime* were inadequate for dealing with the revolutionary armies of France. There must, he declared, be a *levée en masse*, such as the French themselves had organized, of all the countries bordering France. The mature Metternich was to be less eager to seek the help of the people, but his mind at the age of twenty-one was evidently still flexible. In 1795 he married extremely wisely. His bride was the granddaughter of Kaunitz, Maria Theresa's distinguished chancellor, and she brought to Metternich considerable landed wealth and contacts with the ruling class in Vienna. But he had himself a great deal to contribute – intelligence, charm and good looks. He moved with natural ease into a diplomatic career in the service of the Habsburgs, being made their envoy to Saxony in 1801. Less than three years later, by a somewhat dramatic promotion, he was appointed ambassador to Berlin, and in a further two years – in 1806 – at Napoleon's request, he was given the embassy in Paris. He remained on good personal terms with Napoleon until 1809, when war broke out again between France and Austria. Napoleon rightly suspected Metternich of having recommended war to the Austrian government. Metternich was arrested, and when Napoleon entered Vienna in the summer of that year Metternich was taken with him under armed guard. On 8 October 1809 he was made foreign minister, but at a time when Austrian power was in eclipse. The alliance between France and Russia placed Austria in a perilous position, and Metternich decided the only solution was for Austria to try to replace Russia as France's ally. Napoleon seemed to play into Metternich's hands when, in 1810, he proposed marriage to Francis II's daughter, the Archduchess Marie-Louise. Metternich persuaded a reluctant emperor to accept a marriage alliance with Bonaparte. When Napoleon invaded Russia in 1812 Metternich steered Austrian policy along a typically tortuous path. Without declaring war on Russia, Austria contributed 30,000 men to the French invasion, but the Austrian generals were ordered to act only on the defensive. With the disaster which overcame the French during the retreat from Moscow, Metternich slowly detached Austria from the *alliance limitée* with France, and opened negotiations with the other Powers. Although Austria, Russia, Prussia and Britain were, by 1813, firmly allied against Napoleon, Metternich was far from happy: Czar Alexander I seemed too successful and too ambitious, and in Germany the so-called 'War of Liberation' was accompanied by extravagant demands for German unification. Metternich need not have worried: the 'War of Liberation' merely liberated the German princes from Napoleon; it did not liberate the German people. But it is interesting that at that moment Metternich was far more preoccupied with the early glimmerings of German nationalism than with those of Italian nationalism. At the Congress of Vienna, however, his preoccupations were to be mainly with Italy.

Such was the background to the man who, in 1815, exerted more influence on Italian affairs than any other individual. Highly intelligent, but insufferably vain, Metternich was perhaps the first doom-watcher of modern times. He was convinced that the nascent ideologies of liberalism and nationalism would lead Europe to disaster, and he believed that the best that could be done was to slow down the process. Yet in 1815 all the physical forces in Italy were on his side. His only real enemies were small groups of retired army officers and disenchanted professional men working underground in secret sects.

The activities of the secret societies have already been noticed in Lombardy,[1] Tuscany,[2] the Papal States,[3] and Naples.[4] They never had a mass following, but by 1820 they were a very significant pressure group. In Piedmont they continued the tradition of the Jacobin conspiracies of the 1790s. The secret societies there, as in other parts of Italy, had originally been plotting against the French, and their members hoped that the departure of the French would be accompanied by liberal reforms. When they realized that this was not to be, they remained in existence to conspire against the régimes of the Restoration. In Piedmont, where the influence of the Church was as strong as in the Papal States or Naples, and much stronger than in Austrian Italy or Tuscany, the Masons were specifically forbidden to meet. Many former members of the Masons, knowing that they were under observation by the authorities, stopped attending Masonic meetings and joined other sects. One such sect was the Adelfi, who had originally been directed against Napoleon, and after 1815 came under the influence of Buonarroti.

Filippo Buonarroti, a direct descendant of Michelangelo, had been born in Pisa in 1761. Educated in the law, like so many revolutionaries, he had been so closely identified with the French Revolution that he was obliged to leave Tuscany in 1789. He was already in Paris in 1793, a Jacobin and follower of Robespierre. He took part in the socialist rising of Noël Babeuf's 'Conspiracy of Equals' in Paris in 1796, and when Babeuf was executed Buonarroti was imprisoned. His imprisonment in Cherbourg seems not to have been a very rigorous one. The woman with whom he lived for some twenty years, Teresa Poggi, was allowed to stay with him for long periods, and without difficulty carried Jacobin propaganda away from the prison. He was released in 1806, and spent most of the years 1806–23 in Geneva, but he remained constantly in touch with cells in Italy where his revolutionary organization had its headquarters in Alessandria. In a meeting of the sects in Alessandria in 1818 the Adelfi, and remnants of the earlier sect of the Filadelfi, were united into a new society, called the 'Sublime Perfect Masters', a title the absurdity of which seemed not to be apparent to its members. They operated in profound secrecy. The three grades of the society had three basic aims, which were kept secret from each other: they were, in fact, deism and the sovereignty of the people for the first grade; republicanism for the second grade; the establishment of a communist society for the third grade. That communism was an aim of the Sublime Perfect Masters was in particular to be kept a total secret, even from many members of the society. Buonarroti realized that the idea of sharing all property and goods in common would antagonize and terrify the majority of people, and that it could only be whispered of, as an ultimate and not an immediate aim. Although Italian nationalism did not appear among the three declared aims of the society, there is no doubt that Buonarroti believed that Italian independence from Austria must be a first step, and that a second step – before communism could be openly pursued – must be the establishment of a democratic republic. Because of the extreme secrecy surrounding the Sublime Perfect Masters historians are by no means certain of its extent and ramifications. It seems, however, clear that there was an important centre in Turin which was in touch with cells not only throughout Piedmont, but also in Lombardy, the Veneto, Parma and Modena. Probably also there were cells in Tuscany and the Papal States, but there is no evidence that the society reached as far as Naples, where the Carbonari were easily the largest secret society. In spite of a good deal of research which has been directed towards

Buonarroti, it is still by no means clear how important his rôle was. Metter-nich certainly feared him as 'that secret centre, which has directed the greater part of the secret societies of Europe for years'.[5] Buonarroti lived until 1837. After the July Revolution of 1830 he was allowed to return to Paris, but he was not deceived by this act of clemency into believing that the July Monar-chy had any relationship with democracy.

A secret society which satisfied a demand for more immediate, if more limited, action, was the 'Italian Federation' which developed in the years 1818–20 in Piedmont and Lombardy. Its aim was to secure the liberation of Lombardy and the Veneto, and to link them with Piedmont in a constitutional monarchy. The most prominent figure in the Italian Federation was Count Federico Confalonieri, from Milan, who was to be condemned to death in 1821 but subsequently to have his sentence commuted to life imprisonment. It was rare for a nobleman like Confalonieri to be involved in the secret sects, which were more often dominated by the bourgeoisie. Confalonieri was also in touch with the Carbonari.

Most famous of all .the secret societies, the Carbonari had already been in existence in Naples in 1807, but historians are by no means certain of their origin. The name has usually been translated into English as 'charcoal-burners', and so has conjured up the image of small groups of men conspiring around charcoal fires in the night, but it was once thought, and is at least feasible, that the nucleus of the society in Naples were the producers rather than the consumers of charcoal, in other words they were men who sold char-coal for use as domestic fuel, an activity common in the wooded hills of Calabria. The Carbonari followed rituals as elaborate and fanciful as those of the Masons; they had to swear complete and blind obedience to their leaders; even so, it has been roughly calculated that their numbers in Southern Italy reached some 60,000. The main contrast between the Carbonari and the Freemasons was that the former were definitely planning an armed revolution, while the latter intended to spread humanist, anti-clerical values by peaceful means. In the eyes of the Catholic establishment both societies appeared, of course, equally subversive. In theory the Carbonari were a cosmopolitan so-ciety, with a Supreme Lodge in Paris, and branches as far apart as Ireland and Greece. In practice they were far more active in Italy than anywhere else, and there is little evidence that the Italian cells had close contact with Carbonari outside Italy. Unlike secret societies inspired more directly by Buonarroti, and unlike Mazzini's later 'Young Italy', the Carbonari did not aim necessarily for a republic. In Piedmont they hoped to be able to make Carlo Alberto king, with, of course, a constitution. They had supported the restoration of the Bourbons in Naples in 1815, and even when they had become disillusioned with Ferdinand they still did not, in 1820, want to establish a republic, but simply to force Ferdinand to accept a constitution.

The revolutions of 1820–21 in Piedmont and Naples have been considered from the point of view of the domestic histories of those states in Part Two.[6] Their international significance and their importance in the history of the 'Congress System' must now be illustrated.

Metternich was determined that nothing approximating to a constitution should be allowed to exist in any Italian state. Thus when the revolutions of 1820–21 succeeded in creating constitutions in Naples and Turin Metternich was prepared for Austrian intervention. Initially he was apprehensive, however, of using the 'Congress System', which would virtually involve the recognition of an international body for the simultaneous suppression of liberalism and the keeping of the peace. Castlereagh, in control of British policy, was also happy to regard Italy as a sphere of Austrian influence, and was averse to using the 'Congress System' as an international police force. Czar Alexander I, however, had since 1815 developed a great fear of revolution in Southern or Central Europe, and wanted to involve Russia in any police actions which Metternich might undertake. Metternich therefore decided to comply with the Czar's wishes, and to call a congress which would legitimize Austrian intervention on an international plane. Thus was it agreed that a congress should meet in the little spa town of Troppau in that part of Silesia which was in the Habsburg Monarchy. But when the congress met, in October of 1820, Britain and France were represented only by ambassadors, so that the findings of the congress were essentially those of Russia, Austria and Prussia. Those findings were grim and brutal: 'If in states belonging to the European Alliance changes of government are produced by a revolution, and if their consequences threaten other states, then they are excluded from the Alliance until their situation offers guarantees of legitimate order and permanence.' What came to be known as the Troppau Doctrine went on to proclaim that the Allied governments would 'refuse recognition of changes brought about by illegal methods', and would therefore take measures to rectify such changes 'first by friendly representations, then by measures of coercion, if the employment of such coercion is indispensable'.

The Congress of Troppau, then, did not make specific recommendations for dealing with the revolutions in Italy, but laid down a general doctrine, which was applied to Naples when the arrival of Ferdinand at the Congress of Laibach in January 1821 presented the Eastern Powers with the opportunity for such an application. The British Government was beginning to move away from the policy of the Eastern Powers. Castlereagh had already protested at the declaration of the Troppau Doctrine, which he said was 'directly opposed to the political and constitutional system of Great Britain'.[7] But there is reason to suppose that Castlereagh was not so much averse to the destruction of constitutions in Italy as opposed to the idea of the establishment of an international body – the 'Congress System' – which claimed the right to intervene in the internal affairs of sovereign states. He regarded Italy as a sphere of Austrian influence, and would have liked Metternich to pursue a repressive policy there off his own bat without involving the other Powers.

Once absolutism had been restored in Naples and Piedmont there was no further need for active Austrian intervention in Italy throughout the 1820s, but the revolutions of 1831 made the Italian Question once more an international one, international so far as revolutionaries and foreign ministries were concerned. The Italian exiles in Paris grouped around Buonarroti considered themselves the leaders of a future European revolution, but they had not forgotten Italy. They reacted to the revolutions of 1831 in Parma and Modena by publishing a manifesto 'to the Italian people, from the Alps to Etna': 'we are hurrying to unite our voices and our arms in support of Italian liberty'. Italy, they declared, must be 'Independent, One and Free'. In Italy, 'the People must be master; equality and love must reign; the happiness of all must have a firm resting-place'.[8] But Italians were warned not to accept any gifts – like the granting of a constitution – from the ruling princes. The group around Buonarroti were thus putting forward an advanced doctrine of Italian nationalism – if in very general terms – at a time when Mazzini's name was still virtually unknown. But although Buonarroti's *Giunta*, as it was called, had declared that they were 'hurrying to unite their arms in support of Italian liberty', Buonarroti himself advised that no physical intervention was yet possible. It was left to Misley to prepare some kind of revolutionary expedition. His preparations were at first tolerated by the government of the newly established July Monarchy but then, suddenly, on 24 February 1831, the French government halted Misley's expedition, as they did again shortly afterwards when he tried to leave Marseilles with a shipful of arms. The French doctrine of non-intervention, already referred to in Chapters 3 and 4, still seemed, however, to the revolutionaries in Central Italy to be the best guarantee against Austrian intervention. The Papal Government had asked for Austrian intervention on 19 February. A few days later the French ambassador in Vienna informed Metternich that Austrian intervention would lead to war with France, to which Metternich had replied that orders for intervention had already been given to the army. One factor persuading the French to withdraw from their radical and threatening position was the involvement of the young Bonapartes in the Italian revolution. In the event Italy was to wait until Louis-Napoleon was himself the ruler of France before she could secure material aid from the French against Austria.

On 18 March 1831 Louis-Philippe's prime minister, Casimir Perier, made a statement which became famous, and which chilled the hearts of the revolutionaries in Central Italy: 'We do not recognize the right of any people to force us to fight for its cause: the blood of Frenchmen belongs to France alone.' But Perier's government did not intend to remain totally inactive. On the contrary, it decided to send a French expeditionary force to Ancona: the force disembarked on 22 February 1832. The French were concerned only with preventing Austria from dominating the government of the new Pope. Perier also made it clear that he would support the new King, Carlo Alberto, in Piedmont against Austrian attack. But beyond that the French government certainly did not intend to go. 'Italian independence' was not yet on the cards. Nor did Carlo Alberto want French support; he regarded the French occupation of Ancona as dangerous, because likely to encourage subversive elements. But the French presence in Ancona certainly had the effect of discouraging the Austrians from advancing any nearer to Rome than was absolutely necessary to suppress the revolution, and encouraging them to withdraw sooner than they would probably otherwise have done. But the British government were very unhappy at the presence of foreign armies in what were supposedly independent Italian states. The new foreign secretary in London, Lord Palmerston, did not start his long and remarkable career at the Foreign Office with any show of sympathy towards Italy. On the contrary, he complained to the French government that they should not tolerate dangerous Italian revolutionaries in Paris while professing a policy of non-intervention. But once the Austrians and French had established forces in Central Italy Palmerston agitated for the withdrawal of both with equal vigour. He wrote privately to his colleague, Lord Granville:

I am sorry for the determination of Austria about Italy; it is wrong and foolish; and brings on at once a general war, which one had hoped might have been avoided. The inevitable consequence will be, the expulsion of the Austrians from Italy; and for that, one shall not be sorry, provided the French are not established there, in their stead.[9]

Palmerston, of course, was naive in supposing that the revolutions of 1831 in Italy would bring on 'a general war', but he was perceptive in his realization that he was witnessing the beginning of a process which would lead to the expulsion of the Austrians from Italy. Yet Metternich assumed that Britain was on his side against France in Italy. In April 1831 he asked Palmerston to reinforce the British fleet in the Mediterranean. In his career as the pilot of British foreign policy, a career just beginning, Palmerston was certainly not going to be averse to using the British navy. He was not, however, likely to use it at the bequest of Metternich. Palmerston's immediate concern was with the running of the Papal States. It was not difficult to convince the political leaders of Protestant Britain that the administration of the Papal States was inefficient and corrupt. That it happened to be true was a bonus that the English Whigs did not altogether deserve. After the 1831 revolution in Central Italy Palmerston was therefore happy to be able to encourage a demand by the Great Powers that the Pope should reform his administration by allowing municipal governments to be more independent of Rome, by introducing laymen into local government, and by modernizing finance. The demand took the formal shape of a Memorandum from the Great Powers to the Pope. The Powers themselves, and especially Britain, were often to refer to the Memorandum in the future. There is no evidence that Gregory XVI ever gave it a passing thought. That he was becoming isolated in Europe did not worry him over-much. He was, after all, a monk.

A more significant result of the revolutionary turmoil in Italy in 1830–31 was the arrest of a young member of the Carbonari in Genoa, a certain Giuseppe Mazzini, on 13 November 1830. He was arrested on the charge of having recruited another member of the Carbonari. He had been betrayed by Raimondo Doria, one of his superiors in the sect, who had given his name to the police and secured his arrest: this Mazzini surmised from the questions put to him by the police, questions which could have been based only on information from Doria. Mazzini pleaded not guilty, and the evidence against him was so slim that the Piedmontese minister of the exterior ruled that he should be released but not allowed to live in Genoa, Turin, or any point on the coast.

With the turmoil of 1830 bursting upon Europe the idea of staying in a provincial Piedmontese town was too much for Mazzini, and he decided to leave for France.

But from November 1830 until February 1831 Mazzini was in prison in Savona, a little way along the coast from Genoa, and it was here that his ideas of democratic-nationalism were given shape — ideas which formed the most dynamic stimulus to Italian nationalism, and indeed to nationalist movements all over the world.

At that time Mazzini was twenty-six, and the lines of his personality had already been formed. Everyone who had ever met him or who was ever to meet him left a record of an appearance and personality which were both striking and agreeable, and the verdict is sustained by numerous portraits in both painting and photography. Although a short, slight man, his presence always made him the centre of attention. He had large, dark eyes, finely cut features, and could change his expression in a moment from one of deep seriousness and severity to one of great kindness and light-heartedness. Although there were to be people who would find his self-righteousness exasperating, of those who knew him no one ever disliked him, but very many — men and women of all classes and races — developed for him a respect and affection not given to the common run of humanity. So far as his political associates went, however, the reaction tended to be one of two extremes: either they idolized him and followed him with devotion, or they broke with him and quarrelled acrimoniously. It was evidently easy to like and admire him, less easy to work with him. From his student days onwards he lived an austere life, but was not a puritan. He smoked cigars, and could sing well to his own guitar. Later in life he was to develop acute depressions, and to wake in the night with fits of convulsive sobbing. But in 1831 there were no such signs of psychological imbalance.

Giuseppe Mazzini had been born on 22 June 1805 in Genoa. His father, Dr Giacomo Mazzini, was an academic — a professor of anatomy at the University of Genoa, and at the time of Giuseppe's birth still a believer in the democratic ideas of the French Revolution. Dr Mazzini had collaborated in the publication of a Jacobin journal, the *Censore Italiano*, in Genoa in 1797–9. But Giuseppe's mother had the stronger personality, and her interest in European politics was to prove more tenacious than her husband's. However, Maria Mazzini was perhaps a little unbalanced mentally, believing that she had given birth to some kind of Messiah who was, apart from anything else, immune from any physical danger. She was clearly the more powerful influence on Giuseppe. While his father was worried about his son's evidently delicate disposition — probably unnecessarily — his mother was convinced that God intended some great mission for her son, and that her own function in life had become that of sacrificing herself to his needs and, after he had left Genoa for exile, repeating his ideas in the teeth of any hostile or sceptical criticism. Yet Mazzini's parents were evidently happy together, and although they were to disagree on Giuseppe's wisdom in accepting the life of a revolutionary exile, Maria Mazzini retained a gently mocking affection for her husband. Dr Giacomo Mazzini himself became a complete sceptic after the restoration of 1815. He had no hopes for Italy and was appalled when his son later became involved in nationalist insurrectionary activities. He believed – perhaps rightly – that his son was basically a poet, and should establish himself in Italy as a creative writer. Even after a Piedmontese court had condemned Giuseppe to death in his absence, his father believed that the Piedmontese establishment would pardon him if he promised to give up politics and become a respectable literary man. But Giuseppe was not to be tempted by such suggestions. The purpose of life, he wrote to his father, was not happiness but duty.

Giacomo Mazzini had always been worried about his son's health, and the frailty of Giuseppe's constitution in his early years was genuine enough. He suffered from a weakness of the spine, and could not walk until he was five. On the other hand he could read easily at the age of four. He clearly grew up in a healthy atmosphere of political and intellectual vitality. He had three sisters, who were kind to him, but no brothers. A delicate and highly sensitive little boy, he quickly gave evidence of intelligence far above the average. He later recorded that his parents were wholly free of class prejudice, in that they treated everyone with respect. They had warm memories of the French republican period, memories which without doubt complemented his readings in Latin which encouraged him to regard the republic as a civilized constitutional form, and monarchy as an institution of barbarism.

But it was an incident caused by contemporary developments in Italy which, according to his own account, first inflamed Mazzini's imagination with regard to the future of Italy. After the failure of the Piedmontese revolution of 1821 many revolutionaries passed through Genoa on their way to exile – on the whole going to Spain where the revolution still survived. These unfortunate men, begging for cash to enable them to escape, impressed themselves upon the young Giuseppe as he walked with his mother in the streets of Genoa. For the first time he realized that people could struggle and suffer for a political ideal. The failure of the revolutionaries became an obsession with him in his sixteenth year. He started to dress in black and never abandoned the practice. Without realizing it this young, sensitive, intelligent man was providing a stereotype for generations of romantic revolutionaries.

As a small boy Mazzini was privately educated. Initially he was persuaded to follow his father's example and study medicine. But he fainted at the first witnessing of an operation, and his father reluctantly agreed that he should switch his study to that of law. From November 1819, when he was fourteen, he was attending university courses in the faculty of philosophy and literature, eventually fully enrolling and securing a diploma on 31 May 1822. For four and a half years – from November 1822 until April 1827 when he graduated – Mazzini studied law at the university. But if surgery had nauseated him, law bored him. Even so, he managed to pass his law exams with highly respectable results. However, it is surprising how small an impact his academic studies of these years made on his mind. Never legalistically minded, he retained a passionate interest in literature and history, as well as politics. These were the subjects which he discussed with the group of intelligent young friends who gathered around him and of whom the closest to Mazzini were three brothers, Jacopo, Giovanni and Agostino Ruffini. As an undergraduate he was already something of a rebel, refusing to attend the compulsory religious services, not so much in an anti-religious spirit as because he resented the regulation.

The earliest surviving writing of Mazzini is of this period – 'Dante's love of his country', written in 1826 or 1827. It was intentionally polemical, taking sides firmly with Romanticism against Classicism, a struggle which was being fought bitterly by Italian writers.[10] But it was also overtly nationalist, and interpreted Dante's *De Monarchia* as a plea for the unification of Italy. Mazzini wrote, quite simply: 'the father-land of an Italian is not Rome, Florence or Milan, but the whole of Italy'. He sent the piece to the Florentine journal, *Antologia*, but it was not published.

In 1829 he wrote a long review of a French translation of Goethe's *Faust*, a translation published the year before. He interpreted the play as a judgement on the egoism of the age. Feudal tyranny encouraged egoism and was represented by Mephistopheles. The individual who concentrates only on his own interests puts himself in the power of the Devil. Goethe's Margaret represented the other kind of individual – 'simple, candid, confident' – who accepts joys and sorrows naturally, spontaneously, tenderly. 'Between the two extremes, between the refinement of Egoism and the innocence of Nature', were the ignorant superstitious rustics who knew neither 'the delights of virtue, nor the malignance of crime'.[11] With this view of human nature and society it was clear that when Mazzini constructed a political philosophy it would be one appealing to a people's moral sense rather than to its interests.

Mazzini had joined the Carbonari in 1827. He was quickly given the right to enlist recruits and soon he became secretary of the Genoese Lodge. But he was equally quickly suspicious of the basic ideas of the society. He was not told the aims of the Carbonari in any coherent manner, but was simply exhorted to give them complete obedience. The young Mazzini wanted to debate whether a federal Italy or an integrated Italy would be preferable, whether Italy were better suited to be a republic or a monarchy. Such subtle debating points were not encouraged by the Carbonari, who believed that complete obedience to their authority, with its vague aspirations, was essential.

One of the leaders of the Carbonari whom Mazzini met at Genoa was the Raimondo Doria who was to betray him. Doria was in touch with the cells in Spain, France and – a presumably very small one – in London. Mazzini was given the task by Doria of writing an open letter to Charles X of France condemning the French intervention of 1823 against the Spanish revolution. He wrote at great length but never had the satisfaction of knowing if his letter had been sent to France, or read by anyone. His disillusionment with the Carbonari quickly grew.

But as we have seen, his interests in the late 1820s were still primarily literary. He was fond of the concept of the 'Genius', believing that a few rare geniuses – Homer, Dante, Shakespeare, Byron and Goethe – could be clearly distinguished from the rest of mankind. Civilization was, indeed, their construction. The concept was typically Hegelian, yet Mazzini seeems not to have come across the writings of Hegel. He was, however, interested in the purely philosophical writings of Kant and Herder, and the influence of Herder was to be more profound and lasting than all the others. The modern Italian work of literature which affected him most at this time was Foscolo's *Jacopo Ortis*.[12] Mazzini's own inflated and highly emotional style owed much to Foscolo's prose.

Mazzini's disillusionment with the Carbonari increased when they appeared not to respond to the July Revolution of 1830 in Paris. Partly to appease his restlessness Doria gave him the task of travelling to Tuscany and making contact with Guerrazzi, who was already known for his nationalist revolutionary ideas. Guerrazzi was under house arrest at Montepulciano, but was allowed to receive visitors. The young Mazzini was shrewd enough to realize that Guerrazzi was a vain and arrogant man but also, more significantly, a pessimist and cynic who smiled at Mazzini's talk of progress and the love of humanity. Yet the two men were to work together in the future, and Guerrazzi was even to join Mazzini's 'Young Italy'. But in 1830 Doria had already decided to hand Mazzini over to the authorities in Genoa, and in so doing had unwittingly opened a new phase in the history of the Risorgimento.

Mazzini was in prison in Savona for only about three months, but in that short space of time his thoughts crystallized, he realized that the central passion of his life was to work for the independence and unification of Italy, and that to do so he must forget about the Carbonari and found a fresh movement of his own. It was to be called *La Giovine Italia* – 'Young Italy' – and was to be based on firmly defined principles. The main lines of his own political philosophy were by now fixed and were never to change. To begin with, he was convinced of the existence of God, for which he felt that there was no need of proof: any attempt at proof would be 'blasphemy; any denial, madness'. Secondly, he believed in the unity of humanity: no race of man was superior to any other. In this conviction he followed the doctrine of Herder, and so stood in a close relationship with eighteenth-century ideas of the Enlightenment. With the more aggressive ideas of romantic nationalism – those, for example, of Fichte – he had no sympathy. Thirdly, he believed in Progress. Man is 'a being who learns, through the faults and errors of individuals, continually to improve in wisdom and morality'. Here, also he seemed closer to the ideas of the Enlightenment than to those of nineteenth-century Romanticism. A more original basic idea of Mazzini was what he called the principle of 'association'. The French Revolution, he believed, had established and won recognition for the rights of the individual. What was now needed was a recognition of the duties which individuals owed to each other and to society. There was a crying need for 'general co-operation and the harmony of work'. Why the conviction did not lead Mazzini to call himself a socialist will be discussed later when his political convictions as an old man are considered.[13] Here it is sufficient to recognize that he was not a simple Jacobin or liberal; he believed that the obligations as well as the rights of the individual must be taught.

His attitude to religion was an ambivalent one. He believed that young, dynamic religions usually advanced mankind along the road of progress, but only for one phase of history. When a religion became decadent it would have to be discarded — or rather its 'forms and symbols' would have to be discarded, while the 'residue of Truth contained' by the religion, 'a residue immortal, immutable' would be preserved. In this sense Chritianity had already served its purpose, and although Mazzini was careful to avoid offending Christians, he was equally firm in declaring that he himself was not a Christian.

The religion of the nineteenth century was democracy. God, Mazzini believed, was no longer speaking through priests or holy writings, but through the People. What the People demanded, therefore, was also the will of God. And since the People demanded that they should be sovereign within their own national groups, popular sovereignty and the principle of nationality had to be secured, and they could be secured only by revolution, a revolution fought by an alliance of European peoples against their princes. In a sense, then, Mazzini was a nationalist only because he was first a democrat, but a democrat who believed that the popular will demanded that each sense of national identity be respected. It was his mission to construct a revolutionary society which would on the one hand teach the Italian people to have a sense of national identity, and on the other hand would prepare the revolution which would establish an independent, democratic, Italian republic. To this ambitious end 'Young Italy' was to be dedicated.

On his release from Savona in February 1831 Mazzini left Italy and settled for the time being in Marseilles, where there was already a small colony of Italian exiles, and it was in Marseilles that he launched his secret society, 'Young Italy', or, as he called it initially, 'the Federation of Young Italy'. In a letter written to a sympathizer, Giuseppe Gigliolo, from Marseilles, on 21 July 1831, Mazzini gave details of his new revolutionary sect. Members of 'Young Italy' had to swear to consecrate themselves to 'the regeneration of the Father-land', and 'their word, thought and action to the conquest of Independence, Unity, Liberty for Italy'. They had also 'to fight in every way inequalities between men'. Every member had to secure for himself a rifle and fifty rounds of ammunition. There was to be a central *Congrega*, for the time being at Marseilles, and in every Italian province there was to be a provincial Congrega of three members. The 'ultimate scope' of the Federation was 'the republic one and indivisible'. 'Constitutional monarchical governments' would be accepted as 'governments of transition', while 'Young Italy' had insufficient power to take over. 'So far as religion goes, the final aim is the destruction of all the high aristocracy of the Priesthood, and the introduction of a simple parish system . . . . All aristocracy abolished: all privileges which do not depend on capacity, or actions, nullified. Public education encouraged without limit.' All this, however, would have to wait until the 'barbarian had evacuated Italy'. In some respects 'Young Italy' was to retain the theatricality of the Carbonari. There were to be secret handshakes, and passwords: 'What time is it?' – 'The time for struggle' . . . 'Now' – 'And always'. There was even to be a uniform, a green blouse, a red leather belt, white trousers, and a beret with the national cockade. Exactly when this uniform was to be worn was not clear – presumably only after the initial insurrection had succeeded.

Mazzini concluded his letter to Gigliolo with these words: 'You must tell the young men that this is not a Society like the other ones: there are no mysteries, no hierarchies of rank, no symbols – it is a brotherhood of young people, who have come together to work in common with frankness, sincerity and confidence . . . . We have need of everyone, and of no one: the affair will move forward . . .'[14]

In 1831 Carlo Alberto became king of Piedmont. At about the same time as he was writing to Gigliolo about 'Young 'Italy' Mazzini addressed an open letter to Carlo Alberto. The exact date of the letter is not known, but it was written in Marseilles at some time in June or July 1831. Mazzini started by saying that he would not address Carlo Alberto at all if he thought that he was the normal 'vulgar' type of king. But 'we have looked at your face to find the traces of a tyrant, and they were not there'. All the same he continues in a threatening tone, warning the king of a coming popular revolution in Europe, an 'inevitable war . . . not of men but of principles'. In this confrontation Carlo Alberto would have to decide – either to fight the popular revolution with a reign of terror or to make 'concessions', a course which would be proposed to him by some of his courtiers. But concessions which did not include a clear declaration of the sovereignty of the people would achieve nothing. Such concessions would merely antagonize the Austrians without reconciling the Italians. Mazzini then comes to the crux of the matter in telling Carlo Alberto what, in his opinion, la plebe really wants. 'They want liberty, independence and union.' 'The cry of 1789 has roused the people from its sleep.' Carlo Alberto therefore had to face the fact that his destiny was to wage war, 'a European, long, ferocious war of principles'. He had to lead 'the people' and 'the young'.

The question which has to be asked with regard to Mazzini's letter of 1831 to Carlo Alberto concerns its sincerity. He himself commented on his appeal to the new king in a private letter written on 29 June 1831, and added 'not that I have any hopes in him: he is a coward, if not worse'.[15] Since Mazzini had always declared himself basically opposed to monarchy and a staunch republican it must be asked what he would have done in the extremely unlikely event of Carlo Alberto listening to his plea. He was, of course, not unaware of this paradox himself, and makes it apparent when he writes that Carlo Alberto must return 'if not to republican forms, at least to the republican spirit'. But his final advice to the king is to put himself 'at the head of the nation; and write on your banner: UNION, LIBERTY, INDEPENDENCE! . . . Free the country from the barbarians! . . . Give your name to a century!'[16]

From 1831 to 1833 Mazzini devoted himself to the organization of 'Young Italy'. The title reflected the decision that no one over forty should be admitted, but before the end of 1831 Mazzini had discovered that there were older men whom it would be foolish to reject, and he therefore announced that exceptions could be made, but that the general principle must remain so that 'Young Italy' should not be chilled by the scepticism of the middle-aged.

Propaganda was despatched from Marseilles by sea to Italian ports, especially to Genoa and Leghorn. The Ruffini brothers and Mazzini's close group of friends were still in Genoa, where they formed an active cell. They were successful in securing recruits for 'Young Italy' among junior army officers, so that within a year or two they could feel assured of control of the fortress. The most zealous of the Ruffini brothers was Jacopo, who was even prepared to let his medical work suffer so that he could spend time in furthering the cause of 'Young Italy'. Before long Mazzinian propaganda was reaching the rest of Piedmont, Tuscany and the Papal States. But the Papal States was the one part of Italy where Mazzini could not hope for an immediate insurrection, since the Austrian and French forces were firmly encamped there. With Piedmont, however, he felt familiar, and there he had his friends. It was his natural base. It was therefore in Piedmont that the first Mazzinian insurrection was staged. The Piedmontese government was slow in suspecting that the journal, the *Giovine Italia*, had acquired an effective circulation in the kingdom; but fights and troubles in the barracks spread throughout Piedmont, not only in Turin and Genoa, but on the frontier at Alessandria and throughout the country. The conspiracy within the army in 1833 was betrayed by one embittered officer to the authorities, who carefully collected the many details available and then crushed the conspiracy. The repression by Carlo Alberto's government was savage and included torture, a barbarism practised much less often in the nineteenth than in the twentieth century. Sixty-seven people were arrested, and about 200 fled into exile. Twenty-one were condemned to death, and twelve were executed in June of 1833. Jacopo Ruffini, imprisoned and suspecting that he would be tortured in an attempt to secure the names of his friends, killed himself. The news of Jacopo's death brought Mazzini to the verge of a nervous breakdown. No man had been closer to him than Jacopo Ruffini. By nineteenth-century standards the repression was a very savage one, but it did not deter Mazzini from hurrying to Genoa in July 1833 to organize a new movement of insurrection against Piedmont.

On 29 September 1832 Mazzini had reached with Buonarroti an agreement by which they were to unite their revolutionary forces – Buonarroti's long-established contacts and Mazzini's 'Young Italy'. The pact had always been an uneasy one because Buonarroti was by then too old to favour the immediate and dangerous action for which Mazzini was impatient. By 1834 the split between the two men and their organizations was too serious to be concealed, and Buonarroti not only refused to support Mazzini's efforts, but deliberately undermined them by advising his supporters to keep clear of Mazzini's conspiracies.

The main thrust of Mazzini's movement against Piedmont was to come from Switzerland into Piedmontese Savoy, the 'cradle', as it was always called, of the Duchy. For the enterprise Mazzini collected funds from numerous sources. The manpower was to come from Italian exiles in France and Switzerland, strengthened by a few Polish and German exiles. The military command was entrusted to Gerolamo Ramorino, from Genoa, who had served as an officer in Napoleon's army and then in the Piedmontese army until his exile in 1821. He had commanded a Polish revolutionary army in 1831. But the choice of General Ramorino turned out to be unfortunate. Entrusted by Mazzini with funds to organize a fighting force, Ramorino journeyed to Paris and there lost most of the cash in gambling. He returned to Geneva at the end of January 1834, having failed to collect the fighting force which Mazzini expected from him. Mazzini therefore had to depend on the few hundred men he had himself collected in Switzerland. Just before the expedition was to set out the governments of the cantons of Geneva and Vaud, which were virtually independent bodies before the Swiss federal constitution of 1848 was drawn up, surrounded and disbanded the group of Polish and German volunteers. On Ramorino's return less than 200 men remained and he understandably felt that the enterprise should be given up. But Mazzini was emotionally too committed to it. While the two men argued the remainder of the 200 obeyed Ramorino's orders and dispersed. Meanwhile another group of Mazzinian exiles had advanced into Piedmont from Grenoble, the original plan being that they would join up with the force from Geneva. This second group was met and defeated by Piedmontese *carabinieri* – the semi-military, semi-police force which still exists in Italy today. Only two of the revolutionaries and one *carabiniere* were killed in the fighting, and two other revolutionaries were subsequently shot.

A movement scheduled to coincide with that in Savoy was planned in Genoa. The young sailor, Giuseppe Garibaldi, had, early in 1833, joined 'Young Italy', had met Mazzini in Marseilles, and had enlisted in the Piedmontese navy, evidently with the express purpose of organizing a mutiny at the time of the rising planned for February 1834. But the Genoa rising, like the Savoy expedition, failed to materialize. The authorities had been warned and took steps to defuse it. Garibaldi himself escaped and was sentenced to death in his absence.

In 1833 and 1834 the Mazzinian movement had failed more dismally than the Carbonari had done. The Carbonari had contributed notably to the revolutions of 1820–21 and 1831, which had at least temporarily succeeded in establishing revolutionary governments; the Mazzinians in 1834 had not even approached such an achievement. 'Young Italy' as a closely organized and well knit society scarcely any longer existed. Mazzini himself remained in Switzerland until 1836, but his influence, if still great, had now become more diffuse.

In Berne in April 1834 Mazzini founded 'Young Europe', a grandiloquent name for a group of seventeen young men – Italians, Poles and Germans – who swore that they would fight for democracy in Europe. Of no practical importance, 'Young Europe' is of interest as an indication that Mazzini's nationalism was only a part of a broader international philosophy. That his nationalism was not an exclusive or limited one had already been made apparent by one of his writings in 1829 – 'Of European Literature'. In this piece it was already clear that he was looking far beyond the creation of an Italian nation-state. 'I know', he wrote, 'that to many people the words "European Literature" sound destructive of any national spirit, of any individual character of the peoples; to others they will sound strange, a utopian dream. They first confuse the independence of a nation with its intellectual isolation – and this is an error of the intellect; the second despair of men, and of things – and this is a failing of the heart.'[17] He had first used the phrase 'Young Europe' in a letter written in July 1831 where, after discussing the aspirations of the young in France, he added: 'Young Europe'. Here then is the field for Freedom in the nineteenth century . . . Italy must carry her standard to the common field: the Italian legion must be drawn up alongside the French, the Belgian, the Polish legions.'[18]

It was not altogether true, then, that Mazzini believed the Italians to have no need of allies in their struggle against Austria and the princes. He did not want help from any existing government, but he did look for collaboration with other revolutionary movements. Like Buonarroti before him, and Lenin after him, he hoped for a European revolution which would liberate other peoples besides his own.

He remained in Switzerland for three unhappy years and then left for England. He arrived in London on 12 January 1837 with his friends Giovanni and Agostino Ruffini and Angelo Usiglio. They sailed up the Thames while the sun was setting, so that Mazzini's romantic soul could recognize that London on the eve of Victoria's reign was something special – bizarre, sinister, yet beautiful: to use his word, 'phantasmagoric'. They were soon faced, however, with the reality of life in London: they were desperately poor and both food and rent seemed exorbitantly expensive to them. Mazzini hardly ever left his room, finding the streets of London too foul and noisy. The leaden colour of the sky, he decided, was what made the English 'mad, eccentric and absent-minded'. Only the fog pleased him. When, in 1854, he was back in Switzerland, he wrote: 'Under this radiant sky I always think with nostalgia of the London fogs.' Slowly but surely he made interesting contacts in London. Already in September 1837 he had met John Stuart Mill. But by then he was desperately in debt, having decided not to receive more money from his father in Genoa, and depending now on slender earnings from journalism. He refused to exploit contacts with more successful Italian political exiles – like Anthony Panizzi, who had a post in the British Museum, was in 1837 to be made keeper of printed books, and in the 1850s to plan and arrange for the construction of the famous and beautiful Reading Room. Mazzini preferred to live in poverty than to solicit for jobs or income, and much of what little cash he acquired he gave to beggars, who quickly discovered where to find a soft-hearted and unworldly source of funds.

Throughout the many years of exile spent by Mazzini in London his physical conditions were not greatly to change, although his circle of friends and political influence were to broaden. He continued to live in modest surroundings, reading, writing, smoking cigars, with his canaries fluttering around the room, since he could not bring himself to shut birds up in small cages. The impression given by one of his most devoted English followers, Jessie White Mario, would be valid for any moment of his long exile:

My first visit to his tiny room . . . remains ever present . . . . Birds were flying about the apartment, a few lilies of the valley stood in a vase on the mantelpiece, books and papers were scattered everywhere, and there, writing on his knee, on the smallest fragment of the thinnest imaginable paper, sat Mazzini . . .[19]

He was to remain in exile in London for more than a decade, and then to return for an even longer period after the tragedy of the Roman Republic in 1849. But throughout these long years his name and movement were not forgotten in Italy.

NOTES

On the diplomatic history of the Congress System there is a considerable bibliography. Perhaps the best general survey is still that contained in the opening chapters of Pierre Renouvin, *Histoire des relations internationales*, Vol. 5, *Le XIXe siècle. I: De 1815 à 1871*, Paris, 1954. In a sense the standard life of Metternich is still Heinrich von Srbik, *Metternich, der Staatsmann und der Mensch*, Munich, 1925. There was a new edition in Paris in 1956. C. de Grunwald's *La vie de Metternich* was published in 1938, and an English translation in 1953. Another excessively sympathetic study of Metternich is Algernon Cecil, *Metternich, 1773–1859. A study of his period and personality* London, 1933.

G. F. -H. Berkeley, *Italy in the Making*, vol. I, *1815–1846*, Cambridge, 1932, reprinted 1968, is another older book worth reading for this period. On the secret societies there is C. Francovich, *Albori socialisti nel risorgimento. Contributo alla studio delle società segrete (1776–1835)*, Florence, 1962, and on Buonarroti two works, A. Saitta, *Filippo Buonarroti*, Rome, 2 vols, 1950, and Alessandro Galante Garrone, *Filippo Buonarroti e i rivoluzionari dell'Ottocento*, Turin, 1951. In English a vivid impression of Buonarroti is given by W. J. Fishman in *The Insurrectionists*, London, 1970. For Mazzini, A. Codignola, *Mazzini*, Turin, 1946, is a sympathetic study. Less sympathetic is a work by the Catholic historian, E. E. Y. Hales, *Mazzini and the Secret Societies*, London, 1956. Still the best whole biography in English is by a Welshman, Gwilym O. Griffith, whose *Mazzini: Prophet of Modern Europe*, London, 1932, was perhaps excessively laudatory, although not without an occasional note of criticism. The thought of Mazzini was brilliantly summarized in a work by Gaetano Salvemini, *Mazzini*, published in Florence on the centenary of Mazzini's birth. An English translation was made by I. W. Rawson and published half a century later (London, 1956). By far the best book on Mazzini's period of exile in England – which was for the better part of his life – is Emilia Morelli, *L'Inghilterra di Mazzini*, Rome, 1956.

1. See Ch. 1, p. 32.
2. See Ch. 3, p. 86.
3. See Ch. 4, pp. 104–5.
4. See Ch. 5, pp. 134, 136–9.
5. W. J. Fishman, op. cit., p. 46.

6. See Ch. 2, pp. 54–6, and Ch. 5, pp. 136–8.
7. C. K. Webster, *The Foreign Policy of Castlereagh*, London, 2nd edn, 1934, vol. II, p. 301.
8. Quoted by Giorgio Candeloro, *Storia dell'Italia moderna*, Milan, 1958, II, pp. 183–4.
9. This letter is printed in Kenneth Bourne, *The Foreign Policy of Victorian England 1830–1902*, Oxford, 1970, p. 218.
10. See Ch. 11.
11. *Scritti editi ed inediti di Giuseppe Mazzini*, ed. M. Menghini, vol. I, Imola, 1906, pp. 142–3.
12. See Ch. 11, pp. 263–4.
13. See Ch. 14, pp. 296–7, 300.
14. *Scritti . . . di Mazzini*, op. cit., vol. 5, pp. 26–33. vol. 2, pp. 45–56 have the General Instructions for the members of 'Young Italy'.
15. *Ibid.*, vol. 5, p. 9, letter to Michele Palmieri di Micciche.
16. *Ibid.*, vol. 2, pp. 17–41.
17. *Ibid.*, vol. 1, pp. 177–242.
18. *Ibid.*, vol. 5, p. 16.
19. Quoted by G. O. Griffith, op. cit., p. 270.

CHAPTER EIGHT

Rival movements of nationalism and the delusions of 1848 (1840–52)

After 1834, then, Mazzini had devoted his attentions to the concept of 'Young Europe'. The years 1834–7 had been unhappy ones for him – years when he had to remain in hiding from Swiss cantonal governments, and when he had to a great extent lost touch with the cells of 'Young Italy'. Those cells themselves in many cases continued to survive, often in courageous isolation. Historians have understandably failed to record their activities in detail, so that they have remained a grey area in the history of the Risorgimento.

From London Mazzini once more built up his contacts outside Italy by writing to other Italian exiles in France, Belgium, Switzerland and the USA. On 30 April 1840 he could announce that 'Young Italy' was once more alive. But the Ruffini brothers had already broken with him, and for the first few years in London he had concentrated on literature and journalism – to earn a slender living, rather than to have political influence. His favourite sister, Chichina, had died in January 1838. So sad and solitary had his life become that he had at first accepted the breaking of his links with Italy as inevitable. But his London existence was soon softened by a widening circle of friends. He had first met Thomas Carlyle in November 1837. Carlyle had recently published his *History of the French Revolution*, but was not yet as famous as he was to become. Although the two men had found each other interesting at this first meeting, they did not again meet for two years, when they happened to be among guests at the same dinner party. On 5 December 1839 Carlyle visited Mazzini in his humble lodgings, and a close, if paradoxical, understanding developed between the two men. Mazzini found Carlyle 'a man of heart, of conscience and of genius'. That the two men disagreed on most political issues did not prevent them from having immense respect for each other. Jane Carlyle was clearly attracted to Mazzini and became extremely possessive about him. Later Mazzini moved to Chelsea to be nearer the Carlyles. In spite of his unassailable intellectual convictions, Mazzini was emotionally vulnerable, and friendship from the eccentric but formidable Carlyles was without doubt of immense psychological importance for him. Carlyle could write contemptuously of Mazzini's mystical dreams of human progress, but at other times he would pay the Italian great respect. And Carlyle would allow only himself to speak ill of Mazzini; if anyone else did so, he would be silenced by Carlyle's terrible invective. In 1849 Carlyle said of Mazzini that 'his word was sincere as steel, his thought pure and limpid as water', and in this, surely, Carlyle was not mistaken.

By 1840, then, Mazzini was ready to return to political agitation, and was encouraged to do so by contacts with London working-class groups. In March 1840 he had founded the *Unione degli operai italiani* – a union of Italian emigrant workers – as a branch of 'Young Italy'. For the Union he published a daily sheet, the *Apostolato popolare*, 'apostolate' being a favourite word of Mazzini's. The journal was published from November 1840 until September 1844. Perhaps more useful for the Italian emigrant society in London was the school he founded in November 1841. The school functioned in the evenings and on Sundays, and helped the children of poor Italian exiles to read and write, and even become familiar with Italian literature and history. It stayed open until 1848, was, of course, free, and depended upon voluntary help from Italian and English teachers. Mazzini himself taught in the school and was greatly loved by the children and by the adult pupils who were admitted later on.

A friendly rival to 'Young Italy' appeared in 1839 when Nicola Fabrizi founded the 'Italian Legion' on the island of Malta. Fabrizi suggested to Mazzini that 'Young Italy' should consider itself responsible for upholding and passing on the doctrine of Italian republican-nationalism, but that the 'Italian Legion' should now accept responsibility for militant activity. Mazzini rejected the idea, but Fabrizi's organization was nearer Italy and could not be ignored. Fabrizi's idea was to organize a united insurrection at once in the Kingdom of Naples and the Papal States. Nothing immediately came of the scheme but, although Fabrizi's name was not to acquire the familiarity with posterity acquired by those of Mazzini and Garibaldi, his contacts – especially in Sicily – were not to be without their significance in the years ahead. He was to be with Garibaldi and the Thousand in 1860.

After 1843 the Mazzinian movement in Italy was to lose ground to other nationalist movements which were moderate in their aims, but often not more realistic. A last attempt by two young Mazzinians from Venice, Attilio and Emilio Bandiera, however, was to seize the imagination of Italians, and to form another heroic theme in the mythology of the Risorgimento. In 1840 the Bandiera brothers were respectively thirty and twenty-one years old. They were the sons of an admiral in the Austrian navy, and they themselves had acquired commissions, but both had been converted to Italian nationalism by the arguments of Mazzinian acquaintances. Being somewhat isolated from other would-be revolutionaries, and not in contact with Mazzini himself, Attilio Bandiera decided in 1840 to found a secret society, which he called *Esperia*, and whose members would be other officers and sailors of the Austrian navy. The society was controlled by a triumvirate consisting of the Bandiera brothers and another naval officer, Domenico Moro. Although the Bandiera brothers were themselves convinced of the validity of Mazzini's aims for a republic and complete Italian unity, they were prepared to work with other types of nationalists, and were rather more élitist than Mazzini: '*la plebe*' – the common people – they said were 'almost always imprudent by nature, and corrupt from necessity'. Apart from a few sailors Esperia was thus an aristocratic and middle-class society.

In 1842 Domenico Moro's ship visited London, where Moro met Mazzini, with the result that the Bandieras' society Esperia was federated to 'Young Italy'. In 1843 Attilio Bandiera was planning to seize the frigate *Bellona* on which he was commissioned, and which was at the time in the Aegean. The plan was revealed to the Austrian ambassador in Constantinople by a spy, and the Bandiera brothers decided to desert in February 1844. They met Moro at Corfu, where they surrounded themselves with a group of Italian exiles. Through the intercession of their mother with the Austrian authorities in Venice they secured at this point the promise of a pardon, but refused to give themselves up. They decided instead immediately to attempt a rising in Calabria. From Malta Fabrizi, with whom they were in touch, was wise enough to see that the chances of success were slim and the preparations hopelessly inadequate. Unfortunately an agent of Mazzini, Nicola Ricciotti, who arrived in Corfu with cash provided by Mazzini, was convinced by the Bandieras' arguments. Mazzini was thus, without his knowledge, involved.

On 12 June 1844 the Bandiera brothers with a mere nineteen followers left Corfu for the Kingdom of Naples, and disembarked near Crotone on the east coast of Calabria, without being seen by the authorities. Warnings, however, reached the Neapolitan government from Corfu, and from one of the twenty-one in the expedition, a traitor who left the party before the Bandiera brothers had collected a single follower in Calabria. Neapolitan forces therefore encountered the group, two of whom were killed in the skirmish that followed. Seventeen others were condemned to death; eight had their sentences changed to imprisonment, but nine, including the Bandiera brothers and Moro, were shot. All of them young, they died with dignity. It was magnificent, but it was not revolution.

The propaganda value of the Bandiera attempt was immense. While realizing that the venture had been a suicidal one, very many Italians without doubt felt proud that an act of defiance against the princes had been undertaken. Garibaldi was to succeed sixteen years later with a thousand men, but even a figure as small as a thousand – which was quickly to swell into 20,000 – is a rather different matter from a figure of twenty-one.

The Bandiera tragedy was in a sense an anachronistic one, carried out in the spirit of the 1830s rather than the 1840s. The period 1840 to 1848 is characterized rather by nationalist speculation than by militant action. The nationalist movement was becoming more varied and complex. The national question was discussed in scientific congresses which met all over Italy from 1840 to 1847, and in publications of all kinds, and under many guises. But the publication which had an impact greater than all the others was a book written by a Piedmontese priest in exile – Vincenzo Gioberti's *Del primato morale e civile degli italiani* 'Of the moral and civil primacy of the Italians', published in 1843 in two volumes in Brussels.

Gioberti was born in Turin in 1801. He was educated for the priesthood and was ordained in 1825. After leading a somewhat secluded life in his younger years, he was eventually attracted by the doctrines of Mazzini. But after Carlo Alberto's accession in 1831 Gioberti was made one of the King's Chaplains. This strange interlude in his life did not last long. He was unpopular at court, where he was rightly suspected of being a radical, and in 1833 he resigned from the post. Shortly afterwards he was arrested, charged with conspiracy, and exiled without being formally tried. He went first to Paris and then, for eleven years, settled in Brussels. He taught philosophy, but his writings also had a political dimension. In his philosophical teaching he adopted a strictly Catholic approach to ontology. Victor Cousin protested that Gioberti was not a philosopher at all, but a theologian. Gioberti certainly believed that civilization was impossible without religion, and this led him to claim that the Church was a basic necessity for human well-being. His first book, *La Teorica del sovran-naturale*, published in 1838, had been written specifically to reassure a friend of the truth of Christian revelation and the certainty of an afterlife. He published an *Introduction to the Study of Philosophy* in three volumes from 1839 to 1840. When *Del primato morale e civile degli italiani* was published in 1843 he was, then, already known in the academic world, although his works had been published in exile.

In one respect Gioberti agreed with Mazzini. Both men wanted to emancipate Italian thought from French influence. They were concerned equally with the intellectual as with the political independence of Italy. Already in the *Teorica* Gioberti had expressed the wish for an Italy 'one, strong and free from her domestic tyrants and from the ignominious yoke of the foreigner'. But while Mazzini was not so foolish as to claim that Italians were morally superior to other peoples, part of the theme of Gioberti's *Primato* was precisely that the moral and civil supremacy of the Italians was proved by the existence of the Papacy in Rome. The lowly condition of Italy in the nineteenth century was an aberration of history which had to be ended.

There was a vast amount of somewhat disorganized learning behind the *Primato*, and as a work of propaganda for Italian nationalism it was persuasive to the point of brilliance. It founded what become known as the 'neo-Guelph' school of Italian moderate nationalism, the term 'Guelph' being appropriated from the pro-papal party of the Middle Ages. The *Primato* was moderate in the sense that it did not confront the problem of the Austrian occupation of Lombardo—Venezia directly, nor did it discuss the need for reform in the Papal States. In a correspondence with Terenzio Mamiani, Gioberti had already said that he felt that it was not for a Catholic priest to complain about the admittedly unsatisfactory condition of the Papal States. There were larger and more serious problems in the world, and to debate the domestic problems of the Papal States would merely antagonize the younger priests with whom Gioberti hoped to have an influence. Nor did he recommend constitutions, but only consultative bodies, for Italy. The central recommendation of the *Primato* was for a confederation of Italian states under the presidency of the Pope. The devout Catholic state of Piedmont would also have an important part to play in the confederation. The 'holy city and the warrior province' were to be the nucleus of a resurgent Italy. The book was aimed perhaps primarily at the priesthood, but also at the princes, the aristocracy, and the more cautious members of the middle class. In other words it was intended to convert to Italian nationalism precisely those groups who had been most opposed to it. In a confused yet impressive manner, it succeeded. With the publication of this inflated, chauvinist and extraordinary book, the Italian cause suddenly became respectable. Not all Mazzini's extravagances, nor the martyrs whom he had inspired, could have achieved so striking a result. The historian Adolfo Omodeo, in a critique of Gioberti, brilliantly summarized the effect of the *Primato*: 'the fundamental achievement of the *Primato* – to introduce into Italy the national question under the papal banner . . . was really the Trojan horse, which compromised the régime of the Restoration in Italy'.[1]

Gioberti did not have a brilliantly original mind. In spite of his declared aversion for French ideas, he had clearly been influenced by the thought of Saint Simon. He had passed through a Mazzinian phase, before his most productive era as the founder of neo-Guelphism. Later he was to return to a more secular kind of democracy, and ultimately to fall under the influence of French socialists, and especially of Proudhon. Omodeo was surely right in thinking that these phases of Gioberti's writings were not so much matters of basic conviction as responses to changing political situations.

One writer inspired by Gioberti was of a more practical turn of mind – Count Cesare Balbo. In 1844 Balbo published *The Hopes of Italy*, which was to have an impact second only to that of Gioberti's *Primato*. Balbo had been born in Turin in 1789. His father, Prospero Balbo, was a nobleman and the mayor of Turin. His mother was a member of the Azeglio family, to whom Massimo d'Azeglio, whose career will be considered below, belonged. But as Cesare's mother died when he was three, he was brought up by a grandmother. During the period of the First Empire he held public office, as a very young man, in Italy and Paris under Napoleon. This did not prevent the Balbo family from gaining office once again under the Piedmontese monarchy during the Restoration, when Prospero Balbo was made minister of the interior, and Cesare Balbo entered the army. In spite of his service under the French, Balbo had inherited none of the traditions of the Revolution. He was in fact opposed to the revolution of 1821, but fell under suspicion and was for a short while exiled. On his return in 1824 he was kept under house arrest for two years. On his release he tried to secure government posts, without success.

In no sense, then, a revolutionary, Balbo was nevertheless a nationalist, feeling strongly that Lombardy and Venice should be liberated from the Austrians. In a sense he foresaw much that was to follow, and in particular that the Piedmontese monarchy was destined to acquire leadership in Italy. He agreed with that part of Gioberti's theme which recommended a federation of separate Italian states under the presidency of the Pope, and he dedicated *The Hopes of Italy* to Gioberti. Balbo, the lay nobleman, was a far more devout Catholic than Gioberti, the priest. But Balbo differed from Gioberti in showing also greater concern for the wrenching of Lombardy and Venice from Austria. The novel aspect of *The Hopes of Italy* was the proposal to find a diplomatic solution to the Italian question – to Europeanize it, and this was the path which Cavour was later to follow. More specifically, Balbo believed that Austria could be persuaded to give up her Italian provinces if she were compensated in the Balkans. For this, too, Cavour was momentarily to hope, eleven years later, after the Crimean War. In the short term no such arrangement was made, but in the long term Austria was to be edged out of Italy altogether, and many years later, over the years 1878 to 1908, Austro-Hungary was to establish herself in the considerable Balkan province of Bosnia and the smaller one of Herzegovina. It could, then, be argued that ultimately Balbo's plans were to be realized, though not in the manner nor at the pace for which he had hoped. It was to be in the Bosnian town of Sarajevo that the assassination of the Archduke Franz Ferdinand took place in 1914, the assassination which was the immediate cause of the First World War. The expansion of Austria into the Balkans was thus not without its significance in world history. It would be far-fetched to blame Balbo for the First World War, but the national egocentricity which *The Hopes of Italy* expressed was the fatal flaw in nineteenth-century nationalism which was to lead to the horrors of the twentieth century. Of these horrors Mazzini, at least, was wholly innocent. The idea of compensating Austria for the loss of her Italian territories by placing other peoples under Austrian sovereignty had a certain cynicism about it, and was alien to the spirit of democratic nationalism which Mazzini had created. Balbo did not believe in revolution, and his contribution to the nationalist movement was of a purely literary kind. He was strongly opposed also to democracy. His ideal, so far as constitutions went, was a régime like that of Britain between the two great reform acts of 1832 and 1867; in other words, it was a monarchical régime in which a two-chamber legislation gave the nobility and the middle class a firm hold on government, with a balance kept between them. Only a constitutional monarchy, he believed, could preserve a balance between authority and liberty. He was therefore warmly to welcome Carlo Alberto's Statuto, with its conservative constitutional character, and for four months, from March to July 1848, was to be prime minister of Piedmont. He was to die in 1853, before the ultimate drama of the struggle for Italian unification.

While the movement of propaganda for moderate nationalism was developing, a militant conspiratorial movement was forming in the Papal States. The rising of 1844, already referred to in Chapter 4, had a paradoxical character. Among the leaders were men who had for some time had contacts with secret societies, but who were now influenced by the moderate movement. Although Gioberti and Balbo were firm in their condemnation of militant revolutionary activity, they thus had followers in the Papal States who were still preparing to disregard their recommendations. Others, accepting the advice of Gioberti and Balbo more strictly, were hoping to secure reforms from the Pope by more peaceful agitation. The key figure in the transition in the Papal States from insurrectionary conspiracies to reformist agitation was a Piedmontese nobleman, Massimo d'Azeglio.

A sophisticated man with a cosmopolitan outlook, d'Azeglio had in 1844 only recently shown an interest in politics. He had been born in Turin in 1798. His father, Cesare d'Azeglio, one of the ruling class of the nobility in Piedmont, had wanted Massimo to have a military career, perhaps the last thing the boy wanted to do. He was obliged to hold a commission in a cavalry regiment for a short while, but soon resigned it with the excuse of ill-health. His first ambition was to be an artist, and with this in mind he escaped to Rome. To become an artist was regarded by his family as a vulgar eccentricity. He painted romantic landscapes, which were not without a sense of drama and movement, and earned him a certain reputation. He went back to Turin in 1830, and when, the following year, his father died, he settled in Milan for twelve years. From art he turned to literature, and wrote two historical novels, *Ettore Fieramosca*, published in 1833, and *Nicolò de' Lapi*, published in 1841.[2] Both novels had Italian nationalist overtones, and it was becoming clear that his interests were increasingly political ones. What made him unique among the Piedmontese moderates was that he was familiar with much of the rest of Italy, especially with Rome, Florence and Milan. It was not uncommon for the Piedmontese moderates to have lived in Paris or London, but to know the other Italian cities was exceptional. D'Azeglio had also travelled in Western Europe. He had married Manzoni's daughter, Giulia, who had died in 1835, and he was a close friend of Balbo. To a historian in the twentieth century he seems an altogether more attractive figure than either Balbo or Gioberti, more socially and culturally emancipated, but not less conservative in his basic political ideas.

The Romagna was the hotbed of political unrest in the Papal States, and it was to the Romagna that Massimo d'Azeglio went in September 1845. There he discovered that a further insurrection was being planned. His contact with the revolutionary society of the Romagna was significant, since it was the first contact between a moderate, respected by the more cautious middle classes, with militant nationalists. In no sense could he be regarded as a part of the diehard Piedmontese establishment; he had lived among the impoverished artists of Rome; he hated the Jesuits and the military; he was a man of charm and sensibility; above all, his honesty was beyond suspicion. The advice he took with him to the revolutionaries in the Romagna was that they should postpone any plans for revolution and entrust the Italian cause to Carlo Alberto. Perhaps surprisingly his advice was to be respected, but a conspiracy had already been made before his arrival and could not be halted. On 23 September 1845 a revolutionary group, among them Luigi Carlo Farini, took possession of Rimini, but remained in possession for only four days, after which the papal forces re-entered the city.

D'Azeglio meanwhile returned to Turin and secured a meeting with Carlo Alberto. He has left a detailed and vivid account of the occasion. The king was as chilling and distant as ever, but surprised d'Azeglio by telling him to convey to the revolutionaries in the Romagna a message with a somewhat unexpected content: if they waited, and for the time being did nothing, the king, when the occasion offered, would give 'my life, the lives of my children, my arms, my treasures, my army, everything, for the Italian cause'.

D'Azeglio published *Degli ultimi casi di Romagna* ('Of the latest events in Romagna'), in March 1846 in Florence, and dedicated it to Cesare Balbo. Its message was that the insurrection in the Romagna had been a mistake, because Italian and European opinion had been inadequately prepared for it. The men who had died in the rising, however, were martyrs, who deserved the profound respect of Italy. They were victims of papal misgovernment and the Austrian influence in Italy. The pope's temporal power must be reformed or, if not, abolished. But the way forward for Italian nationalism was not by means of violent insurrection but by a continual pressure of public opinion. D'Azeglio's conviction that Italy's aims could be achieved 'with our hands in our pockets' was not proved by the events of 1848–60, but equally it was not disproved. Whether it was necessary for so many people to die in 1848–9 and, on an even larger scale, in the two terrible battles in the spring of 1859, can never be demonstrated. D'Azeglio was a civilized man who was averse to bloodshed, although he was to fight, and to be wounded, in 1848. But whether Italy could have been united while the Italians kept their hands in their pockets, and their tongues and alert minds active, is a question which by its nature can never be answered.

After the publication of *Degli ultimi casi di Romagna* d'Azeglio was promptly ordered out of Tuscany. He went to Rome, where the election of Pius IX brought general rejoicing and a sense of nationalist solidarity. At this stage in his career d'Azeglio, in spite of his anti-clericalism, could be considered a part of the neo-Guelph movement. The straightforward and honest character of *Degli ultimi casi di Romagna* ensured that thousands of copies were sold. Even Mazzini, who clearly could not agree with the policy d'Azeglio was recommending, wrote to his mother that d'Azeglio had 'expressed the great national idea with decision, without reticences, and with a courage worthy of admiration'.

Events in the history of the Risorgimento followed in quick succession from 1846 to 1848. The election of Pius IX and his reforms before 1848 have been considered in Chapter 4; the revolution in Sicily in January 1848 has been considered in Chapter 5; Carlo Alberto's Statuto has been considered in Chapter 2. As important as each of these developments was the rising in Milan in March 1848.

A rising in Lombardy or the Veneto meant a rising against the occupying Austrian army – rather a different proposition from a rising in Palermo or Naples. But the whole Italian position changed with the revolution in Vienna and the fall of Metternich on 13 March 1848. The Austrian army in Italy, commanded since 1831 by Count Josef Radetzky, who in 1848 was eight-one years old, was now left in a somewhat isolated position, with the virtual breakdown of authority in Vienna. Radetzky himself, in spite of his age, was still a highly competent commander, personally popular with his troops. His army numbered between 70,000 and 75,000 and included Hungarian, Czech, South Slav and Austrian battalions, but by far the largest group was the Italians, who accounted for 39 per cent of Radetzky's infantry, and 33 per cent of his army as a whole. The Italians were to desert in great numbers during the revolution and wars of 1848–9.[3]

The 1848 rising in Milan started in the form of a boycott of tobacco, which was an Austrian state monopoly. It was felt that if the population of Milan could stop smoking it would make an appreciable impact on the revenue of the Habsburg government. The troops, however, of course continued to smoke cigars on the streets. Scuffles ensued, followed by riots which quickly developed into a general rising. From 17–22 March, subsequently to be remembered as the glorious *cinque giornate*, there was bitter fighting between Italian civilians and the troops. On 22 March Radetzky made the painful decision to withdraw the army from Milan. Rarely in history had an urban rising against a large well equipped army succeeded more quickly or more brilliantly. One factor in the revolutionary victory was clearly the large number of Italian infantrymen in Radetzky's army; another was the ambivalent attitude of the Hungarians, who felt great sympathy for the Italian cause.

The leaders of the insurrection of the *cinque giornate* had included Mazzinians, who had already on 17 March demanded the calling of a representative assembly, a civic guard and freedom of the press. Another leader of the rising in these early days, a man with very different views from those of Mazzini, was Carlo Cattaneo. When the first histories of the Risorgimento were written Cattaneo was not given a very prominent place in them, but more recently he has been seen as one of the most original and profound of the theorists of his day. Born in Milan in 1801, Carlo Cattaneo had started his career as a schoolteacher. He had then developed an interest in economics and politics and from 1839 to 1844 had edited a review called the *Politecnico*. In a sense he was always more an economist than a politician, perhaps more a Lombard than an Italian. He had immense respect for the Lombard engineers who had constructed the irrigation canals in his homeland. His own ideal was a federal Italy, but a federation of democratic republics. The events of the *cinque giornate* drew him into the militant political world, and with Enrico Cernuschi[4] and two colleagues he formed on 20 March a Council of War, which directed the insurrection, as a rival body to the existing Municipality of very cautious men who had originally worked under the Austrians, but were looking for union with Piedmont. But for Cattaneo and Cernuschi the Municipality would have come to terms with Radetzky, who would soon have been able to nip the movement in the bud. The Municipality was made up of Lombard noblemen, who desperately wanted to avoid an independent republic. They were prepared for Carlo Alberto, but they would have preferred the return of the Austrians rather than the republic. Cattaneo, on the other hand, wanted a democratic, national, if federal, Italian republic, but felt that he could not cause dissension in Milan at this moment of acute crisis. He therefore did not resist the formation of a provisional government, which was at least prepared to continue the fight against the Austrians but looked forward to the arrival of Carlo Alberto.

The policy of the King of Sardinia was almost certainty not conditioned by sympathy for the citizens of Milan. In the heightened atmosphere of Italy in March 1848 he was afraid only that revolution might spread to Piedmont, and more particularly to Genoa. War against Austria would make him into a national hero and give him a good chance of victory, which would enable him to acquire, at least, Lombardy. The Piedmontese press, and great crowds of demonstrators in the streets, demanded intervention. On the afternoon of 23 March, Carlo Alberto, presiding over his council of ministers, decided on war.

Meanwhile in Venice developments had taken a dramatic turn. Hearing of the fall of Metternich the Venetians concentrated on the release of the man who was to be the leader of the Venetian revolution – Daniele Manin. A lawyer of Jewish extraction, Manin had fought legal battles in defence of the Italian cause and had consequently been imprisoned by the Austrians in the famous Venetian prison to which the picturesque Bridge of Sighs leads. But the revolution of March 1848 in Venice lacked the violence of the *cinque giornate* in Milan. A rowdy demonstration was enough to persuade the Austrian authorities to allow Manin to be released from prison. The Austrian fleet was officered by Italians, and wholly unreliable. Even the arsenal – near the centre of Venice – was, before the revolution, virtually in the hands of Italians. The only person in the arsenal who resisted the Italian take-over was a brutal and much hated officer, Captain Marinovich, who was murdered. There was therefore much less bloodshed in Venice than in Milan. The Austrian military and civil authorities in Venice capitulated in a timid and civilized manner, and the Venetians established an independent Republic of St Mark on 22 March, with Manin as its president. An assembly was elected, and began democratically to debate immediate policy. Manin himself was opposed to union with Piedmont, preferring to retain the Venetian Republic until such time as a united Italy – preferably a republic – could be brought into existence. But, very correctly, he assured the assembly that he would accept their majority decision. The vote went in favour of union with Piedmont. It seemed, for the moment, that the Republic of St Mark would be very short-lived indeed.

The Piedmontese started the war with numerical superiority over the Austrians, and in the initial skirmishes did not perform badly. But in the long run – as that brilliant cynic, Napoleon I, had said, quoting Voltaire – God would be on the side of the big battalions. And before long Radetzky was to secure big battalions from Austria. Carlo Alberto commanded the Piedmontese army himself, but had neither the experience nor the ability of Radetzky. The Piedmontese king also seemed more concerned to secure a political victory over the republicans in Milan and Venice than a military victory over the Austrians.

It is interesting to consider how the population of rural Lombardy had reacted to the war. Radetzky, at the beginning of 1848, had written a memoir to the effect that the Italian peasants in 1848 were loyal to Austria, and that the Austrians should therefore recruit troops from the countryside. But the peasants were really becoming increasingly antagonized against the Austrians, and one of the reasons for their antagonism was precisely the conscription which the Austrians had already indulged in, conscription for eight years.

That the rich peasant could avoid conscription by paying a sum of money only made the practice more obnoxious to the poor peasant. The peasants also resented the very heavy taxes imposed by the Austrians. That the peasants hated the Italian noble landowners, and consequently hated the Piedmontese 'liberators', who were the friends of the Lombard landowners, did not make them love the Austrians any more. The peasant whom Ferrari heard crying 'Long live Radetzky' may well have been an isolated case. In the event, the working classes rallied to the revolution both in Milan and in the countryside. The urban poor helped to man the barricades. Two thousand armed peasants took possession of Lecco on 20 March, and other columns of peasants marched on Como and Bergamo. But the wretched Radetzky still believed that the peasants were his allies. After his reoccupation of Milan in 1848 he reduced the crushing taxes on the poor and organized charitable institutions for them. His treatment of the Milanese aristocracy was very different: he tried to ruin them by extorting large sums from them, and by using their palaces as barracks or hospitals. But this deliberate attempt to stir up a class war in Lombardy did not succeed.

In the Papal States the Pope's army had been placed under the command of an Italian nationalist – a soldier of fortune, General Giacomo Durando. His orders were to guard the papal frontiers; the Pope was not at war with Austria. But on 25 April, with the moral support of Massimo d'Azeglio, who wrote his proclamations for him, Durando marched the papal forces out of the Papal States to join the Piedmontese against the Austrians. From Naples an army under the veteran General Pepe also marched to the north to join in the war, which was thus becoming in a real sense a war of the Italian nation.

Pius IX was understandably outraged at Durando's hijacking of his army, and on 29 April issued his famous allocution dissociating himself from the war against Austria. Durando's force continued to fight, but the Pope's allocution marked a serious setback for the Italian cause blessed by the Pope, as it had seemed to be for the past two years. The second blow to Italian nationalism came from Naples. On 15 May, using his Swiss mercenaries, Ferdinand carried out a successful *coup* against the constitutional government, and reestablished his absolute authority. Pepe was ordered to bring his army back from the north. He ignored the order, but about half of his forces, recognizing their perilously isolated position, drifted back to Naples.

The regular forces of Carlo Alberto secured an initial victory over the Austrians on 30 May at the battle of Goito. But Carlo Alberto was a deeply worried man. Added to his fear of republicanism in Lombardy and the Veneto – a fear which was now no longer quite so acute – he was embarrassed by the presence of irregular and disowned allied armies under Durando and Pepe, and considerably more concerned by the build-up of a large French army on his western frontier. The friendship of the French Republic was perhaps as frightening to him as the Austrian army with which he was grappling. The French and British governments, however, limited themselves to diplomatic activity. Palmerston lectured the Austrians on the need to abandon their Italian provinces, and on 15 June the government in Vienna decided to give up Lombardy to Piedmont, and sent orders to this effect to Radetzky. But the decision was an ill-fated one. In the first place Carlo Alberto – perhaps with some sense of honour – refused to desert the Venetians, who were still courageously resisting; and in the second place Radetzky had no intention of giving up Lombardy, where he had spent so much of his career. Radetzky and a kindred soul, Prince Felix Schwarzenberg, soon to be prime minister of Austria, persuaded the government in Vienna to continue the war in Italy, and on 24 July Radetzky's tenacity was rewarded by the total defeat of the Piedmontese at the battle of Custozza. In the course of the next two weeks the Piedmontese army was withdrawn from Lombardy. The Venetians, who had, by their own decision, been so briefly united to Piedmont, hastily re-established the Republic of St Mark and continued the struggle, but the Piedmontese agreed on an armistice with the Austrians. The armistice was known by the name of Salasco, the Piedmontese general who conducted the negotiations. For the time being Lombardy was returned to Austrian sovereignty, but negotiations continued with Anglo-French mediation for several weeks, in the hope that the Austrian government could be persuaded to surrender Lombardy. After Schwarzenberg came to power in Vienna the likelihood of such a surrender faded.

In Mazzini's eyes the war of the princes against Austria had failed, and the war of the peoples was now to be waged. After the revolt of the *cinque giornate* he had rushed to Milan. With the summoning of a Costituente in Rome his dream seemed near realization, and with the proclamation of the Republic on 9 February 1849 he hastened to Rome. The achievements of the Roman Republic have been noted in Chapter 4. Its defence against its several enemies, and its destruction by the French, was rather a part of the history of the Risorgimento than of the Papal States. But before that disaster for Italian democracy occurred, the Piedmontese government scrapped the Salasco armistice and renewed the war. Carlo Alberto had been obliged to allow Gioberti to form a government, and Gioberti made the serious blunder of assuming that France, where Louis-Napoleon had been elected president, would come to the help of Piedmont when she again attacked the Austrians. In the event Radetzky defeated the Piedmontese in this second war in a single battle, the battle of Novara on 23 April. Carlo Alberto, a broken man, abdicated, and hastened from Italy to Portugal, where he entered a monastery and died three months later aged only fifty. A morbid and tragic figure, he had contributed only a somewhat confused part of the myth of the Risorgimento.

Carlo Alberto's son and successor, Vittorio Emanuele II, bore little resemblance to his father. Yet he was a product of his father's court, in the sense that he had been tuned into a superstitious Catholic, and an exclusively military leader, with no intellectual accomplishments. But he was more cheerful and extrovert than Carlo Alberto, and consequently had far better personal relationships. An uncouth and vulgar man, Vittorio Emanuele was at least free of any pomposity, and had no difficulty in getting on close terms, for example, with Garibaldi, who had come from very humble circumstances. The new king took over his kingdom at a very unhappy moment. After Novara there was no longer any question of Piedmont retaining Lombardy, and by the peace terms, which were not signed until 9 August, she was saddled with a very considerable indemnity.

By the end of March 1849 it was thus clear that the princes had failed in their role as leaders of the Italian national cause; the Republics of Rome and Venice, on the other hand, were still alive. It was when the news of Novara reached Rome that the decision was made to hand over executive power, effectively, to Mazzini, but in theory to a triumvirate consisting of Mazzini, Saffi and Armellini.[5] It now seemed extremely probable that French or Austrian intervention in the affairs of the Roman Republic was imminent. That the Neapolitans and Spaniards would also intervene against the Republic was likely, although it is doubtful if that particular likelihood caused Mazzini to lose much sleep. The real threat came from the sister republic in Paris, where universal manhood suffrage had produced a conservative and clerically minded assembly and government, and the untrustworthy presidency of Louis-Napoleon. A considerable minority in the assembly of the French Second Republic certainly had no ill-will towards the Roman Republic, and accepted the idea of a French expedition to Civitavecchia only because they assumed that its main aim would be to discourage Austrian intervention. But the majority in the French assembly almost certainly wanted to see the pope restored in Rome, as did Louis-Napoleon's ministers. Louis-Napoleon himself was probably an unbeliever who could not care less about the pope, but he was soon to acquire a perhaps unnecessary respect for Catholic opinion in France.

On 24 April 1849 a French army, under General Oudinot, was disembarked at Civitavecchia. Oudinot and the French government assumed that it was merely a question of marching into Rome while Mazzini's absurdly idealistic regime crumbled. But this was one moment in the history of the Risorgimento – another was to be in 1860 – when a force of untrained and ill-equipped youths was to defeat a well trained and professionally equipped army. What distinguished the force of enthusiastic youths from other such forces was the remarkable man who led them, a man whose charisma was to do at least as much for the Italian cause as the propaganda of Mazzini or the diplomacy of Cavour.

Giuseppe Garibaldi had been born in 1807 in Nice, at that time a Piedmontese port. His father had started life as a very poor fisherman, but had been successful enough eventually to purchase his own boat. Garibaldi's origins, however, were evidently humble, one indication being that his godmother – an aunt – had signed the baptismal certificate with a simple cross. Giuseppe himself had little formal education, but when very young earned his living as a sailor. After being condemned to death for his part in the unsuccessful Mazzinian rising of 1834 he had escaped to South America. He fought initially for the independence of Rio Grande do Sul from Brazil, was captured by the Brazilian authorities, and tortured, but escaped. In his next campaign he met Anita, who may already have been married but certainly subsequently considered herself Garibaldi's wife. They were to have three children – Anita, Ricciotti, and Menotti. His most important service to liberalism in South

America was to fight for the independence of Uruguay from the Argentinian dictator, Rosas, at first by sea, and then, in command of an Italian legion, by land. He won the fierce and brilliantly fought battle of San Antonio in the spring of 1846. That Uruguay became an independent state, as it has remained ever since, owed much to Garibaldi, and his share in the war of independence has always been generously recognized by the people of Uruguay. Throughout his long years in South America Garibaldi never forgot his hopes for Italy. It was typical of the man that he refused any reward or honour from Uruguay, and hastened back to Italy in 1848, when he rightly suspected that he could help. He landed in his home town of Nice in June 1848 and offered his services to Carlo Alberto in the war against Austria. He was already known as a brilliant leader of guerrilla forces, and in a purely military sense there is no doubt that he would have been a valuable asset to Piedmont. But in a political sense Garibaldi's offer of support was acutely embarrassing to Carlo Alberto. After some bureaucratic unpleasantness it was rejected.

The Roman Republic knew better how to use the services of this wild, brilliant and lovable man. While Carlo Pisacane, an intellectual who had studied military science, was placed in command of all the Republic's armed forces, Garibaldi was given command of the army in the field. In this position he had certain advantages. The social policy of Mazzini's Roman Republic had been such that the peasants were entirely on its side. Garibaldi operated in a world which was friendly to him, and which had no wish for the return of the pope. It was ironical that Louis-Napoleon was about to restore the pope to please the French peasants, while the pope's own peasants had no wish to see him restored. It was often the case that monarchs and popes were more popular with those who were more remote from them. Familiarity with spiritual as with temporal authorities tends to breed contempt. On the other hand, the Roman Republic was a more radical régime than that which had ultimately emerged from the revolution of 1848 in France. Marx wrote: 'The Roman revolution was an attempt against property, against the bourgeois order, as terrible as the revolution of June', by which he meant the unsuccessful workers' rising in Paris in June 1848. And Marx goes on to say: 'The restored bourgeois authority in France insisted on the restoration of the papal authority in Rome.'[5]

When the French expeditionary force under Oudinot attacked the army of the Roman Republic on 30 April 1849 the French were defeated, and suffered severe casualties. Garibaldi was not yet in full command – but fought with his usual brilliance and tenacity. He might well have totally destroyed the French force, but Mazzini now hoped that the French would come to an arrangement with the Roman Republic. It was not yet clear that Louis-Napoleon and his ministers intended simply to destroy the sister republic. It seemed possible that they would be content to establish a bridgehead in Italy, primarily to discourage Austrian intervention in the Papal States, and perhaps to arrange some form of intervention by Piedmont. It is certainly true that not all the French ministers wanted to restore the pope as an absolute monarch. The other invaders of the Papal States – the Neapolitans and Austrians – occupied a less ambiguous position, since they were clear enemies of the Roman Republic and allies of the pope. Mazzini's policy of attempting to come to terms with the French, and even conciliating them by releasing the prisoners who had been taken, proved futile in the end but, given the data at Mazzini's disposal, it seemed reasonable at the time. At least the pause in the fighting with the French allowed Garibaldi to move to the south and confront the Neapolitans. Having defeated the Neapolitans, Garibaldi returned to the northern front to face a strongly reinforced French army. If Louis-Napoleon had agreed to the initial expedition – planned before his election as president – merely because he wanted to secure the sympathy of Catholics in France, after the defeat of his forces on 30 April he became far more emotionally involved. The question had now become that of the defence of the honour of the French army. For a Bonaparte to begin his period of office with a military defeat was unthinkable. Originally the French army in Italy had numbered only 6,000; it was now increased to some 20,000, which made it twice as large as the forces of the Roman Republic. This considerable French army launched its attack on 3 June. Garibaldi's defence of Rome rightly became one of the great epic stories of the nineteenth century. His irregular force of ill-equipped and virtually untrained enthusiasts resisted the much larger French professional army for a month. After savage fighting, with considerable losses on both sides, on 30 June, Garibaldi made a dramatic entry into the Assembly of the Republic, with a sword so bent that it would not fit completely into its sheath. He had to tell the Assembly that further resistance was impossible. The Assembly gave him dictatorial powers to make whatever arrangements were possible before the French broke into the city. Garibaldi explained that there were now three courses open: to surrender to the French, to fight inside Rome, which would cause great destruction and loss of life, or to retreat with a fighting force away from Rome and to continue the struggle for the Risorgimento elsewhere in Italy. The first possibility he did not even discuss; his preference was for the third. He appealed, therefore, for followers in a desperate retreat from Rome, initially in the direction of Venice, where another republic was still holding out. He could offer his followers, he said, only 'hunger, thirst, forced marches, battles and death', a phrase from which Churchill must surely have derived his 'blood, sweat, toil and tears' of 1940. With a splendid impertinence Garibaldi then stole an old claim of the popes: 'Wherever we are, there will be Rome', and for many years he was to claim that, since the only democratically elected government the Romans had ever had had made him dictator, he remained the only legitimate ruler of Rome. Astonishingly, some 4,000 men – in effect most of his army which had not been killed in the bitter defence of Rome – agreed to follow him in his desperate venture. His wife, Anita, had arrived in Rome before the end of the siege and joined him in the retreat. She was five months pregnant with a child who was never to be born. She died in August, by which time his small army had dissolved, but Garibaldi himself escaped, to fulfil a more impressive destiny a decade later.

Meanwhile in Venice the Republic of St Mark survived. Although Manin took repressive action against some of the more radical groups, including the Mazzinians, he remained immensely popular with the Venetian population as a whole. Considering that he had so little experience of the working classes, his popularity with all the people of Venice was remarkable. He himself was even more surprised at the popularity he acquired with the peasants of the mainland. Several measures of social reform taken by his government – and especially the reduction of the tax on salt – endeared him to the peasants, who had eagerly formed national guards during the war and had joined in the fighting against the Austrians. But agents sent out from Venice were somewhat contemptuous of the efforts of the rural civilian forces, and it must be admitted that their military performances were not successful. They did not, however, receive much assistance from Manin's government. Many of them had previously been conscripted into the Austrian army, and so had received some training as soldiers. Manin had at his disposal considerable arms in the Venetian arsenal. With a little more energy he might well have created and armed a large popular army. But he was a lawyer and a townsman, the successful leader of an urban revolution, but an unpromising choice as the head of a peasant army.[6]

Venice remained besieged by the Austrian fleet. After the second defeat of the Piedmontese by the Austrians the Austrian commander, Haynau, on 28 March 1849, wrote to Manin to inform him of the armistice and to invite Venice to accede to a similar settlement. Shortly thereafter news reached Venice of the abdication of Carlo Alberto and the accession of Vittorio Emanuele. The response of Venice to these catastrophic items of news was to invest full powers in Manin in order to continue the struggle. Manin, for his part, was realistic enough to realize that Venice alone could not indefinitely resist the Austrians. He was therefore prepared for Anglo-French mediation, leading, if necessary, to an autonomous, constitutional state of Lombardo-Venezia, under a Habsburg archduke. Since Venice was a port, British influence there was more important than French influence. Throughout the siege of Venice British ships came and went; the Austrians, of course, did not attempt to intercept them. But unfortunately for Manin the only British representative in Venice was George Dawkins, the former Consul-General in Lombardo-Venezia, who had been moved from Milan to Venice at the start of the wars, because there were more British residents and property in Venice than in Milan. The sympathies of Dawkins were entirely with the Austrians. Palmerston, in the Foreign Office, was thus fed with regular accounts of how Venice was on the verge of anarchy, and the British government never extended diplomatic recognition to the Republic of St Mark. Already in August 1848 Dawkins had referred to the Italian revolution as 'this infernal business'. By the spring of 1849 he had some reason for feeling that the fates had deserted him. On 4 May the Austrians began to shell Venice and on 5 May Radetzky, who had joined Haynau at Mestre, invited the Venetians to surrender. Palmerston had already told Dawkins to recommend surrender to the Venetians, on the grounds that they would get better terms if they surrendered then than they would if they resisted for longer. Dawkins carried out Palmerston's instructions with enthusiasm, but on 19 May he had to admit that he had failed: Manin's stubborn government continued to resist. On 27 June the Austrian bombardment became much more intense. Poor Dawkins wrote to the Foreign Office that he was at the mercy of 'unprincipled adventurers'. 'I know that I am a marked man in consequence of having advised coming to terms, and that only three nights ago the best time and occasion for giving me a "coltellata" [knifing] was discussed in one of the Cafés.'

Meanwhile to the Austrian bombardment was added an intensification of hunger, and of the cholera. The Venetians, a gentle and pacific people, astonished the Austrians in the determination of their resistance. To Consul Dawkins it seemed that the Venetians had gone mad. He wrote to the Foreign Office:

You cannot conceive the wretched state we are in or how heartily sick I am of this confinement which is really knocking me up. Cholera is raging here, Manin, our President, is I fear going mad, or at least acting like a madman and I am nearly driven mad and get no comfort from anyone.[7]

But Manin was not going mad, and Dawkins was soon to be rescued. Venice finally surrendered late in the evening of 22 August 1849. Only the Hungarians had measured up to her standards of resistance. The long, slow decline of Venice in the seventeenth and eighteenth centuries had been vindicated in a few months of suffering.

By the summer of 1849 it was clear that the national revolutionary movement in Italy had failed, as it had failed in Germany and as revolutions elsewhere in the Habsburg Monarchy had failed. The only reminders of what had happened in Italy were the constitution in Piedmont and, in a negative sense, the presence of French troops in Rome. The traditional interpretation of the survival of the Piedmontese Statuto was that Vittorio Emanuele courageously refused Austrian demands to abolish it. The truth is now seen to have been almost exactly the opposite. Vittorio Emanuele was not at all eager to retain the constitution, but the Austrians were disinclined to persuade him to abolish it. Although the new régime in Vienna was soon to abolish its own constitution, and although the decade 1849 to 1859 was to be a rigidly authoritarian one in the Habsburg Monarchy, the Austrians believed that the young king of Piedmont would become too unpopular if he abolished the Statuto. A constitutional monarchy in Turin was at least preferable to a republic in Austrian eyes. Austrian policy had become a little more flexible since the passing of Metternich.

The Piedmontese constitution gave political existence to only a small fraction of the population, but at least it guaranteed that a dynamic, if restricted, political life would continue in one corner of the peninsula. The emigration of Italians from other parts of the country to Piedmont also ensured that political activity in Turin was more than a purely Piedmontese concern. The suppressions of the revolutions of 1820–21 and 1831 had led to emigration away from Italy altogether – to France, Belgium, Switzerland, Britain and the USA. There would have been no point in 1821 or 1831 in going to Piedmont where there was no more freedom than elsewhere in Italy. But in 1849, with the Statuto and a free press still in existence in Piedmont, there seemed to a great number of Italians to be no point in going further. In Piedmont they could speak their own language, vote (provided they were rich enough), and even stand for election to parliament. The year 1849 was merely the starting date of the emigration: a steady flow continued until 1860. It has been roughly calculated that more than 30,000 immigrants settled in Turin or Genoa in the decade before the establishment of the Kingdom of Italy.[8] Many of them secured good professional posts, especially as teachers. A few of them edited their own journals, and many of them wrote for the press. They brought a more cosmopolitan atmosphere to Turin. Yet they did not become Piedmontese; they became, rather, Italians. They had lost one homeland – Naples, the Papal States, Lombardy. The one they had found – Italy – they had to help to create.

But the man who was to dominate the political life of Piedmont in its last decade of independent existence was a native nobleman – Count Camillo Benso di Cavour. Born on 10 August 1810 Camillo was the second son of the Marchese Michele Benso di Cavour, and his mother, before her marriage, had been Adèle de Sellon. The Marchese Michele was a rich landowner. His wife came from a Protestant family which had been French in the time of Louis XIV, but had been obliged by that king's religious persecutions to emigrate to Switzerland. Their home in Geneva was to remain a second home for Cavour. His father was an intelligent man, very active, and highly successful in business. Although a minister in the king's government, he was essentially an administrator and did not want political change. He believed that it was not yet time for Piedmont to modify her absolutism, nor for her to switch from an agricultural to an industrial economy. On both points Camillo was later to disagree with his father, but the difference was perhaps simply one between two generations. If Cavour had belonged to his father's generation perhaps he, too, would have felt that the time was not yet ripe for the undeveloped little state of Piedmont to attempt dangerous experiments. Cavour was a noisy and mischievous child, continually running up and down the stairs of the family palace, and banging its doors. The numerous women in the palace – mother, grandmother and aunts – taught him to read and write in spite of a lively resistance on his part. As a second son he was intended for the army, and sent to the Royal Military Academy when he was ten. Here he quickly became a rebel against what he rightly saw to be a mindless routine and unreasonably severe discipline. Already his personality – arrogant, dynamic, quick-witted and egocentric – was beginning to take shape. From the Royal Military Academy he became, briefly, page to Carlo Alberto, a role which soon filled Cavour with disgust. To the prince the young man seemed to be a 'Jacobin'. Soon he had left Carlo Alberto's service for a commission in the army. Here, too, he was thought to be a dangerous rebel. To remove him from Turin the army sent him to Ventimiglia, ostensibly to help supervise the construction of frontier fortifications. He was still only eighteen, but was now to discover the basic intellectual interests of his life. In the loneliness and boredom of his existence high in the forts of the Corniche, and at the forts on the frontier from the Mediterranean to the Val d'Aosta, he started to read economics and political science. His introduction to democratic ideas, which he never fully accepted and was later to reject, was the result of his love affair with Anna Giustiniani, whose salon in Genoa he attended, while still in the army, in 1830. He renewed his relationship briefly with Anna Giustiniani eleven years later, and on this last occasion the affair ended tragically. After Cavour had again left her, Anna Giustiniani committed suicide by throwing herself from a window.[9] In 1832 Cavour was to write that his opinions two years earlier had been 'very exaggerated' ones. To the Marchese di Barolo he wrote:

at the risk of making you laugh for a long time at me, I will confess to you, that there were times when I believed nothing beyond my powers, when I would have believed it quite natural to wake up one fine morning and find myself prime minister ['Ministre dirigeant'] of Italy.[10]

Since in 1830 – or for that matter in 1832 when these words were actually written – there was no possibility nor likelihood of anyone becoming 'prime minister of Italy' in the foreseeable future, and since Cavour was a second son holding no public office, his dream was a remarkable one. Nor did he have any intention of seeking public office at that time. Although he left the army in 1831 he did not immediately find other employment, having no wish to serve an absolute monarch and no desire to play any role in a country which had no free institutions. But free institutions existed in Paris and London, and late in 1834 Cavour left Turin to visit the two great western capitals. With his friend, Piero di Santarosa, he stayed for some time in Paris, where he met Guizot, the conservative statesman who believed in very limited parliamentary institutions, and who became one of Cavour's heroes, Sir Robert Peel being another. In Britain Cavour concentrated on the industrialized regions – London, the Black Country and Lancashire. He and Santarosa seem not to have been in the least depressed by the evil living conditions which they witnessed, but rather to be favourably impressed by the sense of power created by the forest of chimneys and clouds of smoke. But Cavour did not wholly ignore the social problems of Britain: he visited a workhouse and a prison in Liverpool. He was delighted by the Liverpool–Manchester railway, the first passenger line in the world, opened only five years before.

Returning to Piedmont from his travels in 1835, Cavour had to find an occupation for his considerable intellectual energy, and a more reliable source of income than the profits he made from gambling in cards, in casinos and on the stock exchange. He was to remain a gambler all his life, in politics as in everything else – but he was also able to apply himself to a task with great diligence. In 1835, and until 1848, his main occupation was to run the considerable estate of Leri given to him by his father, and the smaller farm of Grinzani. It was typical of Cavour, who was wholly free from pomposity or affectation, that his idea of running an estate was not simply to sit in his office calculating the finances, but also to ride around the fields on a horse and cart, wearing an old straw hat. This rich, ambitious man was prepared to play the role of the peasant farmer when that seemed the appropriate one. As would be expected of him, he used modern agricultural methods − what farming machinery that was already available and artificial manure imported from America.

During these years Cavour did not abandon his studies of the broader politico-economic world of Western Europe, even though he was not yet playing an active part in it. He had published articles on the Irish question and Peel's first steps towards free trade, but his first important article on an Italian question was not published until 1846. Count Ilarion Pettiti had published a fat volume entitled *The Italian railways and an improved plan for them* in 1845. Cavour's writing took the form of an article in the Parisian *Revue nouvelle* and professed to be a review of Petitti's book, although it considered issues not touched on by Petitti. Cavour started his article by referring to the railway as 'this marvellous conquest of the nineteenth century', equal in importance to the invention of printing or the discovery of America. He then expressed his approval at the lines planned by the Piedmontese government, but pointed out that the Austrian government, having failed to build a line to the border of Piedmont, were preventing Lombardy from having rail access to the sea at Genoa, or to France. He applauded the idea of a railway tunnel under the Alps at Mont Cenis, which he said would be 'the master-piece of modern industry', 'the most beautiful triumph of steam'. He took Italian writers to task for opposing any Austrian plan to link Trieste and Vienna by rail, and on this point seemed to pass beyond any narrow Italian nationalism. To link Italy and Germany must, in the long run, bring advantages to both countries.

If the future reserves a happier fate for Italy, and, as we may be permitted to hope, this beautiful country is one day destined to reconquer its nationality, this can be only as the result of a European upheaval,

and in such an upheaval one railway line connecting Vienna with Italy would have little significance.[11] Thus, in the course of discussing one of his favourite topics − the railways − Cavour inserted in parenthesis the hope that Italy would one day become an independent nation.

With Carlo Alberto's freeing of the Piedmontese press in 1847 there was no longer any need for Cavour to confine his writings to French journals. With Cesare Balbo he founded his own journal, *Il Risorgimento*, and in its pages published his own recommendations for Piedmont and for Italy. Initially one of his main recommendations was for a constitution. When in March 1848 Carlo Alberto granted his Statuto, its cautious, conservative nature pleased Cavour well. In the first elections to the new Piedmontese parliament Cavour failed to get elected, but he was successful in June, in a by-election. He had recommended Carlo Alberto go to war with Austria, and had opposed the idea of securing any alliance with the Second French Republic. 'The entry of new foreigners into our country' would be the 'most shameful' of all methods of securing Italian independence. Only after Carlo Alberto's defeat did he begin to suspect that Piedmont alone would never be able to defeat Austria.

Cavour's ability in parliament was quickly recognized. Massimo d'Azeglio, as prime minister, in October 1850 appointed Cavour minister of agriculture, commerce and the navy, and in 1851 the yet more important ministry of finance was added to the list. D'Azeglio did not enjoy administration, and had in effect handed over the working functions of the government to Cavour.

D'Azeglio was at the head of a centre-right government, whose position was strong because it had the support of Vittorio Emanuele, who had virtually promised Radetzky to exclude the left from power. It was by no means yet clear whether the ministers were responsible to parliament or to the king, but the question was not of importance at the moment because d'Azeglio was supported by a majority of the deputies. The general election of 9 December 1849 had given the conservatives an even larger majority. In that election the king had played a somewhat unconstitutional role by letting it be known, in no uncertain terms, that he wanted d'Azeglio to remain prime minster with a strong parliamentary support. Probably many voters had feared that if a conservative majority were not returned there could well be a royal *coup d'état*, as there had been the previous year in Naples. The survival of the constitution, even with a centre-right government, seemed preferable to the reassertion of monarchical absolutism.

The parliament elected in December 1849 contained ultra-clerical reactionaries, and a solid block of slightly more moderate deputies, who nevertheless wished to operate the constitution in a very conservative manner and to defend the privileges of the church. The leader of the latter group was Count Ottavio Thaon de Revel. All these were to the right of d'Azeglio himself, as was Cesare Balbo, who felt that in the reactionary atmosphere of Europe in 1850 any show of liberalism would be dangerous. In 1850 the church was to become the main issue in Piedmontese politics, and her privileges were to be fought over until 1852. The limitation of ecclesiastical power brought about by reformers of the Enlightenment in Naples, Austrian Italy and Tuscany had not been experienced in Piedmont. Napoleon's anti-clerical legislation had been repealed in 1814. Under Carlo Alberto the Jesuits had become more influential. Ecclesiastical courts still existed, and even the right of asylum could still be claimed in certain instances. In the revolutionary days of 1848 there had been popular demonstrations against the Jesuits, who had been formally expelled by a law of August 1848. It now seemed both to liberals and moderates that the feudal nature of the Piedmontese church must be eliminated. In December 1849 Cavour persuaded d'Azeglio to appoint Count Giuseppe Siccardi minister of justice and ecclesiastical affairs with the recognized purpose of reforming the laws governing relations between the church and the state. In February 1850 Siccardi introduced three bills, eliminating the ecclesiastical courts and the right of asylum, reducing the very numerous religious holidays to six days a year, and giving the government the right to veto gifts or bequeathments of cash to the church. The first Siccardi law, dealing with the ecclesiastical courts and the right of asylum, was opposed by Revel and Balbo, but defended by Cavour, who spoke on 7 March, in a speech which greatly increased his prestige in parliament. The law was passed by an overwhelming majority in the lower house, by a considerable one in the senate, and signed by Vittorio Emanuele on 9 April. The other two, less important, Siccardi laws were also passed by both houses. But the papacy and the church in Piedmont were bitterly antagonized by the laws. Fransoni, the archbishop of Turin, circulated to his priests the somewhat contorted instruction that they should secure the permission of their clerical superiors before appearing at a lay court. The circular was judged to be an incitement to the priests to break the law, and Fransoni was imprisoned for a month. Subsequently he was exiled, and never returned to Piedmont. The conflict between church and state was thus at fever pitch when Cavour was brought into the government in October 1850.

As minister, however, Cavour's first concerns were with the affairs of his own departments, and in particular with the preparation and conclusion of commercial treaties with other countries. He had already registered his approval of the free trade policy which was, for a comparatively brief period, adopted by British governments influenced by the economic theories of the Manchester School. In Britain tariffs had been lowered or abolished as a unilateral policy, regardless of the commercial policies of other governments. For a small and semi-developed country like Piedmont a less dramatic policy had to be followed, and Cavour decided to reach specific agreements with those countries with whom political understanding would also be beneficial. In November 1850 an agreement was reached with the Second French Republic. In economic terms it seemed unfavourable to Piedmont, and Cavour did not conceal his belief that a political alignment with France would in the long run justify the acceptance of terms which made it appreciably easier for France to export certain specified goods to Piedmont, and only slightly easier for Piedmontese goods to flow to France. A treaty with the British government rather more favourable than that with the French government was signed on 3 January 1851, and followed by a treaty with the liberal government in Belgium on 27 February. Defending his policy of freer trade in parliament, Cavour argued that a government which claimed the right to interfere in the economic life of the country in a protectionist sense justified the socialist view, which he found abhorrent, that the government could also control capital, production and wages. On 15 October 1851 Cavour signed a commercial treaty with Austria which allowed a cheaper flow of Piedmontese goods – and especially wine – to Lombardy; on the whole Piedmontese wines were superior to Lombard wines, and at least the equal of Venetian wines.

After Louis-Napoleon's *coup d'état* in Paris in December 1851 the political climate in Europe became yet more repressive. D'Azeglio and his more right-wing colleagues in the government prepared a law slightly diminishing the freedom of the press. Fearing a change of policy in an increasingly conservative direction, Cavour decided to reach an understanding with the centre-left, which was led by Urbano Rattazzi. An agreement was reached to the effect that Rattazzi would make a clear break with the more extreme left, and Cavour with the more extreme right, with whom he had in fact never had links, and that the alliance would be announced to the house at an opportune moment.

214

D'Azeglio was not informed of the arrangement, although Cavour hoped that it would not lead to a break with him. When the press law came before the house both Rattazzi and Cavour expressed a moderate attitude towards it, Cavour explaining the need to discourage the press from attacking foreign governments – the relevant one being Louis-Napoleon's – but aiming his strongest attack against the extreme right, who wanted much stronger measures. Thus was formed the *connubio* or 'marriage' between the centre-right and centre-left. Like all strong centre parties, that which Cavour created had the effect – so long as it lasted – of preventing a choice between two parties based on clear-cut principles. On the other hand it provided a large degree of unity in Piedmont for the coming struggle with Austria.

D'Azeglio listened to the debate on the press law with growing surprise, since he had not been told of the agreement between Cavour and Rattazzi. To avoid scandal and embarrassment he concealed his surprise, so that, although he could never trust Cavour again, there was no open break. With Cavour's support Rattazzi was elected president of the house on 11 May 1852. His election was the occasion of a victory for parliament over the crown. The king tried to prevent him from being nominated, but moved too slowly. Once he had been elected the king gave up the attempt to impose his will on parliament, even though Rattazzi offered to resign. Imperceptibly Piedmont was becoming a genuinely parliamentary state.

Before the end of May Cavour decided that his position in d'Azeglio's government was too blatantly a false one, and resigned his office. He seized the opportunity for a quick visit to Paris where he met, for the first time, the Prince President Louis-Napoleon, who was to be so important for Cavour's future plans, and who was to make himself emperor before the end of the year.

Back in Turin a crisis was quickly developing. The government had decided to follow the first two Siccardi laws with a third introducing civil marriage. It passed the lower house easily enough, but then ran into determined clerical opposition. The pope wrote to Vittorio Emanuele, over whom he had considerable influence, and the king decided that his government's policy was a blasphemous one. He put sufficient pressure on the senate to get the bill rejected. D'Azeglio resigned and, putting his country's interests before his personal inclinations, recommended the king to consult Cavour. In asking Cavour to form a government, Vittorio Emanuele laid down conditions: the dropping of the civil marrige bill, and the opening of discussions with Pius IX for a new concordat. Cavour could not accept these conditions. After Balbo and Revel had made a joint effort, unsuccessfully, to form a government, the king again summoned Cavour, who now agreed, in effect, to drop the civil marriage bill, but not to open negotiations with the pope. The Siccardi laws already passed would not, of course, be repealed. Cavour, the man of the *juste milieu*, had shown himself to be flexible in negotiation. Rattazzi remained president of the house and entered the government in 1853. Cavour took up office as prime minister on 4 November 1852. The other colleagues he appointed to office were rather mediocre men of the centre-right. There was no doubt that Cavour was in control.

NOTES

Excellent for Mazzini for this period is Franco della Peruta, *Mazzini e i rivoluzionari italiani, Il 'partito d'azione' 1830–1845*, Milan, 1974. On Gioberti a classic essay by Adolfo Omodeo should still be read: 'Vincenzo Gioberti e la sua evoluzione politica', in *Difesa del risorgimento*, Turin, 1951. A fluent life of Massimo d'Azeglio in English is Ronald Marshall, *Massimo d'Azeglio. An artist in politics, 1798–1866*, London, 1966. Volumes 2 and 3 of a work of which Volume 1 has already been mentioned in the notes to Chapter 7 are still important authorities in English: G. F.–H. and J. Berkeley, *Italy in the Making*, vol. 2, *1846–1848*, Cambridge, 1936, and vol. 3, *1848*, Cambridge, 1940. Both volumes were reprinted in 1968.

Two studies of Cattaneo appeared in 1971 – N. Bobbio, *Una filosofia militante. Studi su Carlo Cattaneo*, Turin, and Biancamaria Frabotta, *Carlo Cattaneo*, Lugano. Cattaneo's own scattered political writings are collected together in four volumes as *Scritti politici*, Florence, 1964–5.

On the social aspects of the revolutions of 1848 Domenico Demarco's article, 'Le rivoluzioni italiane de 1848', in *Studi in onore di Gino Luzzatto*, Milan, 1950, is valuable, as are Franco della Peruta's essays in *Democrazia e socialismo nel risorgimento*, Rome, 1977.

A fair amount has been written on the international dimension of the 1848 revolutions in Italy. For British policy towards Italy in 1848–9 two works are important: A. J. P. Taylor's early book, *The Italian Problem in European Diplomacy, 1847–1849*, Manchester, 1934, and Ottavio Barie, *L'Inghilterra e il problema italiano nel 1848–49*, Milan, 1965, a book which deals well with the British involvement in Naples, a question which Mr Taylor left aside. On the diplomatic side there is in addition R. Moscati, *La diplomazia e il problema italiano nel 1848* Florence, 1947.

On war and revolution in the North in 1848 two recent publications in English are of major importance. Alan Sked, *The Survival of the Habsburg Empire. Radetzky, the Imperial Army and the Class War, 1848*, London, 1979, gives a vivid impression of the composition of the Austrian army, and of Radetzky's ham-handed attempts to win the Lombard peasants to his side, while Paul Ginsborg, *Daniele Manin and the Venetian Revolution of 1848–49*, Cambridge University Press, 1979, considers the peasants on the mainland, but also the urban poor of Venice, and Manin's relations with them.

On the revolution of 1848 in Tuscany there is C. Ronchi, *I democratici fiorentini nella rivoluzione del '48–49*, Florence, 1963. Domenico Demarco has written interestingly on both Naples and Rome in 1848. On Rome there is his *Pio IX e la rivoluzione romana del 1848*, Modena, 1947, and the short work *Una rivoluzione sociale. La repubblica romana del 1849*, Naples, 1948. Equally important for developments in Rome in 1848–9, but written with a quite different approach, are the articles by Alberto M. Ghisalberti in his *Momenti e figure del risorgimento romano*, Milan, 1965, articles which provide insight and understanding of the Roman scene. On the emergence of the Roman Republic for English-speaking readers there is an article by H. Hearder – 'The Making of the Roman Republic, 1848–1849', in *History*, LX, June 1975, and the first half of G. M. Trevelyan's great trilogy on Garibaldi, *Garibaldi's Defence of the Roman Republic*, London, 1907, is, of course, relevant here.

Three volumes of Rosario Romeo's important life of Cavour have now been published: *Cavour e il suo tempo*. The first volume (Bari, 1969) deals with the period 1810–42, and the second and third (Bari, 1977) with the period 1842–54. The most recent life of Cavour in English is a short fluent work by an American historian, Frank J. Coppa, *Camillo di Cavour*, New York, 1973. The debates of the Piedmontese parliament were edited in nine volumes by Adolfo Omodeo and L. Russo – *Discorsi parlamentari*, Florence, 1932–42. A short selection of Cavour's parliamentary speeches was made by Delio Cantimori: *Camillo Benso di Cavour. Discorsi parlamentari*, Turin, 1962. Rarely cited nowadays, but not without a note of brilliance, is a long essay by Lord Acton on Cavour, which can be found in a volume entitled *Historical Essays and Studies*, London, 1926. It was originally published in *The Rambler* in 1861, shortly after Cavour's death. A good antidote to the traditional picture of the *re galantuomo* is provided by Denis Mack Smith, *Vittorio Emanuele*, Bari, 1972.

1. Adolfo Omodeo, op. cit., pp. 91–2.
2. For Massimo d'Azeglio as an artist and novelist see Chapters 12 and 11.
3. Alan Sked, op. cit., p. 49.
4. For Cernuschi's ideas see Giuseppe Monsagrati, *Federalismo e unità nell'azione di Enrico Cernuschi (1848–1851)*, Pisa, 1976.
5. Quoted in Candeloro, op. cit., vol. III, p. 439.
6. This argument is convincingly put across by Paul Ginsborg, op. cit.
7. Harry Hearder, 'La rivoluzione veneziana del 1848 vista dal console generale inglese', *Rassegna storica del risorgimento*, XLIV, 1957, p. 741.
8. A well documented study of the movement is Gian Biagio Furiozzi, *L'emigrazione politica in Piemonte nel decennio preunitario*, Florence, 1979.
9. This tragic event in Cavour's life has been fully told for the first time in Rosario Romeo's work mentioned above.
10. Luigi Chiala ed., *Lettere edite ed inedite di Camillo Cavour*, Turin, 1884, vol. I, p. 280.
11. Ibid., pp. 49–56.

CHAPTER NINE

Cavour and the achievement of unity (1852–61)

The first major trial to face Cavour after he had become prime minister of Piedmont was an attempted insurrection in Milan, organized by Mazzini. The insurrection was intended to coincide with other risings against the Habsburg Monarchy, and in Germany and France. In Paris Louis-Napoleon assumed the title of 'Emperor Napoleon III' in December 1852, on the anniversary of his *coup d'état*. He had, of course, many bitter enemies, many of whom were in exile but, equally, many were still in Paris. With this republican opposition to the Second Empire Mazzini was in touch, and in Italy there were plans for Mazzinian risings in the Papal States, the Central Duchies and Sicily. The Hungarian revolutionary leader, Louis Kossuth, was also now an exile in London, and Mazzini could co-ordinate plans with him in July 1852.

The conspiracy was thus a complicated one. Its drawback, however, lay in the fact that in the course of 1851 and 1852 the Austrians had arrested a great number of Mazzinian supporters, a few of whom they had shot, with the result that former conspirators were prudently going into exile. By the beginning of 1853 the Austrians knew far more about the Mazzinian network than they had known two years earlier.

In January 1853 Mazzini left England for Switzerland, where he stayed at Lugano, which often served as his headquarters when he wished to be as near Italy as possible. It seemed to him that an insurrection in Milan had a good chance of succeeding, and that it would then spread throughout Italy and, possibly, Europe. The insurrection was planned for 6 February, a Sunday at the end of the carnival, when most of the troops would be in the bars and debilitated by too much wine. Mazzini was in close touch with working-class leaders who, although not enrolled in his organization, appeared to be prepared to lead a popular rising, which would take possession of the barracks and procure arms. Some of the middle-class leaders, however, were sceptical of success, and their pusillanimity infected the working-class leaders when the moment for action came. Trust between the two groups was lacking. A few hundred workers attacked the Austrian sentries but were quite inadequately armed for the task. Some, indeed, were not armed at all, and most had only knives. Only four of the insurgents and ten Austrian soldiers were killed; the

218

fighting, then, was on a small scale and the insurrection a total failure. But large numbers were arrested, and fifty men executed. Later trials at Mantua and Ferrara led to more revolutionaries being shot. Mazzini returned in great dejection to London. Many of his followers now began to fall away, but he defiantly announced in April that his party would be reorganized, given the new name of the 'Party of Action', and would consist only of dedicated revolutionaries prepared for an armed struggle. He now hoped to attract a larger working-class following and to depend less on the predominantly middle-class following which had previously provided members for the party.

Cavour reacted to the attempted rising in Milan by arresting a number of Mazzinians, among them Francesco Crispi, the future prime minister of Italy, who was briefly imprisoned. For this Cavour received official thanks from the Austrians, thanks which would probably have embarrassed him had they not immediately given him the opportunity to escape from their friendship. A week after the attempt in Milan the Austrians published a decree expropriating the property of all emigrants, including those who had quite legally and correctly emigrated to Piedmont, and those who had acquired Piedmontese citizenship. Cavour protested strongly at this act. The emigrants most affected by the decree were members of the aristocracy who had left behind palaces and rich possessions, which they now lost without compensation. The British government also took up their cause, but without avail. The 'Sequestrations Question', as it came to be called, was to be a vital issue in the complex diplomacy between the Western Powers, Austria and Piedmont during the Crimean War.

War between Russia and Turkey started on 8 October 1853. France and Britain were not to go to war with Russia until 28 March 1854. In the interim prolonged negotiations ensued, and continued even after war had started, since Austria remained neutral and could attempt to mediate between the two sides. The preoccupation of the French and British governments was with the securing of Austrian help, if possible in the form of a full military alliance against Russia, or at least in the form of an exerting of diplomatic pressure on Russia to come to terms. That France was seeking an alliance with Austria placed Piedmont in a dangerous corner. Cavour could envisage his country becoming isolated from the Great Powers. On the other hand he was not, initially, prepared for Piedmontese intervention in the war, since he knew that such intervention would be unpopular both with some of his own colleagues in the government and with the left in parliament, who felt that if Piedmont had to go to war it should be against Austria on the plains of Lombardy, not against Russia on some remote peninsula, in a struggle which did not involve Piedmontese interests. The traditional interpretation by which Cavour was seen as gleefully entering the war in order to secure the sympathy of France and Britain and a seat at the peace conference has not survived the research of the last few decades. Rather was Cavour pressurized by Britain and France to enter the war, partly because more troops were needed against Russia, partly to reassure the Austrian government, who had groundless fears that, with the Austrian army guarding the Danube and in occupation of the

Romanian Principalities, Piedmont might seize the occasion to stir up revolution in Lombardy unless she were involved in the war in the east.

In April 1854 Sir James Hudson, British minister in Turin, started to put the pressure on Cavour, only two weeks after the Western Powers had gone to war with Russia. At first the French government was less eager for Piedmontese intervention than the British, but eventually the French minister in Turin persuaded Vittorio Emanuele to favour the sending of an army to the Crimea. The king actually believed that Cavour would resign rather than carry through the policy of intervention, but in this he was mistaken. On the contrary, once Cavour had signed an agreement to send a force to the Crimea, he himself became the most enthusiastic salesman of the idea of intervention. The force, numbering 15,000 – precisely the figure Sir James Hudson had suggested a year earlier – arrived in the Crimea in the spring of 1855.[1] They fought only one engagement of any importance, the Chornaya Rechka, but in it performed creditably. It has been usual for British historians to treat Piedmont's military contribution in the Crimea as a rather trivial affair, but it should at least be recognized that when the 15,000 Piedmontese troops arrived, the British army in the field numbered only about 20,000, since British forces had been so tragically depleted by the cholera. The French army in the field, admittedly, numbered some 90,000.[2]

The Russians accepted defeat in January 1856, and the peace congress was held at Paris from 25 February to 16 April. Cavour was not hopeful about its conclusions so far as Piedmont was concerned. He had received no promises from his allies, and at first was disinclined to attend. He asked Massimo d'Azeglio, who was liked and respected in London and Paris, to represent Piedmont, but at the last moment changed his mind and went himself. In Paris Cavour had several meetings with the British plenipotentiary and foreign secretary, Lord Clarendon, and exchanged letters with him throughout the congress. Clarendon appeared to be very sympathetic to the Italian cause, but Italy was not discussed until after peace with Russia had been signed. Even then Count Buol, the Austrian plenipotentiary and foreign minister, tried to prevent discussion by protesting that no 'Italian Question' existed. Cavour played a very modest role. He knew that there was no point in suggesting that Lombardy should be given to Piedmont. He limited his argument to the mild, but valid, suggestion that the Austrian troops in the Papal Legations had no legitimate right to be there. He was posing as a legitimist, not as a nationalist. Clarendon, primed by Cavour, took up the argument. In a dramatic speech he argued that there would be no need for foreign troops to be in the Papal States if the pope's government was less corrupt and incompetent. He then attacked Naples, and insisted that Ferdinand should reform his primitive kingdom. Clarendon had scrupulously avoided attacking Austria, yet Cavour was evidently delighted by the Englishman's performance. But once back in London and under the influence of the hard-headed prime minister, Palmerston, Clarendon's enthusiasm for Italy became distinctly tepid. In the long run it was much more important for Cavour that at the Congress of Paris he had made a contact – though not yet a close one – with Napoleon III.

In 1857 one last, tragic, attempt at republican insurrection was made. Carlo Pisacane has already been mentioned in connection with his role in the Roman Republic, and must be mentioned again in the context of the birth of Italian socialism. But his most important role in the history of the Risorgimento is that of his attempt to raise the revolution in the Kingdom of Naples in 1857, and his death in the attempt. He was perfectly aware that the concept of socialism meant nothing to the poor people of Naples, but he believed that they were sufficiently impoverished, and yet sufficiently alive, to respond to a call to revolution. The peasants of Lombardy and the Veneto had fought for the Risorgimento in 1848. It was true that the peasants of the south had never fought for the bourgeois revolution but, rather, had fought against it with great savagery, in 1799. In more recent times, however, they had been fighting, in an incoherent way, for a quite different, agrarian, revolution, and it was this that Pisacane wished to give them. He was working, however, in close co-operation with Mazzini, who did not usually expect help from the peasants. Mazzini returned to his native town of Genoa on 11 May 1857, where he intended to organize a rising to correspond with a rising started by Pisacane in the Kingdom of Naples. Another insurrection was to be started in the radical port of Leghorn.

Rubattino and Company, a Piedmontese shipping firm, ran a mail service from Genoa to Cagliari, Sardinia, to Tunis, and back. The small ship, the *Cagliari*, which performed this service, also carried about thirty passengers. Pisacane and twenty-four followers bought tickets for the *Cagliari*. When the ship was on the high seas the passengers produced revolvers and daggers and hijacked the vessel. They then sailed to the island of Ponza where the Neapolitan government had a large prison. Over 300 men were released from the prison. Not more than fifteen of them were political prisoners; the rest were normal criminals, but were quite prepared to contribute to a revolution rather than to stay in the primordial conditions of a Neapolitan prison. With its considerably augmented human cargo the *Cagliari* sailed on to the Neapolitan coast and arrived at Sapri on the evening of 28 June. The local population greeted the invaders at first with suspicion and then with open hostility. In his first encounter with the Neapolitan forces Pisacane lost some 150 killed. The next day he himself was wounded and, aware that the expedition had been a disaster, killed himself. In Genoa and Leghorn Mazzini tried to call off the insurrections, but could not avoid the arrest of some of his followers. The death of Pisacane, one of the most intelligent of the leaders of the Risorgimento, was a major disaster. There was a terrible irony in the fact that Garibaldi in 1860 was to succeed in a typically Mazzinian adventure, yet an adventure in which Mazzini played no part. To attempt to overthrow a kingdom with 300 untrained men may in retrospect seem to have been a hopeless folly. Cavour can perhaps be excused for thinking in 1860 that Garibaldi's attempt to destroy the Kingdom of the Two Sicilies with an initial force of 1,000 was only marginally less foolish.

A last republican attempt of a rather different kind was made in January 1858 – an attempt on the life of Napoleon III. It was made by four Italians, the leader of whom was Felice Orsini. Of the other three one was simply a hired assassin, paid by Orsini, and the other two were young Mazzinian enthusiasts. Like Mazzini, Orsini had been living as an exile in England, but Mazzini himself knew nothing of the plot, Orsini having broken all links with him some years before. Three large bombs were made for Orsini in England, and taken by the four conspirators to Paris by way of Brussels. The London police informed the French authorities that known revolutionaries had left England for Belgium, possibly *en route* for Paris. The French police halted traffic on the roads from Belgium, but overlooked one small possibility – that the conspirators might travel to Paris by train, which, of course, they did. The bombs were thrown at Napoleon and the Empress Eugénie as their coach arrived at the Opera on the evening of 14 January. Seven people were killed, and one died later in hospital. About 150 people were hurt. Napoleon and Eugénie were unharmed. Orsini's theory had been that if Napoleon were killed a republic would be restored in France, and a republican régime would come to the help of Italy. This contorted plan was no stranger than what, in the event, happened.

During the trial Orsini's counsel, the republican lawyer Jules Favre, read a letter in which Orsini affirmed that he knew he was about to die and that this was no longer of any concern to him, but he added an appeal to the emperor to secure for Italy her independence. If Napoleon listened to the plea of 'a patriot on the steps of the scaffold', 'the blessings of twenty-five million citizens would follow him to posterity'. Exactly how it was that this plea should have had its desired effect on Napoleon is perhaps for the psychologist rather than the historian to explain.

From the Congress of Paris until 1858 Cavour did not have a direct correspondence with Napoleon, but kept in touch through several channels. One was Cavour's and Napoleon's doctor, Conneau, another was Napoleon's nephew, Prince Jérome-Napoleon, nicknamed 'Plon-plon', who became a close friend of Cavour; but most important was Cavour's highly intelligent private secretary, Costantino Nigra, who was to have a distinguished career in the diplomatic service, but in these years acted as a secret and informal agent of Cavour in Paris. An agent of a different kind was the Countess Castiglione, a nineteen-year-old girl whom Cavour despatched to Paris, and who slept with the emperor. Napoleon subsequently made the rather unkind remark that she was 'very pretty, but had no charm'.[3]

The next initiative towards a Franco-Piedmontese alliance was apparently taken by Napoleon, although Cavour had been sufficiently primed by Nigra to be able to keep a firm control of developments. Plombières had always been a favourite spa resort of the Bonapartes. It was near the Swiss frontier, so that when Cavour was in Geneva he could be unobtrusively invited to meet Napoleon at Plombieres.

The meeting took place in July 1858. Basically the agreement reached was for a war to be waged against Austria by France and Piedmont for the acquisition by Piedmont of the provinces of Lombardy and Venetia. Since Cavour had been invited to Plombières by the emperor the first assumption must be that the proposals came from France. Yet there is documentary evidence that Cavour took with him a memorandum which anticipated with remarkable precision the course of the discussion. There can be little doubt that the creative mind behind the decisions reached at Plombieres was Cavour's rather than Napoleon's. And the ground had been well prepared by Nigra.

To begin with, some time was spent in a search for a possible excuse for war with Austria: it is here that the more callous and hypocritical element in the agreement becomes apparent. They settled on a crisis to be created artificially, involving the Duke of Modena and the tiny Duchy of Massa; in the event this pathetic excuse for war was never to be used. On the real objectives for war they agreed without difficulty. The Austrians were to be driven out of Italy. A Kingdom of Upper Italy under Vittorio Emanuele was to be created, consisting of Piedmont, Lombardy, Venetia and the Papal Legations. There would be a Kingdom of Central Italy consisting of Tuscany and the Papal Romagna. The Pope would retain the area around Rome known as the 'Patrimony', and the Kingdom of Naples would be left intact, mainly because Napoleon had a not altogether justified fear that Czar Alexander II regarded himself as the protector of the Neapolitan Bourbons. The four Italian states which would thus emerge would be formed into a confederation of which the Pope would be president 'to console him for losing the best part of his territories'. Napoleon then asked for his pound of flesh, which, as pounds of flesh go, was a surprisingly modest one. He wanted only Savoy and Nice, two very beautiful corners of the world but, before the days of mass tourism, not particularly valuable. Although the kings of Sardinia had originally been only dukes of Savoy, Cavour knew that the people of Savoy were French-speaking, and looked towards France. Savoy was certainly of greater strategic value to France than to Piedmont. Nice, however, was a rather different matter, since the majority of its population was Italian-speaking. Cavour would therefore not commit himself on Nice. 'The Emperor', Cavour wrote, 'stroked his moustache several times', and agreed to leave the question open.

To achieve these ends France would provide 200,000 men, Piedmont 100,000. The small state of Piedmont was to provide half as many troops as the large land of France; in the event neither country was quite to produce its complement. The final point of the Plombières agreement was one very close to the heart of Napoleon III. He wished to have a marriage alliance with Piedmont, in the shape of a marriage between his nephew, Prince Jérome, who was no longer young, and the fifteen-year-old daughter of Vittorio Emanuele, the Princess Clotilde. The Bonapartes had always been social climbers. Just as Napoleon I had wanted a marriage alliance with the Habsburgs, so, now, Napoleon III wanted a marriage alliance with the ancient House of Savoy. Cavour, who had dropped his own 'de' and called himself simply 'Camillo Cavour', knew the foibles of the Bonapartes. He was not likely to have any sentimental concern for the little Princess Clotilde: probably he thought that she would be only too lucky to escape from Turin to the splendour of Paris under the Second Empire. Nothing was signed at Plombieres, but the marriage between Plon-plon and Clotilde was quickly arranged.

Cavour now saw his task as that of building up a war of nerves with Austria. To this end he drafted an emotional speech for the king to read to the first session of parliament in 1859. Napoleon was shown Cavour's draft which ended with a fairly bland and vague sentence about 'the Great Mission entrusted by Divine Providence' to the king of Piedmont. Napoleon thought the sentence 'too strong' and suggested another one which Cavour privately, and rightly, noted was 'a hundred times stronger'. Napoleon's concluding sentence ran: 'we cannot remain insensible to the cries of pain which come to us from so many parts of Italy'. Vittorio Emanuele himself made a few changes in the wording, one of which, though small, was an improvement in a literary sense, and not without significance politically. He changed 'cries of pain' to the singular *grido di dolore*, or 'cry of pain'. The phrase *grido di dolore* echoed around Italy. The Austrian government started to prepare for war. But it was not yet by any means certain that Cavour could arrange for a war of aggression against Austria. Napoleon was unreliable, and not fully committed to war. In London there was a Tory government under Lord Derby, with Lord Malmesbury at the Foreign Office. Malmesbury had been made foreign secretary briefly in 1852, and then again in 1858, because he had been a close personal friend of Napoleon. As very young men the two had been in Italy together in the 1820s. They have moved in the revolutionary circle of the Countess Guiccioli, Byron's mistress, and Malmesbury, in 1859 a respectable middle-aged Tory peer, still felt nostalgia for Italy and a love–hate attitude to Napoleon. He distrusted Cavour but, unlike his colleagues in the cabinet, and especially Derby himself and Disraeli, Malmesbury had no sympathy for Austria. Above all Malmesbury wanted to preserve peace, and went to considerable lengths to do so.[4] When the Russian government proposed a European congress on the Italian Question, Malmesbury grasped at the proposal, and tried to sell it to the other European powers. Napoleon was very fond of congresses. The Congress of Paris had been a good moment in his life, the birth of his first child, a son, corresponding with the arrival of the political élite of Europe in Paris to settle the Eastern Question. Although Napoleon III had studied military science he was not really a man of war. He would have preferred to settle the Italian Question in a great congress over which he would preside, rather than on some bloody battlefield. But Cavour was convinced that a congress could only shelve the Italian Question once more, as the Congress of Paris had done. At first the Austrians even queried Piedmont's right to be represented at the congress. When the Austrians had been convinced by the French and British governments that if there was to be a congress Piedmont must be represented, they argued that in that case all the other Italian governments – the Pope, the King of Naples, the Grand Duke of Tuscany – must also be represented. Cavour followed the intense diplomacy of these months with growing alarm. As the crisis deepened both the Austrian and Piedmontese governments placed their armies on a war footing. Malmesbury was now trying desperately to reverse the trend – to get what he called 'disarmament' in Northern Italy, by 'disarmament' evidently meaning demobilization. Cavour's war policy was eventually saved by the precarious financial condition of the Austrian government. Having mobilized their considerable army in Northern Italy, the Austrians could not afford to keep it mobilized indefinitely. On the other hand they could not risk demobilizing it while the Piedmontese army remained on a war footing. They therefore took the extreme step which they must have realized was highly likely to lead to war. They sent an ultimatum, drawn up on 19 April 1859 by the foreign minister Count Buol and with the approval of Emperor Francis Joseph, to Turin, demanding that the Piedmontese government should demobilize its army, and that a reply should be given to the demand within three days. Cavour replied, quite correctly within the three days, saying that the King's government could not accept the ultimatum. The Italian Question was to be settled by war, not by congress.

The Austrians should have had the advantage initially in the fighting. Piedmont could produce an army of only 60,000 against a very much larger Austrian army. Napoleon III took a few days to declare war on Austria and had then to move an army of some 110,000 to Italy – partly by sea to Genoa, partly over the Alps. Cavour's dream of a railway tunnel under Mont Cenis was still on the drawing-boards.[5] But the Austrian commander-in-chief, Gyulai, was slow to move, hampered by heavy rain which was unusual in the spring in Italy. Instead of occupying Turin, which he could probably have done with a little more moral courage, he delayed, and even suffered a minor defeat at the hands of the Piedmontese before the French arrived. The war was short and localized geographically, but nevertheless horrible and bloody. The numbers involved were greater than those involved in the Crimean War, and in only a few days the casualty rate was appalling. No arrangements were made for looking after the maimed and wounded, who often lay for hours on the battlefield with their limbs shot away, or in other respects hopelessly disfigured. For the first time the railway had been used to move large numbers of troops, but it moved them only to a scene of great suffering and horror.

The war was decided in two major battles: Magenta and Solferino. The Piedmontese played no part at Magenta, but performed well at Solferino. Both battles were defeats for the Austrians, but not overwhelming defeats, since the French losses were also very heavy. Napoleon was nauseated at the carnage, and it is surely to his credit that he decided that nothing – not even the independence of Italy – could justify this kind of outrage against humanity. But his decision to end the fighting had other, more calculating, motives. There were, perhaps, four in all:

The first was certainly his revulsion at the carnage of Magenta and Solferino. The second was his realization that the Austrian army, though sadly depleted, was still intact, and that there was no question of an easy march to Vienna, or even to Venice. The third concerned developments in Central Italy. On the first day of the war a working-class demonstration in Florence had persuaded the Grand Duke Leopold II to leave for Vienna. Subsequently an upper-class group, dominated by Baron Ricasoli, had assumed control in Tuscany and had declared their readiness for union with Piedmont. Revolution had also spread to the Papal Legations, where an agent of Cavour, Farini, had assumed control. None of these developments in Central Italy had secured the approval of Napoleon III, who consequently felt that the Italian Question was slipping from his grasp. His fourth motive for seeking peace was perhaps the decisive one. The Prussian government was a bitter rival with the Austrian for predominance in Germany, but it had no desire to see a French army marching into Vienna, which would have meant an alien army marching into the lands of the German Confederation. The Prussians therefore mobilized their army on the Rhine, and the German Confederation mobilized a very considerable army to stand beside the Prussians. Napoleon's reasons for seeking peace with Austria were not slender ones.

Napoleon III met the young Austrian emperor, Francis Joseph, at Villafranca on 11 July 1859. In a very short time they drew up the terms for an armistice, without consulting any representative of Piedmont. In some respects the armistice reflected the terms of the Plombières pact, but in other respects it was considerably more reactionary. An Italian confederation was to be created, under the presidency of the Pope. Lombardy, of course, was to be ceded to Piedmont, but Venetia was to remain under Austrian sovereignty. Then came the most reactionary feature of the armistice: 'The Grand Duke of Tuscany and the Duke of Modena will return to their states'. Since his restoration in 1849 Leopoldo II, who had seemed a tolerant, not to say enlightened, ruler in his earlier days, had come to be considered by the Tuscan moderates to be on the side of reaction. Having lost faith in the Grand Duke, the Tuscan moderates were inclined to turn to Piedmont, although before 1859 they certainly had no desire to be annexed by Piedmont. The outbreak of Cavour's 1859 war and the popular rising of 27 April in Florence, however, hardened the attitude of the moderates. Led by the strong-minded Baron Ricasoli, they now decided that union with Piedmont was the only policy which could save them from democracy and republicanism. The grim, old-world authoritarian, Ricasoli, thus found himself as much opposed to the armistice of Villafranca as was Cavour or, for that matter, Mazzini. Cavour, for his part, after an hysterical scene with Vittorio Emanuele, tendered his resignation. There then followed a dangerous hiatus in the history of Italy. Cavour had stepped aside, and for the moment it seemed that Napoleon III was aligned with Austria in an attempt to halt further developments in the Italian Question. In the absence of Cavour two strong, aggressive men kept a movement towards Italian unification alive – in Tuscany, Ricasoli, and in the two small duchies and the Papal Legations, Farini. In Modena Farini took power on 19 June as Governor. The Piedmontese government was nervous about assuming power in Tuscany and preferred to delay decision, but the annexation of the smaller duchies of Parma and Modena did not seem such a precipitate step. After the battle of Magenta the Austrians had left Bologna on the night of 11–12 June. On the morning of 12 June there had been a revolutionary demonstration in this most revolutionary of cities. Cavour's government had sent Massimo d'Azeglio to take control.

In London a new government had come to power during the war, with Palmerston as prime minister and Lord John Russell as foreign secretary. They were furious at the terms of Villafranca, believing that Napoleon had betrayed the Italians, and there was some truth in the belief. In particular Palmerston and Russell were opposed to the idea of a restoration of the Grand Duke of Tuscany, and Palmerston even talked wildly of Britain going to war with Austria if any such attempt at restoration were made. The attitude of the British government was not without influence on Napoleon.

After Cavour's resignation, Alfonso Lamarmora, the general who had led the Piedmontese army in the Crimea, formed a government, which was somewhat timid in its approach to the question of the Central Duchies, because it feared offending Napoleon III. That there was, in the second half of 1859, any forward movement towards the unification of Italy depended not on Turin but on the two dominant figures in Central Italy – Ricasoli and Farini, and to a lesser extent on the sympathetic attitude of the Whig government in London. After Villafranca Ricasoli acquired virtually dictatorial powers in Florence. Arrangements made for electing an assembly in Tuscany ensured that no reactionary representatives who might have wanted a return of Leopold II, and equally no representative of the left, would be elected. The newly elected assembly passed a motion, unanimously, on 20 August, requesting annexation of Tuscany by Piedmont, the approval of Napoleon III, and the benevolent mediation of Britain, Prussia and Russia. For the time being Ricasoli's government was to remain in power.

A rather more popular assembly was elected in Modena, and met on 16 August. Five days later it voted for annexation by Piedmont, while leaving dictatorial power, for the time being, in the hands of Farini. The term *dittatore*, or dictator, was to acquire a sinister ring in twentieth-century Italy during the Fascist era. In nineteenth-century Italy it was applied as in Roman antiquity exclusively to the temporary holding of power. A 'dictator' was simply someone given full powers during a brief period of crisis or transition, and Garibaldi was to use the term in this sense in Sicily in 1860. In Parma, also, Farini had assumed dictatorial powers on 18 August, and arranged for the election of an assembly which, on 12 September, voted unanimously for annexation by Piedmont.

In the Legations the problem raised by the revolution was an even more delicate one, since the Great Powers – and especially France – were bound to be acutely concerned as to whether papal sovereignty were to be restored or not. D'Azeglio, sent as Piedmontese agent by Cavour before the latter's resignation, left Bologna on 16 July, leaving behind as his successor Colonel Leonetto Cipriani, who was a personal friend of Napoleon III, and whose control of Bologna would therefore, the Piedmontese government hoped, appease the French emperor. Cipriani arranged for the election of an assembly under rules which would ensure a distinctly middle-class body. The assembly, on 6 and 7 September, declared the Pope's rule to be ended, and the Legations prepared for annexation by Piedmont.

The armistice of Villafranca had been signed without the co-operation of Piedmont. But already on 8 August a peace conference met at Zurich and Piedmont was now invited to send plenipotentiaries. The peace of Zurich, however, was not signed until 10 November 1859. It dealt with the cession of Lombardy by Austria, first to France and then to Piedmont, not with the complex question of Central Italy. The other clauses of the armistice of Villafranca – those concerning Central Italy, and the proposed confederation – were to be discussed by a European congress. Napoleon evidently felt that he had lost the initiative in the Italian question, and looked to a congress to win it back for him. In December 1859 he took an unexpected step. An anonymous pamphlet called *Le Pape et le Congrès* was published in Paris, and official leaks informed the public that it had been written by a confidant of the emperor, La Guéronnière, and under the emperor's instructions. It recommended the pope to depend for his independence on a smaller state than his present one, for his defence on the army of an Italian confederation, of which he would be a member, and for his income on grants from the Catholic powers. The immediately operative part of these recommendations was that the pope should recognize that he could not retrieve the Legations. The pamphlet was in effect Napoleon's blueprint for the agenda of the proposed congress, so far as the Papal States were concerned. Understandably the pope was outraged, but his position was becoming an impossible one, since the survival of the Papal States to a great extent depended on the French army in Rome. The Austrian government made it clear that they could not take part in a congress in which French policy followed the line of *Le Pape et le Congrès*. The most important immediate effect of the pamphlet was, therefore, that the idea of a congress had to be abandoned. In January 1860 Lord John Russell, at the Foreign Office, for the moment seized the initiative with proposals based on the principle of non-intervention in Italy, proposals which the other powers accepted, although Austria did so under protest, since the proposals clearly anticipated an ultimate Piedmontese annexation both of the Central Duchies and of the Papal Legations.

Partly because of the influence of Sir James Hudson, Cavour returned to the premiership on 21 January 1860. He had regained faith in Napoleon III's friendship, but believed that it would be dependent upon a gesture from Piedmont, and the obvious gesture to make was to allow France to regain her natural frontiers by the cession of Savoy and Nice, in this case the concept of 'natural frontiers' relating to geographical and strategic factors rather than to human ones. The Palmerston–Russell government was bitterly opposed to the French annexation of Savoy and Nice, believing that it would herald the opening of a Napoleonic phase of expansion. Both men could remember the First Empire, and were misled by their memories. But it was true that Piedmont was under no obligation to cede Savoy and Nice to France, since Venice was still Austrian, so that the terms of Plombières had not been fulfilled by Napoleon.

At the opening of 1860 Central Italy was awaiting decisions, with Ricasoli exercising dictatorial powers in Tuscany, and Farini in the newly created state of 'Emilia', which comprised the two smaller duchies and the revolted Papal Legations. Although the problem of Central Italy was not logically linked to that of Savoy and Nice, Cavour saw them as being inextricably connected,

228

since he knew that Napoleon would be opposed to a Piedmontese annexation of Tuscany and Emilia unless he were bought off by the gift of Savoy and Nice. In February the idea became current that plebiscites might be held by universal manhood suffrage in Tuscany and Emilia to see if the population would approve Piedmontese annexation. At first Cavour disliked the concept of universal suffrage, which had for him a Mazzinian flavour, but he came to feel that it might be a gamble worth taking to secure annexation of Central Italy.

Ricasoli in Tuscany and Farini in Emilia published decrees on 1 March 1860 announcing that plebiscites would be held in ten days' time, offering a choice between 'Annexation to the constitutional monarchy of the King Victor Emmanuel II', or 'A separate Kingdom'. All men over twenty-one could vote. Neither government made any attempt to be non-partisan: both indulged in active propaganda in favour of annexation. The phrase 'separate Kingdom' ('*Regno separato*') seemed to rule out a republic, although not the restoration of the dukes, although the point was a somewhat academic one. The possibility of a second restoration was now remote; in eight months Villafranca had become little more than an unpleasant memory. The results of the plebiscites marked a resounding victory for the annexationists. In Tuscany 386,445 voted for union with Piedmont, 14,925 for a separate kingdom; in Emilia 427,512 for union with Piedmont, 756 for a separate kingdom. In Turin decrees were quickly published declaring Tuscany and Emilia parts of the Kingdom of Piedmont.

An organization which had played a prominent role in favour of the annexations was the National Society, a group which was small in number but considerable in influence. The man who could lay the strongest claim to being considered founder of the National Society was Giorgio Pallavicino, a rich nobleman. He had been imprisoned in the notorious Austrian prison, the Spielberg, for his part in the revolution of 1821 in Piedmont. At that time he had been on the radical wing of the revolution, but already in 1849 he had announced that he would abandon his previous republican aims to work for the unity of Italy, if necessary as a monarchy. He claimed that he was still a democrat but that, above all else, he wanted Italian unification: 'So long as Piedmont preserves the tricoloured flag, in Piedmont I see Italy.' The former president of the revolutionary Republic of St Mark, Daniele Manin, brought a greater weight of intellect and a more commanding personality than Pallavicino's to the leadership of the National Society. Manin, too, had abandoned his republicanism, believing that so long as there was some hope that the Piedmontese monarchy would work for Italian unification it must be supported. By 1860 the significance of the National Society was that it had contact both with Cavour and Garibaldi. It constituted one of the factors which were to push Cavour along the path to unification.

A secret treaty by which Piedmont ceded Savoy and Nice to France was the complement of the annexation of Tuscany and Emilia by Piedmont. The treaty was signed by Vittorio Emanuele on 12 March in Turin, and by Napoleon on 14 March in Paris. It laid down that the approval of the populations concerned must be consulted 'as soon as possible': a sceptic could argue that it should have been consulted before the treaty was signed. An announcement of the cession of the two provinces was made to the public on 30 March, and the plebiscites were held in the middle of April. Once again there were enormous majorities in favour of annexation. In Savoy those favouring annexation to France numbered 130,583, those against 235. In Nice the number in favour of French annexation was 24,448, those against 160. The result in Savoy, where the population looked towards France since the highest range of mountains in Europe prevented them from looking towards Italy, was not surprising. But in Nice, where the population was predominantly Italian-speaking, the figure of 160 was clearly spurious and can be explained only by the bullying activity of French agents, and the presence of a French army which was on its way home from Lombardy. The Piedmontese surrender of Nice was unfortunate for another reason – because the town was Garibaldi's birthplace, and he was one of its two deputies in the Piedmontese parliament. An MP who finds that his constituency has been given to a foreign power is very likely to feel a grievance. Garibaldi's reaction was to contemplate an irregular military expedition to prevent the annexation from taking place. It was with this absurdly unrealistic idea in mind that he started to form the irregular force which was to become the 'Thousand', on the coast a few miles east of Genoa, at a little place called Quarto, now a suburb of Genoa.

Meanwhile revolution had broken out in Sicily on 4 April 1860. It started as a working-class movement in Palermo, but did not survive for more than a fortnight. Other risings, however, started throughout Sicily, some in the towns, some among the peasants in the countryside, and these risings proved difficult for the royal troops to suppress. The events in Sicily had the fortunate effect of persuading Garibaldi to abandon his plans for liberating Nice and to concentrate on Sicily. Among his followers the Sicilian, Francesco Crispi, played an important role in persuading Garibaldi to lead an expedition to Sicily, as did another Sicilian who had played a leading part in 1848, Rosalino Pilo. One of the more interesting secondary figures of the Risorgimento, Pilo was an emotionally disturbed young man who died heroically after making a significant contribution to the unity of Italy. Some years earlier he had decided to commit suicide and had written dramatic and emotional letters to his friends bidding them goodbye. He had then changed his mind and decided to live a while longer. In 1860 he carried through what was in effect a double bluff. Before leaving Genoa he had persuaded Garibaldi that the revolution in Sicily was succeeding – which was not, strictly speaking, true. On 12 April he sailed, with one companion, to Sicily, where they found that the main risings had been suppressed, but that in a few rural centres resistance was continuing. Pilo assured the revolutionaries that Garibaldi was on his way, an assurance which was based on faith rather than knowledge, or even conviction. Meanwhile Pilo was regarded as the leader of the revolution.

Garibaldi sailed from Quarto on 6 May in two small steamers with a force of slightly more than a thousand volunteers. Only after they had sailed did he announce that they would fight under the banner of 'Vittorio Emanuele and Italy'. Some of the more dedicated Mazzinians among the Thousand were not prepared to fight for the King of Sardinia, even though Garibaldi saw him simply as a figurehead for a united and democratic Italy. It was partly with the idea of dropping these fanatically republican men, and partly to confuse the Neapolitan forces, that Garibaldi anchored at Talamone, on the Tuscan coast just north of the frontier with the Papal States. Sixty-four men were disembarked at Talamone, to attempt an insurrection in the Papal States. Not surprisingly, this small group failed miserably, and were eventually arrested by forces in Tuscany – forces, it should be noted, who were under the authority of Cavour's government in Turin. But Garibaldi's main force – still numbering about a thousand – sailed on to Sicily. The Thousand came, mostly, from Northern Italy. Nearly half of them were Lombards. The city of Bergamo, in particular, could claim to have sent 180 men. A large number were students and, among the older volunteers, professional men of one kind or another. But many also were artisans or industrial workers. The Thousand originated overwhelmingly from the cities. There was one woman, Francesco Crispi's wife. The youngest of the Thousand was a boy of eleven, Giuseppe Marchetti, who accompanied his father. The boy was to survive the campaign, but to lead a sad life and die in poverty in his twenties.[6]

From Talamone the Thousand sailed to Marsala, on the far western coast of Sicily, and landed unopposed. Of this tiny force many had fought in 1859, but it would be an exaggeration to say that they were experienced soldiers. They were poorly armed. The Piedmontese government had allowed them some ancient muskets, which were not rifled, and many of which were unsafe to use. Against them was the royal Neapolitan army, which in Sicily numbered some 25,000 and had been newly equipped and armed, and well supplied with artillery. But Garibaldi, who had defeated the French in 1849 and the Austrians in 1859, was no ordinary commander. With a thousand young men, and a few rusty rifles and bayonets, he was about to destroy an ancient kingdom. The nineteenth century is short on romance. Garibaldi in 1860 did something to modify the shortage. Hearing of Garibaldi's arrival, Pilo wrote to his girl friend that now everything would be all right. His optimism was to be justified, but Pilo himself was killed a few days later on 21 May.

With the original Thousand, plus 200 or 300 Sicilian revolutionaries who had joined him, Garibaldi had his first encounter with the Neapolitan Bourbon troops at Calatafimi on 15 May. The Neapolitans were a slightly larger force, far better equipped, and occupied a stronger position on higher ground. Even so the Thousand defeated the Bourbon forces, mainly because of the courageous use made by Garibaldi's men of that ugly weapon, the bayonet. The psychological impact of Garibaldi's victory at Calatafimi – in Sicily, in the Kingdom of Naples, and throughout Italy as a whole – was immense. By the end of June very large reinforcements of volunteers had arrived to swell the numbers of Garibaldi's original Thousand. After fierce fighting Garibaldi entered Palermo on 27 May, and was greeted by a popular insurrection in his favour. The Bourbon command decided to seek an armistice, which was arranged through the mediation of the British admiral, Mundy, and by which Garibaldi was left in control of Palermo.

Garibaldi's success in Sicily meant that Cavour had lost the initiative. A week after Garibaldi sailed from Quarto, Cavour wrote to Costantino Nigra in Paris explaining his attitude to the expedition very precisely. Elections were being held in Piedmont, and positive action by Cavour to prevent Garibaldi from sailing would have been condemned by Piedmontese public opinion. Nevertheless, Cavour wrote, 'I omitted nothing to persuade Garibaldi to drop his mad scheme'. Cavour assumed that in the end Gribaldi would not go. When he did so, and when his expedition started to succeed in Sicily, Cavour decided to regain the initiative, if possible, by allowing arms to be sent – somewhat belatedly – and by sending an agent of his own, Giuseppe La Farina, to contact Garibaldi. But La Farina's aim was to secure the annexation of Sicily to Piedmont as soon as possible. He had quarrelled with Garibaldi and Crispi before the sailing of the Thousand, and for Cavour to send such a man was a grave error of judgement. Crispi and La Farina fought for a while against each other, with Garibaldi being too occupied with military matters to decide between them. Eventually, on 7 July, he had La Farina arrested and expelled from Sicily. Cavour's influence on events had thus sunk to an even lower point. Garibaldi then persuaded Cavour to send to Sicily, as representative of Piedmont, Agostino Depretis, one-time Mazzinian, and one day to be prime minister of Italy.

In Naples Francesco II took a few desperate steps to give his regime a liberal appearance. On 1 July he restored the constitution of 1848 and allowed a free press to come into existence. On 15 July he appointed Liborio Romano minister of the interior. Romano was believed to be a liberal, although he had contacts with the *camorra*, the *mafia* of Naples. The people of the kingdom of Naples regarded these measures with the scepticism they deserved; for them Garibaldi had become the only reality.

After Garibaldi had occupied Palermo there was a spontaneous rising throughout Sicily against the Bourbons, whose forces were obliged to concentrate themselves at Messina. But the Garibaldini had to fight the bitter battle of Milazzo, in which they lost 800 dead and about 5,000 wounded, against less than 200 dead and wounded on the Neapolitan side. Yet Milazzo was another moral victory for Garibaldi, and on 27 July his forces entered Messina. Once Garibaldi was in control of the whole island of Sicily the question of his invasion of Continental Naples presented itself to the European Powers. Napoleon III would have prevented Garibaldi from crossing the Straits of Messina, but the Palmerston/Russell government in London was determined not to intervene. The British point of view – an eminently sensible one – was that if Garibaldi succeeded in crossing the Straits and occupying Naples he must have considerable popular support. That Garibaldi entered Naples unopposed, and with immense acclamation, on 7 September 1860, was due to his own charisma and the brilliance of his achievements; that he had crossed the Straits was due to the goodwill of the British government and the British

Mediterranean fleet. In the long run the wickedness of Nelson's policy at Naples had been expiated.

Cavour had tried, through several agents in Naples, or sent to Naples from Turin, to anticipate Garibaldi's arrival by starting a pro-Piedmontese movement in Naples. He was in touch with Romano, who was quite prepared to betray the Bourbons, but no following could be found for such a movement. Nor did Cavour want openly to oppose Garibaldi; he realized the extent of Garibaldi's achievement. On 9 August he wrote to Nigra: 'Garibaldi has rendered Italy the greatest services that a man could give her: he has given Italians confidence in themselves: he has proved to Europe that Italians know how to fight and die on the battlefield to reconquer a fatherland . . . . All the same it is eminently desirable that a revolution in Naples should take place without him.' Although Garibaldi was fighting for 'Vittorio Emanuele and Italy' the 'Italy' he had in mind was a democratic state which would immediately liberate Rome and Venice. Cavour believed that Italy would not be ready for democracy, and that an attack on Rome and Venice would embroil her in a war with France and Austria, a war which she could hardly hope to win. Yet the extent of Garibaldi's success lay in the fact that a normally cautious statesman like Cavour was, in August 1860, talking of 'Italy' as though she already existed as a political entity.

The still very considerable Bourbon army was withdrawn from Naples towards the north before Garibaldi's arrival in the capital. Francesco II and his queen journeyed by sea from Naples to Gaeta, not far south of the frontier with the Papal States. They left Liborio Romano in virtual control of Naples and he, true to form, promptly invited Garibaldi to come as quickly as possible. Such was Garibaldi's confidence that he would be well received in the vast teeming city of Naples that he travelled the last part of his journey by train, and arrived when most of his army was some distance away.

The democrats had held the initiative since May 1860. Dr Agostino Bertani, working with Mazzini, had even succeeded in collecting together some 9,000 armed and equipped men for an assault on the Papal States, but Cavour had successfully undermined this attempt. Cavour was now prepared himself to move against the Papal States, ostensibly to prevent revolution there, but really to ensure that Garibaldi's march towards Rome was halted. Costantino Nigra was still in Paris, in constant touch with Napoleon. On 26 August Nigra could reassure Cavour that Napoleon was prepared for Turin to regain the initiative. There is no documentary evidence of the precise assurance given by Napoleon to Cavour, but Cavour was convinced that he could take the last and greatest gamble of his career without provoking French intervention. Probably Napoleon merely laid down that the Piedmontese troops, in moving through the Papal States, should keep as far away from Rome — and the French garrison there — as possible.

The Piedmontese army invaded the Papal States on 11 September, four days after Garibaldi had entered Naples. There was, of course, no possible justification for the invasion in terms of international law. Whatever private assurances Napoleon had given Cavour, publicly he had to disapprove so blatant an act of aggression. Diplomatic relations between Paris and Turin were partially broken, in that the heads of legation returned to their respective home capitals, but the legations remained open under a *chargé d'affaires*. The army which Cavour's government moved into the Papal States was a considerable one – some 33,000 men – under the command of General Manfredo Fanti, soon to be minister of war of united Italy. The Pope's army had been to some extent renovated and placed under the command of a French general, Louis de Lamoriciere, who had completed the conquest of Algeria for Louis-Philippe. But Lamoricière had at his disposal a force of only about a third the size of the Piedmontese force. In a week Fanti had occupied most of Umbria. The decisive battle was fought on 18 September at Castelfidardo, a little hill town near Ancona. The papal forces were defeated, and the greater part of them surrendered. Lamoricière himself, with a handful of men, continued to resist for a few more days in Ancona itself.

Meanwhile the Neapolitan army, numbering some 50,000, was still intact, and Garibaldi was about to face what was to be perhaps his most demanding military encounter, at least since Calatafimi. The Bourbon army took up a position on the northern bank of the broad river Volturno. At Calatafimi Garibaldi had been in command of a ludicrously small force of ill-equipped and untrained youths; at the Volturno his army was about twenty times as large and consisted mostly of seasoned campaigners, but it was still probably smaller than the army of the Bourbons, and less well equipped with artillery. Garibaldi's first attempt to establish himself on the northern bank of the Volturno was unsuccessful. He was thrown back with very considerable losses. The Bourbon army was thus given the opportunity to counter-attack and perhaps to reoccupy Naples. This they failed to do. But the next stage of the battle of the Volturno was bitterly fought and cost Garibaldi more casualties than the Bourbons. Even so, there was no doubt that Garibaldi's forces were the victors and any possiblity of a Bourbon restoration was eliminated. Until the battle of the Volturno Garibaldi had been recognized only as a brilliant leader of guerrilla forces. But in this, his last major battle, Garibaldi showed that he could effectively and victoriously handle a large army, using the railway to move troops, and the terrain to conduct complex strategy.

With the Bourbons defeated and a Piedmontese army on its way to the South discussion centred on the problem of whether a parliament should be elected for Sicily, or whether both Sicily and the Neapolitan mainland should decide, by plebiscite, for or against an immediate annexation by Piedmont. The democrats in the South, and at first Garibaldi, favoured the election of local assemblies and the postponement of annexation. But Cavour's policy of Piedmontese military intervention in September virtually decided the matter in favour of his programme – the holding of plebiscites, a programme which had paid off so well, from his point of view, in Central Italy. The plebiscites were held on 21 October, the voters being asked to decide in favour, or opposition to, 'Italia Una Vittorio Emanuele'. The crude question of annexation to Piedmont was thus obscured by the reference to 'Italy', coupled with the king's name – the slogan under which Garibaldi had fought.

There was no reference to the name or constitution of Piedmont, not was a numeral attached to the king's name: the numeral II would have identified him as a Piedmontese monarch. In Continental Naples 1,302,064 people voted Yes, and 10,302 No. In Sicily 432,053 voted Yes, 667 No. In theory the voting was by secret ballot, but in practice separate voting slips, some saying 'Yes' some 'No', were provided and two separate ballot boxes – 'Yes' or 'No' – were also provided.[7] It must be remembered, however, that the secret ballot was introduced for elections in Britain only in 1872. Elections held in 1860 cannot be judged by the standards of twentieth-century democracy.

The Piedmontese army in Ancona was joined by Vittorio Emanuele on 3 October. The presence of the king made it extremely improbable that there would be a clash with Garibaldi. The two men met at Teano, north of the Volturno, on 26 October, Garibaldi at the head of a column of his followers in their red shirts, and the king surrounded by generals, ministers and numerous officers. The meeting was apparently friendly, and the two oddly assorted groups fraternized happily. For the moment at least political differences and divergent aims were forgotten. But the king had immediately made it clear that Garibaldi's army must now act under the royal command, and Garibaldi's reactions were inevitably mixed ones. The work of rounding up and defeating the remaining Bourbon troops was completed by the Piedmontese army. On 7 November Vittorio Emanuele, accompanied by Garibaldi, made a formal entry of Naples. Garibaldi refused all honours and gifts, but suddenly, and perhaps by then unexpectedly, asked to be given dictatorial powers in Southern Italy for one year. They were refused him, and on 9 November he left for his island home of Caprera. Wholly above corruption of any kind, he took no financial rewards with him, returning to the simple peasant life which he preferred, but leaving a promise – or threat – that he would return in a few months to undertake the liberation of Rome and Venice.

Plebiscites in the central and eastern parts of the Papal States – the Marches and Umbria – which had been occupied by the Piedmontese, were held on 4 November. Again enormous majorities in favour of annexation were recorded. In the Marches 133,765 returned a positive vote, 1,212 a negative one. In Umbria 97,040 were positive, 360 negative.

None of the Great Powers had intervened actively in the dramatic developments of 1860 in Italy. As has been seen, Napoleon III gave some kind of secret approval to Piedmont's invasion of the Papal States, although officially he took a tentative step towards breaking diplomatic relations with Turin. Russia formally broke diplomatic relations with Piedmont in October, and Austria increased her military forces in Venetia. Only the British government openly showed sympathy for the emergence of an independent and united Italy. On 27 October Russell sent Hudson a despatch which was published and greeted with great rejoicing in Italy. It explicitly stated that Britain had no intention of breaking off diplomatic relations with Vittorio Emanuele's government, but referred, on the contrary, to 'the gratifying prospect of a people building up the edifice of their liberties, and consolidating the work of their independence'. Russell had sent the despatch with Palmerston's approval, but without consulting the rest of the cabinet. The precaution had been taken of showing the despatch to Queen Victoria and Prince Albert, who had much more sympathy for Austria than had the British cabinet, and very little sympathy for Italy. The royal couple did not veto this first demonstration of British sympathy for the emerging Italian kingdom. Russell then composed a circular for the Powers, a circular recommending non-intervention in Italian affairs, and referring, somewhat provocatively, to Rome and Venice: 'It is to be hoped that these two Cities, so thoroughly Italian in their character, may finally enjoy as great a degree of well-being and good government as the rest of Italy.' More significantly, Russell's draft went on to warn that if 'any other Power' should indulge in 'forcible interference' in Italian affairs, 'Her Majesty's Government will hold themselves free to act in such manner as the rights of nations, the independence of Italy, and the interests of Europe may seem to them to require.'[8] Unfortunately this splendid despatch was never sent, because the Queen insisted that it should first be submitted to the cabinet, and Russell then preferred to forget about it. The fulsome sympathy of Russell and Palmerston for Italy in October 1860 was thus never known in Italy, but the despatch of 27 October did much to counterbalance the coldness of the rest of Europe. Apart from the two ugly decades of fascist aberration Italy and England were thereafter to remain close friends.

On 27 January 1861 elections were held for the first parliament of the Kingdom of Italy, and the parliament met in Turin on 18 February. Cavour had never left Turin, which had remained the centre of power. Vittorio Emanuele was recognized as King of Italy by parliament on 17 March. There were no ecclesiastical or feudal rituals like those accompanying a coronation in the United Kingdom or in earlier feudal monarchies. The new king was an essentially secular sovereign, just as Louis-Philippe had been in France. And, like Louis-Philippe, he was to rule because of the achievements, with the good will, and for the well-being, of the richer classes. The Kingdom of Italy which came into being in 1861 was an essentially pragmatic *ad hoc* institution and, like all such institutions, it was to be more stable than was at first expected; it was to survive for eighty-six years, but those eighty-six years were to include involvement in two world wars and the interlude of Fascism.

Garibaldi had promised that he would return from Caprera in a few months. His main preoccupation was that the soldiers who had fought under him – and who had, in the event, secured the unification of Italy – should not be forgotten in the final settlement. The minister of war in the government of the new kingdom of Italy, General Fanti, wanted to exclude Garibaldi's officers from commissioned ranks in the royal Italian army. They were, of course, far better educated than Fanti's own officers, and far more dedicated to the concept of 'Italy'. But they were also, as Fanti rightly foresaw, likely to be subversive in the army of a limited monarchy under the House of Savoy, especially if, for the time being, there was no question of an Italian acquisition of Venice or Rome. Fanti preferred the officers of the old Bourbon army of Naples, who had never been taught to think and so were better soldiers. That they had fought on the wrong side in the Risorgimento, Fanti thought –

236

perhaps with some reason – was not entirely their fault. In April 1861 Garibaldi came back from Caprera. He made a dramatic intervention in a debate of the Italian parliament, an intervention which led to uproar and confusion. The public galleries cheered his every remark, while the deputies shouted against him: it was an ominous forecast of the clash between the people of Italy and the ruling class. The immediate issue, the question of what should be done with Garibaldi's officers, was lost sight of in the general debate. Nino Bixio, whose rôle as a lieutenant of Garibaldi in the expedition of the Thousand had been a brilliant one, spoke with some wisdom, and restored an element of stability to the parliamentary scene, but Garibaldi had spoken with great passion against Cavour, whom he saw as an evil influence on Vittorio Emanuele, and as an enemy of the ideals of the Thousand.

Cavour was deeply distressed by this episode in the early life of the Italian parliament. But his main preoccupation in these last months of his life was with the Roman Question, about which he was surprisingly optimistic. His attempts to solve the Roman Question were cut short by his death, but are anyhow a part of the history of relations between church and state in Italy, and will be discussed in that context in Chapter 13.

Cavour died on 6 June 1861. His death took Italy and Europe by surprise. In the medical vocabulary of the day he died of a 'fever', which probably meant malaria. In his last delirious remarks he was concerned with the Southern Question. The Neapolitans, he said, were extremely intelligent, but corrupt. It would be necessary to cleanse them. And this could be done not by the imposition of martial law, but by ten years of freedom. Cavour, with all his faults and with all his limitations, had always believed in freedom. A few months before his death he had written to the Comtesse de Circourt a letter which has often been quoted, but which deserves repetition because it bears the mark of sincerity:

I have never felt so weak as when parliament is not in session . . . I am a child of liberty and owe it everything that I am. If ever it should be necessary to forget the constitution, it will not be for me to do it. If ever Italians should need a dictator, they will choose Garibaldi, and they will be right.[9]

NOTES

One aspect of Cavour's foreign policy was his interest in the Eastern Question. It is examined by Angelo Tamborra in *Cavour e i Balcani*, Turin, 1958. On the Italian Question during the Crimean War and Congress of Paris two books which broke new ground were Franco Valsecchi, *Il Risorgimento e l'Europa. L'alleanza di Crimea*, Florence, 1948, and Ennio di Nolfo, *Europa e Italia nel 1855–56*, Roma, 1957. The official account of the Piedmontese military expedition to the Crimea has been totally ignored by English-speaking historians, but deserves to be noticed: Cristoforo Manfredi, *La spedizione sarda in Crimea nel 1855–56*, originally published by the Italian Army Headquarters in 1896, reprinted by an anonymous publisher in 1956.

A splendid book on the earlier years of Felice Orsini is Alberto Ghisalberti, *Orsini*

Minore, Rome, 1955. The best account of the Orsini attempt itself is still the one which occupies book XIII, vol. II of P. de La Gorce, *Le Second Empire*, Paris, 7 vols, 1894–1908.

A classic in English on Tuscany in these culminating years of the movement for unification is W. K. Hancock, *Ricasoli and the Risorgimento in Tuscany*, London, 1926. Two essays by Denis Mack Smith are extremely important for Tuscany in 1859: 'Radicals and Moderates in Florence, April 1859', and 'Cavour and the Tuscan Revolution of 1859', in *Victor Emanuel, Cavour, and the Risorgimento*, Oxford, 1971.

Much interesting discussion, both of research and interpretation, can be found in the Acts of the Congress of the *Istituto per la storia del risorgimento italiano*. Often the congresses have dealt with a centenary theme. Thus the *Atti del XXXVIII congresso* consists of papers read in 1959, and published in Rome in 1960, and deals with the developments of 1859; especially valuable papers were those given by Franco Valsecchi, Heinrich Benedikt, Henri Contamine, Luigi Salvatorelli, Ruggero Moscati, and Piero Pieri. A central figure in 1859 was the erratic and excitable Luigi Carlo Farini. He has not been too well served by historians, but there is a life by Piero Zama, *Luigi Carlo Farini nel risorgimento Italiano*, Faenza, 1962. For Rome in 1859 Anna Maria Isastia, *Roma nel 1859*, Rome, 1978, gives a vivid picture of the political and social scene in the papal city while the war was raging in the north. Interesting on British policy in 1859 is Denis Mack Smith, 'Palmerston and Cavour: some English doubts about the Risorgimento, 1859–60', in *Italian Studies presented to E. R. Vincent*, ed. C. P. Brand, K. Foster, and U. Limentani, Cambridge, 1962. The small group of men who constituted the National Society played their most influential role in 1859. Historians had tended to pay more attention to the individual leaders of the National Society than to the policies and activities of the Society as a whole, until an American historian, Raymond Grew, published *A Sterner Plan for Italian Unity. The Italian National Society in the Risorgimento*, Princeton, 1963. Works which deal with 1859, but which also go beyond 1859, should be mentioned here. In this bracket there is an excellent work on British policy and opinion towards Italy – D. E. D. Beales, *England and Italy 1859–60*, London, 1961.

On the events of 1860 there is, of course, a vast literature, larger even than that for 1859. Once again a start can be made by considering the Acts of the congresses of the *Istituto per la storia del risorgimento italiano*. The XLII congress in 1960 dealt with the theme 'Da Villafranca ai plebisciti del marzo 1860', and shed considerable light on this confused period. Adam Wandruska dealt with 'L'Austria dopo Villafranca', Harry Hearder with 'Politica e opinione pubblica inglese verso l'Italia da Villafranca ai plebisciti dell'Italia centrale', Emilia Morelli with 'La sinistra rivoluzionaria da Villafranca ai plebisciti', and Louis Girard with 'La politique française de Villafranca aux plebiscits de l'Italie Centrale'.

For Garibaldi a good, short life is Denis Mack Smith, *Garibaldi*, London, 1957. The last two volumes of G. M. Trevelyan's classic trilogy are relevant to this chapter: *Garibaldi and the Thousand* (1909) and *Garibaldi and the Making of Italy* (1911). Originally published by Longman, they have since appeared in several editions. For developments in 1860 generally the relevant volume of the *Atti del congresso di storia del risorgimento italiano* is XXXIX (Rome, 1961); it contained many useful articles; those particularly worth noting were by Friedrich Engel-Janosi, Ettore Passerin d'Entrèves, Jacques Godechot, Denis Mack Smith and Angelo Tamborra. For a Sicilian view of 1860 there is Gaetano Falzone, *Sicilia 1860*, Palermo, 1962. There are several exciting accounts by people who took part in the expedition of the Thousand. Two which have been translated into English are G. C. Abba, *The Diary of One of Garibaldi's*

Thousand, trans. E. R. Vincent, London, 1962, and F. Brancaccio di Carpino, *Tre mesi nella Vicaria di Palermo nel 1860*, trans. and ed. John Parris as *The Fight for Freedom: Palermo, 1860*, London, 1968. A British Admiral, George Rodney Mundy, gave his account of the fall of the Kingdom of Naples in 1860, and of his own part in that event, in *H. M. S. 'Hannibal' at Palermo and Naples during the Italian Revolution, 1859–1861*, London, 1863. There has been no modern edition in English of this interesting book, but Antonio Rosada translated it into Italian, and edited it as *La fine delle Due Sicilie e la marina britannica*, Naples, 1966. Finally, an article dealing well with the international context of the expedition of the Thousand is Franco Valsecchi, 'European Diplomacy and the Expedition of the Thousand: the Conservative Powers', in Martin Gilbert (ed.), *A Century of Conflict 1850–1950. Essays for A. J. P. Taylor*, London, 1966.

1. A discussion of the rôles of Sir James Hudson and the British foreign secretary, Lord Clarendon, is contained in Harry Hearder, 'Clarendon e l'Italia', in *Il Risorgimento e l'Europa*, edi. Vittorio Frosini, Catania, 1969.
2. Cristoforo Manfredi, op. cit., p. 73.
3. Giuseppe Massari, *Diario dalle cento voci 1858–1860*, edi. Emilia Morelli, Rocco San Casciano, p. 59.
4. For the details of Malmesbury's policy before the war of 1859 see Harry Hearder, 'La politica di Lord Malmesbury verso l'Italia nella primavera del 1859', in *Rassegna storica del risorgimento, XLIII*, 1956, pp. 35–58.
5. A first blast for the Mont Cenis tunnel had been made in 1857. But the tunnel was not opened until 1871, after Cavour's death. It was nearly eight miles long – even by twentieth-century standards an impressive achievement.
6. Anton Maria Scarpo, 'Giuseppe Marchetti, il garibaldino undicenne', in *Rassegna storica del risorgimento, LXVII* 1980, pp. 297–307.
7. A 'Yes' voting slip from Naples in 1860 was sent to Prince Albert, and has been preserved in the Royal Archives at Windsor.
8. H. Hearder, 'Queen Victoria and Foreign Policy. Royal Intervention in the Italian Question, 1859–1860', in *Studies in International History. Essays presented to W. Norton Medlicott*, ed. K. Bourne and D. C. Watt, London, 1967, pp. 184–5.
9. *Cavour e l'Inghilterra*, vol. II, book 2 Bologna, 1933, p. 284.

The integration and centralization of institutions (1861–70)

The first decade of the life of the Kingdom of Italy was darkened by a savage civil struggle in both Sicily and Continental Naples. The struggle has usually been called, somewhat inadequately, 'the brigands' War'. It was much more than a 'brigands' war', being a mixture of a spontaneous peasant movement and a Bourbon-clerical reaction directed by the old authorities.

Already in the last days of September and the first half of October 1860, peasants operating under the command of Bourbon agents occupied several towns of the mainland Kingdom of Naples, defeating the pro-Garibaldi national guards who had been formed. Thousands of peasants took part in the fighting. After Garibaldi's final success on the Volturno, and the arrival of the Piedmontese army, the towns were, of course, retaken, but the peasants did not surrender, retreating into the hills where they became 'brigands' in the eyes of the new authorities. The bitter struggle continued.

In Sicily the peasants in 1860 had sided with Garibaldi, because they saw him as a revolutionary against their old masters. But when peasant movements had attacked local and municipal authorities Garibaldi had suppressed the risings with unexpected firmness, and the peasants had then become disillusioned with the red-shirted men from the north. But in Sicily there had been little enthusiasm to return to a loyalty to the Bourbons. Instead they had fallen into a sullen hostility to their new masters from Turin, and it was an easy transition for them to join a 'brigands' war' against the Kingdom of Italy. The representatives of the new regime, on the other hand, showed much greater enthusiasm in liquidating Garibaldi's army than in dealing with the old Bourbon forces. This was particularly the case during the lieutenancy (*luogotenenza*) of Farini, who had shown such energy in Emilia, but who treated the Bourbon officials, whose authority he was supposed to be replacing, with remarkable respect. The Bourbon army had held a very special position in the Neapolitan state, and its main function had been rather to suppress the population than to defend the kingdom. Cavour was determined that this influential part of the old establishment – the high-ranking military commanders – should be won over to loyalty to the new kingdom. To an extent he succeeded.

The Neapolitan high command did not oppose the new régime. But the great numbers of their troops who were disbanded took to the hills. By February 1861, 2,191 Bourbon officers had been given commissions in the Italian army while their men were being rapidly dispersed and deprived of their livelihood. Many Bourbon officers preferred to retire than to serve the new régime, but they had been treated gently by the Piedmontese authorities and it is significant that very few of them took part in the 'brigands' war' against the new authorities. The policy of Cavour's government towards the Bourbon army without doubt gave a class character to the 'brigands' war'. Often the war resembled a mass movement of poor peasants against a combination of their old and their new masters. Above all it was a movement against the military establishment which later imposed conscription and a state of siege. It was not controlled centrally by any Bourbon authority, since no such authority any longer existed. However, local authorities still loyal to the Bourbons encouraged and helped to organize the insurgent peasants. Mayors and civil servants of the old régime who, for one reason or another, had a particularly strong grudge against the new régime, gave their support. Funds were also supplied for the 'brigands' from the Papal States, and the Pope's government gave refuge to insurgents from the Kingdom of Italy.

The 'brigands' operated usually on horseback, sweeping down on the villages, killing the officials of the new régime, and destroying the archives in the town halls, archives which, they assumed, contained title-deeds to property usurped from common ownership. The newly elected mayors of the villages, and the national guard, were their first victims. The national guard and the army returned violence with violence. A savage brutality characterized the struggle on both sides. There were reports of men being crucified or burnt alive. How far such reports were exaggerated it is impossible to tell, but there seems sufficient evidence for the conclusion to be reached that behaviour more typical of the seventeenth than the nineteenth century became common. Apart from the great number of people killed in the fighting, very large numbers became helpless refugees, agricultural land was abandoned, shops and businesses closed, unemployment spread. In short, civilization receded. The 'brigands' war' continued throughout the 1860s, and is believed to have killed more people than all the wars of independence between 1848 and 1861.

In one sense the tragedy was a deeper one in Sicily than on the Neapolitan mainland, because in Sicily the 'brigands' war' merely intensified troubles which had always existed, and which were to continue after 1870. General Gorone, who was in command of the Italian army in Sicily in 1863, reported to parliament in December of that year. He claimed that much of the fighting was between rival villages or the result of family vendettas. Whole families were killed or forced to leave their homes, which were burnt down. During the 1860 campaign, Gorone said, about ten thousand criminals had escaped from prison to swell the numbers of brigands. He admitted that conscription had exacerbated the situation by increasing the number of deserters from the army. Murders were taking place at the rate of a thousand a year. People were afraid to given evidence against criminals for fear of a vendetta: they preferred to start or continue their own vendetta rather than rely on the authorities. In Sicily brigandage had always been endemic, and the lawlessness associated with the mafia was to become a characteristic of twentieth-century Sicily.

After Cavour's death in 1861 the party which he had led, now called 'the Right' (*la Destra*), remained in office, and Ricasoli became prime minister. But Ricasoli did not long retain the confidence either of the king or of parliament. On 3 March 1862 he was replaced as prime minister by Urbano Rattazzi, whose period of office lasted for only nine months, but was the occasion for one dramatic episode.

Although frustrated by Cavour's policy in 1860, Garibaldi had not abandoned the idea of taking Rome. Rattazzi seemed more accommodating than Cavour had been, and did not prevent Garibaldi from raising another volunteer army in Sicily for what was intended to be a crowning achievement – the securing of Rome as the capital of Italy. Without opposition from the government Garibaldi transported his army from Sicily to the mainland. Rattazzi's government then changed its mind and decided that Garibaldi must be forcibly dissuaded from the venture. There was a short skirmish at Aspromonte, in the far toe of Italy, between Garibaldi's irregular force and the regular Italian troops. Garibaldi himself was wounded in the leg, and for some five weeks imprisoned. The episode was an unfortunate one; Rattazzi resigned in December 1862 and was replaced as prime minister by Farini. The premiership of Farini was even shorter than that of Rattazzi. In March of 1863 he suffered a complete mental breakdown, which manifested itself in an attempt to knife the king, an act not readily tolerated even by a constitutional monarch.

Farini was followed as prime minister by an intelligent politician and economist from Bologna, Marco Minghetti, who survived for slightly longer than his predecessors – from March 1863 until the end of September 1864. Towards the end of his term of office a secret agreement of some importance was reached with Napoleon III, an agreement known as the September Convention. Napoleon agreed to complete the evacuation of Rome in two years, provided that the Italian government moved the capital from Turin to Florence. Napoleon assumed – with somewhat dubious logic – that if Florence became the capital of Italy the Italians would never be tempted to take Rome from the Pope. There was a good strategic justification for such a move. Florence, unlike Turin, was protected from a possible Austrian attack by formidable mountains. But the debate in parliament as to where the capital should be was a heated and complex one. Many deputies – and not only Neapolitans – felt that Naples, which was by far the largest of Italian cities, should be the capital. One deputy even argued that Perugia, the beautiful city in the province of Umbria, should be the capital until Rome could be acquired. But Florence was the more obvious choice for the time being, although the move was violently resisted by the people of Turin, where riots leading to deaths broke out. Florence was to be the capital of Italy until 1870; the consequence for the city itself will be considered in Chapter 12.

The September Convention was concerned, basically, with the Roman Question. But the question of Venice was to be resolved sooner than that of Rome.

After the Kingdom of Italy had been created, without her, in 1861, life in Venice acquired an unreal character. An American resident, William Dean Howells, wrote:

The carnival, with all the old merry-making life of the city, is now quite obsolete, and, in this way, the conventional, masquerading, pleasure-loving Venice has become as gross a fiction as if . . . it had never existed . . . . There is no greater social dullness and sadness, on land or sea, than in contemporary Venice.

There was virtually no social intercourse between Austrians and Italians. The owners of the famous Fenice theatre refused to open it after 1859, and although there continued to be an active theatrical life of all kinds elsewhere in Venice, this owed nothing to the Austrians but everything to the rich dramatic tradition of the Venetians.[1] After 1859 Austrian occupation of Venice was clearly doomed.

Italy's acquisition of Venice eventually resulted from complex diplomacy involving Napoleon III and Bismarck, who had become prime minister of Prussia in 1862, and Italy's Third War of Independence. Alfonso Lamarmora succeeded Minghetti as prime minister in September 1864, and on 8 April 1866 Lamarmora's government signed a treaty with Bismarck, with the blessing of Napoleon. Bismarck was involved in a crude struggle with Austria for power in Germany, and was prepared for Italy to acquire Venice in return for the creation of a second front in an Austro-Prussian war. The terms of the treaty were clear-cut; if Bismarck went to war with Austria within two months, Italy was to join him as an offensive ally and, after Austria's defeat, was to acquire Venice. Napoleon played a subtle diplomatic game, which was to bring him no reward but a powerful enemy in the shape of a Germany dominated by Prussia. On 12 June he signed a secret treaty with the Austrian government who promised to cede Venice to him, who would then pass her on to Italy whatever the result of the coming war; in return France would remain neutral. Lamarmora knew of the Franco-Austrian treaty, which in one sense rendered it unneccesary for Italy to go to war. But Lamarmora had the sense of honour of an old-world military man, and felt that the treaty with Bismarck could not be broken. For this part Bismarck, at the height of his powers, engineered a war with Austria within the required two months. Generally known as the 'Seven Weeks War', but to Italians as the 'Third War of Independence', the war started on 14 June. Six days later Lamarmora returned to his command of the army, handing over the premiership to Ricasoli.

In military and naval terms the war was a disaster for Italy. On 24 June the Italian army was defeated by the Austrians at the battle of Custozza. The Austrians suffered far heavier casualties than the Italians, who were routed mainly because of inadequate generalship. Fortunately for Italy, von Moltke, the greatest military genius since Napoleon I, and a man whose intelligence altered the whole concept of warfare, was working for them on the other front. The Austrians were defeated by Moltke at Sadowa on 3 July, and on that same day ceded Venice to Napoleon III, who promptly handed the province to Italy. Italy's humiliation at the manner by which she had acquired Venice was exacerbated two or three weeks later when her fleet was defeated at the battle of Lissa by a smaller and less modern Austrian fleet. One terrible aspect of the battle of Lissa was the proportion of Italians killed to those wounded: 620 killed to 80 wounded – even for a naval battle a grimly exceptional proportion.[2] Persano, the admiral in command, was subsequently found guilty of negligence and inefficiency and deprived of his rank and honours. To what extent he was simply a scapegoat for the disasters of 1866 is still a subject of debate; at the time recriminations on all sides were extremely bitter, but the undeniably Italian nature of Venice was at last recognized by international law, and the complete unification of Italy moved one step nearer.

Nationalist sentiment in Italy now inevitably centred on Rome. Urbano Rattazzi became prime minister in April 1867, and the mishap of Aspromonte, which had taken place during Rattazzi's first ministry, was now to be repeated on a rather larger scale. The last French troops had left Rome in December 1866, as Napoleon had promised they would in the September Convention. Garibaldi raised another irregular army in October 1867 but was, surprisingly, defeated by papal forces. Napoleon immediately sent a French army back to the Papal States. The French were armed with a newly designed rifle, the *chassepot*, which was loaded at the breach and had a range more than twice that of previous rifles. When Garibaldi attacked again, at Mentana, with a reconstituted force, he was easily defeated. He was captured but allowed to return to Caprera. As at the time of Aspromonte Rattazzi's involvement had been secret and ambivalent, but he could not survive the fiasco. Late in October he resigned and General Luigi Menabrea, a favourite of the king, formed a rather more conservative government. The crisis of Mentana left the French army firmly installed in Rome, but if it had been a grave misfortune for Italy it was equally a misfortune for Napoleon. After the Seven Weeks War Bismarck had created the North German Confederation, the strong nucleus of a united Germany. With the growing power of a Germany under Prussian leadership Napoleon was becoming increasingly insecure. In the years 1867–70 he hoped to create a triple alliance with Austria and Italy. Austria could not afford to ally herself with France, unless Italy were also a member of the alliance and the danger of another war on two fronts were removed. But Italy could not enter an alliance with France so long as Napoleon's troops were in Rome. The Roman Question thus undermined Napoleon's position in Europe.

Menabrea remained in office until December 1869, when he was replaced by the able Piedmontese medical doctor, Giovanni Lanza, who remained prime minister throughout the Franco-Prussian War of 1870, and until 1873.

When the government of the French Second Empire blundered into war with Prussia and all the other German states except Austria in July 1870, Italy remained neutral. Vittorio Emanuele II believed that the marriage alliance which had been arranged at Plombières between his court and that of Napoleon gave him a moral obligation to go to the help of the French emperor in his hour of need, but Lanza's government knew that Italy could not afford to become an enemy of Bismarck, quite apart from the unresolved Roman Question. Napoleon, for his part, needed all the troops he could get, and hastily withdrew his forces from Rome even before he had suffered any defeats. Then, on 1 September, a large French army commanded by the emperor himself capitulated to the Prussians at Sedan, and Napoleon became a prisoner of war. The Italians had held back from marching on Rome, but after Sedan there was no further need of caution. Papal forces resisted briefly, the Italians were obliged to shell the walls of Rome, a few lives were lost, but a breach was made at Porta Pia, and on 20 September 1870 the troops of Vittorio Emanuele entered Rome. Inevitably Rome was made the capital of Italy, and her acquisition by the Italian Kingdom was confirmed by plebiscite in October. The most significant chapter of Italian history, usually referred to as the Risorgimento, had reached its natural conclusion.

The party of the Right, the heirs of Cavour, had ruled Italy from 1861 until 1870, and were to continue in power until 1876. After the drama of the years 1848–60 Italian history had moved into a less colourful phase. Names with the familiar ring of Mazzini, Cavour or Garibaldi do not appear among Italy's rulers from 1861 to 1876. Yet Benedetto Croce was to argue that the leaders of the Right after 1861 could claim impressive achievements in integrating the institutions of the new Kingdom: their work, Croce believed, though far less glamorous, was no less important than that of the heroes of the Risorgimento. Croce also believed that the dour, conservative men who ruled Italy from 1861 to 1876 were singularly innocent of corruption, but it may be that their reputation in this respect has been aided by the lack of detailed research. Whether corrupt or incorrupt, the leaders of the Right certainly succeeded in integrating and standardizing diverse institutions to an extent, and sometimes with a ruthlessness, which has not always been appreciated by historians.

The Italy which had come into being in 1861 was, of course, a constitutional monarchy. The sovereign body was the king in parliament, as defined by Carlo Alberto's Statuto of 1848, which has already been considered in Chapter 2. By no stretch of the imagination could the new state be considered a democracy. To have the vote it was necessary to be male, at least twenty-five years old, literate, and to pay at least 40 lire a year in taxes. This meant that less than 2 per cent of the population could vote in the first elections which were held in January 1861. It is therefore not surprising that a predominantly conservative body of men were elected. So far as her political constitution was concerned Italy was based on an English rather than a French model. The Italian parliament, like the British one, represented, and was composed of, the upper classes, but it was a dynamic body which allowed freedom of expression, and provided – within the limitations of a bourgeois state – for individual rights.

The administration, on the other hand, was based on the French model, which had already been copied by the Belgians. It was a highly centralized system, following the ideas of Napoleon. Prefects and sub-prefects with considerable local powers were, and have ever since been, appointed by the government. Many people believed that the system was ill-suited to a country with such ancient divisions in traditions and customs as Italy had. But the ruling party of the Right – and for that matter many nationalists of the left also – believed that the Kingdom of Italy had to be quickly centralized, and its institutions integrated into a single system, if it were to survive. Men with opinions like those of Carlo Cattaneo and Giuseppe Ferrari, who believed that a greater degree of regional autonomy should be granted, were in a small minority. Both Piedmont and the Kingdom of Naples had come under a sufficiently strong Napoleonic influence since the beginning of the century to accept a centralized system of administration. The tradition in favour of centralization was less strong in the Papal States, and considerably less strong in Lombardy. In Piedmont the restored monarchy in 1814 had dispensed with most things revolutionary or French, but had clung to Napoleon's centralized type of administration, which served equally well for one type of authoritarian state as for another. In France Napoleon's method of regional administration by prefects had been simply a new form of Louis XIV's government by 'intendants', and in the Piedmont of the Restoration the term 'intendente' was used although the experience of the Napoleonic period was not forgotten. In 1842 Carlo Alberto had intensified the control of the central government over the regions. It is true that in November 1847 he allowed local councils to be elected, but elected on an extremely restricted basis. The electors were the rich and respectable. And they met only twice a year, for a fortnight each time. The Piedmontese government had established the tradition that local government should be weak and central government all-powerful. The government of the Kingdom of Italy after 1861 carried forward the Piedmontese tradition.

Both the constitution of the Kingdom, with its English-type parliament, and the administration, with its French-type centralization, stemmed from Piedmont. But both the constitution and the administration of a country can be sustained or undermined by the magistrates who conduct the courts from day to day. Democracy needs an independent magistracy: so long as judges or magistrates can be sacked arbitrarily by a government there is neither law nor democracy. In Carlo Alberto's Statuto of 1848 there was a contradiction between the apparently all-powerful constitutional state created at that moment and the independence of the old judicial power which emanated from the crown. The Statuto said that justice 'emanated from the king and is administered in his name by judges appointed by him'. In effect this meant that the Statuto of 1848 referred only to executive and legislative powers. The judicial powers remained in the hands of the king, but for that reason – in a constitutional monarchy – were independent of the government. To an Englishman who has been to the right kind of school the idea will seem rather attractive; to an Italian of the bourgeoisie in the nineteenth century it seemed rather less so. That judges should be immovable may seem a good thing to an Englishman who has come to trust his deep-seated traditions, but for an Italian in 1861 judges appointed in the past were a considerable danger to the state. But traditionalism was not a monopoly of the Piedmontese monarchy. The 1848 constitution in Naples had declared that 'justice emanated from the king', and it is probably true of any monarchy that justice ultimately resides in the personal sovereign. In Italy only republican constitutions – for example the constitution of the Roman Republic of 1849 – could make the magistracy really autonomous. Two traditional attitudes thus emerged. In Piedmont the debate was openly and explicitly conducted. The question involved people as well as ideas: should the existing judges, appointed by the old autocracy, be purged, or should they be considered as permanent fixtures, independent of any existing government.

In the first debate on the subject in May 1848, Count Federico Sclopis had eloquently defended the existing magistrates, saying that they should be regarded as immovable. Rattazzi, himself a lawyer of the new regime, had argued that the magistracy had to recognize that the Statuto had introduced a new order of things: those magistrates who could not accept the new regime could not expect to remain in office. A bitter debate in the Piedmontese parliament followed, and the freedom of expression thus provided in Turin before unification made it less likely that the Italian judiciary after 1861 would be subjected to executive control.

The magistrates simply had to enforce the law. The legislative unification of Italy after 1861 might well have seemed a desperately difficult, if not impossible, task. Yet the dour successors to Cavour accomplished it without a major upheaval. The two main difficulties in unifying the Italian legal systems lay in the fierce controversy over civil marriage and divorce. In retrospect these may seem rather marginal issues but history has its own strange priorities. Only a little less contentious was the problem of how, if at all, a uniform penal system could be enforced. The Piedmontese model of penal law was no better than those of the other Italian states, and appreciably less enlightened than that of Tuscany. Giovanni Baldasseroni's government in Florence had introduced a new penal code in 1853, a code which had brought back the death sentence for murder, but which in other respects was more civilized than the Piedmontese penal code. In practice no Tuscan court had ever again found a person guilty, if the judicial murder of execution could have resulted from the verdict. The Italian government in 1861 wisely decided not to impose the Piedmontese penal code on Tuscany. The Tuscans were allowed to preserve their own penal system, rather as the Scots – for a much longer period – have preserved theirs in the United Kingdom.

The various legal codes – civil, penal and commercial – which existed in Italy at the moment of unification were immensely complex and certainly need not be listed here. Their apparent complexity, however, was in a sense misleading, since all the Italian states had been to a considerable extent influenced by the Code Napoléon, a code which had been a civilizing one in many respects, but which had been over-careful in its concern to protect the rights of property. After 1861, with the one exception of Tuscany, a uniform penal code was quickly adopted throughout the Kingdom. To create a unified civil code on the other hand was far more difficult. If the government in Turin was often callous in the speed with which it imposed Piedmontese institutions on the rest of the country, it at least realized that too many interests – some of them powerful ones – were involved in the drawing up of a civil code for the nation, for them to proceed without great care and a thorough study of the problems involved. In the field of civil law they were even accused of moving too slowly and too timidly. A project was eventually presented to parliament in the first months of 1865, at the very end of the life of the first Italian parliament, which had been working desperately hard for four years, and was not likely to create too many difficulties. The law which finalized the legal unification of Italy was passed on 2 April 1865. The civil code bore a remarkable resemblance to the Code Napoléon. Civil marriage was introduced in the teeth of bitter resistance from the clericals. On the other hand divorce remained illegal, and in this respect there was no return to the Code Napoléon, which had permitted divorce. In other respects the patriarchal authority within the family, which was one characteristic of the Code Napoléon, and which without doubt deprived women of civil rights, was upheld. Illegitimate children had no civil rights, and debtors were to be arrested and treated as criminals. The civil code of 1865 reflected the politico-social philosophy of Cavour and his heirs in the party of the Right. In some ways it was cruel, but it was not wholly barbaric. It was to survive into the Fascist era.

In one respect, if Italy was to be recognized as an integrated nation-state, she had to have unity – in her foreign policy. And in this respect, at least, Piedmont could claim priority over the other parts of Italy. Cavour's Piedmont had been a state with which the Great Powers had been obliged to deal, whether they wanted it or not. The fat, ebullient little man in Turin had proved difficult to deal with and, in the end, impossible to control. That had been part of the story of the making of Italy. Cavour had himself been slow to believe that a political entity called 'Italy' could exist but, once convinced, he had been quick to convince Europe of its existence. Once Europe had recognized the existence of Italy, it could not fail to recognize the existence of an Italian foreign policy. In this sense the successors to Cavour owed him a great debt. Inevitably the foreign policy, and with it the institutions of a foreign ministry and a diplomatic service, of the new Kingdom, were simply inherited from Piedmont. The Piedmontese foreign ministry became the Italian foreign ministry, and was not touched until 1866, when a few bureaucratic changes were introduced. But in the field of foreign relations, more than in other fields, the government of Turin had taken over.

The integration of Italy's institutions after 1861 followed a path already conditioned by her previous history: it could not be purely the result of abstract reasoning. In no field was this more true than that of the armed forces. Three generals created the army of the Kingdom of Italy, and Garibaldi was not one of them. Since Napoleon I Europe has perhaps seen only two men of military genius: Moltke and Garibaldi. But the 1861 Kingdom of Italy was too small in spiritual stature to encompass a Garibaldi. Instead it owed much to three tough, competent military men who gave Italy a single, genuine army, which did not perform too well in 1866, but was nevertheless a force to be reckoned with. The first of the three generals was Alfonso Lamarmora, who

248

has already figured in this history. He had reformed the Piedmontese armies after the disasters of 1848–9, taking the French army as his model and, if his achievements in 1866 had been mainly negative, his record in the Crimea and in 1859 had been far from negligible. The second general, Manfredo Fanti, was the real creator of an Italian army. In 1860 he had three considerable armies to cope with – his own, Piedmontese, army: the very considerable army of the Neapolitan Bourbons; and the 'army of the South', as Garibaldi's army, which had in fact played the major role in the unification of Italy, was called. Before Garibaldi entered Naples in September 1860 Fanti had succeeded in uniting with the Piedmontese army the Lombard volunteer forces of 1859, remnants of the armies of Parma and Modena, and almost the entire army of the Grand Duchy of Tuscany. As has already been seen, the absorption of the 'army of the South' and of the remains of the Bourbon army was much more difficult. Fanti was a hard man, and he carried through his assignment without pity. The third general, Ricotti-Magnani, falls just outside the scope of this volume, since he was minister of war from 1870 to 1876. But it was Ricotti-Magnani who reorganized the Italian army on the Prussian model, and who therefore enabled it to survive the grim ordeal of the First World War, from which it emerged victorious. The integration of the Piedmontese and Neapolitan navies into a single force was accomplished more slowly, and with much bitterness. The problem of uniting the fleets was accentuated by the fact that in three years there were great changes in the character of navies, with steel replacing wood, and steam replacing sail. Even after the disastrous defeat of Lissa there were few reforms, but rather a period of discouragement and defeatism. Only after 1876 was there a thorough reconstruction of the Italian navy.

The institutions of education were a more delicate plant than the armed forces, but were not for that reason treated with greater respect. In this field, at least, the new régime was working from pure motives: it decided that it must eradicate illiteracy, even if this involved conflict with local and traditional forces. It was decided that the state should take over responsibility for providing schools and should centralize control of universities, several of which had very long independent histories. Before his death Cavour appointed as minister of education the Neapolitan philosopher Francesco De Sanctis, who was not only a brilliant literary critic but also an administrator of a high calibre. In spite of the immense respect he felt for his own ancient University of Naples, De Sanctis was convinced that both the universities and the schools should be absorbed into a state system. Once the process of nationalization had been completed, however, he believed that universities should be allowed a certain amount of autonomy, and headmasters and headmistresses should not be continually pestered with circulars from the ministry. The fight against illiteracy had at least started by 1870. While 75 per cent of the population was illiterate in 1861, the figure had been reduced to 69 per cent by 1871, but the progress was mainly in the north.[3] The standard of living was so low in the south, in Sardinia, and in remote rural areas elsewhere that, even when free elementary education was provided, the peasants could not utilize their rights since they needed their children's labour. There was a cruel irony in the fact that peasants paid crushing taxes with which schools were built and teachers employed, but the peasants were too poor to benefit from the exercise. Another tragic fact was that children often learnt to read and write only to lose the ability later, since the quality of their lives was so primitive that literacy could serve no purpose. The terrible contrast between north and south was not to be easily overcome.

NOTES

A good history of the so-called 'Brigands' War' is Franco Molfese, *Storia del brigantaggio dopo l'unità*, Milan, 1964. The opening chapters of Raffaele Romanelli, *L'Italia liberale (1861–1900)*, Bologna, 1979, are interesting for this period, especially the tables and statistics in the appendices. For the Venetian question from 1859 to 1866 an extremely important collection of documents was published on the centenary of the acquisition of Venice by Italy: *Il problema veneto e l'Europa 1859–1866*, Venice, 1966. The volume dealing with Britain's role in the Venetian question, *Documenti diplomatici. Inghilterra*, was edited by Noel Blakiston. Also for the diplomatic history of the years after 1860 an American historian of the Second Empire, Lynn M. Case, wrote the important study, *Franco-Italian Relations 1860–1865* Philadelphia, 1932. Important also for the period when Florence was capital of Italy is G. Spadolini (the prime minister of Italy at the time of writing), *Firenze capitale. Gli anni di Ricasoli*, Florence, 1979.

A volume of primary sources for the Roman Question in the 1860s is Noel Blakiston (ed.), *The Roman Question. Extracts from the despatches of Odo Russell from Rome 1858–1870*, London, 1962. A Garibaldian who fought in 1866 and again in the Mentana campaign of 1867 has left a valuable record: Cesare Aroldi, *L'ultimo dei vecchi Garibaldini. Note e ricordi 1862–82*, Viadana, 1973.

A study of the diplomacy surrounding the acquisition of Venice is John W. Bush, *Venetia Redeemed. Franco-Italian Relations 1864–1866*, New York, 1967.

An analysis of election results in Piedmont from 1848, but more particularly in Italy from 1861, is provided by Vincenzo G. Pacifici, *Le elezioni nell'Italia unita*, Rome, 1979.

For the economic history of the last decade of the period one book is significant: Piero Bolchini, *La Gran Bretagna e la formazione del mercato italiano (1861–1883)*, Genoa, 1968.

On the integration and centralization of institutions in the period 1861–70 a very important series of documents was published in the 1960s, with full introductions, under the general editorship of Alberto M. Ghisalberti and Alberto Caracciolo. The volumes, published by Giuffré of Milan, are as follows:

1. *Il Parlamento nella formazione del regno d'Italia*, ed. Alberto Caracciolo, (1960).
2. *Amministrazione centrale e amministrazione periferica, da Rattazzi a Ricasoli (1859–1866)*, ed. Claudio Pavone (1964).
3. *Politica e Magistratura (1848–1876)*, ed. Mario d'Addio (1966).
4. *L'unificazione legislativa e i codici del 1865*, ed. Alberto Aquarone (1960).
5. *Il Ministero degli Affari Esteri (1861–1870)*, ed. Ruggero Moscati (1961).
6. *Le Forze Armate nella età della Destra*, ed. Piero Pieri (1962).

7. *La Scuola dalla Legge Casati alla inchiesta del 1864*, ed. Giuseppe Talamo (1960).

8. *Stato e Chiesa. La legislazione ecclesiastica fino al 1867*, ed. Giuliana d'Amelio (1961).

9. *La finanza pubblica nel primo decennio dell'unità italiana*, ed. Luigi Izzo (1962).

1. William Dean Howells, *Venetian Life*, London, rev. edn 1907, pp. 7–50.

2. Gaston Bodart, *Losses of Life in Modern Wars: Austria-Hungary; France*, Oxford, 1916.

3. Raffaele Romanelli, in *L'Italia liberale (1961–1900)*, Bologna, 1979, p. 436.

The culture of nineteenth-century Italy

CHAPTER ELEVEN

Literature and the opera

Italian nationalism in the nineteenth century was one aspect of the romantic movement. Yet to make such a generalization at once creates difficulties, since development of Italian literature in the period 1790–1870 involved the purifying and simplifying of an Italian national language, which can be seen as an essentially classical movement operating against the diversities of provincial dialects. The purification of the language can perhaps best be considered within the context of a study of the writing of Manzoni's masterpiece *I Promessi Sposi*, and will therefore be postponed until the novels of the period are surveyed. The creation of a genuinely national Italian literary language certainly owed more to creative writers than to grammarians or philologists. Yet the creative writers themselves were usually more concerned with politics than with linguistics, and the broad generalization can be made that liberals and nationalists in the early nineteenth century were products of the romantic movement in literary as well as political terms, while conservatives still wrote in the classical tradition. In the last decade of the eighteenth century, however, Italian classical writers were still identified with the Enlightenment and were far from being reactionaries in a political sense.

Two journals were central to the politico-literary history of romanticism in Italy. *Il Conciliatore*, founded in September 1818 by Luigi Lambertenghi and Federico Confalonieri in Milan, was ostensibly a scientific-literary journal, but its romantic, liberal sentiments became increasingly obvious. It was suppressed by the Austrians in October 1819, but its influence in its short life had been considerable. The *Antologia* has already been mentioned in the context of the history of Tuscany in Chapter 3. In the pages of the *Antologia* ideas and manners inherited from the Enlightenment met the newer ones of the Romantic movement. Especially after Niccolò Tommaseo took over the editorship of the journal in 1827 did it acquire a stronger spirit of romanticism, and with it of Italian nationalism.

The tension caused by the struggle between classicism and romanticism added greatly to the vitality of Italian literature during the period covered by this volume. As in the rest of Western Europe, the emergence of the Romantic movement led to remarkable achievements in the writing of lyric poetry.

There is also a profusion of plays to be briefly surveyed, but Italian drama of the period has survived the test of time rather less well than has the poetry of Leopardi or Foscolo. As in Russia, France and Britain, the period marks the great age of the novel, although many works of the secondary Italian novelists have dated rather quickly: perhaps only Manzoni and Nievo have retained their freshness and brilliance into the late twentieth century.

The first poet who deserves consideration in a survey of this brevity is Giuseppe Parini. Born in 1729 near Como, into a poor family, Parini was trained for the priesthood in Milan. But he was a child of the Enlightenment, and although he never overtly rejected Christianity, his approach to religion was the abstract, sceptical one of his generation. His father died when he was still young, and he then knew acute poverty. His early life gave him a strength of character which enabled him to feel contempt for the purely peda-gogic and academic aspects of the Enlightenment but also, later, to resist the fanaticism of the Jacobins. His integrity enabled him to span the two worlds of eighteenth-century classicism and revolutionary romanticism rather as Goethe did in Germany. Parini's major work, *Il Giorno*, belongs to an earlier period than that covered by this volume, and to a civilized tradition of satire more typical of the eighteenth than of the nineteenth century. But by 1790 he had already recognized the need for change in Italy, although he was opposed to revolutionary or violent change. His judgements were always healthy, bal-anced ones. He rejected the more arid lapses of eighteenth-century classi-cism, but was determined to preserve its rationality, clarity and ability to compromise. When the French entered Milan in 1796 Parini was eager to receive them. He had no desire for Italy to be united, or even politically independent, but he welcomed the more generous of the ideas of 1789. He opposed the violent methods, rather than the principles, of the Jacobins. He died on 15 August 1799, when the Austrians had already re-entered Milan.

Besides *Il Giorno*, the *Odi* are usually considered to be his other major achievement, though they are not in fact a single work, but rather a collection of lyric poems composed between 1757 and 1795. The later of the *Odi* were written after the French Revolution – the *Dono* in 1790, *La Musica* in 1793, and in 1795 *A Silvia o sul vestire alla ghigliottina*, and *Alla Musa*. In particular, the *Messagio* and *Alla Musa* have a new sense of human tenderness which is beginning to break away from the formalism of Parini's own century, and from the artificial nature of some of his own earlier *Odi*. An episode often told of Parini can be perhaps repeated here, since it encapsulates the enlightenment and the humanity of the man. During the revolutionary period in Milan a noisy radical, or 'Jacobin' audience in the theatre were shouting 'Long live the Republic. Death to traitors.' An old gentleman stood up in one of the boxes and momentarily silenced the shouting by thundering 'Long live the Repub-lic. Death to no one.' The old gentleman was Parini, and his courage was the measure of his independence of judgement and the surviving vitality of the world of the classical Enlightenment.

An equally courageous, though less balanced and more tormented, poet was Vittorio Alfieri. Born at Asti in Piedmont in January 1749, into a rich family of the nobility, Alfieri frantically desired success for himself as an individual. As a child he attempted suicide, and his autobiography suggests that for long periods of his life he was virtually deranged. His importance lay in the full extent to which he anticipated Italian romanticism and the cultural nationalism of the Risorgimento. He has already been mentioned in the context of the emergence of Italian nationalism, and he must be considered later in this chapter when Italian drama of the period is surveyed, but here his place as a precursor of the Romantic movement must be suggested.

Parini had still used the weapon of satire which the eighteenth century had brought to so fine an art. Alfieri, twenty years Parini's junior, stated his convictions with a brutal directness, thinking and writing at white heat. He was, in the words of De Sanctis, 'a gigantic and solitary figure, pointing a finger in accusation'.[1] Yet he had not started his formidable revolt against society as a young man. Until he was twenty-six he lived the idle and dissipated life of an Italian nobleman, but with increasing dissatisfaction. He believed that in 1775 he experienced a 'conversion' in that he suddenly decided to concentrate on the writing of tragic drama, and so to provide Italy with a tradition which she had hitherto lacked. Yet his preparation for this task had been more thorough than he himself pretended. The deliberate training for a literary career came after his 'conversion' but, in his own feverish way, he already knew the world. He had travelled throughout Europe for some five years, getting involved in numerous love affairs, fighting duels and, again, attempting suicide. He developed a great contempt for the Europe of the *ancien régime*, considering the customs of Paris disgustingly false, and the Berlin of Frederick the Great a 'universal barracks'. The Vienna of Maria Theresa and the St Petersburg of Catherine the Great pleased him no better. As might have been expected, he was highly critical of the writings of Montesquieu and Voltaire. More surprisingly he reacted also against Rousseau, who was in so many respects a kindred spirit. Perhaps the strongest influences on him were Plutarch, Machiavelli, Cervantes and Shakespeare; for writers who were his own contemporaries he felt only antipathy.

Alfieri's main weakness was his lack of self-criticism, so that there is no steady development in the body of his work. His ideas, too, remained constant and unchanging. He felt great respect for the heroic individual – rather as Carlyle and Nietzsche were to do – and contempt for the universalism, philanthropy and even the humanitarianism of the Enlightenment. He believed that the individual must rebel with violence against the corrupt, formal and tyrannical world of eighteenth-century Europe. He had grown up, like most of the Piedmontese nobility, speaking and writing French: his Italian was not good. After his 'conversion' in 1775 he tried desperately to rectify this lack by reading the Italian classics, and in 1776 by moving to Florence, where the Italian accepted as the correct version of the national language was spoken.

From 1785 to 1792 he was living sometimes in Alsace, sometimes in Paris. In 1792 his house in Paris was sacked by the crowd. He moved again to Florence, where he stayed until his death in 1803. He had, like so many creative writers of Western Europe, welcomed the French Revolution but his experiences during the Jacobin period in Paris had embittered him, and in his last years he was even more lonely and depressed than he had been throughout the earlier part of his life. He is buried in Santa Croce, in Florence, the Westminster Abbey of Italy. His tomb was the work of Canova: that so turbulent a personality as Alfieri should have so serene and classical a tomb is perhaps the final incongruity.

In the history of Italian poetry there is also a contradiction in Alfieri in that he was determined never to write 'lyric' poetry in the strict sense of the term. He despised poetry which was simply a verbal accompaniment to music. Yet the rest of the world can recognize his *Rime* as genuine and sometimes great lyric poetry. It may well be that his concentration on tragic drama was a mistake.

If Alfieri was too obsessed with himself, Vincenzo Monti sold himself too completely to the external world. Monti was born in February 1754, in the Romagna. After studying medicine and law, with little conviction, at the University of Ferrara, he lived from 1778 until 1798 in Rome, working as a secretary for Luigi Braschi, a nephew of Pius VI. While Alfieri had fought his own private revolt against the universe, Monti was essentially a poet of the establishment — at first that of the Papacy, and then those of the Cisalpine Republic and the Italian Kingdom. But establishments rarely have at their disposal poets with the imagination and verbal dexterity of a Monti. Yet Monti's poetry, often of great beauty, is a façade, and the man behind it is never visible. Whether he had any basic convictions is open to doubt. In the pope's Rome he defended monarchy and Catholicism against the Terror in Paris; in Milan in 1797 he defended French and Cisalpine 'democracy'. In *Prometeo*, written in 1797, he paid his respects to Napoleon as the scourge of tyrants. By then his verse had turned against Catholicism and he had become concerned for the independence and freedom of Italy. In 1801, after Marengo, he wrote the short poem *Per la liberazione d'Italia*, which has a freshness and sincerity about it that at least puts his patriotism beyond doubt. Thereafter, however, he was essentially the official poet of the Napoleonic régime. Sadly, after 1815, he continued to be the Vicar of Bray, writing poems in honour of the Austrians. Yet his work remained fresh and vivid. In a sense Monti's achievement represented the triumph of art over honesty.

Italian Romanticism reached its fulfilment in Foscolo, and its peak in Leopardi. Foscolo and Leopardi were deeply sincere poets in a way that Monti could never have understood. Perhaps even Alfieri, tied up in his huge egoism, could not have understood the limpid honesty of these two great Romantic poets. But it would be a mistake to link Foscolo and Leopardi too closely together. Foscolo was more important in the history of the Risorgimento: Leopardi was more important in the history of humanity. Yet both of them used the Italian language to achieve a perfection which had not been achieved since the days of Dante and Petrarch.

Ugo Foscolo was born on the Greek island of Zakinthos or Zante in 1778, the son of an Italian doctor. Zante was at the time of Foscolo's birth under the sovereignty of the Republic of Venice. Foscolo was always to claim a classical

257

inheritance from Greece, and a romantic modern one from Venice. Perhaps because his father died when he was only ten, Ugo had a sense of purpose and moral responsibility at a very early age. When the French Revolution broke out, Ugo, young as he was, could sympathize with its aims. He had already read Alfieri, and his very first youthful rhymes were written in 1794. At 1797, when he was still only nineteen, he had a play, *Tieste*, performed in Venice, with great success. The romantic expression of sympathy for the French Revolution in these early writings of Foscolo obliged him to leave Venice. He returned very briefly when the *ancien régime* of the Doge fell, later in 1797, but had to depart once more when Napoleon sold Venice to the Austrians. This act of treachery on the part of Bonaparte was clearly a traumatic event for Foscolo, yet he was still prepared to fight for French-controlled Genoa in the campaign of 1799–1800. Meanwhile he had written the 'Last Letters of Jacopo Ortis', which was to be published in Milan in 1802, and will be considered later in the context of the Italian novel. But it is as a poet, not a novelist, that Foscolo holds so central a place in the history of Italian literature. A major work, the *Sepolcri*, was published in Brescia in 1807. During the Napoleonic period he lived a life of great political, military and literary activity. After the Restoration, in 1816, he settled in London, where his last years were ones of poverty and misery, although he was lionized by the Whig aristocracy. He died at Turnham Green in 1827, but in 1871 his remains were taken from London to Santa Croce.

Foscolo's genius was perhaps most perfectly expressed in his sonnets. The concept of poetry as 'the poet speaking to himself', which is still, in the late twentieth century, the more usually accepted one, was in Italy forcefully established by Foscolo. One of his best known sonnets is entitled, precisely, *Di Se Stesso* (Of Himself). While Alfieri had denied that his poetry had anything to do with music, Foscolo's control of the Italian language was such that he could not avoid writing verse of great verbal beauty. One example must suffice here, his sonnet *To Evening*, of which the first eight lines are:

> Forse perché della fatal quiete
> tu sei l'immago a me si cara vieni
> o sera! E quando ti corteggian liete
> le nubi estive e i zeffiri sereni,
>
> e quando dal nevoso aere inquiete
> tenebre e lunghe all'universo meni
> sempre scendi invocata, e le secrete
> vie del mio cor soavemente tieni.

To attempt to translate Foscolo or Leopardi seems almost blasphemous, but the attempt must be made. These lines of Foscolo's *Alla Sera* might be rendered:

> Perhaps it is because you are the
> image of the fatal quiet of
> death that you are so dear
> to me, O evening. Whether you

come with happy summer clouds and
soft breezes, or from a snowy
sky, bringing restless and long shadows
to the world, you always
come when you are sought
and gently fill the secret paths of my heart.

One of the great patriotic Italian poets, Foscolo had a strong influence on Mazzini, who arrived in London after Foscolo's death and went to some length, successfully, to track down notes Foscolo had left on Dante. Another patriotic poet, not of the stature of Foscolo but worth more than many other poets of the Risorgimento, was Giovanni Berchet. Born in Milan in 1783, he played an important role in the early stages of the Romantic movement rather as a polemicist than a poet, and, in particular as a contributor to the *Conciliatore*. He attacked the provincialism of many of the classicists, and appealed for a popular, national literature, which would be a worthy part of a European literature. But writers should learn, he believed, to write in a simple and direct manner which would appeal to the mass of the people. Poetry had a social function to perform, a function which could not be achieved by esoteric or scholarly allusions. He himself employed no subtle or complex imagery, but as in *Il Trovatore*, one of his most popular poems, wrote with an almost childish sentiment. Berchet was exiled from Italy in 1821 and lived in London, Belgium and France before returning to play an active role in his home city during the *cinque giornate* of 1848. He was subsequently elected to the Piedmontese parliament and died in Turin in 1851.

Perhaps the greatest, if also the saddest, Italian poet of the nineteenth century was Giacomo Leopardi. Born in 1798 at Recanati, a little hill town near Ancona, in what was then the Papal States, Leopardi came from a family of the minor nobility. His father was an educated man and took pains to educate his eight children, of whom Giacomo was the eldest. In a sense, he was too successful. Giacomo remained glued to his father's well-stocked library. By the time he was sixteen he had written two tragedies and much poetry in Italian and short works in Latin. Whereas a sedentary scholar's life does little harm to most people, it was clearly dangerous to Giacomo, who became hunchbacked, suffered from very weak eyesight, and for much of his life was virtually an invalid.

His first successful poem, *All'Italia*, published in 1818, showed him to be at the age of twenty a part of the romantic patriotic movement, a movement which he was to go far beyond in later years:

O patria mia, vedo le mura e gli archi
E le colonne e i simulacri e l'erme
Torri degli avi nostri,
Ma la gloria non vedo . . .

(O my fatherland, I see the walls
and the arches and the columns and
the crumbling towers of our ancestors,
but the glory I do not see . . .)

259

The youthful Leopardi's approach to his country was thus one of regret for a lost past. The subsequent approach in his poetry to the human predicament was distilled from his own suffering. His extraordinary erudition – his knowledge of Latin, Greek, Hebrew, and the principal modern languages of Western Europe – never intruded into the purity of his poetry. Involuntarily he adopted Berchet's doctrine that poetry should be direct, never opaque, in its emotional appeal, but he employed imagery of an intensity beyond Berchet's wildest dreams. And, like Foscolo's, Leopardi's poetry created its own music, though perhaps less self-consciously than Foscolo's had done, because it was the product of a passive, repressed suffering, unlike that of Foscolo which had been active and aggressive. Leopardi was the victim of parents who loved him in a suffocating yet distant, a remote yet possessive, manner. They were determined that he should not leave home even when he was in his twenties, so that the Leopardi library became for Giacomo a prison, though a prison which nurtured a genius.

Finally in 1822 Giacomo's father agreed that he should leave Recanati and stay for a few months in Rome. But Leopardi's soul was by then restless and acutely pessimistic. He lived for periods in Milan, Bologna, Florence and Pisa. Perhaps, for the first time in his life, he found some peace and happiness in Pisa where, in 1828, he wrote *A Silvia*, a moving and remarkable poem of nostalgia. In 1827 he had worked briefly with the *Antologia* group of writers, and had quarrelled with Tommaséo, a man totally unworthy of the friendship of Leopardi.

In December 1828, in desperately ill health, he returned to Recanati. Only then, in contact with the bitter memories of his youth, and by some kind of desperate paradox, did he produce his truly great poetry. Three poems must be mentioned here: *La quiete dopo la tempesta*, and *Il sabato del villaggio*, both written in 1829, and the haunting and beautiful *Canto notturno di un pastore errante nell'Asia* in 1830, written seven years before his death.

Il sabato del villaggio miraculously conjures up peasant life in the little village before the holiday: the preparations of Saturday evening before the Sunday festivities. Leopardi concludes the poem with a deep melancholy which is implied rather than stated:

> Questo di sette é il piu gradito giorno,
> pien di speme e di gioia:
> diman tristezza e noia
> recheran l'ore, ed al travaglio usato
> ciascun in suo pensier farà ritorno.
>
> Garzoncello scherzoso,
> cotesta età fiorita
> è come un giorno d'allegrezza pieno,
> giorno chiaro, sereno,
> che precorre alla festa di tua vita.
> Godi, fanciullo mio; state soave,
> stagion lieta è cotesta.

altro dirti non vò; ma la tua festa
ch'anco tardi a venir non ti sia grave.

(This is the most welcome of seven days,
full of hope and joy. Tomorrow the
hours will bring sadness and boredom,
and everyone in his mind will go back to
his accustomed toil.
    But for you, playful
lad, this fresh age of yours is like
a day full of happiness, a clear
cloudless day which comes before the
holiday of your life. Enjoy it, my
child; it is a sweet state, a happy
season. I will not tell you more; but
do not mind if the waiting for your
holiday is long).

The suggestion here that the expectation of joy is always greater than the joy itself is a poignant one, and the unspoken sadness of 'Altro dirti non vò' makes the poem one of Leopardi's most tragic statements. Yet this is only one which could be quoted from the rich store of Leopardi's powerful works. It was unlikely that another Italian poet in the nineteenth century would reach this degree of human understanding.

Between Leopardi and the culmination of Italian nationhood in 1870 there was perhaps only one other major poet who deserves attention here: Manzoni.

Alessandro Manzoni must be considered later as the most brilliant Italian novelist of the nineteenth century. As a poet his achievement was also far from negligible. He was born in 1785 in Milan. His mother, Giulia Beccaria, was Beccaria's daughter, so that Alessandro could hardly escape the inheritance of the Lombard Enlightenment. But his parents' marriage was legally ended in 1792, and his mother had settled in Paris with Carlo Imbonati, who is known to posterity mainly because famous writers – Stendhal and Manzoni himself – wrote so favourably of him. Alessandro's father was not over-concerned about the welfare of his son, who was taken care of, for some years, by an aunt. Manzoni's first poem, written at the age of sixteen in 1801, was *Il Trionfo della Libertà*, an exaltation of the French Revolution and its triumph over tyranny and superstition. Stylistically an imitation of Monti, it showed little promise. Its main importance was precisely that it secured the approval and gained the encouragement of Monti. When Imbonati, with whom Manzoni had developed a close understanding, died in 1805, Manzoni wrote *In morte di Carlo Imbonati*, published in Paris in 1806 and marking a very considerable development from his juvenile works. He lived in Paris for most of the period 1805 to 1810, marrying Henriette Blondel, the sixteen-year-old daughter of a Swiss Calvinist banker, in 1808. Within a few years both Henriette and Alessandro developed devoutly Catholic convictions, and in 1810 were married again according to Catholic rites. In that same year Manzoni returned to Milan, which remained his permanent residence – in spite of trips away from time to time – until his death in 1873.

In 1815 Manzoni had published the first four of his five *Inni Sacri*; no one had paid any attention to them. Yet, as De Sanctis was to point out, they constituted an important aspect of the romantic movement, in that they brought a return of a religious sensibility, and of medieval Christian preoccupations – with the Madonna and the saints – but in a modern form. Manzoni could not escape the rationality and secularism of the Enlightenment, nor could he escape the egalitarianism of the ideas of 1789, which he had already praised in his earlier youth. Throughout his life he was to believe – as Lammenais, but few other Catholics, were to believe – that there was no contradiction between the doctrines of Christ and the belief in the brotherhood of man. The fifth and last of the *Inni Sacri*, the *Passione*, was published in 1822, and was a more mature and profound work than the first four.

In 1821 he had written a patriotic poem, *Marzo 1821*, in which he had declared that the Ticino, the river marking the boundary between independent Piedmont and Austrian Lombardy, should 'no longer run between two alien shores'. In the optimism of the moment, he wrote: 'Let there never again be a place where there are barriers between Italy and Italy'. Although written in 1821 when he believed that the Piedmontese revolution would lead to the liberation of Lombardy, *Marzo 1821* was not published until 1848. His *Cinque Maggio* (May the 5th) was also written in 1821, that being the day of Napoleon's death. It is a strange poem, neither sympathetic nor hostile to Napoleon, but seeing him in the light of eternity and of Manzoni's profound religious convictions.

The first edition of *I Promessi Sposi* had appeared in 1827, and must be considered later in this chapter. Manzoni's role in the Risorgimento was an ambiguous one. His devout Catholicism made it difficult for him to agree with the anti-clericalism of most of his nationalist contemporaries. But he believed that the pope should give up the temporal power; he refused all honours offered him by the Austrian government; during the *cinque giornate* of 1848 he encouraged his sons to fight on the barricades; in 1861 he accepted the rôle of a senator in the new Italian Parliament, thus ignoring Pius IX's instructions to Catholics to have nothing to do with the godless Kingdom of Italy. He lived on until 1873, dying at the age of eighty-nine.

There were, of course, a great number of lesser poets in nineteenth-century Italy, and a few of them acquired national fame. Luigi Mercantini, born in 1821 in the Papal States, was exiled after 1848 as a liberal. He returned in 1852, was a university professor at Bologna and Palermo, and died in 1872. One of his poems, *La Spigolatrice di Sapri* ('The Gleaner of Sapri'), had an immense popular success. Dealing with Pisacane's tragic expedition of 1857, it is written as though spoken by a Neapolitan girl, in simple language, although not in dialect. It is shamelessly sentimental, yet authentically catches the right note, with its chorus:

Erano trecento, eran giovani e forti
e sono morti!

(They were three hundred, they were
young and strong, and they are dead!)

La disser ladri usciti dalle tane
ma non portaron via nemmeno un pane.

(They were said to be thieves escaped
from prison but they did not take away
even a loaf of bread.)

Even more famous than Mercantini was Goffredo Mameli, born in 1827, the son of a Genoese naval commander. Mameli wrote the *Fratelli d'Italia*, which became the Italian national anthem. He was killed, at the age of twenty-two, fighting with Garibaldi in the defence of the Roman Republic in 1849. That he may well have written more profound works is indicated by his long poem, *Un'idea*.

Apart from the poets who were to become popular in a patriotic sense, there was a subculture of dialect poetry, consisting mainly of lyrics of popular songs. In some cases the author is known, in many cases not. A long verse which was probably never sung in its entirety, but which was certainly intended to be sung rather than read or recited, was *Su patriotus sardu a sos feudatarios*. Written by the Sardinian Francesco Manno in 1794, it was popular during the peasants' revolt of 1796:

Try to moderate your tyranny, you barons.... Be aware that there is a fire being lighted against you. Be aware that this is no game . . . that there is a storm brewing.

In the South there was a great proliferation of such verse of protest. In and after 1860 many songs were written in support of Garibaldi, but many, also, against him and in support of the Bourbons.[2]

In spite of the great heights reached by poetic expression during the romantic movement, it is still true that the literary form most typical of nineteenth-century Europe was the novel. It was in the nineteenth century that the novel was to settle into its classic form as a piece of direct prose narrative divided into chapters, written sometimes in the first person but more often in the third person. But the first influential novel published in nineteenth-century Italy, the 'Last Letters of Jacopo Ortis' by Foscolo, took the form common in the eighteenth century of a sequence of letters which provide their own narrative. *Ortis* was published in Milan in 1802, during the life of Napoleon's Italian Republic. It was a central, if extreme, example of European romantic prose. Foscolo was influenced, as so many of the Romantics were, by Goethe's *Werther*, but *Ortis* is in no sense derivative. It is, in its extravagant way, a wonderful piece of writing. Jacopo, the fictitious letter-writer, has been deeply embittered by Napoleon's betrayal of Venice (this aspect of the book is clearly autobiographical), and having fallen deeply and hopelessly in love with a woman who cannot marry him, kills himself. In spite of its extravagance and melodrama, *Ortis* keeps the disbelief of the reader permanently suspended; it has an authenticity and a sincerity which many more restrained novels lack. Like Rousseau's *Rêveries d'un promeneur solitaire*, or Emily Brontë's *Wuthering Heights*, it is the work of a chaotic genius.

But it was with Manzoni that the novel reached its highest peak of achievement in nineteenth-century Italy, and it is perhaps at this point that something should be said of the final adoption of the Tuscan form of Italian as the written form of the national language. It could be said that the process by which the language of Florence became recognized as 'correct' Italian had started with Dante and was concluded by Manzoni's re-writing of *I Promessi Sposi* ('The Betrothed').

Manzoni had strong views on the establishment of a national language. He believed that any attempt to create or evolve one by combining features of several different dialects was doomed to failure. The language spoken in one particular city had to be recognized as the national language, just as the language spoken in Paris – not, of course, the *patois*, but the language spoken by educated Parisians – had become recognized as correct French. The language, then, had to be an existing, organic one, but one capable of being adopted by writers who had hitherto written partly in dialect. The decision to choose one particular language would not be an arbitrary one, but would be suggested by historical factors. For Italy, because of the development of her literature, the national language could only be the language of Florence. These views were expressed in several writings, most of them of the years 1868–71, in other words long after the publication of *I Promessi Sposi*. But to write his great novel he had, of course, already had to select a language which would be popular and accepted on a national level.

The first edition of the novel was published over the years 1825 to 1827, in three parts. Manzoni then rewrote it in the correct Tuscan according to the linguistic doctrine he was beginning to evolve. He removed archaic expressions and dialect words which would not be understood in many parts of Italy. The revised edition was published between 1840 and 1842.

The scene of *I Promessi Sposi* was Lombardy under Spanish occupation in 1628–30. Manzoni was a modest man, and although he sometimes criticized Walter Scott, he admitted his debt to Scott and protested that he himself had simply written another of Scott's novels. Scott's reply – 'Yes. But it is my best' – was certainly nearer the mark. Scott's novels rarely went beyond pleasing adventure stories, although their reputation throughout Europe in their day was immense. Manzoni's characters have an extra dimension of credibility – with the possible exception of Lucia, the heroine, who follows the stereotype of the virtuous and innocent maiden. The exploits of Manzoni's humble young hero and heroine are set against the broader picture of the horrors of the early seventeenth century – the Thirty Years War and the plague of 1630. The effectiveness of the novel lies in its lucid, vital narrative style, never rhetorical and only occasionally sentimental, his use of primary sources – mostly seventeenth-century memoirs – to get the feel of the period, and the richness of his canvas, as he himself put it in a letter to a friend, 'stuffed with peasants, nobles, monks, nuns, priests, magistrates, scholars, war, famine'.[3] There are many sequences and episodes in the book which are vividly memorable; two deserve mention here: the painful but convincing tale of the nun of Monza, and the brilliant account of the food riot and attack on the bakeries in Milan during the famine.

The Piedmontese novelist, Massimo d'Azeglio, has already been mentioned several times for his political role. As an historical novelist he was of far smaller stature than Manzoni, but by no means a negligible figure. Azeglio published *Ettore Fieramosca* in 1833, and it had an immediate success. His second complete historical novel, *Niccolò de' Lapi*, was published in 1841. *Ettore Fieramosca* is set in the Franco-Spanish wars in Italy at the turn of the fifteenth century, the age of the Borgias. Cesare, indeed, is brought into the novel, rather unconvincingly. On the surface it appears to be a romantically patriotic work, as does *Niccolo de' Lapi*, which is concerned with the fight by the Florentine Republic for her survival in 1530. But Azeglio's other writings, and in particular his perceptive autobiography, *I miei ricordi*, first published in 1863, suggest that the somewhat naive element in his novels is due to his desire to appeal to nationalist sentiments in readers less sophisticated than himself. In Azeglio's novels the smiling face of the author can be seen shining through the mist of the melodrama. Occasionally in *Ettore Fieramosca* he apologizes for the violence and horrors he is decribing: he knows that the reader, like the author, is tired of them, and he therefore moves to another matter. While these asides are rather endearing, they are reminiscent of an earlier literary style and cannot be said to contribute to a suspension of disbelief. In addition to his two finished novels, Azeglio left an unfinished one, *La Lega Lombarda*, which he was writing in 1843, and which he abandoned because of his growing interest in the political situation in the Papal States. Although only the first few chapters of *La Lega Lombarda* were written, they are enough to suggest that it would have been markedly superior to *Ettore Fieramosca*, and even more so to *Niccolò de' Lapi*. It is this fragment, in which the influence of Manzoni is clearly visible, which makes Azeglio worthy of mention in a brief survey of the Italian novel in the period.

Another novelist who played an important role in the political history of the Risorgimento, and who has already been mentioned in that context, was Francesco Domenico Guerrazzi. Two of his novels had great success in his day – the *Battaglia di Benevento* published in 1827–8, and the *Assedio di Firenze*, published in 1836. Guerrazzi was strongly influenced by Byron, and has the extravagant, morbid and desperate features of romanticism carried to extremes. The *Assedio di Firenze*, however, is a powerful, if chaotic and frenetic, work. As with Azeglio, the author is always too near the surface of his creation, but Guerrazzi is far more sincere and serious than Azeglio. Although Guerrazzi was a Tuscan, his language was not the one to be recommended by Manzoni. *L'Assedio di Firenze* is full not only of archaic words and sentence constructions, but also of expressions from the dialect of Leghorn. It serves as a warning that it is not strictly accurate to say that 'Tuscan' became recognized as the correct Italian; it was the language of Florence, rather than Tuscan, which filled this rôle.

If the novels of d'Azeglio and Guerrazzi have dated rather rapidly, the single masterpiece of Ippolito Nievo, *Le confessioni di un italiano*, has acquired increasing respect with the passing of the decades. The psychological penetration of Nievo's novel is more to modern taste than anything written by Azeglio, Guerrazzi or, for that matter, Alfieri.

Ippolito Nievo was born in Padua in 1831. He fought with Garibaldi in Lombardy in 1859, and in Sicily in 1860. He was a Mazzinian, but by no means a simple Mazzinian. In a short work entitled *La rivoluzione nazionale* he argued that it would not be enough to unite Italy in a political sense: another kind of unification was needed, the unification of town and countryside, the unification of the literate population with the rural population. He wrote *The confessions of an Italian* between 1857 and 1858. The novel purports to be the autobiography of an old gentleman in his eighties who had lived from the last days of the ancient Republic of St Mark into the mid nineteenth century. Clearly parts of the novel are genuinely autobiographical, but what gives the novel some of its poignancy is the fact that Nievo himself died at the age of thirty. On 4 March 1861 Nievo set sail from the Italian mainland for Palermo. Neither Nievo nor the boat on which he was sailing were ever seen again.

That Nievo's novel has survived the ravages of time is partly due to his egocentric, complex, but in the end self-sacrificing, heroine, la Pisana, who is so much more interesting than Manzoni's Lucia. But it is also due to his subtle understanding of human reactions to events. The great sense of relief of the inhabitants of the castle of Fratta at the end of a siege results in everyone chattering at once:

The state of mind of someone who has, or believes himself to have, escaped a mortal risk, is like that of someone who has received a favourable reply to a declaration of love. The same loquacity, the same willingness to give anything requested, the same lightheartedness. To put it in another way, all great joys are similar in their effects, while great sufferings have a very varied scale of manifestations. Human souls have a hundred senses for feeling misfortune, and only one for good fortune; and nature reveals not a little of the character of Guerrazzi, who has greater imagination for the miseries than for the precious things of life.[4]

Later in the novel Nievo contemplates the fact of death, and inserts a passage which is closer to Samuel Beckett's pessimism of the mid twentieth century than to anything written in Nievo's own lifetime:

> after the light the darkness,
> after the hope the oblivion,
> after everything nothing . . .[5]

It is, of course, impossible to say how Nievo would have developed had he lived. But it can surely be said that when he was drowned at the age of thirty, European literature lost a figure of profound significance.

The realist school of novelists had, in a sense, already started in France with Balzac, and was to continue with Flaubert and Zola. In Italy Giovanni Verga was to bring the realist novel and short story to their highest points of achievement. In 1865 he had left his native Sicily and in 1870 was living in Florence, which had been, for several years, the capital of Italy. This young man was to become, in several ways, the founder of modern Italian literature, but in 1870 his genius was still unrecognized, in spite of the publication of his first two novels.

In the nineteenth century, and especially in Italy, there is a strange paradox with regard to drama: much drama was written and performed, yet little of it was of real value. The Venetian dramatist Carlo Goldoni was still alive in 1790. He had written delightful plays of great subtlety and rich humour, but he belonged essentially to the earlier period. The only dramatist of any stature who clearly belongs to the Risorgimento is Vittorio Alfieri, the man who coined the very term 'risorgimento'.

In the course of twelve years – from 1775 to 1787 – Alfieri wrote nineteen tragedies. The scene for most of them was the classical world of Greece or Rome. A few were concerned with more recent history – *Filippo, Maria Stuarda* – and one, *Saul*, with biblical history. That *Saul* was perhaps his greatest play suggests that Alfieri was closer in spirit to the Old Testament than to Greco-Roman civilization. If the spirit of the tragedies is romantic, the form is strictly classical. The three unities are observed, the scansion is regular, and the characters are very few in number. The plays are pared to the bone: no episode or scene takes place which is not essential to the single tragedy. Alfieri does not indulge in sub-plots or superfluous characters. In this sense his tragedies were closer to classical Greek drama than to anything written since. But if these were his strengths, his weaknesses were the two-dimensional nature of his characters, who lack any psychological subtlety, and the sheer monotony of his verse. Astringency in the writing of tragedy is not enough; somewhere in a great play there should be some real human beings. But the impact of his drama in its day was enormous, mainly because of its simple, direct political message: the heroes of his tragedies are almost always fighters for freedom against tyranny, and fighters who are doomed to become victims of the tragedy. Only when a slightly different flavour is added to this recipe – especially in *Saul* and *Mirra* – does Alfieri's art rise above its usual level.

Whatever might be said by way of negative criticism of Alfieri it has to be admitted that no drama which was written later during the Risorgimento had, or deserved, the same impact. A few dramatists, like the Tuscan Gian Battista Niccolini, were extravagantly praised in their day. Niccolini was given a huge tomb in Santa Croce, an absurdly extravagant recognition for his turgid plays, but none of Alfieri's successors had such an influence as Niccolini in popularizing the idea that tyranny must be fought in the cause of freedom.

If the prose and verse drama of the period has had a short life, one theatrical form – the opera – produced works which are still familiar to audiences all over the world. Opera was a comparatively recent art form, dating from the early seventeenth century, but it had been essentially an Italian invention, and if anyone can be called the 'inventor' of opera it must surely be Claudio Monteverdi, who had lived from 1567 to 1643. But it was in the nineteenth century that the opera reached its peak of popularity, and so far as Italy is concerned four composers deserve mention here: Donizetti, Rossini, Bellini and Verdi.

Gaetano Donizetti was born in 1797 in the lovely Lombard City of Bergamo. His father was a worker in the textile industry, but Gaetano's musical gifts gained him a place in the Philharmonic Lyceum at Bologna. His first success was with the opera *Anna Bolena* (Anne Boleyn), produced in Milan in 1830, and subsequently in Paris and London. In 1833 came *Lucrezia Borgia* in Milan, an opera based on Victor Hugo's work. *Lucia di Lammermoor*, based on Scott's novel, was first performed in 1835 in the San Carlo Theatre in Naples. Donizetti composed many operas at an incredible rate. If *Lucia* is his best known and most characteristic opera, *Don Pasquale*, composed in 1843, and first performed in Paris, was a light-hearted masterpiece. Donizetti's end was unhappy. He had probably suffered from syphilis for many years, and in 1848 had a complete mental breakdown, resulting in his being confined to an asylum near Paris. He and his music were typical products of the romantic age, but in Donizetti's case romanticism had no political overtones. He died in Bergamo in 1848, quite unaware of the nationalist storm which was brewing all around him. On his tomb in the church of Santa Maria Maggiore in Bergamo it is said of him that he was 'a fruitful discoverer of sacred and profane melodies'. The idea that he 'discovered' rather than 'composed' melodies is a pleasing one: the melodies, sacred or profane, must, of course, already exist in the ear of God; the individual composer, with the help of his muse, merely has to discover them. That Donizetti's voyage of discovery was a fruitful one can hardly be doubted.

An older contemporary of Donizetti, Gioacchino Rossini, lived twenty years longer and had a lifespan – 1792–1868 – which almost exactly corresponds with the period covered by this book.

Born in the little coastal town of Pesaro, in the Papal States, Rossini started his career, while still a boy, as an instrumentalist of some virtuosity. His first – and last – enthusiasms were for Mozart and Haydn. Like Donizetti's, Rossini's parents were humble people, and his childhood was an insecure one, but he, too, had gained a place at the Lyceum at Bologna. In 1810 Rossini left the Lyceum to go to Venice, where he had been commissioned to write a one-act opera. The result, the *Cambiale del Matrimonio*, was sufficiently successful to allow him to remain in Venice writing popular one-act operas. It was in Venice that Rossini wrote *Tancredi*, based on Voltaire's play, which spread his fame to all classes in the city. His next opera, *L'Italiana in Algeri*, is much better known today, yet he was still only twenty-one years old. In 1815 he moved to Naples, where he was given leave, in November, to go to Rome to write a single opera, which in the event turned out to be his most brilliant – *The Barber of Seville*. He wrote the score of *The Barber of Seville* in less than a fortnight. The use to which Rossini put Beaumarchais's play produced perhaps the most splendid comic opera of all time. Like Donizetti, Rossini continued to write operas at an amazing rate. That they could compose at such speed is indicative not only of their professionalism, but also of the popularity of opera as an entertainment in the nineteenth century, especially in Paris and Vienna, and more especially in Italy, where the great opera houses – La Scala in Milan, the San Carlo in Naples and the Fenice in Venice – were becoming more important than cathedrals in the spiritual life of the people.

The Barber in the long run was to prove to be Rossini's most successful opera. It was followed in 1816 by *Otello*, and in 1817 by *La Cenerentola* and *La Gazza Ladra* ('The Thieving Magpie'), the last two as original musically as the *Barber*. Praised by Beethoven and Schubert, Rossini was by the 1820s immensely popular throughout Europe. At one moment in 1823 twenty-three of his operas were being performed in different European cities. His culminating, and his most influential, work was *William Tell*, based on Schiller's play, and first performed in Paris in 1829. He felt, however, with some reason, that his popularity was on the wane, and for the last thirty-nine years of his life wrote no other opera.

If Rossini's impact on the world was greater than Bellini's, the latter composer could claim to have had a greater influence on younger composers, notably on Chopin. Vincenzo Bellini was born in Catania in 1801. His first successful opera was *Il Pirata*, which secured for him an international reputation. Performed for the first time in La Scala in 1827, it had a gentle simplicity combined with great technical skill which made it immediately appealing. His next opera of significance, *La Sonnambula*, was performed in Milan in 1831, not at La Scala, but at the Teatro Carcano. Far more important than these two operas was *Norma*, produced at La Scala in December 1831. Until that moment it had seemed unlikely that Bellini could produce an opera as powerful as *Norma*. Yet he followed it with one almost as powerful – *I Puritani*, first produced in Paris in 1835. Before the year was out Bellini was dead. He cannot be considered among the greatest of composers, but in his brief life of thirty-five years he had made a simple musical statement of very real value.

Most Italian poets, painters or sculptors came from the middle or upper classes. The most successful operatic composers came from humbler backgrounds. Giuseppe Verdi's father was an innkeeper, and in spirit a peasant. Verdi was born, in 1813, in the countryside of Parma. The early years of his career were ones of desperate struggle, but at the age of twenty-six he had his first opera performed at La Scala – *Oberto, Conte di San Bonifacio*. His life was then blighted by personal tragedy on an appalling scale: his wife and his two children died within two years. At that moment he could well have abandoned his career, but without enthusiasm continued to write music. In 1842 Verdi's *Nabucco* was produced at La Scala: it had an immense popular success. His next opera, *I Lombardi*, performed at La Scala in 1843, could be interpreted in a nationalist sense, and got him into trouble with the Austrian authorities. Donizetti, Rossini and Bellini had been apolitical. The same could certainly not be said of Verdi. The people of Milan were quick to recognize the distinction. But Verdi was much more than a political propagandist.

His *Macbeth*, produced in Florence in 1847, was to survive into an age which had long forgotten the Risorgimento.

In 1851 *Rigoletto* was produced in Venice. It was based on Victor Hugo's *Le Roi s'amuse*, and eventually secured Hugo's warm approval. Its permanent success since Verdi's death need hardly be stated here. *Il Trovatore* was first performed in Rome in 1853 – a reminder that the Rome of the popes was not entirely dead between 1849 and 1870. In 1853 *La Traviata* was produced in Venice. Critics – especially in England – thought it was wickedly erotic. *Simon Boccanegra* was produced in Venice in 1857, and was not well received, although Verdi himself – rightly – always believed that it was one of his best works. In 1858 he hoped to produce *Un Ballo in Maschera* in Naples, but the Bourbon authorities prevented its production on the ridiculous grounds that the story involved the assassination of a monarch. Thus, almost by accident, Verdi became increasingly identified with the revolutionary movement, and a hero in the eyes of the liberals and nationalists. *Un Ballo in Maschera* was produced in Rome in 1859, with a changed plot to satisfy the censors. With the creation of the Kingdom of Italy Cavour persuaded Verdi to stand for parliament, which he did, much against his inclination. He was a deputy for five years, though not an active one. In 1862 the tragic opera, *La Forza del Destino*, was produced in the St Peterburg of Alexander II, who had just, by a stroke of the pen, emancipated millions of serfs. It could well be argued that *La Forza del Destino* was Verdi's most beautiful opera. His next opera, *Don Carlos*, produced in 1867, was uncharacteristic.

The true Verdi reached his culmination on Christmas Eve, 1871, with the production of *Aida* in Cairo. It was a daring and remarkable work, which confused and sometimes exasperated the critics when it was performed a few weeks later in Milan. But the critics have now been dead for some decades, and *Aida* is still very much alive.

Wagner believed that the combination of music and drama made opera the highest of the arts. The four Italian composers who have been considered here would all have been too wise to countenance such nonsense. Yet it is true that opera in nineteenth-century Italy was a vital part of national life, and a part of national life which cut across class divisions.

NOTES

Obviously an enormous literature of editorial and critical work in many languages has been lavished on Italian poetry, drama and novel of the nineteenth century. Here only a few hints can be given of the kind of material which is available. A starting-point must still be Francesco De Sanctis, whose *Storia della letteratura italiana*, edited by N. Gallo, is contained in a comparatively recent edition of the *Opere* of De Sanctis (Turin, 1958). More completely relevant to this chapter is the work of De Sanctis, *La letteratura italiana nel secolo XIX*, edited by Giorgio Candeloro and Carlo Muscetta under the titles of *Mazzini e la scuola democratica*, Turin, 1951, and *La scuola cattolico-liberale e il romanticismo a Napoli*, Turin, 1953.

An early study of Confalonieri was A. d'Ancona, *Federico Confalonieri*, Milan, 1898, and an enlightening study of three great eighteenth-century writers is Walter Binni, *Settecento maggiore: Goldoni, Parini, Alfieri*, Milan, 1978. For Monti there is Donata Chiomenti Vassalli, *Vincenzo Monti nel dramma dei suoi tempi*, Milan, 1968.

The national edition of the works of Ugo Foscolo deserves mention. Edited by a number of scholars, it was published in Florence in 14 volumes from 1932 to 1961. A fine biography of Leopardi in English is Iris Origo, *Leopardi. A biography*, London, 1935, and a collection of Leopardi's works has been edited by Walter Binni: *Tutte le opere di Giacomo Leopardi*, Florence, 2 vols, 1969.

For Manzoni there is a beautifully written work by Archibald Colquhoun, *Manzoni and his Times* London, 1954. Relevant for Massimo d'Azeglio as a novelist is a work already mentioned for Chapter 8: Ronald Marshall, *Massimo d'Azeglio. An artist in politics, 1798–1866*, London, 1966. An early work on the novels of Guerrazzi has already been mentioned in the notes to Chapter 3 – Furio Lopez-Celly, *Francesco Domenico Guerrazzi nell'arte e nella vita*, Milan, 1918.

Writing on the opera has been, perhaps not surprisingly, rather less extensive than writing on literature. But musicology of the Italian nineteenth century is far from negligible. Herbert Weinstock has written on Donizetti and Rossini – *Donizetti and the world of opera in Italy, Paris and Vienna in the first half of the nineteenth century*, London, 1964, and *Rossini. A biography*, Oxford, 1968. In the same year Luigi Rognoni published a full biography, *Gioacchino Rossini*, Turin. For Bellini a good study is Francesco Pastura, *Vincenzo Bellini*, Turin, 1959, and an interesting recent work on Verdi is David R. Kimbell, *Verdi in the Age of Romanticism*, Cambridge, 1981.

1. Francesco De Sanctis, *Storia della letteratura italiana*, Turin, 1951 edn, vol. II, p. 317.
2. A fine selection of protest songs can be found in Giuseppe Vettori ed., *Canzoni italiane di protesta 1794/1974 dalla rivoluzione francese alla repressione cilena*: Rome, 1976.
3. Quoted by Archibald Colquhoun, *op. cit.*, p. 170.
4. Ippolito Nievo, *Le confessioni di un italiano*, Milan, 1973, vol. 1, pp. 187–8.
5. *Ibid.*, vol. II, p. 450.

CHAPTER TWELVE

The arts and urban development

As with literature, so with painting, the main development of the period is the movement away from the formality and neo-classicism of the eighteenth century to the romanticism and spontaneity of the nineteenth. And as with literature, so with painting, the classicists tended to be conservative in politics and the romantics tended to be radicals and nationalists. This neat picture, however, is a little blurred because Napoleon I, who claimed to be the heir to the Revolution, made classicism the official style of the Empire, and his triumphs reinforced in Italy an enthusiasm for classical styles of painting, sculpture and architecture. Italy, of course, had known classical art and architecture when the natives of what was to become France were still primitives, but she had, in recent decades, passed through the fashions of the baroque and the rococo, which, in their way, had anticipated romanticism, and these fashions became unacceptable in the Napoleonic period. Indeed, they were associated with the *ancien régime*. The history of taste and art is full of paradoxes.

From the thirteenth to the eighteenth centuries Italy had produced in each century at least a few painters whose names are familiar to educated people all over Europe. The same cannot be said of the nineteenth century. This was less because of the poor quality of Italian nineteenth-century painting (it is, after all, not that poor), than because Italy, after 1815, lost her artistic contacts with the rest of Europe. It was the result, then, of political factors, and in particular of the dominance of the Habsburg Monarchy, a state with no strong artistic traditions – none, at least, which could even remotely be compared with those of Italy.

One school of Italian painters, at least – the Macchiaioli in Tuscany – deserve far more attention from art historians than they have ever received. But before the Macchiaioli were operating, a few other Italian painters produced works which would probably have secured them some fame had they been Parisians.

Within the neo-classical school of Napoleonic Italy one painter showed a sensibility of a kind which reaches beyond schools and fashions. Andrea

Appiani was born in Milan in 1754, the son of a doctor. He became a respected official artist of the Cisalpine Republic and the Italian Republic and Kingdom. If some of his work – like the *Apollo and Daphne* in the Brera in Milan, or the *Apotheosis of Napoleon* in the Palazzo Reale in Milan – was self-conscious and derivative, his portraits had perception and penetration. His self-portrait deservedly has a place in the Uffizi in Florence. He was a friend of Foscolo, and his work was admired by both Parini and Monti. He was at the centre of the artistic group around Eugène de Beauharnais, Napoleon's viceroy in Milan, a civilized, if slightly spurious, court.

One reaction against the neo-classicism of the Napoleonic era came with two religious movements in painting – the Nazarene school, founded in Rome by a brotherhood of young Germans, but with adherents in Turin, Milan and Florence, and the *Puristi*. The religious movements were bound to be sterile artistically, since they reflected merely the backlash of the Restoration, and had no links with any dynamic political or social forces in Italy. Regrettably the Papacy continued to patronize deplorable artists in this tradition: Francesco Podesti, born in Ancona in 1800, was allowed to paint a work in recognition of Pius IX's dogma of the Immaculate Conception, beside Raphael's work in the Vatican. But the religious painters had one thing in common with the neo-classicists: they too were capable of painting sensitive and interesting portraits. Before the invention of photography portrait-painting was regarded as a craft rather than an art, and the portrait-painter mercifully forgot his neo-classical, or pseudo-religious, partisanship, and tried, often with remarkable success, to interpret personality.

One artist of worth moved from neo-classicism to romanticism. Francesco Hayez was born in 1791 in Venice, his father being French but his mother Venetian. His first works were biblical, but when he returned from Rome to Venice he shifted his interest to another aspect of the romantic movement – the patriotic one. His next move – to Milan – completed his conversion to Italian nationalism. In Milan he became part of the circle which revolved around the dynamic journal, the *Conciliatore*. He met and painted the portrait of Manzoni, but it must be said that the portrait is not the most successful of his works. The Manzoni depicted by Hayez could not conceivably have written *I Promessi Sposi*. But the more ambitious paintings of Hayez were beginning to show distinction. His *Sicilian Vespers*, in the Gallery of Modern Art in Rome, has a tension and drama which most Italian painting of the period lacked. But the painting which made him famous was a sensuous and passionate study – the *Last Kiss of Romeo and Juliet* – painted in 1823. Even more striking is a self-portrait in the Uffizi, showing a wise, sensitive, disillusioned old man.

In the mid nineteenth century, when the historical novel had become so popular, it is not surprising that paintings of historical scenes were in demand. That *uomo universale*, Massimo d'Azeglio, contributed to both genres. As a young man he had decided to be an artist, and his paintings of scenes of dramatic action never quite go beyond the bounds of credibility. They have dated less unhappily than his novels. His decision to abandon painting for the novel was a deliberately political one: he believed that the message of national-ism could be more fully expressed in prose.

Romanticism dominated Italian art in the mid nineteenth century. But at an exhibition in Florence in 1861 a group of canvases scarcely noticed by the crowd or, if noticed, treated with condescension, gave evidence of a new de-parture and several of them were awarded prizes. They were the work of a group of artists known as the Macchiaioli. They met in the Caffè Michelan-giolo in the Via Larga, and very self-consciously evolved new theories of art. They rejected neo-classical and romantic traditions equally, believing that painting had become too academic and mannered. It was important to involve art with everyday life and break away from literary or historical narrative. In many ways they anticipated the French Impressionists, and if they did not produce a Monet, a Degas or a Van Gogh, they certainly deserved more atten-tion than art historians have ever given them. The Macchiaioli were inclined to consider that the artistic past was irrelevant to them, that ignorance of history would be a positive advantage for an artist, since it would enable him to develop an original imagination, to see the world about him in all its colour, vitality and freshness. And the world which they saw was not one filled with saints or heroes, but with working people — beggars, peasants, tradesmen. In this sense the Macchiaioli were essentially democrats, and in their political sympathies were radical and republican. They painted directly from life, which meant going outdoors into the street or the countryside, or recording what they saw before their eyes in the studio or the café. It was especially in this respect that they anticipated French impressionism. The search for immediacy went to remarkable lengths. Vincenzo Cabianca's picture *A pig against a white wall* had a defiant note about it, but Adriano Cecioni's work of sculpture, *Dog defecating*, carried artistic protest to its ultimate point.

But the break with the past could not be a total one. There were inevitably links between the Macchiaioli and the earlier romantic school. Thus Egisto Sarri frequented the Caffè Michelangiolo, and learnt the technique of the Mac-chiaioli — that of using splodges or spots of bright paint to convey light, movement and atmosphere — but then used the technique to paint traditional historical scenes. And the Macchiaioli themselves were not averse to painting battle scenes, though it is significant that they depicted battles of their own day rather than those of earlier ages. Massimo d'Azeglio had himself been present on the battlefield in 1848, but preferred to paint an impression of the twelfth-century battle of Legnano, while the Macchiaioli painter, Giovanni Fattori, chose for subjects the battles of Magenta and Custozza.

The Macchiaioli produced three artists of real distinction: Telemaco Signor-ini, Giovanni Fattori and Silvestro Lega. Signorini was born in 1835. He fought in the war of 1859 and recorded some of his impressions in violently coloured paintings. But he found his true expression in simple, humble scenes, like the *Morning toilet*, a late work in which one figure would not have been a disgrace to Degas, and *Little girl writing*, a painting which is deeply moving precisely because it is devoid of any sentimentality. Signorini was the best known of the Macchiaioli outside Italy. He lived briefly in London and

Paris, where indeed, he knew Degas, as well as Corot and Manet. He had, however, evolved his own style before meeting the French artists. If the human figures in his work are sometimes reminiscent of Degas, the delicate handling of light and colour in his paintings of the countryside is more reminiscent of Monet.

Born in 1825, Giovanni Fattori was ten years older than Signorini, but lived into a later period. Fattori was less of a theorist than Signorini or than some of the secondary figures of the movement. But that he could paint with great panache was already apparent from a youthful self-portrait now in the Gallery of Modern Art in Florence. Unlike some of the other Macchiaioli he was not eager to take part in revolutionary political movements, although he came from the working class of the highly politicized city of Leghorn and had worked with Mazzinians as a boy. He had started his career by painting large, cluttered canvases of historical scenes in the style of the romantic nationalists, but he quickly adopted the new techniques of the Macchiaioli. He worked, however, slightly apart from the rest of the group, although greatly admired by them. One of his most successful works was another portrait – of his stepdaughter – a gently penetrating psychological study, also now in the Gallery of Modern Art in Florence. But his landscapes are more powerful, emptier, bleaker and less intimate than Signorini's.

If the Macchiaioli can be said to have a central figure it was neither Signorini nor Fattori, but Silvestro Lega. He was not a Tuscan by birth, but was born in the Romagna in 1826, and came to Florence at the age of nineteen to study art. Like Fattori, Lega started his career as a typical nationalist romantic, and fought against the Austrians in 1848. But he, too, was soon converted to the ideas of the Macchiaioli, especially by the National Exhibition of 1861. The exhibition was still dominated by the huge canvases of Hayez and artists of his romantic persuasion. But Lega was impressed by the more modest, but much more interesting, works of Signorini. His conversion was to give a rich harvest for European art, a harvest still not fully recognized. Where the romantics had chosen scenes of great drama or tragedy, Lega chose scenes of excessive ordinariness – like his *Houses at San Gervasio* – and transformed them by his vision and his sensibility. *Coffee in the garden*, now in the Brera in Milan, is an extraordinary achievement in the conveying of space and light. Lega's happiest works are comparable with those of Manet, and sometimes he resembles Renoir, but Renoir without the sugar.

Italian painting in the period covered by this book deserved greater reputation in Europe than it obtained. The only artist who secured universal respect – perhaps even more than he deserved – was primarily a sculptor, Antonio Canova. He lived from 1757 to 1822, one of the most disturbed periods of European history. Born near Treviso, in the far north-east of Italy, he became an establishment figure of the Napoleonic age, but deserved to be much more than that. Praise was lavished on him by the French artist, David, and the French novelist, Stendhal, and Foscolo said that he 'invested his marble with eternal youth'. He was a student of the Academy at Venice, and some of his more powerful works – especially his *Dedalus and Icarus* – were inspired in these years. But from Venice he moved to Rome, and there experienced more fully the impact of the classical world. His first important commission was to create the tomb for Pope Clement XIII. It was an enormous success. The idea of having two very naturalistic lions weeping marble tears at the death of the pope seems today slightly ludicrous, if a little touching. But at the unveiling of the tomb the crowd were deeply moved by this gentle show of sentiment. Canova's immense fame, while still a very young man, was due to his observance of a severely classical style at the moment when such a style was at the height of fashion. In a later, less classically-minded age, his nude figures from Greek mythology were to seem lifeless and mannered. In 1802 he travelled to Paris, at Napoleon's request, to carve a marble bust of the first consul, but refused to accept the Legion of Honour from the man who had stolen so many works of art from Rome. Perhaps his most famous work was the *Venus*, now in the Villa Borghese. Even in that permissive age the Romans were shocked to learn that Napoleon's sister, Paolina Borghese, had posed as the model for the nude goddess. In 1815 when many of the works of art stolen from Rome by Napoleon were to be returned under the terms of the Second Treaty of Paris, Canova was given the task of supervising the operation. He showed great tact and diplomacy in this delicate task. In the romantic era it almost came to be expected that an artist would be a tormented, anti-social creature. Canova, on the other hand, was a serene, good-natured, kind man, immensely generous to artists less fortunate than himself, and to the peasants of his native Veneto. But, although today many of his works seem static and lifeless, there are at least two which depict, in one case great suffering, in the other violence. His early *Dedalus and Icarus*, now in the Accademia di Belle Arti in Venice, is a painful and deeply moving study, while his *Hercules and Lichas* vividly portrays an horrific act of murder. But only in a few rare works did Canova break free from the conventions of neo-classicism. He died in Venice in 1822; no other sculptor in the period covered by this book was to have fame which even approached Canova's.

Sculpture was not a medium well adapted to the historical and patriotic narrative so popular with the Italian romantics. The neo-classicists had enjoyed a field-day in carving nude pagan figures in marble, but the overdressed people of the medieval and early modern periods did not easily lend themselves to three-dimensional art. Partly for these reasons the romantic reaction against neo-classicism had fewer followers in sculpture than in painting. Lorenzo Bartolini, who was born in Prato in 1777, attacked classical traditions but can scarcely be considered a romantic. After a period in Paris Bartolini was appointed master of sculpture at the Academy of Carrara, a convenient spot for anyone working in marble. He recommended an abandoning of Greek and Roman models and a concentration on the sculpture of the early renaissance. But his art was religious and anti-pagan rather than nationalist. His tender kneeling female figure, *Faith in God*, was a deliberate response to Canova's Venuses. But the immense respect he acquired in the mild nineteenth century seems today to have been misplaced. His large monument in Florence to Nicholas Demidoff, the Russian hero who raised a private regiment to fight

Napoleon, has a distinct whiff of the Albert Memorial about it. But that Bartolini could sometimes rise above sentimentalism is demonstrated by the strange and disturbing tomb of Princess Zamojski in Santa Croce in Florence.

A much younger man, Giovanni Dupré, born in Siena in 1817, carried the movement against neo-classicism a stage further with two works in bronze, a dead *Cain*, and an aggressively alive *Abel*, both now in the Gallery of Modern Art in Florence. The two figures, and a *Pietà* in the cemetery in Siena, verge on the melodramatic, but at least marked a new departure in Italian sculpture.

The Macchiaioli, like the French Impressionists, were primarily concerned with light and colour, and so produced fewer works of sculpture than of painting. Adriano Cecioni, a very doctrinaire member of the group, whose *Dog defecating* has already been mentioned, modelled a somewhat less eccentric theme, although still an original one – a small boy holding a cockerel who is frantically beating his wings in a struggle to escape. It is a masterpiece of observation, the final naturalistic answer to all the *putti* and cherubim of the past. Another secondary figure of the group, Augusto Rivalta, has left a delightful study of a girl reading a letter – *Return of the post*. Both are in the Gallery of Modern Art in Florence, and like the rest of that remarkable collection, are overlooked by the countless tourists who flood through Florence every summer, and who religiously visit the Uffizi and the other Pitti galleries.

The quantity of sculpture produced in Italy as elsewhere in Europe in the nineteenth century was certainly more impressive than the quality, and the same may be said of architecture. The rise in population and the beginning of industrialization were two factors which explain the vast amount of building carried out. Developments in town planning were perhaps more significant than the design of individual buildings by architects, and a few examples of urban development will therefore be considered separately at the end of this chapter.

The Napoleonic period brought an outcrop of triumphal classical arches, of which one of the most ambitious was Luigi Cagnola's vast 'Arch of Napoleon' in Milan. In 1815 the Habsburgs, who never destroyed the architecture of their enemies, simply renamed it the 'Arch of Peace'. In contrast to Napoleonic rhetoric Canova left one exquisite little building of his own design. In Possagno, the village where he was born, he built, with the help of two young collaborators, a classical temple of great beauty and simplicity, to house some of his works and, in the end, his own remains.

One notable building operation in Naples was the church of San Francesco di Paola, built as a thanksgiving for the Restoration of 1815. The plan to build a massive church for this purpose drained money away from much needed public works. Building started in 1816. The contract was given to Domenico Barbaja, director of the San Carlo theatre, a Milanese who had arrived in Naples during the French period and had made a comfortable fortune. He was not the most devout of men, and was certainly more interested in increasing his fortune than in building a church. The 1820 revolution held up operations. In 1831 the church was still not completed, and the government had run out of funds, having already spent a great sum on the church. Ferdinando II insisted, however, that a loan must be procured to enable work to continue. Dr John Davis, who has made a detailed study of investment in Naples in the period, concludes that the church of San Francesco di Paola was 'the most expensive example of investment in public works of the restoration period, and a fitting epitaph to the decline of the Bourbon dynasty'.[1] Designed by Pietro Bianchi, born in 1787 in the far-away Ticino, the church is an impressive latter-day Pantheon, but silent, grim, dead, and strangely out of place in the centre of the overflowing vitality of Naples. Apart from this enormous folly there was less building in Naples in the first half of the nineteenth century than in other Italian cities. This was because there was so little capital available. The few men who made money in the Kingdom of Naples in her last decades of life did not want to build splendid palaces as their forerunners had done. They were quite content to buy, or even to rent, palaces already existing.

In striking contrast to the ordeal of the building of San Francesco di Paola, an architect of twenty-nine, Gaetano Baccani, had the Palazzo Borghese in Florence built in six months in 1821.[2] The Palazzo Borghese is not an architectural masterpiece, but it has dignity and is not a disgrace to Florence. In the nineteenth century Florence saw a great deal of building, the results of which were often happy or, at worst, innocuous. In the Renaissance it had been assumed that important churches should be given marble facades. But there had been exceptions: San Lorenzo's façade had been left bare, and has remained bare, because the original commission had been given to Michelangelo, who had failed to execute it; to find a substitute for Michelangelo would have seemed a blasphemy and so San Lorenzo was left free of marble. The great medieval barn of Santa Croce was a different matter, and in the mid nineteenth century the church was at last given its façade. It was the work of an architect from Ancona, Niccolò Matas, who lived from 1798 to 1872. It is in a restrained Gothic style, balanced and dignified. In one sense Matas achieved his purpose: almost certainly most tourists imagine that the façade dates from the late Middle Ages.

As the nineteenth century progressed, engineers became more important as designers of large constructions than architects were. The Eiffel Tower, the Crystal Palace and the Albert Hall were the work of engineers. In Italy another striking example of the work of an engineer was the extraordinary *Mole Antonelliana* in Turin. Alessandro Antonelli had been born, like Matas, in 1798, and lived to be ninety. His 'Thing' or *Mole* (which simply means 'large structure') was started in 1863, and on its completion was the tallest building in Europe. Quaintly repugnant, it has both classical and Gothic details but is essentially a work of eccentric engineering.

Architecture, however, survived alongside engineering. But no longer was it architecture patronized by popes or princes. One of the most delicately beautiful buildings of nineteenth-century Italy was a coffee-house – the Caffè Pedrocchi in Padua, designed by Giuseppe Jappelli and Antonio Gradenigo, and built in 1842. A more ambitious and active architect of the 1860s was the

Florentine, Giuseppe Poggi, who combined his designing of single buildings with landscape planning and engineering. Born in 1811, Poggi, like Antonelli, lived to be ninety: engineering architects lived long. Besides his own architectural creations, several highly successful restorations are owed to Poggi, in particular the basilica of the Annunziata and the Palazzo Strozzi. But three of his own original works deserve mention. The Villa Favard is a perfect, civilized, symmetrical work, as is little loggia on the Piazzale Michelangelo, which serves today as a restaurant and cafe. Finally Poggi's gateway on the Piazza San Gallo is a strangely gaunt, dramatic structure. Whether it is a hangover from early medieval architecture, or an anticipation of new brutalism, is a matter of opinion, but at least it demonstrates that Poggi could break away from classical elegance, if he so decided.

The nineteenth century was not a great age of architecture, but in Italy, as in Paris, there were big developments in town planning. In the very first years of the century Milan experienced the impact of Napoleon. Our knowledge of the plan of Milan in the period starts with a map by a cartographer called Pinchetti, a map executed in 1801. The walls of the city are intact, and outside them are only two small suburbs, and a cemetery for the poor: the rich still tended to bury their dead inside churches. The map bears a striking resemblance to ones drawn two and a half centuries earlier. In 1801 the architect Giovanni Antolini drew up a typically Napoleonic plan for the building of a vast *piazza*, half a kilometre in circumference, around the castle of the Sforza. Perhaps it was as well that this monstrous plan was never carried out, but a modified version, the crescent-shaped Foro Bonaparte, which partly encircles the Piazza Castello, was built shortly afterwards. Cagnola's 'Arch of Napoleon' has already been mentioned. This, and other arches designed in the Napoleonic period, were not, of course, intended to serve any defensive purpose, but were merely to mark the limits of the city, to embellish it, and to serve as memorials of Napoleon's achievements. In the same spirit, in 1807, Eugène de Beauharnais, as viceroy of the Kingdom of Italy, commissioned five architects, one of whom was Cagnola, to draw up a plan for the rebuilding and rationalizing of Milan. Their plan has survived and suggests that, without destroying the ancient spirit of the city, it would have created a more beautiful Milan. No historic buildings would have been destroyed, but fine vistas would have been opened up, and broad streets, and new piazzas. With the fall of the Empire and the Kingdom of Italy the plan was not only laid aside but completely forgotten, only to be rediscovered, as a curiosity, in 1906.[3]

The other part of Austrian Italy, Venezia, declined economically from 1797 to 1824, the population actually shrinking when, in most parts of Europe, it was growing rapidly. But after 1824 there was a marked recovery. In 1846 the railway bridge across the lagoon to the mainland came into operation — again a work of engineering, rather than of architecture, being the main event in the growth of a city. In that same year Venice could boast eleven hotels, and a bathing establishment, not on what is now the Lido, but at the mouth of the Grand Canal, near the Customs House.[4]

Developments in Turin were less impressive than in Napoleon's Milan, but they were not without interest. A description of Turin published in 1840 by Davide Bertolotti gives a vivid account of the life of the city. Bertolotti stresses that the population of Turin had acquired more hygienic habits in recent years. At the beginning of the century there were only two public baths. In 1840 there were six, 'comfortable and elegant and much used'. Turin had suffered some destruction in the 1790s. When the Austro-Russian army had entered the city on 26 May 1799, the French had withdrawn to the citadel, and Turin had become the scene of a heavy bombardment. A certain amount of rebuilding was thus inevitable, but it was not carried out on a particularly grandiose scale. But Bertolotti, writing in 1840, is very proud of the growth of Turin since the return of the Savoy monarchy in 1814. 'Of all the cities of Italy', he claims, 'Turin is without doubt the one which, in this happy period of universal peace, has grown and flourished with most obvious progress.' As an example of the modernization of Turin he writes: 'Turin today is lit by 481 oil lanterns, which burn all night, from the evening to the morning, whether the moon is shining or not.'[5] Twenty-one lamplighters lit all the lights in twenty minutes. All of which could be expressed in a negative way by the observation that gas-lighting had not yet been introduced, but Bertolotti points out that many shops were lit by gas. A fire-fighting service of fifty men had been formed in 1824. Carlo Alberto always went to the scene of serious fires in person. A large new cemetery had been opened in 1828, in which about 4,000 bodies were being buried annually by 1840. Bertolotti seems not to realize that this was evidence as much of the high death rate as of the efficiency of the funeral arrangements. He is proud of the fact that there was very little architecture indeed from the Middle Ages in Turin, and he correctly points out that a great deal of the city as it was in his day was the product of the seventeenth century, developed and embellished in the eighteenth. But he claims that at least a quarter of the buildings in the city had been built in his own century. He accepts the fact that there had been developments in the Napoleonic period, noticing for example that a bridge over the Po in Turin had been built then by a gang of Spanish prisoners-of-war. Bertolotti's boast that Turin had grown more quickly than other Italian cities in the Restoration period may have some justification, though it would obviously be difficult to prove. What can be said is that urban growth in Milan and Florence was greater in the 1860s, when they had become parts of the Kingdom of Italy, than it had been in the earlier period.

There was, however, some urban development in Florence in the 1820s and 1830s. Gaetano Baccani, who has already been mentioned as the architect of the Palazzo Borghese in 1821, was subsequently entrusted with the broadening of the Piazza del Duomo on the side of Giotto's campanile. If he had been permitted, he would have provided a broader vista of that end of the cathedral, but whether his plan would have been an improvement or not is an open question. Part of the character of Florence depends upon sudden, dramatic glimpses of the massive cathedral, down comparatively narrow streets. In the 1830s some of the streets in central Florence were broadened and the Via Larga, now called the Via Cavour, was built. In the 1850s the Via Calzaioli and the Via Cerretani were broadened, but the new buildings constructed on these streets were unimaginative. In the last years of the independent duchy there was no systematic town planning. A few new suburbs had appeared, without any green belts being left between them and the city. Then, in 1864 Florence became the capital of Italy. There was already a considerable housing shortage, and, in spite of her rich architectural heritage from the Middle Ages and the Renaissance, there was an uneasy feeling that Florence lacked the scale and dignity to be a fitting capital city of a great power. To remedy this Giuseppe Poggi, who has already been mentioned as a successful neo-classicist architect, was asked to apply his good taste and imagination. His most important work was the landscaping of the hill to the south of the Arno – and the planning of the Piazzale Michelangelo and the network of paths between it and the Palazzo Pitti, where the king was housed for the three years when Florence was the capital. The Pitti was certainly worthy to be a royal palace, and the Palazzo Vecchio made a dramatic seat for the two houses of parliament and the foreign ministry.

When the capital moved to Rome in 1870 there was no need for renovations, since Rome had always been the capital of a great power, whether imperial or spiritual, and since the Renaissance it had had the appearance of one. The major developments in Rome during the period covered by this book had been in the early nineteenth century, and had been the work of an archaeologist and street-planner, Giuseppe Valadier. He worked on the restoration of the Colosseum and the Arch of Titus, and if his methods were not the scientific ones employed by archaeologists today, they at least saved the monuments from further decay. But perhaps his happiest achievement was the planning of the delightful Piazza del Popolo.

One last creation of nineteenth-century Italy, something between architecture and street planning, must be mentioned – the *galleria*. An English translation of *galleria* would presumably be 'arcade', though it is an inadequate translation since the British 'arcade', of which the best examples are in Cardiff, are small, intimate affairs, while the Italian *galleria* is a generous and sumptuous one. As early as 1831 Andrea Pizzola had built the classical *Galleria de Cristoforis* in Milan. The *Galleria Mazzini* in Genoa is elegant and beautiful, but by far the largest and most significant of these glass-covered streets is the *Galleria Vittorio Emanuele* in Milan. Designed by Giuseppe Mengoni, a Milanese, born in 1829, the *Galleria* of Milan connects the Piazza del Duomo with the Piazza della Scala. Symbolically linking religion and the theatre, it lies at the heart of the life of Milan.

NOTES

A survey of the history of Italian art in the period is provided by C. Maltese, *Storia dell'arte in Italia, 1785–1943*, Turin, 1960. Piero Bargellini's *L'arte dell'ottocento*, Florence, 1965, which is Volume II of his *Belvedere. Panorama storico dell'arte*, is a work of popularization, but is comprehensive and especially valuable for its 205 photographic reproductions of paintings, sculpture and architecture. Two works published in 1955 dealt with nineteenth-century painting in Italy: P. d'Ancona, *Pittura dell'Ottocento*, Milan, and G. Deloga, *Pittura italiana dell'Ottocento*, Bergamo. An earlier work is still worth nothing: E. Cecchi, *Pittura italiana dell'Ottocento*, Rome, 1926, new edn 1946, while G. Castelfranco, *Pittori italiani del secondo Ottocento*, Rome, 1952, has a useful bibliography.

For Massimo d'Azeglio as an artist a work already twice cited must be mentioned again: Ronald Marshall, *Massimo d'Azeglio. An artist in politics, 1798–1866*, London, 1966. Benedetto Croce wrote *Una teoria della macchia. Problemi di estetica*, Bari, 1923. Other works on the Macchiaioli are M. P. Cazzullo, *La scuola dei Macchiaioli*, Florence, 1948, and M. Giardelli, *I Macchiaioli e l'epoca loro*, Milan, 1958. On Fattori there is M. Tinti, *Giovanni Fattori*, Rome, 1926.

There are many articles on Canova and studies of single works, though few full lives; P. Scarpellini, *Canova e l'Ottocento*, Milan, 1968, however, deserves mention.

On urban development two books are extremely interesting – one on Milan: G. De Finetti, *Milano, costruzione di una città*, Milan, 1969; and one on Florence: Franco Borsi, *La capitale a Firenze e l'opera di G. Poggi*, Florence, 1970.

1. John Davis, *Società e imprenditori nel regno borbonico 1815/1860*, Bari, 1979, p. 190.
2. Giuseppe Conti, *Firenze vecchia. Storia cronaca aneddotica—costumi (1799–1859)*, Florence, 1899, p. 387.
3. Giuseppe De Finetti, *Milano, costruzione di una città*, Milan, 1969.
4. Paul Ginsborg, *Daniele Manin and the Venetian Revolution of 1848–49*, Cambridge 1979, p. 31.
5. Davide Bertolotti, *Descrizione di Torino*, Turin, 1840, facsimile reprinted by Arnaldo Forni, 1976, p. 47.

CHAPTER THIRTEEN

Religion and the Church

In the eighteenth century the Catholic Church had been on the defensive. The spirit of the Enlightenment had been accepted by powerful princes, and even by one or two of the popes themselves. The Jesuits had been disbanded. In France the Civil Constitution of the Clergy had almost destroyed the Catholic Church, and in spite of Napoleon I's cynical belief that the Church could be used to retain some spurious kind of social stability, by 1815 the number of priests in France had fallen dramatically. Yet after 1815 a surprising Catholic revival took place, a revival associated with the romantic movement and its attraction towards the Middle Ages. It owed a great deal to a French priest, Lamennais.

Hughues Felicité Robert de Lamennais was born in Britanny in 1782. As a boy he read Pascal, but also Rousseau, and in his somewhat inflamed imagination was eventually to believe that the egalitarianism of Rousseau could be linked to the mysticism of the Catholic Church. Initially, however, he saw Rousseau as the enemy. In 1808 he published *Reflexions sur l'etat de l'église en France pendant le 18ième siècle*. Napoleon, who saw the Church as a useful department of state, did not want a movement of romantic Catholic revivalism. Lamennais's book was seized by the police. He himself subsequently became professor of mathematics at an ecclesiastical college at Saint-Malo, and entered the priesthood. He was recognized as an important figure in the Catholic revival in France when the first volume of his *Essai sur l'indifférence en matière de religion* was published in 1817. It attacked liberalism and religious toleration, and even argued that the states of the Restoration were guilty of attempting a compromise with the spirit of the Revolution. The decline of Catholic faith, started by Luther, continued by Cartesian traditions, and the ideas of the Enlightenment and of Rousseau, had resulted in the spiritual death of Europe. The only hope lay in a return to Catholicism, and especially to the authority of the pope. It was his ultramontane convictions – his belief that the pope must be the absolute authority in the Church – that made Lamennais as much a part of Italian, as of French, history. From 1818 to 1824 three more volumes of the *Essai* appeared. In France the older bishops, with their Gallican traditions, regretted Lamennais's influence which was very strong with the new generation of young priests which was appearing. Leo XII approved Lamennais's doctrines, and received him as an honoured visitor in Rome. To liberal non-Catholics Lamennais's teaching inevitably seemed reactionary, but there was already one aspect of it which could not be so lightly defined. Since he believed that the pope should have full authority over national Catholic churches, he was opposed to absolute monarchy. The logic of this attitude was to lead him in an unexpected direction.

Meanwhile an equally important figure in the Catholic revival had made his presence felt. Joseph de Maistre was, in a sense, half Italian, although his first language was French. Born in Savoy in 1754, he had studied in Turin and held official posts in Piedmont. When the French Republic invaded and annexed Savoy, De Maistre went into exile in Lausanne. His *Considérations sur la France*, published as early as 1796, had taken a legitimist and strongly Catholic line against the ideas of the Enlightenment, but his most important work, *Du Pape*, came in 1819. It dealt not only with the pope's role in the Church, but also with his relations with temporal sovereigns and with Protestants, especially the Church of England. If anything, it was more violently ultramontane than Lamennais had been. There was a streak of madness in *Du Pape* which made it as much a part of the romantic movement as were later writers at the opposite pole politically, like Foscolo or Mazzini. The foundation of the social order, De Maistre declared, was the executioner. And the inquisition was needed for the spiritual health of mankind. It is interesting to notice that De Maistre was not a priest, and yet was obsessed with the importance of the pope's rôle in the world. During the revolutionary period he had come to believe that moral and public anarchy was the greatest threat to civilization – rather as Hobbes had concluded in the days of Charles I. The only universal moral authority available in nineteenth-century Europe was the pope; De Maistre, like Lamennais, had no confidence in absolute monarchs. In the restoration period the influence of this highly cultured, intelligent, but fanatical man was immense. In Italy the writings of both Lamennais and De Maistre were known and influential from about 1818.

Both Pius VI and Pius VII had possessed a certain saintliness and nobility of character. There thus seemed some justification for claiming for them a significant rôle in the world. But their successors, Leo XII, pope from 1823 to 1829, and Pius VIII, pope briefly in 1829–30, were small-minded men, who did not fit comfortably into the role given them by De Maistre. Leo XII's main preoccupations were that people should not enter a church lightly clad, or get drunk on Sunday.[1] Pius VIII was primarily concerned with the banning of unofficial – that is, Protestant – translations of the Bible. These popes, and their successor Gregory XVI, pope from 1831 to 1846, were in a sense less ambitious for Catholicism than were Lamennais and De Maistre. The popes were so appalled at the thought of revolution in Europe, and so hostile to liberal ideas, that they recommended Catholic subjects of non-Catholic sovereigns – the Poles, the Belgians, the Irish – to obey their governments and not to cause trouble. However, Pius VIII was quick to recognize that the July Revolution in Paris in 1830 was an innocuous one from the Papacy's point of view. Although Louis-Philippe was a very secular kind of monarch, refusing coronation by the Church, and sending his numerous offspring to state schools, he was accepted by Metternich and other conservative rulers as a bulwark against social revolution. Pius VIII was not slow in extending diplomatic recognition to the July Monarchy. This meant ignoring the advice of his nuncio in Paris, Cardinal Lambruschini, who was later to be made secretary of state by Gregory XVI. Lambruschini was opposed to recognition of Louis-Philippe, but Pius VIII, the only pro-Austrian pope of the nineteenth century, preferred to follow Metternich's advice.

Lamennais also encouraged Pius VIII to come to terms with the July Monarchy, if only because he was glad to see the authority of the French Gallican bishops undermined. Lamennais believed in a strict separation of church and state, with the Catholic Church, all over the world, free from temporal authority and firmly under the authority of the pope. The irony was that Lamennais preferred to have as his sovereign a complete sceptic like Louis-Philippe rather than a devout Catholic who wanted to control the French church and to keep the pope's influence at arm's length. But the revolutionary years 1830–31 were profoundly important in the life of Lamennais, as they were in the life of the papacy. Pius VIII died, and Gregory XVI was elected pope. In the Low Countries and in Poland there were revolutions, supported by Catholic peoples, against non-Catholic sovereigns. Gregory XVI did not hesitate in deciding where his sympathies lay. They lay with the non-Catholic monarchy against revolution. He knew about revolution because he had it on his door-step. He wrote to Czar Nicholas I defending the rights of the Catholic Church in Poland, but he was careful to avoid any reference to the political rights of the Poles as a people.

Meanwhile Lamennais's thought had taken a dramatic step forward. His belief that the spiritual authority of the pope was immensely more important than any temporal authority had led him to believe that in purely political matters demands for freedom and democracy were justified. He had come to think that there was no reason why the pope and the church should not be allied with the people against the princes. It was an exciting but dangerous doctrine, and Lamennais had gathered around him a few of the more formidable theological intellects in France. Henri-Dominique Lacordaire, whose portrait shows him to have had a highly intelligent but unnervingly ascetic face, co-operated with Lamennais on the liberal Catholic journal, *L'Avenir*. Charles Forbes René de Montalembert, a less fanatical and more respectable follower of Lamennais, also wrote for *L'Avenir*. They believed in a free press, freedom of speech, universal suffrage, and the separation of church and state. In other words, they had come to terms with nineteenth-century civilization, and were intelligent enough to realize that the Catholic Church could come to terms with it also. In the columns of *L'Avenir*, in 1830 and 1831, Lamennais defended the Polish cause against Czarist Russia, and the Belgian cause against the Protestant king of the United Netherlands. Montalembert wrote in defence of the Irish against British Protestant imperialism. At the end of 1831 Lamennais, Montalembert and Lacordaire travelled to Rome in the somewhat vain hope of persuading Gregory XVI to help movements of liberation by Catholic peoples, and in particular the Polish revolution against the Czar. The pope did not give them an audience until March 1832. The audience, for which they had thus waited for several months, lasted a quarter of an hour, and was limited to pleasantries: Catholics apparently accept that they cannot introduce a topic of conversation with the pope. Gregory XVI was certainly not going to introduce the revolution in Poland, or a free press, as themes for discussion. Still hoping for a change of mood by the papacy, the three men stayed on in Rome until August, but were not granted a second audience. Instead the pope issued the encyclical *Mirari vos*. On the surface the encyclical appears to be a simple denunciation of liberalism, but the pope believed that, in making no reference to Lamennais or *L'Avenir* by name, he was showing a paternal affection for a stubborn member of his flock. It could also be argued that Lamennais represented a part of the romantic movement's assault on rationalism. He had written: 'the consensus of all is for everyone the only criterion of certainty' – a statement which appeared to reject equally the authority of the Church and respect for human reason. Lamennais's belief in democracy thus seemed to be destroying his belief in the spiritual supremacy of the papacy. For the time being he announced his submission to the doctrine of *Mirari vos*, but in June 1834 he published his most famous work *Les Paroles d'un croyant*, which defended more strongly than ever the need for freedom of expression. Gregory XVI replied with the encyclical *Singulari nos*, in which Lamennais's work was condemned, this time directly. Lamennais then left the Church, welcomed the revolution of 1848, and was elected to the assembly. When he died, in 1854, he was buried without funeral rites. Montalembert continued to preach liberal doctrines but without breaking with the Church. Lacordaire became a Dominican monk, but also without giving up his faith in democracy. However, the liberal Catholic movement had failed to secure the support of the papacy, and in Italy was absorbed by Gioberti's neo-Guelphism. Already in 1835 Niccolò Tommaseo's *Dell'Italia* had given a Christian call for the unification of Italy and the departure of the Austrians, but it was, of course, Gioberti who put across dramatically and influentially the message that the pope should place himself at the head of the Risorgimento.

The writings of Tommaseo and Gioberti were, in a sense, parochial. It was Lamennais who had anticipated the twentieth-century Catholic Church – the separation of church and state, the existence of the church without any temporal power in spite of the infallibility of the pope in spiritual matters, and the acceptance of liberal and democratic régimes. Lamennais had simply appeared on the scene half a century too soon. It is a little difficult to believe that he is for that reason condemned to eternal hell-fire, as the teachings of the Catholic Church would have had its congregations believe.

After 1848 the history of the relations between church and state took a different turn. Some Italian states during the second restoration reached a *modus vivendi* with the pope by means of separate concordats. The restored Grand Duke of Tuscany, Leopoldo II, signed a concordat with the Holy See in

April 1851. More significantly, in August 1855 a concordat was signed with the Habsburg monarchy. Francis Joseph was the first genuinely devout monarch Austria had experienced for many years, and his 1855 concordat gave back considerable powers to the church. For example, marriage disputes were placed back in the hands of special ecclesiastical courts. The struggle between church and state in Piedmont in the years after 1848 was a bitter one but, since it was an important element in the political history of Piedmont, it has already been considered in Chapter 8.

After the traumatic experiences of 1848 and 1849 Pius IX divorced his interests from political matters, leaving them in the hands of his secretary of state, Cardinal Antonelli. He himself returned to his obsession with that typically Mediterranean image of mythology, the Madonna. The curious desire of some Catholics to have proclaimed the doctrine that the maternal grandmother of Christ had been a virgin at the time of the birth of Christ's mother had been expressed since the seventeenth century, especially in France. In 1830 a girl, Catherine Labouré, claimed to have seen a vision of the Madonna in the Rue du Bac in Paris, bearing a scroll which read: 'O Mary, conceived without sin, pray for us who have need of you.' Gregory XVI, a scholar concerned with less colourful theological issues, had not responded to requests for the proclamation of the dogma, but Pius IX, who was more warm-hearted, more superstitious, and more concerned with popular sentiment than his predecessor, decided to act. On 1 June 1848, when most people in Italy were preoccupied with other matters, he set up a commission of twenty priests to consider the question. They put forward a somewhat Jesuitical argument to the effect that although Mary had been conceived in a normal human way, she had been freed, at conception, of original sin.

Pius IX was deeply worried by the question. By February 1849 he was in exile in Gaeta, and even at that moment of political crisis his preoccupation was with the question of the Immaculate Conception. He published the encyclical *Ubi primum* seeking advice from Catholic bishops. About six hundred bishops replied. A few claimed that it was logically impossible to define the doctrine; some, rather more prudently, suggested that it was not the best moment to do so; but a very large majority begged the Pope to proclaim the dogma. Pio Nono still did not act for several years. Two leading Jesuit theologians, Fr. Perrone and Fr. Passaglia, wrote drafts of the dogma, and finally, in December 1854, the Pope proclaimed the dogma in St Peter's, the key phrase being 'that the most blessed Virgin Mary, in the first instant of her conception . . . was preserved free from all stain of original sin'. The Catholic congregations of Europe were not too worried by the vagueness of the dogma, and decided, without defining 'original sin' too closely, to believe that Mary's had been a virgin birth, just as Christ's had been. The column, with a statue of the Madonna, in the Piazza di Spagna in Rome, was constructed, at Pio Nono's request, to celebrate the dogma.

Thus in the mid 1850s Pius had tried to forget about politics, but the Roman Question remained a very real one in the eyes of the other rulers of Italy and of Europe. So long as the Papal States stretched across Italy from coast to coast there could be no unification of the peninsula. And the Pope continued to believe that his temporal power over the Papal States was necessary for his independence as the head of the Catholic Church. In this he was merely maintaining the traditional policy of the Church. Even his more liberal predecessors – Pius VI and Pius VII – had been more prepared to let Napoleon I control the appointment of French bishops than to accept the loss of the temporal power. The Papal States were the 'seamless garment of Jesus Christ', and it would be a blasphemy to take it away from him. None of the popes reflected that when, in the event, Napoleon I had occupied the Papal States and made the pope a virtual prisoner, the pope's popularity and spiritual authority had increased impressively. None of the popes could know that when Pius IX was eventually, in 1870, to lose the last vestige of the temporal power, the moral prestige of the pope in the Catholic world was to continue to increase.

The creation of the Kingdom of Italy in 1861 was a dangerous moment for the pope. The Piedmontese had left him a diminished stretch of territory, but it was still recognizably a state. The danger lay in the fact that most Italians were by then convinced that Rome was the obvious capital for united Italy. Even Cavour, who had always been very wary of approaching the Roman Question, for fear of antagonizing Napoleon III, believed, in the last months of his life, that some steps towards the acquisition of Rome must be taken. It was impossible to deal directly with Pius IX, but the pope did not forbid an unofficial approach. Before the end of 1860 negotiations were started between Cardinal Santucci, who spoke with Pius IX's tacit approval, and Fr. Passaglia, who had left the Jesuit Order, but remained a respected theologian and was supported by his friend, Diomede Pantaleoni. Passaglia and Pantaleoni were in touch with Massimo d'Azeglio, and so, indirectly, with Cavour. Already in November 1860 Pantaleoni drafted a memorandum proposing the abolition of the temporal power coupled with the promise that the Church would be allowed complete independence from the State. It was the idea which Cavour had encapsulated in the phrase 'a free Church in a free State'. The memorandum passed from Pantaleoni to Passaglia, and from Passaglia to Cardinal Santucci, who submitted it to the pope. Perhaps, surprisingly, Pio Nono did not reject it out of hand, but asked Antonelli to consider it. Pantaleoni's proposal envisaged the pope as remaining an independent sovereign, with his own diplomatic corps, and the end of state interference in the appointment of bishops. In other words it represented the separation of Church and State, a separation for which Lamennais had fought thirty years earlier. It did not take long, however, for the pope to realize the true nature of what was being proposed. On 27 March 1861 Cavour made his famous speech to the assembly, the speech in which he used the much quoted phrase 'a free Church in a free State', but by then Pio Nono had already insisted that the unofficial negotiations should be abandoned.

A few years later, in 1864, the pope circulated the *Syllabus of Errors* and the Encyclical *Quanta Cura*. Even to many very devout Catholics the two documents seemed incredibly unreasonable and a tragic blunder on the part of the papacy. To pretend that the *Syllabus* was simply a circular letter to Catholic priests, and should be ignored by the rest of the world, was naive. The rest of the world were certainly going to hear about it. The *Syllabus* lists eighty propositions which it was considered an error to believe. The propositions virtually embrace all the 'isms' in which the nineteenth century believed except, of course, Catholicism and baptism. They included pantheism, rationalism, socialism, communism and liberalism, and were defined by Antonelli in a note which accompanied the *Syllabus* as 'the chief errors and false doctrines of our most unhappy age'. Proposition 80 was the most comprehensive and damning. The erroneous proposition read: 'The Roman Pontiff can and should reconcile and harmonize himself with progress, with liberalism, and with recent civilization'. Mazzini noted that the pope had hurled down a glove of defiance against nineteenth-century civilization, and perhaps the pope himself would have accepted that conclusion. But a closer study of the *Syllabus* suggests that each of its arguments was a continuation of a previous argument with the Piedmontese state. Pio Nono's thought was somewhat parochial. He was not concerned so much with Charles Darwin and the materialism of the nineteenth century as with Vittorio Emanuele and the annexations of papal territory. But in more general terms the *Syllabus* condemned religious toleration and freedom of expression, which were likely to lead to 'corruption of manners, and minds'. It was to be expected that Protestant governments and non-Catholic groups generally would grab at the *Syllabus* as a stick with which to beat the pope. But Pius should have realized that liberal Catholics would also have found it very distasteful. Poor Lamennais was long since dead, and rotting in unconsecrated earth, but his most distinguished disciple, Montalembert, was still very much alive. A dominant figure in the Catholic world in France, Montalembert was deeply embittered by the *Syllabus*, as were distinguished Catholic scholars in Germany and England – Johann von Döllinger, theologian and historian, and John Acton, perhaps the author of the greatest work of history never written, the *History of Freedom*. After the publication of the *Syllabus of Errors* Montalembert, Döllinger and Acton knew that their ideal of a liberal and intelligent head of the Catholic world would have to wait for a while. But the opinion of a few Catholic scholars in Northern Europe that the pope was leading Catholic thought in a mistaken direction was not reflected by Catholic congregations as a whole. The emotional fervour and veneration felt for the pope as an individual since Pio Nono's day was a product of his pontificate, to a large extent, although it had been partly anticipated by the personal affection shown for Pius VI and Pius VII. During the pontificate of Gregory XVI there had been no such fervour. A priest who visited Rome in 1842 noticed that no one bothered to raise his hat when the pope passed on the street.[2] It was Pius IX who brought about the change of atmosphere in the Catholic world. But total devotion to the pope led to religious intolerance of those who were not so devoted. The *Syllabus of Errors* is inclined to distrust religous toleration, which can lead to 'indifferentism', which is described as 'a pest'. Montalembert, who was by then generally recognized as the most brilliant Catholic preacher in

France, had only the year before – in 1863 at the Catholic Congress at Malines – made a passionate and much applauded plea for religious toleration. For the Catholic Church to depend upon force, which would in practice be the force of an authoritarian state, would be, Montalembert believed, deeply damaging to the church. But for his contribution to the congress at Malines Montalembert received a mild and polite rebuke from Rome, a rebuke which reminded him of Gregory XVI's *Mirari vos*.

One of the other distinguished Catholic scholars who could not accept all the affirmations in the *Syllabus of Errors* was Döllinger. At a congress in Munich in September 1863 Döllinger had put across an argument which was really more profound than Montalembert's. Döllinger had argued that history and science were autonomous disciplines and their findings could not be subjected to ecclesiastical authority. On the contrary, theology itself could only be strengthened by an understanding of history and philosophy. Whether Pio Nono and his intimate advisers followed the subtlety of Döllinger's argument is open to doubt. But Döllinger had already offended the pope by criticizing his rule in the Papal States. In January 1864 Pio Nono wrote to the Munich Congress regretting that they had not asked his permission for holding a major Catholic congress, and arguing in favour of the doctrinal authority of Rome. The German Catholics decided not to hold a similar congress in Munich again. Acton had been a student of Döllinger, and had immense respect for the German historian. He was deeply dismayed at the papal reaction to the Munich Congress. Montalembert, Döllinger and Acton were thus still further dismayed when the *Syllabus of Errors* was published at the end of 1864, though they had by then half expected it. For the time being there was little they could do, and of the three of them only Döllinger was eventually to leave the Catholic Church.

Although he seemed a quiet and humble man Pius IX could fly into fits of rage, and was certainly never dominated by his advisers. The College of Cardinals lost influence during his pontificate; he preferred to seek the advice of individual cardinals rather than of the college as a body. And having sought the advice of a cardinal or official, he would frequently ignore it completely. He was humble before God, but not before man. The dogma of papal infallibility did not fit so strangely on his shoulders as some had assumed that it would.

In 1865 Pio Nono decided to start a full-scale consultation of Catholic bishops to see if opinion was in favour of the proclamation of a dogma declaring the pope infallible in his *ex cathedra* pronouncements. The majority of bishops were in favour of the idea. The decision was therefore reached that a Council of the Church – the first to be summoned since the sixteenth-century Council of Trent – should meet in Rome. The decision was announced in June 1867. Thereafter two men were emphatic in persuading the pope to push through the dogma of infallibility and to have no truck with nineteenth-century liberalism: a French journalist, Louis Veuillot, and an English priest, Henry Manning. Born in 1813, with a humble background, Veuillot had fought his way into eminence in the world of Catholic journalism, and in this context the word 'fought' has a literal significance because Veuillot's Catholic militancy had involved him in duels and a period of imprisonment under the July Monarchy. In 1848 he had become editor of the *Univers*, the most influential Catholic journal in France. He was to live on until 1883 and to defend the pope until the latter's death in 1878. Veuillot was an ultramontane as Montalembert was, but, unlike Montalembert, was violently opposed to liberal Catholicism. Manning had been born in 1808 and, after Harrow and Balliol, had a fairly successful career in the Church of England, being archdeacon of Chichester from 1841 to 1850. But, as Lytton Strachey wickedly remarked in that classic of wickedness, *Eminent Victorians*, one cannot remain an archdeacon all one's life. After a private audience with Pio Nono, Manning joined the Catholic Church.[3] In 1865 he became archbishop of Westminster. The pope had great respect both for Veuillot and Manning, who with their very different backgrounds had each a considerable influence upon him. Veuillot and Manning and the other men who pressed for the dogma of Papal Infallibility were now known as 'neo-ultramontanes' to distinguish them from the ultramontanes of the earlier part of century – Lamennais, Montalembert and Lacordaire, who had linked their demands for the total authority of the pope within the church to a fervent wish that the church should align itself with 'ideas of 1789'.

In Italy the founding of the Jesuit newspaper, the *Civiltà Cattolica*, gave the neo-ultramontanes an even more influential organ than the *Univers*. The editor of the Roman paper, the Jesuit Carlo Curci, differed from Veuillot in that he refused to enter into political argument by condemning liberalism or defending absolute monarchs. Curci simply kept silence on such questions and concentrated on defending the spiritual absolutism of the pope. Only in 1863 did Curci offend Pius by arguing, in typically Jesuitical manner, that whereas the *Syllabus of Errors* had condemned religious toleration for an ideal Christian society, 'toleration is often desirable in actual circumstances'. Pius removed Curci from the editorship, and brought the *Civiltà Cattolica* more closely under papal control. Henceforth it came to be regarded as the voice of the papacy. Jesuit influence in Rome was moving closely into alignment with Pio Nono's own wishes.

The General Council opened in Rome in 1869 on the anniversary of the dogma of the Immaculate Conception, 8 December. Its sympathizers inside Catholicism, and even a few non-Catholics – most notably Guizot, the veteran French Protestant statesman – believed that the moral anarchy of the nineteenth century needed the affirmation of a moral authority. Its hostile critics suspected that the findings of the Council would be out of tune with the spirit and understanding of the age, and would cause only conflict and confusion. All Christian bishops were invited – Protestant and Greek Orthodox as well as those 'in peace and communion'. The universal nature of the invitation contrasted strangely with the passages on religious toleration in the *Syllabus*; however, the invitation was universal only in an ecclesiastical sense:

no secular government was invited to send representatives.

Montalembert died while the Council was sitting. His last thrust was contained in a letter published in the *Gazette de France*, on 7 March 1870:

who could have led us to suspect, in 1847, that the *liberal pontificate of Pius IX, acclaimed by all the liberals of the two worlds, would become the pontificate represented and personified by the Univers and the Civilta?*

And who, he asked, could have foreseen:

the permanent triumph of those lay theologians of absolution who . . . offer up justice and truth, reason and history, as a holocaust to the idol which they are erecting at the Vatican?

At least a few devout and intelligent Catholics had seen through the folly which Pius IX, in his innocence, was enacting. In October and November 1869 the eminent priests of the Catholic world assembled in Rome. About 700 attended the opening ceremony. The Greek Orthodox bishops did not respond to the invitation from Rome, and Protestants clearly saw that attendance at the Council would imply acceptance of Catholic authority. No Protestant arrived. The superb basilica of St Peter, the creation of Michelangelo, Bramante and Bernini, provided a wonderful setting. The first document to emerge from the Council, on 24 April, was entitled *Dei Filius*, rejected rationalism and pantheism, and repeated familiar interpretations of revelation and the relationships between faith and reason. It had been discussed at some length, but was eventually accepted unanimously. Meanwhile, as the Roman summer approached, heated discussions on the question of Papal Infallibility were going on behind the scenes. The pope seemed in no hurry to discuss the matter in open debate, but Manning and the neo-ultramontanes pressed him not to leave it for too long. The question of the role of the papacy in the Church was therefore discussed from 13 May. A minority group had been arguing that, whatever the merits of the doctrine that the pope's official statements were infallible, it was an inopportune moment in which to turn it into a dogma.

Finally, on 13 July, the Constitution *Pastor aeternus* was passed by 451 affirmative votes, and 88 negative ones, with 62 agreeing 'subject to certain amendments', and 76 absent. In spite of long debate and very serious doubts by an appreciable minority, the final clause of the dogma was indeed final:

the Roman Pontiff, when he speaks *ex cathedra*, that is, when as Shepherd and Teacher of all Christians, by virtue of his supreme apostolic authority he defines that a doctrine on faith or morals must be held by the Universal Church, enjoys, by the divine assistance promised to him in the person of Blessed Peter, that infallibility which the divine Redeemer intended his Church to possess when defining doctrine concerning faith and morals; and therefore such definitions of the Roman Pontiff are unalterable in themselves and not by virtue of the assent of the Church'.[5]

So the pope had triumphed over the church. The hot Roman summer had already arrived. In September 1870 the troops of the Kingdom of Italy blasted their way into Rome. Pio Nono became, as he called himself, the 'prisoner of the Vatican', but only a few weeks before he had made himself the infallible source of truth in the Catholic world. History is full of paradoxes, but this is one of the more dramatic ones. In that one year the pope lost the last shreds of his temporal power but secured a spiritual authority which was continually to be reaffirmed over the next century.

NOTES

A recent study in English, sympathetic in its approach to the nineteenth-century papacy, is J. Derek Holmes, *The Triumph of the Holy See. A short History of the Papacy in the Nineteenth Century*, London 1978. For the papacy before Pius IX, E. E. Y Hales, *Revolution and Papacy 1769–1846*, London, 1960, gives a fluent account from the standpoint of a liberal Catholic, while the same author's *Napoleon and the Pope*, London, 1962, vividly recounts the struggle between Pius VII and Napoleon.

On Lamennais's ideas there is Mario Sancipriano, *Lamennais in Italia: autorita e libertà nel pensiero filosofico-religioso del risorgimento*, Milan, 1973, and on Lacordaire and Veuillot there is a work in English – Philip H. Spencer, *Politics of Belief in Nineteenth-century France: Lacordaire: Michon: Veuillot*, London, 1954. A great deal of intelligent writing has been lavished on de Maistre. Three works which reward reading are Adolfo Omodeo, *Un reazionario. Il conte Joseph de Maistre*, Bari, 1939; Richard A. Lebrun, *Throne and Altar. The political and religious thought of Joseph de Maistre*, Ottawa, 1965; and Bruno Brunello, *Joseph de Maistre politico e filosofo*, Bologna, 1967.

For Leo XII's pontificate there is Raffaele Colapietra, *La chiesa tra Lamennais e Metternich. Il pontificato di Leone XII*, Brescia, 1963. The pontificate of Gregory XVI has been, comparatively speaking, neglected by historians, apart from the interlude when Lamennais appeared on the scene. But a recent work has to some extent filled the gap: Maria Luisa Trebiliana, *Il pontificato di Gregorio XVI*, Rome, 1974.

E. E. Y. Hales's *Pio Nono* (London, 1954) has already been mentioned for Chapter 4, and is of course relevant here. A Jesuit historian, Pietro Pirri, produced a recognized classic, *Pio IX e Vittorio Emanuele II dal loro carteggio privato*, vol. I, *La laicizzazione dello Stato Sardo*, Rome, 1944, and vol. II, *La questione romana*, Rome, 1954. But, although a fine scholar, Father Pirri, like the Bourbons, had forgotten nothing and forgiven nothing. An authoritative study of Pius IX is Roger Aubert, *Le Pontificat de Pie IX, 1846–1878*, Paris, 1952. More recently, for the pontificate of Pius IX, and in particular for his attitude to the masonic movement, there has appeared Romano F. Esposito, *Pio IX – La Chiesa in conflitto col mondo. La S. Sede, la Massoneria e il radicalismo letterario*, Rome, 1979.

An important study of Cavour's approach to the Roman Question in the last weeks of his life was Ettore Passerin d'Entrèves, *L'ultima battaglia politica di Cavour*, Turin, 1956.

The text of Pius IX's *Syllabus of Errors* is conveniently found in an English translation in Anne Fremantle, *The Papal Encyclicals in their Historical Context*, Mentor, 1963. There is only one unintentionally amusing indication of ignorance of Italian in this edition. A footnote to the first mention of Pius IX reads: 'Nicknamed and generally known, even during his lifetime, as "Pio Nono"'.

The most recent biography of Cardinal Manning is Vincent A. MacClelland, *Cardinal Manning. His public life and influence, 1865–1892*, London, 1962.

1. These are two of the points in his Encyclical *Caritate Christi* of 25 December 1825.
2. Noticed in J. Derek Holmes, op. cit., who, however, gives no source.
3. It should perhaps be added here that, while personal ambition probably played a part in Manning's conversion to Catholicism, it is of course not the whole of the story. The Gorham case in 1850 had convinced Manning that the Church of England was too fully under the control of a secular judicial and political system. But the matter clearly falls outside the scope of this book.
4. Quoted in E. E. Y. Hales, *Pio Nono*, p. 290.
5. Quoted in J. Derek Holmes, op. cit., pp. 157–8.

CHAPTER FOURTEEN

Beyond nationalism: the end of the Risorgimento

It is perhaps true that history is to a great extent written by the victors. It has already been suggested that until comparatively recently most Italian nineteenth-century history was written by sympathizers of Cavour and the moderate party who succeeded in imposing their solution to the Italian Question. But even in the realm of political speculation there were movements in nineteenth-century Italy which had little or nothing to do with the struggle for independence and unity. Some of them – like socialism – were to be more important after 1870. Some of them – like the Hegelianism which characterized certain Neapolitan thinkers in the early part of the period covered by this book – never quite connected with the main currents of Italian nationalism.

Hegel's role in the history of nationalism has been seen very differently by different historians and political scientists. In his view of history, great world movements – Hellenism, the Roman Empire, the modern European civilization which was dominated by Teutonic peoples – provided the central theme, while the state in its modern form – and he thought especially of the Prussian state – was the most powerful and life-giving unit in history. The nation-state – for example, the nation-state of Germany or Italy – was not anticipated nor important as an idea in Hegel's scheme of things. Thus a distinguished political scientist, in a book entitled *Nationalism*, mentions Hegel only once, and dismisses him in a footnote with the words: 'Hegel is not a nationalist . . . . His political thought is concerned with the state not the nation.'[1]

The Hegelianism which Neapolitan writers embraced in the early nineteenth century was to some extent a reaction against the revolution of 1799 which had brought such horrors upon so enlightened a group of men. Vincenzo Cuoco, who has already been mentioned as the author of the *Saggio storico sulla rivoluzione napoletana del 1799*, expressed in that work the belief that the revolutionaries of 1799, innocent and generous products of the Enlightenment as they were, had placed too much trust in philosophy and too little in a knowledge of tradition and history. Vico in the eighteenth century, and Hegel in the nineteenth, would not have made that mistake. The revolutionaries of 1799 had worked to emancipate the peasant, but according to their own abstract ideas, not with the help of the peasant himself nor with knowledge of his own earthy conditions. And in the event the peasant had turned against his would-be liberators and massacred them. But Cuoco had no intention of rejecting 'philosophy' altogether. It was simply that an understanding of the peasant, and co-operation with him, must be obtained before a revolution, not after it.

In many ways Cuoco anticipated the Neapolitan Hegelians of the mid nineteenth century. Perhaps the most profound of these was Bertrando Spaventa, who was born in 1817. A Hegelian of the left, Spaventa accepted Hegel's conviction that the state was the main motive force of history, but rejected Hegel's theology. He had been educated in a seminary for the priesthood, but was sympathetic to the Neapolitan revolution of 1848. After the revolution he left the priesthood and became a Freemason. He secured a professorial post at the University of Turin, and published articles in the Piedmontese journal *Il Progresso*. His articles were passionately concerned with the freedom of the masses, but also with the power of the state to secure that freedom. He had not forgotten the Hegelian doctrine that only the state can secure and guarantee freedom. But by the end of 1851 Spaventa was becoming more concerned with egalitarianism. He believed that a national revolution in Italy must involve everyone, not just an élite of the middle class. He refused to call himself a 'socialist', just as Mazzini did, but he believed that no movement which did not create a republic of all the citizens could succeed. This, then, was the Spaventa whose thought had stretched beyond the Risorgimento. Sadly, Louis-Napoleon's *coup d'état* in December 1851 disillusioned Spaventa, who then decided that only a strong existing authority could be effective, and this meant, in Italian terms, the Piedmontese monarchy.

The philosophy of Hegel was the starting-point of Marx, even though Marx quickly turned that philosophy upside-down. But long before Marx had been heard of in Italy a considerable influence of a democratic and socialist nature had been exerted by Claude-Henri de Rouvroy, the Count of Saint-Simon. The ideas of the followers of Saint-Simon, who had died in 1825, were better known in Italy than were those of Saint-Simon himself, who had recommended the equal sharing of wealth in an industrial society. His influence, then, was a second-hand one. Even so, Mazzini, Gioberti and Tommaseo were all familiar with Saint-Simon's ideas. After Saint-Simon's death Italian exiles during the 1830s made contacts with his supporters in Paris. The links, first, then, were between members of the Carbonari and the Saint-Simonians. By that time the ritual and mysticism of Saint-Simonism were becoming more important than the socialist element. But, to their credit, the Italians who attended Saint-Simonian séances were interested in the economic doctrines, but found the religious ones somewhat ridiculous. Apart from the formal seances of the Saint-Simonians, the salon of Princess Belgioioso Trivulzio in Rue-Honoré was another meeting-place of the two groups.

Two French followers of Saint-Simon, who broke with the Saint-Simonians after his death, were Philippe Buchez and Pierre Leroux, with both of whom Italians had close relations. Buchez tried to reconcile Saint-Simon's original ideas with a more orthodox form of Christianity, and was admired by Gioberti and Tommaseo, but bitterly opposed by Mazzini. Leroux, on the other hand, was admired by Mazzini, who was introduced to him by George Sand. The first centre of Saint-Simonian ideas in Italy was Tuscany, followed shortly by Liguria. In Liguria also there were followers of Fourier, and a periodical propounding his ideas, called *Pace sociale*, was published. As a university student Montanelli followed the more exotic, mystico-sensual traditions of Saint-Simonism. He founded a Saint-Simonian church in Pisa, where he played the priestly role adopted by 'father' Enfantin in France. But the church was later closed by the authorities. Saint-Simonism was a strange mixture of tendencies of a kind not likely to appeal to the single-minded, not to say simplistic, ideas of Mazzini. On the one hand it had inherited from the Enlightenment a respect for science and a belief that social change could be brought about by scientific reasoning. On the other hand it shared with writers of the romantic movement an enthusiasm for the Middle Ages, an enthusiasm which Mazzini, although a product of romanticism, did not share. The Saint-Simonians had, however, a concept of progress in history which need not have been alien to Mazzini's thinking, and could certainly be reconciled with Hegel's dialectic. They believed that 'organic' periods of history alternated with 'critical' ones. In an 'organic' period there would be progress, but progress in which authority, a faith, and a respect for the advantages of association would dominate. In a 'critical' period there would be a querying, and finally a destroying, of existing institutions, and a rejection of beliefs formerly held. Such a 'critical' period would be necessary before a leap forward by another 'organic' period could be made. The Middle Ages had been an important 'organic' period. This broad historical philosophy of Saint-Simonism could clearly be adapted by theorists of very different persuasions, so that Gioberti and Mazzini, in their early days, and Montanelli later, could be influenced by Saint-Simonian ideas.

The first socialist ideas in Italy had thus come from Saint-Simon, and had been acquired by men who had before 1848 followed Mazzini, but after 1849 found themselves in sharp disagreement with him. Cattaneo, Ferrari, Pisacane and Montanelli all agreed in condemning the abstract nature of Mazzini's thought, his reluctance to accept a class struggle, and his rejection of historical materialism. Of the four of them Carlo Pisacane was the most firmly convinced that the history of the 1848 revolutions had to be written in terms of class.

Pisacane's *Guerra combatuta in Italia negli anni 1848−49* ('The war fought in Italy in the years 1848−49') was written at Lugano and published in 1851. While the book is concerned with a minute analysis of the blunders made by Italian armed forces in 1848−9, the political setting for the military critique is all-important. Carlo Alberto's failure to defeat the Austrians, when they were scattered, disorganized and undermined by revolution in Vienna, was not due, in Pisacane's eyes, simply to incompetence and error. It was due to the spirit in which the Piedmontese entered the war. Precisely because the Austrians had been driven out of Milan by a popular rising, Carlo Alberto had felt that it was necessary to replace them by a Piedmontese army, to prevent a social revolution. Carlo Alberto's war had not been 'the consequence of his war-like ideas against the foreigner, but a precaution to defend the throne against the people'.[2] The faults of the republicans, however, in Pisacane's eyes, had been simply technical and military, not ideological.

So far as the organization of a revolutionary army was concerned, Pisacane was firm that commissions must be obtainable by anyone who deserved them, and all ranks, commissioned or non-commissioned, must be paid the same. The people's army which brings about the revolution, Pisacane argued, must not hand over power to any other authority. The revolutionary authority, which emerges spontaneously from the barricades, must retain power until a democratic regime is instituted. The mistake in Milan in 1848 had been that the Council of War which had conducted the popular insurrection against the Austrians had accepted a constitution which was made by men who did not want a people's democracy. The republican leaders of 1848–9 'had not sought adherents among the people, partly because they despaired of finding them', and partly because they made the mistake of considering national independence more important than the liberty of the people.[3] The republican governments which had come into being in 1849 had done nothing positive to help the people, but had tended to regard the introduction of a constitution based on universal suffrage as the fulfilment of their aims. But, 'whether there be a king, a president, or a triumvirate at the head of the government, the enslavement of the people does not cease, unless the social set-up changes'.[4] The establishment of civil liberties, without the overthrow of the economic and social structure, simply provides new instruments for exploiting and oppressing the people. Political 'equality' is worthless so long as the citizens, in terms of social relations, are divided into classes. 'Metternich smiled when the sovereigns were alarmed by the political question; his acute genius realized that victory for despotism was certain so long as the question did not become a social one.' But here Pisacane perhaps overrated Metternich's acuteness: the record makes it only too clear that Metternich was as scared as any monarch of political change. But Pisacane anticipates Marxist writers – and notably Gramsci – in saying that in the French Revolution of 1789 there had been a drawing together of classes but that the bourgeoisie had then reasserted its control, 'a very unequal society was reconstituted', and the people were 'as unhappy with the new regime as they had been with the old one'. The real enemies of the people were no longer the political rulers but the property owners. It was they who were 'enjoying the fruit of the labour of the peasant and the worker, who can scarcely secure a livelihood'.[5] 'The bourgeoisie in Italy possess the land and the capital; it has the monopoly of commerce, of science, of industry and of employment, it reigns in Italy, as in America, in England, in France.'[6] Pisacane attacked the old revolutionary concept of secret societies operating through conspiracies. Such societies thought in terms of single acts of violence against governments, instead of working from within the masses.

Pisacane believed, further, that the revolution would come where the workers were the most heavily oppressed, not where they were the best educated or the least wretched. Consequently he believed that in Italy revolution would be more likely to break out, and to succeed, in the South rather than in the North, and in the countryside rather than in the town. As has been seen in Chapter 9, his own choice of the Neapolitan countryside as the scene for revolution in 1857 was to prove a tragic mistake, but on the other hand it can be said that the peasants in Sicily in 1860 were sympathetic to Garibaldi, if not exactly eager to fight with him, and there had been plenty of evidence of revolutionary sentiment among the peasants of the South, and of the Veneto, in 1848−9. In the days of the Roman Republic Pisacane had already argued that an attempt should be made to stir up a peasant insurrection to the south, but his advice had not been taken.

Pisacane's socialism went deeper than Ferrari's, but Ferrari's writings were better known at the time. Born in 1811, Giuseppe Ferrari became a close friend of the French socialist Proudhon. So far as Italian history goes, Ferrari anticipated several post-1945 tendencies. A republican and a socialist, a believer in regional autonomy and so a federalist, he became isolated in his own day. Before 1848 he believed that republican revolutions should be organized in each individual Italian state and that only then − though as quickly as possible − should the Austrians be driven from Italy; and the Italians should seek the assistance of France instead of relying on the Piedmontese monarchy. After the failure of the revolution of 1848 in Milan, in which he played a role, Ferrari went into exile in France, and in 1851 published a pamphlet, *La federazione repubblicana*. Also in 1851 he published his *Philosophy of the Revolution*. In both of these writings the great enemy of Italy was the papacy. The great ally of Italy was the coming European revolution, which would be initiated in France. Mazzini also believed that the Italian revolution must be part of a European one, rather as Lenin was to believe that the Russian revolution could survive only as part of a European revolution, but Mazzini believed that the centre of the democratic revolution should be Rome rather than Paris. Ferrari's European revolution, emanating from Paris, was to be a socialist one, and in Italy, too, the social questions would be recognized as being more important than the political ones. Ferrari realized that the socialist movement had developed further in France than it had in Italy, but he believed that there was something which he called 'latent' socialism in Italy, which could emerge with the help of the French. He believed that concepts like freedom and independence were empty ones so long as there were extremes of wealth and poverty. Ferrari's *La federazione repubblicana* was widely read, and stimulated much discussion. Yet by 1860 his was a solitary voice.

Even before 1861, then, some writers had looked far beyond the Italian nationalism of the Risorgimento, and had anticipated later movements. The great protagonists of the Risorgimento − Mazzini, Vittorio Emanuele II, Pius IX, Garibaldi − lived on for some years beyond 1861. Garibaldi, indeed, lived for another twenty-one years. After Cavour, Mazzini was the first to die − in 1872. In his last years he showed himself receptive to some new ideas, though he bitterly rejected others. Thus his interest in the emancipation both of women and of the working class continued to grow, although he persisted in refusing to be considered a 'socialist'. On female emancipation he had written, as early as June 1858: 'Above man and woman there exists something common to them both: the single trunk from which grow the two varieties of human nature. Philosophically speaking, there is no such thing as man or woman: there is only human nature which it is the mission of woman and man to develop.'[7] Elsewhere he had written: 'Half the human family, that half from which we seek inspiration and comfort, and to which we confide the early education of our children, is by a curious inconsistency held to be inferior from the civil, political and social point of view...'[8] Again he wrote, presumably to a man: 'Love and respect woman.... Blot out from your mind any idea of superiority; you have none. There is no inequality between man and woman.'[9]

Mazzini's attitude to the working class is a complex question, and has already been mentioned in this volume. Already in 1837 he had written: 'Freedom without equality is not, and cannot be, a reality for more than a small number of privileged people; for the great majority it is a delusion, a word empty of sense.'[10] His interest in forming a working-class organization dated from 1840. Early that year he founded in London the 'Union of Italian Workers' as a section of *Giovine Italia*, and in the same year provided the 'Union' with its own newspaper, the *Apostolato Popolare*, which was published until September 1843. Although this activity was linked to *Giovine Italia*, and therefore with Italian nationalism, Mazzini made it clear in the *Apostolato Popolare* that the coming revolution should have social as well as political aims, and should include 'moral and material improvement of all'; it was important that the interests of the workers should not be subordinated to those of the middle class, as they had been in the French Revolution. In the years from 1860 to his death in 1872 Mazzini became increasingly concerned with the workers' movement. But his basic political philosophy ensured that he would lose out in debates with socialists, and even with anarchists. He played a small rôle in the formation of the First International in London, through his very warm and sincere contacts with English workers, but his influence was soon replaced by that of Marx, whose contacts with English workers were far from warm, but whose intellectual control of the movement rapidly became formidable. Mazzini persisted in his belief in God, and – perhaps more significantly – in the sanctity of private property. His later, long debate with Bakunin was not resolved in theoretical terms, but marked the end of Mazzini's influence over the workers' movement in Italy.

Mazzini had never accepted the kingdom of 1861 as being the real Italy. Perhaps someone with his exalted concept of what Italy should be could never have accepted any simple man-made institution. He had accepted, and had ruled with great wisdom, the Roman Republic, but that had been only a half-way station. If some state with the tolerance and the humanity of the Roman Republic had been created for Italy Mazzini would have been satisfied. But that, after all, was asking rather a lot.

Mazzini died on 10 March 1872, in Pisa, having returned, clandestinely, to the Italy which he had rejected, and which had rejected him. He was buried in the great cemetery of Staglieno in his birthplace, Genoa, and his epitaph was written by the greatest living Italian poet, Giosuè Carducci:

THE LAST

OF THE GREAT ANCIENT ITALIANS

AND THE FIRST OF THE NEW

THE THINKER

WHO FROM THE ROMANS FOUND HIS STRENGTH

FROM THE COMMUNES HIS FAITH

FROM OUR TIMES HIS IDEAS

THE POLITICAL MAN

WHO THOUGHT, AND WILLED, AND MADE ONE THE NATION

WHILE MANY JEERED AT HIS GREAT PURPOSE

WHO NOW ABUSE HIS ACHIEVEMENT

THE CITIZEN

TOO LATE HEEDED IN 1848

REJECTED AND FORGOTTEN IN 1860

LEFT IN PRISON IN 1870

WHO ALWAYS AND ABOVE ALL LOVED

THE ITALIAN FATHERLAND

THE MAN

WHO SACRIFICED EVERYTHING

WHO LOVED MUCH

AND FORGAVE MUCH AND NEVER HATED

GIUSEPPE MAZZINI

AFTER FORTY YEARS OF EXILE

TODAY PASSES FREELY IN ITALIAN SOIL

NOW THAT HE IS DEAD

O ITALY

SUCH GLORY AND SUCH BASENESS

AND SO GREAT A DEBT FOR THE FUTURE

GIOSUÈ CARDUCCI[11]

Two other central figures of the Risorgimento died in the early weeks of 1878 – Vittorio Emanuele II on 9 January, and Pio Nono on 7 February. In his last years Vittorio Emanuele had tried to bolster up the monarchy by forging close relations with the Austrian and German empires. He had visited both Francis Joseph and William I in 1873. Although he was well received by the crowds in Vienna and Berlin there was no immediate diplomatic consequence. Francis Joseph did not return the visit, for fear of offending the pope. Not until 1882 – four years after Vittorio Emanuele's death – was the Triple Alliance between Italy, Austria, and Germany signed.

Although Pius IX called himself the 'prisoner of the Vatican' after 1870, he continued to play a prominent role in European politics. In particular he fought the bitter struggle with Bismarck for control of the Catholic Church in the new German Empire, the struggle which was known as the *Kulturkampf*, and which had not been resolved when Pius died. Cardinal Antonelli died in November 1876, and it is interesting to notice that Pio Nono's pronouncements against the activities of the Italian government become more virulent after Antonelli's death. Without Antonelli, and deprived of his temporal power, the pope became more of a mystic, and perhaps less of an Italian, in his last years. When the French constructed the beautiful white church of Sacré Cœur, on Montmartre, to celebrate the defeat of the Commune, Pio Nono gave 50,000 francs, from the somewhat limited funds available to him, towards the building of the church. Cardinal Manning went to Rome in December 1877 and stayed at the pope's bedside until the death of Pius some six weeks later. The two men had certainly served each other well.

After 1878 Garibaldi was the one principal figure of the Risorgimento still alive. After the disaster of Mentana he had returned to his home on the island of Caprera, and in 1868 wrote the first of three novels, *Clelia*. His novels were sold and read in Italy, in spite of their intellectual immaturity. Foreign publishers were not eager to produce translated editions, perhaps from a sense of respect for the author. Garibaldi's life on Caprera was mainly that of a poor peasant. A few words from G. M. Trevelyan's masterly trilogy on Garibaldi might be quoted here. Trevelyan describes Garibaldi 'at work among the granite boulders industriously putting seed into the scrapings of earth which he called his fields; sheltering a few sad vines from the sweeping winds of the Straits; calling up his cows by name from their pasturage among the wild, odorous brushwood; and seeking the strayed goats on the precipice-top'.[12] But there is no doubt that this serene, generous man was happy on the little island which he had chosen to be his home.

The events of 1870, both in France and Italy, disturbed his peace once more. The defeat of the French at Sedan, and the fall of the Second Empire, divided Italian republicans. Mazzini and many Italians of the left persisted in hating the French, whether they were ruled by Napoleon or a republican government. Mazzini formed an uncharacteristic and mistaken respect for Bismarck. But the position was a complex one from the point of view of the Italian republican tradition, since it had been a French republic that had destroyed the Roman Republic in 1849, whereas Garibaldi had been quite prepared to fight alongside the forces of Napoleon III in 1859. The difference, of course, was that in 1859 Napoleon had been fighting for Italy; for Garibaldi in 1870 to support the enemy of the Roman Republic was unthinkable. However, as soon as the Second French Empire had fallen, Garibaldi telegraphed to the new republican government that 'what is left of me is at your disposal'. He was sixty-three years old, and suffering acutely from arthritis. The new authorities in France could be forgiven for suspecting that his military usefulness would be outweighed by the disadvantages of allowing a foreign adventurer to command an irregular force in France. At first the French did not reply, but public opinion in France would have been offended by an outright rejection of so selfless an offer from so colourful a man. When Garibaldi arrived in Marseilles he was cheered by huge crowds. Somewhat reluctantly the French republican government placed him in command of a force of some 5,000 many of whom were Italians who had accompanied Garibaldi to France. In three small battles Garibaldi defeated the Germans, in a year when the Germans were unaccustomed to defeat. Most of Garibaldi's followers of 1860 – who had been Mazzinians – had failed to go with him to France, but one, an Englishwoman, Jessie White Mario, joined him. Jessie Mario had in the past helped Garibaldi by organizing his nursing services. A formidable Victorian lady, married to an Italian, she was in a sense Garibaldi's Florence Nightingale. Her account of her arrival in France is a moving one. As she entered the cottage which was Garibaldi's headquarters the old man, crippled with arthritis, approached her with his infectious smile and the words: 'This time I scarcely expected you.'[13]

The French electorate recognized Garibaldi's efforts on their behalf by electing him to the National Assembly which met in Bordeaux. Unfortunately the very conservative deputies who assembled in Bordeaux protested loudly against him as a foreigner and a subversive. Garibaldi returned to Caprera, having, not for the first time, been the victim of deplorable ingratitude. He expressed his sympathy for the revolt of the Commune in Paris, and thereafter proclaimed himself a socialist, in sharp contrast to Mazzini who condemned the Commune and so antagonized many men on the left who could not believe that Mazzini could condemn a revolution of the people. Garibaldi in these last years even went so far as to say that if Italy ever started to oppress other peoples he would take up arms against her. He could not accept the idiocy of the slogan 'My country right or wrong'.

So far as his private life on Caprera in these last years went, it should be said that the woman with whom he slept was Francesca Armosino, who had initially been employed as a nursemaid for his children. He married her just before his death, so that two of his several children, Clelia and Manlio, became legitimate and could take the name of Garibaldi, a name not to be spurned. He died on 2 June 1882. Less than two weeks before an alliance had been signed between Italy, the Habsburg Monarchy and the German Empire. With Garibaldi's death it could be said that the Risorgimento was truly over.

NOTES

Although primarily concerned with Benedetto Croce, Edmund E. Jacobitti, *Revolutionary Humanism and Historicism in Modern Italy*, Yale, 1981, is interesting on the Neapolitan Hegelians. For Giuseppe Ferrari there is Silvia Rota Ghibaudi, *Giuseppe Ferrari. L'evoluzione del suo pensiero (1838–1860)*, Florence, 1969. An essay already mentioned in the notes to Chapter 8 is particularly relevant here: 'Un capitolo di storia del socialismo risorgimentale: Proudhon e Ferrari', in Franco della Peruta, *Democrazia e socialismo nel risorgimento* Rome, 1977. Two works by Nello Rosselli were seminal and are vital for this chapter: *Carlo Pisacane nel Risorgimento italiano*, Turin, 1932, and *Mazzini e Bakounine. Dodici anni di movimento operaio in Italia (1860–1872)*, Turin, 1927, new edn 1967.

For the official Italian reaction to the crisis which caused the Franco-Prussian War, and Italy's decision to remain neutral in it, see S. Walter Halperin, *Diplomat under Stress. Visconti-Venosta and the Crisis of July 1870*, Chicago, 1963.

1. Elie Kedourie, *Nationalism*, London, 1960, p. 36.
2. Carlo Pisacane, *Guerra combatuta in Italia negli anni 1848–49*, Genoa, 1851, p. 155.
3. *Ibid.*, p. 329.
4. *Ibid.*, p. 330.
5. *Ibid.*, p. 338.
6. *Ibid.*, p. 334.
7. The original of this remarkable statement is on a card among the papers presented by G. O. Griffith to the library of University College, Cardiff. For the rather mangled forms in which it was originally published, and the sensitive passage of Italian which Mazzini actually wrote, see Harry Hearder, 'Mazzini e l'Inghilterra', *Atti del XLVI congresso di storia del risorgimento italiano*, Istituto per la storia del risorgimento italiano, 1974.
8. Quoted in Gaetano Salvemini, *Mazzini* (English edn), London, 1951, p. 30.
9. Quoted by Bolton King, *Mazzini*, London, 1903.
10. *L'associazionismo Mazziniano. Atti dell' incontro di studio*, Ostia, 1976, p. viii.
11.

L'ULTIMO

DEI GRANDI ITALIANI ANTICHI

E IL PRIMO DEI MODERNI

IL PENSATORE

CHE DE' ROMANI EBBE LA FORZA

DE' COMUNI LA FEDE

DE' TEMPI NUOVI IL CONCETTO

IL POLITICO

CHE PENSO E VOLLE E FECE UNA LA NAZIONE

IRRIDENTI AL PROPOSITO GRANDE I MOLTI

CHE ORA L'OPERA SUA ABUSANO

IL CITTADINO

CHE TARDI ASCOLTATO NEL 1848

RINNEGATO E OBLIATO NEL 1860

LASCIATO PRIGIONE NEL 1870

SEMPRE E SU TUTTO DILESSE

LA PATRIA ITALIANA

L'UOMO

CHE TUTTO SACRIFICO

CHE AMÒ TANTO

E MOLTO COMPATI E NON ODIO MAI

GIUSEPPE MAZZINI

DOPO QUARANT'ANNI DI ESILIO

PASSA LIBERA PER TERRA ITALIANA

OGGI CHE E MORTO

O ITALIA

QUANTA GLORIA E QUANTA BASSEZZA

E QUANTO DEBITO PER L'AVVENIRE

GIOSUÈ CARDUCCI

The phrase 'left in prison in 1870' refers to the fact that in August 1870, while he was trying to enter Italy, Mazzini's passport was found to be invalid. He was arrested and imprisoned for a few weeks, but treated with great respect and gentleness.

12. G. M. Trevelyan, *Garibaldi and the Making of Italy*, London, 1920, p. 229.
13. Elizabeth Adams Daniels, *Jessie White Mario. Risorgimento Revolutionary*, Athens, Ohio, 1972, p. 109. Mrs Daniels' sensitive and perceptive study of Jessie Mario seems, surprisingly, to have escaped the notice of most historians of the Risorgimento.

Maps

Map 1. Physical features and historic regions of Italy

Map 2. Italy in 1815

Map 3. North and central Italy 1848–59

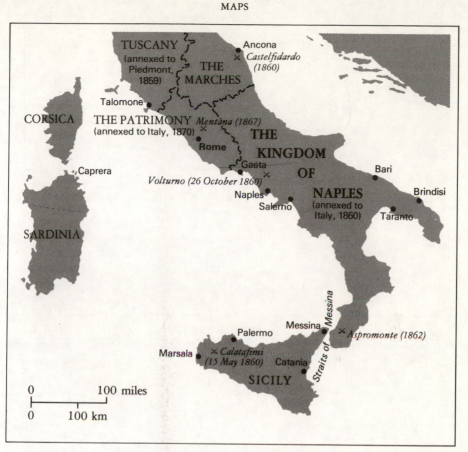

Map 4. South and central Italy in the 1860s

Index

Aci, Prince of, 138

Acton, John, 127, 289, 290

Adelfi, 32, 177

Albert, Prince Consort, his attitude to Italy in 1860, 236

Alexander I, Czar, 74, 135
 at Tilsit (1807), 168
 in 1815, 174
 his changing attitude after 1818, 175, 177

Alfieri, Vittorio, 255, 256, 257, 267
 his part in the origins of the Risorgimento, 161
 reaction to the French Revolution, 44
 Saul, 267

Amiens, Treaty of, 166

Ancona
 declaration of the republic in 1797, 98
 part of Napoleon's Kingdom of Italy, 27
 occupied by revolutionary forces in 1831, 107
 occupied by the French in 1832, 180
 besieged by the Austrians in 1849, 118
 the economy of, 121

Andreoli, Giuseppe, 76

Antolini, Giovanni, 279

Antologia, 73, 74, 90, 254

Antonelli, Alessandro, 278

Antonelli, Cardinal Giacomo
 president of Pius IX's Consulta in 1847, 112, 113
 Pius IX's secretary of state, 119, 287
 and the *Syllabus of Errors*, 289
 death of, 302

Aporti, Abbot Ferranti, 65

Appiani, Andrea, 272, 273

Apulia, economic vitality in the last years of Neapolitan independence, 152

Armellini, Carlo, 110
 triumvir of the Roman Republic of 1849, 117

Armosino, Francesca, 303

Artois, Count of, 44, 45

Asinari, Carlo, 55

Aspromonte (1862), 242

Associazione Agraria, 57

Austerlitz, battle of, 27, 167

Avellino, 136

Baccani, Gaetano, 278, 280

Bagnasco, Francesco, 142

Bakunin, Michael, 300

Balbo, Count Cesare, 58, 197, 198, 200, 213
 The Hopes of Italy (1844), 197
 and *Il Risorgimento*, 212
 prime minister of Piedmont, 61

Baldasseroni, Giovanni, 82, 89
 his penal code of 1853, 247

Balleydier, Alphonse, 109, 110

Banco di Napoli, 151

Bandiera, Attilio, 194, 195

Bandiera, Emilio, 194

Barbaja, Domenico, 277

Bartolini, Lorenzo, 276, 277

Bassville, Hugou de, 98

Bayard, Armand, 152

Beauharnais, Prince Eugène de, 27–30
 the cultural life of his court, 273
 and the plan for rebuilding Milan, 279

with Napoleon's army in Russia in 1812, 169

Beccaria, Cesare, 70, 161

Beccaria, Julia, 261

Belgioioso Trivulzio, Princess, 296

Bellini, Vincenzo, 269
  Il Pirata (1927), 269
  La Sonnambula (1831), 269
  Norma (1831), 269
  I Puritani (1835), 261

Bentinck, Lord William, 131–3

Benvenuti, Cardinal, 108

Berchet, Giovanni, 259

Bergamo
  the silk industry, 38
  the city's exceptionally large contribution of men to the 'Thousand', 231

Bernadotte, Marshal, and later king of Sweden, 74

Bertani, Dr Agostino, 233

Bertolotti, Davide, his account of Turin in 1840, 280

Besini, Giulio, 76

Bianchi, Nicomede, 3, 278

Bismarck, Count Otto von, 243, 301, 302

Bixio, Nino, 59, 237
  and the defence of the Roman Republic in 1849, 118

Blondel, Henriette, 261

Bologna, 96
  occupied by the French in 1796, 98
  Metternich's designs upon, in 1815, 174
  the revolution of 1831, 79, 107
  its industry, 121

Bonaccorsi Anna, 84

Bonaparte, Carlo Luciano, prince of Canino, 110, 114, 115

Bonaparte, Caroline, queen of Naples, 170

Bonaparte, Elisa Baciocchi, grand duchess of Tuscany, 71

Bonaparte, Joseph
  French agent in Rome in 1797, 98
  King of Naples, 130, 131, 149, 167, 168

Borghese, Prince Camillo, 52

Borodino, battle of, 169

'Brigands' War', 240, 241

Brofferio, Angelo, 58–60

Buchez, Philippe, 296, 297

Buol, Count, 220
  sends Austrian ultimatum to Turin in 1859, 225

Buonarroti, Filippo, 18, 48, 177, 178
  his part in Babeuf's rising of 1796 in Paris, 177
  in 1831, 78, 179, 180
  relations with Mazzini, 188

Cabianca, Vincenzo, 274

Cagnola, Luigi, 277, 279

Calatafimi, battle of, 231

Calderari, 134

Campo Formio, treaty of, 164

Canosa, Prince of, 134, 140

Canova, Antonio
  as sculptor, 97, 275, 276
  as architect, 277

Canuti, Filippo, 106

Capponi, Gino, 74, 80, 82, 84–6
  his theories on the Tuscan economy, 92, 94

Caracciolo, Domenico, Marquis of Villamarina, 127

Caramanico, Prince of, 127

Carbonari, 32
  origins of, 178
  in Restoration Tuscany, 73
  in Restoration Naples, 134, 177
  in the revolution of 1820 in Naples, 136–40, 178
  in the Papal States, 103–5
  Mazzini's reactions to membership of, 184, 185

Carducci Giosuè, his epitaph for Mazzini's tomb, 301

Cariati, Prince of, 147

Carlo II, Duke of Parma, 82, 88

Carlo III, Duke of Parma, 88

Carlo Alberto, 77
  in 1821, 54–6
  king of Piedmont, 57, 58, 187
  his assessment of the young Cavour, 210
  in 1831–32, 180
  his reforms of 1847, 59
  his granting of the *Statuto* in 1848, 60, 61
  and the war of 1848, 201, 202
  rejects Garibaldi's offer of support in 1848, 206
  his victory at Goito, 203
  his defeat and abdication, 208

Carlo Emanuele IV, 49–51

Carlo Felice, 54–7, 59

Carlo Ludovico, Duke of Lucca, 81

Carlyle, Jane, her relationship with Mazzini, 193

Carlyle, Thomas, his respect for Mazzini, 193, 194

Caropreso, Camillo, 141

Carra, Antonio, 88

Cassa di Risparmio, 39

Cassisi, Giovanni, 148

Castelfidardo, battle of (1860), 234

Castiglione, Countess Virginia di, 222

Castlereagh, Viscount, 30
  his policy towards Sicily, 133
  and in 1815, 134, 172, 174, 175
  and in 1820−21, 179

Catanzaro in 1835, 151

Cattaneo, Carlo, 35
  his background and ideas, 201
  during the cinque *giornate*, 201

Cavour, Adèle Benso di, 210

Cavour, Count Camillo Benso di
  publications of his writings, 11−12
  his birth and background, 210
  visits France and Britain in 1834−35, 211
  his study of banking, 61
  and the railways, 63, 212
  his running of his estates, 211
  his founding of *Il Risorgimento*, 212
  his opposition to Solaro della Margarita in 1847, 58−60
  on Pius IX in 1848, 113
  elected to Parliament in 1848, 212
  his ministerial posts from 1850, 213
  his commercial policy, 214
  the *connubio* of 1852, 215
  appointed prime minister of Piedmont, 215
  and the Mazzinian rising of 1853 in Milan, 219
  his reaction to the outbreak of the Crimean War, 219
  at the Congress of Paris (1856), 220
  his contacts with Napoleon III from 1856 to 1858, 222
  at Plombières (1858), 222, 223
  prepares for the war of 1859, 224, 225
  resigns after Villafranca, 226
  his relations with the National Society, 229
  his attitude to the sailing of the Thousand, 232
  his attempts to start a pro-Piedmontese rising in Naples in 1860, 233
  decides to invade the Papal States in 1860, 233
  his attitude to the Roman Question in 1860−61, 288
  his death, 237

Cavour, Marquis Benso di, 210

Cacioni, Adriano, 274, 277

Cempini, Leopoldo, 80, 83

Centurioni, 108
  their reactions to Pius IX's reforms, 110

Cernuschi, Enrico, 201

Cerruti, Count Giuseppe, 53

Chiala, Luigi, 3, 4

Chornaya Rechka, battle of, 220

Cicero, his idea of 'Italy', 156

'Ciceruacchio' (Angelo Brunetti), 109, 110
  and the civic guard in Rome in 1848, 112
  executed by the Austrians, 116

cinque giornate in Milan (1848), 201

Cipriani, Colonel Leonetto, 85, 86

Circolo Popolare, Roman revolutionary club in 1848, 112, 115, 116

Circolo Romano, 115

Circourt, Countess of, 237

Cisalpine Republic, 21−4, 25, 28, 164
  re-established in 1800, 166

Civiltà Cattolica, 291

Clarendon, Earl of, 220

Clement XIV, Pope, his suppression of the Jesuits, 97

Clotilde, Princess of Savoy, 223

Clough, Arthur Henry, in Rome in 1849, 118

Como
  the woollen industry, 38
  peasant insurrection of 1848, 203

Conciliatore, Il, 254, 273

Concistoriali, 75

Concordia, 66

Confalonieri, Count Federico, 30, 36, 178
  founder of *Il Conciliatore*, 254

Confederation of the Rhine, 167

Congress System, 175, 179

Conneau, Dr, 222

Consalvi, Cardinal Ercole, 100, 102−4
  signs Concordat with Naples, 135

deprived of his office by Leo XII, 105
Contemporaneo, Il, a Roman journal of 1848, 111
Continental System, its effect on Italy, 29
Corsini, Neri, 76, 80
Crimean War, outbreak of war between Russia and Turkey in 1853, 219
Crispi, Francesco
arrested in 1853, 219
and the Thousand, 230, 232
Croce, Benedetto, 9
his assessment of the rule by the party of the Right from 1861 to 1876, 245
Cuoco, Vincenzo, 131, 150, 166, 295, 296
Curci, Carlo, 291
Custozza, battle of (1866), 243

D'Ancona, Alessandro, 76
Dante, his concept of Italy, 156, 157
Dawkins, George, British consul-general in Lombardo-Venetia, 208, 209
D'Azeglio, Marquis Massimo, 58, 199
as artist, 273, 274
as writer, 265
Ettore Fieramosca (1833), 265
Niccolò de' Lapi (1841), 265
I miei ricordi (1863), 265
La Lega Lombarda (1843), 265
his meeting with Carlo Alberto in 1845, 199
publication of *The recent events in Romagna* (1846), 200
his collaboration with Durando in 1848, 203
prime minister of Piedmont, 1849–52, 213, 214
and Cavour's *connubio* (1852), 215
Davis, John, quoted, 278
De Deo, Emanuele, 128
Delcarretto, Francesco, 141
Denina, Carlo, 161, 162
Depretis, Agostino, sent to Sicily by Cavour in 1860, 232
Derby, Earl of, 224
De Sanctis, Francesco
minister of education in 1861, 249
on Manzoni, 262
D'Este, Archduke Francesco, 132
Di Blasi, Francesco, 128

Döllinger, Johann von, 289, 290
Donizetti, Gaetano, 268, 269
Anna Bolena (1830), 268
Lucrezia Borgia (1833), 268
Lucia di Lammermoor (1835), 268
Don Pasquale (1843), 268
Doria Raimondo, 181, 184, 185
Dupré, Giovanni, 277
Durando, Giacomo, 115, 203

Elba, 73
Erfurt, Congress of, 168
Eugénie, Empress of the French, and the Orsini Attempt (1858), 222
Eylau, battle of, 168

Fabrizi, Nicola, 81
his foundation of the 'Italian Legion' (1839), 194
his contact with the Bandiera brothers, 195
Fanti, General Manfredo, 234, 236, 237
his integration of Italian armies after 1860, 249
Farini, Luigi Carlo, 110
judgement on Cardinal Gizzi, 110
in 1859, 225–7
in 1860, 228, 229
his *luogotenenza* in the South, 240
prime minister of Italy, 242
Fattori, Giovanni, 274, 275
Favre, Jules, 222
Ferdinando IV (later Ferdinando I), King of Naples, 126–8, 134
in exile in Sicily, 130, 132
assumes title of 'Ferdinando I', of the 'Kingdom of the Two Sicilies',
on his restoration in 1815, 133, 134
obliged to pay compensation to Eugène de Beauharnais after 1815, 135
in 1820–21, 137, 139, 179
his death, 140
Ferdinando II, King of Naples
his accession, 141
and the building of the church of San Francesco di Paola, 278
and railways, 151, 152
in 1848, 143, 145, 146, 203
refuses to join Italian League, 85
in 1849, 147, 148

Ferdinando III, Grand Duke of Tuscany (1790–1824), 70–3, 76

Fermo, part of Napoleon's Kingdom of Italy, 27

Ferrara, 96
occupied by the French in 1796, 98
Metternich's designs upon (1815), 174
occupied by the Austrians in 1831, 108
and again, illegally, in 1847, 112

Ferrari, Giuseppe, 299
La federazione repubblicana (1851), 299
Philosophy of the revolution (1851), 299

Filangieri, General, 148

Ford, Franklin, quoted, 166

Foro Bonaparte, in Milan, 279

Fortunato, Giustino, 147

Foscolo, Ugo, 73, 257–60
Alla sera, 258, 259
Last letters of Jacopo Ortis (1802), 263, 264

Fossombroni, Vittorio, 72, 73, 76, 77

Francesco IV, Duke of Modena, 75, 76
and the revolution of 1831, 77–80
death of, 81

Francesco V, Duke of Modena, 81–3, 89

Francesco I, King of Naples
Vicar of Sicily in 1812, 132, 133
becomes king in 1825, 140

Francesco II, King of Naples
grants a constitution in 1860, 232
withdraws from Naples, 233

Francis II, Habsburg emperor (1792–1835), 17, 32, 70, 74, 163
abandons the title of Holy Roman Emperor (1806), 167, 168

Francis Joseph, Habsburg emperor (1848–1916)
approves sending of ultimatum to Turin in 1859, 225
at Villafranca in 1859, 226

Fransoni, Luigi, Archbishop of Turin, 58, 65, 214

Friedland, battle of (1807), 168

Galleria de Cristoforis in Milan, 281

Galleria Mazzini in Genoa, 281

Galleria Vittorio Emanuele in Milan, 281

Galletti, Giuseppe, 108, 116

Garibaldi, Anita, 207

Garibaldi, Giuseppe
in South America, 205, 206
offers Pius IX the help of the Italian Legion in 1847, 112
deputy of the Roman *Costituente* in 1849, 117
his defence of the Roman Republic in 1849, 118, 206, 207
his relations with the National Society, 229
and the cession of Nice to France in 1860, 230
and the sailing of the Thousand in 1860, 230, 231
enters Palermo, 27 May 1860, 231, 232
crosses the Straits of Messina, and enters Naples, September 1860, 232
at the battle of the Volturno, 234
refused dictatorial powers in Southern Italy, November 1860, 235
intervention in parliament in 1861, 237
the Aspromonte episode (1862), 242
the Mentana campaign (1867), 244
his three novels, 302
his life on Caprera (1867–1878), 302
his campaign in France in 1870, 302, 303
his death in 1878, 303

Gavazzi, Alessandro, 85

George III, king of England, 174

George IV, king of England, previously Prince Regent, 174

Georgofili, 80, 90, 92

Ghisalberti, Alberto M., 11

Giachi, P., the *Catechismo al popolo*, 91

Giannini, Vincenzo, 80

Gigliolo, Giuseppe, 186

Ginsborg, Paul, 6

Gioberti, Vincenzo, 286
his background, 196
the publication of *Il Primato* (1843), 195

Giordano, Pietro, 76

Giustiniani, Anna, 211

Gizzi, Cardinal, 109, 111
appointed secretary of state, 110
and the papal press laws in 1847, 111
his resignation, 112

Gladstone, William Ewart
translator of Farini's history of the Papal States, 110
Two Letters to the Earl of Aberdeen, 144

Goito, battle of, 203

Goldoni, Carlo, 267
Gorone, General, 241
Gradenigo, Antonio, 278
Gramsci, Antonio, 7–9, 147
Gregory XVI, Pope, 111, 284, 285, 287, 289
  elected in 1831, 107
  and the revolutions of 1831, 108
  finances during his pontificate, 121
  ignores the Memorandum from the Great Powers of 1832, 181
  his treatment of Lamennais in 1832, 286
Greppi, Paolo, 18
Gualterio, Filippo Antonio, 2
Guelfi, 32
  in the Papal States, 103
Guerrazzi, Francesco Domenico
  as novelist, 265
  Battaglia di Benevento (1827–28), 265
  Assedio di Firenze (1836), 81, 265, 266
  in 1847, 81
  in 1848, 82, 83, 86, 87
  in 1849, 88
  his trial and sentence, 89
Guiccioli, Countess Teresa, 224
Guizot, François, 291

Hamilton, Lady Emma, 128, 129
Hamilton, Sir William, 129
Hayez, Francesco, 273, 275
Hegel, Georg Wilhelm Friedrich, 295–7
Herder, Johann Gottfried von, his influence on Mazzini, 159, 160
Holy Alliance, 174
Holy Roman Empire, dissolution of, 167
Howells, William Dean, American consul in Venice, 243
Hudson, Sir James
  his part in bringing Piedmont into the Crimean War, 220
  his influence on Cavour's return to power in 1860, 228

Illuminati, 32
Imbonati, Carlo, 261
Intonti, Nicola, 141
Italian Republic (formerly the Cisalpine), 26, 27, 30
Italy, Kingdom of, Napoleon's creation of (1805), 27–30

Jappelli, Giuseppe, 278
Jena, battle of, 168
Jérome-Napoléon, Prince ('Plon-Plon'), 222, 223
Jesuit Order
  treatment in Restoration Tuscany, 72, 73
  influence in Restoration Modena, 75
  expelled from Piedmont in 1848, 213
Jews
  in the Roman ghetto, 99, 122
  given civil rights in Rome by the French, 101
  their brutal treatment by Leo XII, 105
  excluded from citizenship by Pius IX's constitution of 1848, 114

King, H. Bolton, 5
Kissinger, Henry
  on Metternich, 172
  on the 1815 settlement, 173
Kossuth, Louis, Mazzini's contacts with him, 218
Kutusov, General, 169

Labouré, Catherine, 287
La Cecilia, Giovanni, 81, 82
Laclaire, Jean-Paul, 62
Lacordaire, Henri-Dominique, 285
  and L'Avenir, 285
  in Rome, 1831–32, 285, 286
La Farina, Giuseppe, sent to Sicily by Cavour in 1860, 232
Lafayette, Marquis de, 77
Laffitte, Jacques, 77
La Guéronnière, anonymous author of Le Pape et le Congrès (1859), 228
Laibach, Congress of, 56, 139, 179
Lamarmora, General Alfonson, 227, 248
  prime minister of Italy in 1864, 243
  signs treaty with Bismarck for war against Austria in 1866, 243
La Masa, Giuseppe, 142, 143, 145
Lambertenghi, Luigi, 254
Lambruschini, Cardinal Luigi, 285
Lamennais, Hughes Felicité Robert de, 283–5
  Reflexions sur l'état de l'église en France pendant le 18ième (1808), 283
  Essai sur l'indifférence en matière de religion (1817–24), 283
  and L'Avenir, 285

in Rome in 1831–32, 285, 286
Les paroles d'un croyant (1834), 286
leaves the Church, 286
death of, 286
Lamoricière, General Louis de, 234
Landucci, Leonida, 89, 94
Lanza, Giovanni, prime minister of Italy in 1869, 244
Lawrence, Sir Thomas, his portrait of Pius VII, 100
Lecco, taken by a peasant revolutionary army in 1848, 203
Lega, Silvestro, 274, 275
Leghorn, 69, 73, 77
in 1847, 80, 81
in 1848, 82, 83, 85, 86
economic growth of, 90
the first railway line to, 92
Leipzig, battle of, 170
Leo XII, Pope, 284
his election in 1823, 104, 105
his repressive policy, 105
approves the earlier ideas of Lamennais, 284
death of, 105
Leoben, peace of, 164
Leopardi, Giacomo, 73, 76, 257, 258
All'Italia
A Silvia (1829), 260
La quiete dopo la tempesta (1829), 260
Il sabato del villaggio (1829), 260, 261
Canto notturno di un pastore errante nell'Asia (1830), 260
Leopold II, Habsburg emperor, 16, 17, 163
see also Pietro Leopoldo
Leopoldo II, Grand Duke of Tuscany, 76
in 1847, 80
in 1848, 84, 87
leaves for Naples in 1849, 87
in exile, 88
the restoration of 1849, 88, 89
his departure in 1859, 225
to be restored according to the terms of Villafranca, 226
signs Concordat with the pope (1851), 286, 287
Leroux, Pierre, 296, 297
Lesseps, Ferdinand de, 118
Letture di famiglia, 58
Ligurian Republic, 49, 50

Lissa, battle of, 244
Lloyd Austriaco di Trieste, 39
Lodi, battle of, 18, 164
Lodovico of Parma, 'King of Etruria' under the French, 71
Louis XVIII, king of France, 172
Louis-Bonaparte, Prince, *see under* Napoleon III
Louis-Philippe, king of the French, 77, 78
his troops occupy Ancona, 108
Lucca, 92
Lunéville, peace of, 25, 166

Macchiaioli, 272, 274, 275, 277
Macerata, attempted rising in, 104
Machiavelli, his concept of 'Italy', 157, 158
Magenta, battle of, 225
in the painting of Giovanni Fattori, 274
Maistre, Joseph de, 284
Considérations sur la France (1796), 284
Du Pape (1819), 284
Malmesbury, Earl of, 78, 224
Mameli, Goffredo, 59, 263
Fratelli d'Italia, 263
Un'idea, 263
Mamiani, Count Trenzio
in 1831, 107
in 1848, 115, 116
Manin, Daniele
and the Venetian revolution of 1848, 202, 207–9
and the National Society, 229
Manning, Cardinal Henry, 290–2, 302
Manno, Francesco, 263
Mannucci, Achille, 118
Mantua, siege of, 1796–97, 164
Manzini, Camillo, 77
Manzoni, Alessandro, 255, 261, 262
as poet, 261
Il Trionfo della Libertà (1801), 261
In morte di Carlo Imbonati (1806), 261
Inni Sacri (1815–22), 262
Marzo (1821), 262
Cinque Maggio (1821), 262
as novelist
I Promessi Sposi (1827/1842), 264, 265
the portrait by Francesco Hayez
Marchetti, Giuseppe, 231
Marengo, battle of, 25, 166
Maresca, Nicloa, duke of Serracapriola, 144

Margarita, Count Solaro della, 58, 59

Maria, grand duchess of Tuscany, 72

Maria Beatrice, duchess of Modena, 75

Maria Carolina, queen of Naples, 126–8
    in exile in Sicily, 130, 132, 133
    death of, 133

Maria Cristina, queen of Naples, 141

Marie-Antoinette, queen of France, 163

Marie-Louise, Empress, later duchess of Parma, 73–5
    her marriage to Napoleon (1810), 169
    and the revolution of 1831, 79
    death of, 82

Marinovich, Captain Giovanni, 202

Mario, Jessie White, 191
    joins Garibaldi in the 1870 war, 303

Marsala, landing of the Thousand at, 231

Martini, Giulio, 81

Marx, Karl
    on the Roman Republic, 206
    and the First International, 300

Masons, 178
    in Piedmont, 177

Massari, Giuseppe, 4

Masséna, Marshal, 165–7

Matas, Niccolo, 278

Maximilian, Prince, 33

Mazzini, Dr Giacomo, Mazzini's father, 182, 183

Mazzini, Giuseppe, 73, 116
    his background and personality, 182, 183
    his first writings, 184
    arrested in 1830, 181, 182
    in prison in Savona conceives Young Italy (1831), 185
    his basic ideas, 185, 186
    his influence from Herder, 159, 160, 185
    in exile in Marseilles founds Young Italy, 186
    his open letter to Carlo Alberto in 1831, 187
    his influence in Piedmont in the 1830s, 57
    relations with Guerrazzi, 81, 82
    the 1833 conspiracy, 188
    the failure of the rising of 1834, 188, 189
    the founding of Young Europe in 1834, 189, 190
    arrives in London, 190
    in England, 194

his opinion of Massimo d'Azeglio in 1846, 200
    arrives in Florence in 1849, 87, 88
    triumvir of the Roman Republic (1849), 117–9, 206, 207
    and the Milan rising of 1853, 218, 219
    and the attempted rising of 1857, 221
    his ideas after 1861, 299, 300
    and the First International, 300
    and the Syllabus of Errors, 289
    his attitude to the war of 1870, 302
    and to the Commune in 1871, 303
    his death (1872), 300, 301
    his epitaph, by Carducci, 301

Mazzini, Maria, Mazzini's mother, 182

Mazzoni, Giuseppe, 86, 87

Medici, Luigi de', 134–6

Melzi d'Eril, Count Francesco, 17–9, 22, 25–7, 29, 35

Memorandum of the Great Powers to the pope in 1832, 181

Menabrea, General Luigi, prime minister of Italy, 244

Mengoni, Giuseppe, 281

Menotti, Ciro, 78–80, 105, 106

Mentana campaign (1867), 244

Mercantini, Luigi, 262
    La Spigolatrice di Sapri, 262

Metternich, Prince Clemens, 72, 75, 78, 140, 164
    his youth and early career, 175, 176
    foreign minister in 1809, 176
    policy towards Naples in 1815, 134, 135
    in 1815, 102, 172, 174
    and the Congress System, 175
    and the suppression of the revolutions of 1820–21, 56, 137, 139, 179
    his recognition of the July Monarchy, 285
    and the revolutions of 1831, 79, 180, 181
    decision to suppress the Antologia, 74
    his decision to occupy Ferrara in 1847, 112
    the absurdity of his characterization of Italy as a 'geographical expression', 156, 157
    requests and is refused permission to send troops across the Papal States in January 1848, 113
    his fall from power in 1848, and its effect in Italy, 200

mezzadria, 93, 94

Milazzo, battle of, 232

Minghetti, Marco
member of Pius IX's *Consulta* in 1847, 112
prime minister of Italy, 1863–64, 242

Minichini, Luigi, 136

Minto, Earl of, 59
in Naples, 144, 145

Mirari vos, encyclical (1832), 286

Misley, Enrico, 77–9, 180

Mole Antonelliana in Turin, 278

Montalembert, Charles Forbes René de, 285
and *L'Avenir*, 285, 286
in Rome, 1831–32, 285, 286
condemns the *Syllabus of Errors*, 289
his ideas on religious toleration, 289, 290
and the work of the Vatican Council, 292
death of, 292

Montanari, Leonida, 105

Montanelli, Giuseppe, 86–8
his judgement of Pius IX's constitution of 1848, 114

Monti, Vincenzo, 257

Morandi, Antonio, 76

Morando, Felice, 45

Moreau, General Jean-Victor-Marie, 166

Morelli, Emilia, 4, 11

Moro, Domenico, 194, 195

Morning Post, 132

Müller, John James, 62

Mundy, Admiral George Rodney, 232

Murat, Joachim, 26, 126, 165
King of Naples, 131, 133
With Napoleon's army in Russia in 1812
returns to Naples in 1812, 169
'King of Italy' in 1815, 72, 170
his execution, 170

Musolino, Benedetto, 147

Napoleon Bonaparte
appointed commander of French army in Italy in 1796, 163
in Italy in 1796, 18, 47, 164
invades the Papal States in 1796, 98
his Egyptian campaign in 1798, 165
in Italy, 1799–1800, 24, 25, 51, 166
elected president of the Cisalpine Republic (1802), 26
'King of Italy', 27, 28, 166, 167

and Pius VII, 100
at the peak of his power (1809), 168
marriage to Marie-Louise (1810), 169, 176
his treatment of Pius VII in 1812, 169
his invasion of Russia in 1812, 169
his defeat at Leipzig (1813), 170
his abdication (1813), 170
on Elba, 73
the Hundred Days, 170

Napoleon 'II', king of Rome, and later duke of Reichstadt, 74, 78, 106
his birth, 169

Napoleon III, emperor of the French, previously Prince Louis-Napoleon Bonaparte
in 1830–31, 78, 106
in 1849, 206, 207
assumes title of 'Emperor Napoleon III' (1852), 218
and the Orsini Attempt, 222
and the *grido di dolore* speech (1859), 224
goes to war with Austria (1859), 225
at Villafranca in 1859, 226
his attitude to Garibaldi in 1860, 232
and the September Convention (1864), 242
his diplomacy in 1866, 243
his foreign policy, 1867–70, 244
withdraws his forces from Rome in 1870, 245

Nardi, Biagio, 79

National Society, 229

Nazarene school of painting, 273

Neipperg, Count Adam, 74, 75

Nelson, Admiral Horatio, 128, 129, 165
death of, 167

Niccolini, Gian Battista, 267

Nicolson, Harold, 172

Nievo, Ippolito, 255, 266
Le confessioni di un italiano, 266
La rivoluzione nazionale, 266

Nigra, Costantino, 222, 223, 233

Nugent, General Count, 136

Omodeo, Adolfo, 9, 10, 197

Onesti, Luigi, 97

Orsini, Felice
in the 1844 conspiracy in the Papal States, 108

the attempt on the life of Napoleon III (1858), 221, 222
Ortolani, Angelo, 105
Oudinot, General, 118, 206

Padua, the silk industry, 37
Pallavicino, Giorgio, 229
Palazzo Borghese, in Florence, 278
Palazzo Pitti, the royal palace when Florence was the capital, 281
Palazzo Strozzi, in Florence, restored by Giuseppe Poggi, 279
Palmerston, Viscount
    policy towards Italy in 1830s, 181
        in 1848, 202
            towards the Republic of St Mark in 1849, 208
            in 1856, 220
            as prime minister after 1859, 226, 227
            towards Garibaldi in 1860, 232
Panizzi, Sir Antony, 5, 190
Pantaleoni, Diomede, 288
Papal Infallibility, Dogma of, 292, 293
Parini, Giuseppe, 255
Paris, Congress of (1856), 220
Paris, First Treaty of (1814), 173
    Second Treaty of (1815), 173
Parthenopean Republic, 128, 165
Passaglia, Fr., 287, 288
Paul I, Czar, 165
Pedrocchi Café, in Padua, 278
Pellico, Silvio, 140
Pepe, Guglielmo
    in 1820–21, 136, 137, 139
    leads force against Austria in 1848, 146, 203
Périer, Casimir, 180
Persano, Count Carlo, admiral, 242
Perugia, occupied by revolutionary forces in 1831, 107
Petiet, Claude, 25
Petitti, Carlo, 63
Pettiti, Count Ilarion di, 212
Piacenza, in 1848, 82
Pietracalla, marquis of, 144
Pietro Leopoldo, grand duke of Tuscany (1765–90), Emperor Leopold II (1790–92), 70
Pilo, Rosalino, 142, 230, 231

Pisa
    University of, 72
    the first railway line to, 92
Pisacane, Carlo
    in 1849, 206
    his attempted rising and death in 1857, 221
    Mercantini's poem on the Pisacane expedition, 262
    Pisacane's socialism, 297
    Guerra combatuta in Italia negli anni 1848–49 (1851), 297–9
Pistoia, 92
Pius VI, Pope, 97, 98
    death of, 99
Pius VII, Pope, 52, 100, 101, 104
    election of, 99
    coronation of Napoleon I, 100
    arrested by the French in 1799, 101
    treatment by Napoleon in 1812, 169
    his restoration in 1815, 101, 102
    refuses to sign the Holy Alliance in 1815, 174
    death of, 103, 104
Pius VIII, Pope, 104, 284
    election of, 105
    his recognition of the July Monarchy, 285
    death of, 106
Pius IX, Pope, 57, 58, 109
    his election as pope, 108
    his amnesty of 1846, 109
    his policy with regard to the press in 1847, 111
    reactions in Turin to his initial reforms, 59
    his proposal for a customs union with Tuscany and Piedmont in 1847, 80, 81
    his protest at the Austrian occupation of Ferrara in 1847, 112
    refuses permission for Austrian troops to cross the Papal States, January 1848, 112
    introduces a constitution, March 1848, 114
    his Allocution of 29 April 1848, 115, 203
    leaves Rome, November 1848, 116
    returns to Rome in 1850, 119
    proclaims Dogma of the Immaculate Conception (1854), 287
    in 1859, 228

issues *Syllabus of Errors* (1864), 119
proclaims papal infallibility (1870), 290–3
contributes to the building of *Sacré Coeur*, 302
his death (1878), 301, 302
Pizzola, Andrea, 281
Plombières, Pact of, 222, 223
Podesti, Francesco, 273
Poerio, Carlo, 143–5, 148
Poggi, Giuseppe, 279, 281
Poggi, Teresa, 177
Ponzoni, Antonio, 76
Pressburg, Peace of (1805) 27, 167
Prina, Giuseppe, 27–9
Puristi, school of painting, 273

Quadruple Alliance, 174
Quanta Cura, encyclical (1864), 288
Quod divina sapientia, bull issued by Leo XII, 105

Radetzky, Field-Marshal Count Joseph, 32, 33
in 1848, 200–3
in 1849, 208
Ramorino, Gerolamo, 188, 189
Rastadt, Congress of, 23, 164, 165
Rattazzi, Urbano
his argument regarding the judiciary in 1848, 247
his *connubio* with Cavour, 214, 215
prime minister of Italy in 1862, 242
and in 1867, 244
Ravenna, occupied by the French in 1796, 98
Revel, Count Ottavio di, 59, 61, 213
Ricasoli, Baron Bettino, 84
in 1859, 225–7
in 1860, 228–229
prime minister of Italy in 1861, 242
and again in 1866, 243
Ridolfi, Cosimo, 80, 82–4
on the Tuscan economy, 92
Risorgimento, Il
founded in 1847, 212
on Pius IX, 113
Rivarola, Cardinal, 105
Romano, Aldo, 8
Romano, Liborio, 232, 233

Roman Republic of 1798, 98, 99, 165
Roman Republic of 1849, 117
Romeo, Rosario, 10
Rossi, Count Pellegrino
appointed chief minister by Pius IX, 115
his assassination, 116
Rossini, Gioacchino, 268, 269
Cambiale del Matrimonio, 268
Tancredi, 268
L'Italiana in Algeri, 268
The Barber of Seville, 268, 269
Otello, 269
La Cenerentola, 269
La Gazza Ladra, 269
La Gazza Ladra, 269
William Tell, 269
Rousseau, Jean-Jacques, his ideas as an anticipation of Mazzini's, 159, 160
Rubattino and Company, and the Pisacane expedition of 1857, 221
Ruffini, Agostino, 184, 190
Ruffini, Giovanni, 184, 190
Ruffini, Jacopo, 184, 188
his suicide in prison, 188
Ruffo, Cardinal Fabrizio, 129, 130
Rusconi, Cardinal Bishop of Imola, 104
Russell, Lord John
policy as foreign secretary in 1859, 226, 227
and in 1860, 228, 232
his despatch of 27 October 1860, 235
his later circular to the Powers never sent, 236
Russo, Vincenzo, 129

Sacchi, Giuseppe, 38, 39
Sadowa, battle of, 1866, 243
Saffi, Aurelio, triumvir of the Roman Republic (1849), 117
St Mark, Republic of, in 1848–49, 202, 207–9
Saint-Simon, Count of, his influence on Italian writers, 296, 297
Salmour, Count Ruggero di, 61, 62
Salvador, Carlo, 19, 20
Salvagnoli, Vincenzo, 92, 94
Salvatorelli, Luigi, 7
Salvemini, Gaetano, 6–7
San Antonio, battle of, 206
Sanfedisti, 104

during the pontificate of Pius VIII, 105
their reaction to Pius IX's reforms, 110
San Francesco di Paola, church of, in Naples, 277, 278
San Marzano, Count Ermolao Asinari di, 59
Sanseverino, Cardinal, 104
Santarosa, Piero di, 211
Santarosa, Santorre di, 55, 56
Santucci, Cardinal, 288
Sarri, Egisto, 274
Schiarino-Rizzino, Convention of, 30
Schönbrunn, treaty of (1809), 168
Schwarzenberg, Prince Felix zu, 53
Sclopis, Count Federico, 247
Scott, Sir Walter, influence on Manzoni, 264
Sedan, French capitulation at (1870), 245
September Convention (1864), 242, 244
Sercognani, Colonel Giuseppe, 107
Serra, Gian Battista, 46, 47
Serra, Gian Carlo, 46
Serristori, Antonio, 70
Serristori, Luigi, 80
Settembrini, Luigi, 125, 140, 141, 148, 151
Settimo, Ruggero, 143, 145
Siccardi, Count Giuseppe, 213
the Siccardi Laws, 214, 215
Siena, University of, 72
Signorini, Telemaco, 274, 275
Singulari nos, encyclical (1834), 286
Smith, Denis Mack, 11
Solferino, battle of, 225
Spaur, Countess, 116
Spaventa, Bertrando, 296
Spaventa, Silvio, 148
Sterbini, Pietro, 110, 115, 116
editor of *Il Contemporaneo*, 111
and the *Circolo Popolare*, 112
Strachey, Lytton, 291
Suvorov, Marshal, 24, 50, 51, 165
Syllabus of Errors (1864), 288, 289

Talleyrand, Charles-Maurice de, prince of Benevento, 74, 75
extracts reward from Naples for help given at the Congress of Vienna, 135, 173
Targhini, Angelo, 105
Teano, meeting of Garibaldi and Vittorio Emanuele II at (October 1860), 235
Testa di Lana, Teresa, 147

Tilsit, treaty of, 168
Tolentino
battle of (1815), 170
treaty of, 98, 164
Tommaseo, Niccolo, 73
editor of the *Antologia*, 254
Dell'Italia (1835), 286
Trafalgar, battle, 167
Trevelyan, George Macaulay, 5
Trollope, Mrs Frances, 80, 121, 122
Trollope, Thomas Adolphus, 76
on Pepe, 136
Troppau, Congress of (1820), 139, 179
Troya, Carlo, 145, 146
Tuscan Athenaeum, 81

Ulm, battle of, 167
Uruguay, Garibaldi's support of Uruguayan independence, 206
Univers, 291
Usiglio, Angelo, 190

Valadier, Giuseppe, 281
Valerio, Lorenzo, 57–60
and social reform, 63, 65
Vatican Council of 1869–70, 291, 292
Velletri, battle of (1849), 118
Verdi, Giuseppe, 269
premier of the *Battaglia di Legnano* in Rome in 1848, 117
Oberto, Conte di San Bonifacio, Nabucco, I Lombardi, 269
Macbeth, Rigoletto, Il Trovatore, La Traviata, Simon Boccanegra, 270
Un Ballo in Maschera, La Forza del Destino, Don Carlos, Aida, 270
Verga, Giovanni, 267
Verona
given to the Cisalpine Republic, 25
the silk industry, 37
Congress of, 56
Verri, Pietro, 16, 17, 161
his influence on Melzi, 26, 27
Veuillot, Louis, 290, 291
Vicenza, the silk industry, 37, 38
Vicini, Giovanni, 107, 108
Victoria, Queen, her attitude to Italy in 1860, 236
Vienna, Congress of
regulations concerning navigation of inter-

national rivers, 40
with reference to Piedmont, 53, 54
Treaty of, 173, 174
Viereck, Peter, 172
Vieusseux, Gian Pietro, 73, 74
Viglia, Michelangelo, 140
Villafranca
armistice of (1859), 226
revision of terms of, by the peace of Zurich, 228
becomes a dead letter, 229
Prince of, 138
Vittorio Amedeo III, 18, 43–9
Vittorio Emanuele I, 52–5
Vittorio Emanuele II, 56, 213
accession of, 208
and the constitution, 209
and the Siccardi Laws, 215
and intervention in the Crimean War, 220
and the *grido di dolore* speech in 1859, 224
signs treaty ceding Savoy and Nice to France in 1860, 229
joins the army in Ancona, October 1860, 235
King of Italy, 17 March 1861, 236

and the war of 1870, 244
his death (1878), 301
Volturno, battle of the, 234

Wagram, battle of, 168
War
of the First Coalition, 128, 162, 163
of the Second Coalition, 24, 128, 165
of the Third Coalition, 27, 167
Crimean War, 219
of 1859, 225
of 1866, 243
of 1870, 244, 302, 303
Waterloo, battle of, 170
Webster, Sir Charles, 133
on the Vienna Settlement, 172
Wellington, Duke of, in command of the allied armies in 1815, 170
Werklein, Baron, 79
Whyte, A.J., 10–11
Wyndham, William, British minister at Florence, 71

Zelada, Cardinal, 98
Zucchi, General Carlo, 79, 80, 108
Zurich, peace of (1859), 227, 228